Improving Children's Competence

Advances in Child Behavioral Analysis and Therapy

Paul Karoly and John J. Steffen, Editors

Volume One	**Improving Children's Competence**
Volume Two	**Autism and Severe Child Psychopathology**
Volume Three	**Child Abuse and Family Violence**
Volume Four	**Adolescent Behavior Disorders**

Improving Children's Competence

Advances in Child Behavioral Analysis and Therapy

Volume One

Edited by
Paul Karoly
Arizona State University
John J. Steffen
University of Cincinnati

LexingtonBooks
D.C. Heath and Company
Lexington, Massachusetts
Toronto

Library of Congress Cataloging in Publication Data

Improving children's competence.

(Advances in child behavioral analysis and therapy; v. 1)
Includes bibliographies and index.
Contents: Conceptualizing social competence in children/Martha Putallaz and John Gottman—Social skills training for socially withdrawn/isolated children/Hyman Hops—Community based interventions for the developmentally disabled/Michael F. Cataldo, Brian A. Iwata, and Eric M. Ward—[etc.]
1. Remedial teaching—Addresses, essays, lectures. 2. Student adjustment—Addresses, essays, lectures. 3. Mentally handicapped children—Education—Addresses, essays, lectures. I. Karoly, Paul. II. Steffen, John. III. Series.
LB1029.R4I65 1982 371.92'8 82-47798
ISBN 0-669-05640-5 AACR2

Published simultaneously in Canada

Printed in the United States of America

International Standard Book Number: 0-669-05640-5

Library of Congress Catalog Card Number: 82-47798

This series is dedicated to our children,
Michael Karoly and Joshua and Rebecca Steffen,
and this volume to our wives,
Linda Ruehlman and Veronica Bleakley Steffen

Contents

Figures

Tables

Series Preface

The contemporary student of children's adjustment confronts an array of theoretical models and investigative tools and can draw upon advances in diverse fields such as medicine, behavioral genetics, engineering, mathematics, computer science, and systems theory in addition to psychology, education, sociology, and related domains. Resting upon a firm tradition of normative research, dating to the descriptive studies of children's growth and development of the 1920s and 1930s and of clinical work such as the pioneering psychoanalytic studies of Anna Freud, Melanie Klein, and others, the modern discipline of clinical child psychology nonetheless faces exciting new directions and choices in the years ahead. Diagnostic-classification systems and clinical-assessment procedures continue to be developed and refined. Studies of high-risk populations and the psychology of prediction (and ultimately prevention) are being pursued. Attempts to define and train the skills and competencies of adaptation across the life span have begun in earnest and show signs of promise.

Advances in Child Behavioral Analysis and Therapy is a series of volumes intended to assist clinicians in psychology, psychiatry, nursing, and social work to cull from the vast experimental literature new and hopefully useful information on description, conceptualization, assessment, and treatment of the disorders of childhood and adolescence. The series is also intended to be of use to students and researchers in child development and education who may want a thorough, timely account of programmatic efforts to investigate child psychopathology. The title of the series is not meant to suggest a strictly behaviorist emphasis. We endeavor to bring together contributions that address structure as well as function, the normal as well as the abnormal, and to illustrate the utility of naturalistic as well as laboratory methods.

Each book in the series contains presentations of current research and/or practice within a single area of interest. While not designed to serve as introductory texts or primers, the volumes contain sufficient background material and clinical examples to orient beginners. The major purpose of each volume is to bring together state-of-the-field papers and to organize them in such a way as to facilitate communication and, ultimately, a synthesis of divergent perspectives.

The editors plan to invite authors from the professions or specialty areas clearly relevant to each topic, although we expect that psychology will be somewhat overrepresented because of our own inherent biases. Nonetheless, we think it fair to characterize our orientation to this series as multidisciplinary. In this regard, we welcome comments and suggestions from readers on the content of future volumes and potential contributors.

Preface and Acknowledgments

The observation of differences among children along with the attempt to discern patterns, causal and correlational, that may map these differences forms the core of modern psychological studies of the child. It is not surprising that differences in children's success with mastering the social and intellectual demands of their environments have attracted the attention of developmentalists, social psychologists, clinicians, and educators. However, with the number of potential entry points to the study of children's competence and the absence of universally accepted criteria for successful functioning, it is understandable that the pathways to a science of childhood competence are somewhat snarled.

Among the many factors that have been postulated to influence children's productive interactions with the social and inanimate world are genetics, parental child-rearing practices, educational opportunities, the children's history of interpersonal successes and failures (with peers and adults), and current constraints on their motivation to perform successfully. All of these hypothesized antecedents or correlates of social and intellectual skills are logical: most have demonstrated that they possess some predictive usefulness. None has proved to be the essential ingredient or the single key to clinical or educative intervention. The contemporary competence researcher must acknowledge that he or she confronts a vast array of undefined terms and that inventing new words or phrases, limiting the field to certain confined spaces (such as the psychological laboratory, the family setting, or the classroom), or compiling lists of desirable versus undesirable attributes of children will hardly improve our overall understanding.

Is there a way to steer our efforts toward a reliable, nonpathologic, developmentally and socioculturally relevant classification of the perceptions, desires, and behaviors that predict children's interpersonal and academic success? Can we not only measure but also change or redirect children's capacities and motives to act and interact socially and intellectually? This volume is predicated on the belief that progress is possible, and it will be heralded by the kind of improvements in conceptual organization, research methodology, and clinical sophistication modeled by our contributors.

Among the major obstacles to progress in understanding children's competencies has been the rather freewheeling attitude taken by investigators toward the practice of offering (or not offering) basic definitions. For some, the cognitive and interpersonal skills necessary for survival are obviously tied to the demands of a situation. What do parents, teachers, employers, or governments expect in the way of behaviors, attitudes, and beliefs? Whatever is demanded becomes the objective(s) of training or clinical intervention. Countless programs (at varying levels of organization and depth) have been mounted over the years to teach children to be cooperative, diligent, receptive, inquisitive, altruistic, assertive, self-confident, and proficient in language, mathematics, and science. The problem for many educators and clinicians is not what to teach, but how.

Theorists (whether psychologists, pedagogues, or biologists) have often interpreted the apparent consensus about childhood survival skills as suggesting evolutionary necessity (for example, all children must learn to read, to control their impulses, to love their neighbors). The result is that, whether one is an avowed situationist or an absolutist in the domain of children's competencies, the tendency to question or evaluate premises is somehow eroded.

One way to avoid local definitions of competence (and the lack of generalizability they imply), as well as universal definitions (so encompassing as to be circular and unwieldy), is to adopt a relativist stance. Such a stance also mitigates against losing sight of premises by forcing a consideration of context; that is, if we define a skill as a capacity to respond so as to obtain a desired goal (either interpersonal or intellectual), we must also understand (as relativists) that success at goal attainment can be judged differently depending on the observer (for example, the child, his or her peers, adults); the task (for example, easy or difficult); the setting (for example, structured or unstuctured); the time frame (for example, long term or more immediate); the level of analysis (for example, molar or fine grained); and the cultural and age norms. These considerations provide the context in which the skill in question is to be interpreted.

The temporal facet in this scheme is particularly salient. If the conditions under which a skill is to be performed are relatively stable, then performance of the skill at time *a* should be predictive of performance at time *b*. Where settings, observers, task dimensions, and so forth fluctuate widely, it is unlikely that success or failure will mean very much insofar as adaptation is concerned. School systems do not expend great amounts of money or energy teaching etiquette, presumably because of the variability across persons and settings in what is considered proper. However, schools seek valiantly to teach reading, presumably because reading maintains as an adaptive skill in situations over time.

The contributors to this book are people who have closely examined basic premises and methods and have, in some sense, found them deficient. Traditional definitions and labels can set unnecessary limits on how one conceptualizes a problem and how one seeks to remedy it (especially when children are the subjects of analysis). These contributors are pioneers in the conceptualization of social and intellectual competencies and in the development of efficient and effective teaching methods.

In their provocative chapter, Martha Putallaz and John Gottman provide a useful guide for the field of social competence. They review the ways in which the concept of social competence has been used and illustrate the definitional chaos that has pervaded the literature. They propose the criterion of "psychological or physical risk" as a means of organizing future research efforts. Putallaz and Gottman argue that problems in peer acceptance and friendship formation represent empirically grounded indexes of risk—in the academic, behavioral, physiological, and mental-health domains. Then they provide an in-depth summary of current knowledge about correlates of unpopularity and inadequate friendship and acquaintanceship processes in children, identifying what they consider to be six fundamental dimensions of competence.

In chapter 2, Hyman Hops delves into the world of socially isolated children and reviews the varied clinical interventions that have been directed at rectifying deviant social-interaction patterns among young children. After thoroughly examining treatments based on reinforcement, modeling, and specific skills-training principles, Hops examines the critical question of the maintenance of recent clinical efforts. Suggestions for improving the durability of treatment effects are offered, stressing the need for more-complete assessment and for the recognition of the inherent complexity of the child's life space.

Chapter 3, by Michael Cataldo, Brian Iwata, and Eric Ward, shifts the focus to children labeled "retarded" or "developmentally disabled." These authors comment incisively about the widespread policy of deinstitutionalization in light of our acknowledged ignorance of the forces at work in the community that influence the adaptive potential of both normal and retarded youngsters. The multidimensional and relativistic perspectives on competence noted earlier mandate a closer examination of the components of various community-living arrangements for retarded children, the specific behaviors required for a successful fit between child and setting, and those factors that promote maintenance and generalization of learning. Cataldo, Iwata, and Ward provide the necessary information to allow social planners as well as clinical practitioners to begin a data-based—as opposed to a purely speculative—assault on the problems of normal and so-called special children.

No one concerned with teaching children can afford to overlook the technology represented by the Direct Instruction model. In chapter 4, Wesley Becker, Siegfried Engelmann, Douglas Carnine, and Alex Maggs present their highly successful programs for teaching academic skills as opposed to purely social, survival skills (although the two kinds of skills are obviously related). In addition to describing methods for the design of instructional materials, the authors provide evidence that documents the value of Direct Instruction programs in the national Follow-Through projects and in programs for the learning disabled and retarded in Australia. In the past, so-called disadvantaged children have had the added burden of teachers who were themselves at a disadvantage insofar as teaching methods were concerned. Becker and his colleagues aptly illustrate that children's competence is built partially upon the instructional competencies of their socializing agents.

Searching the complexities of the learning process, Joseph Campione, Kathy Nitsch, Norman Bray, and Ann Brown (chapter 5) examine the role of memory. To the extent that both academic and social success require the storage and retrieval of information, memory must occupy an important place among the potential child competencies. The approach taken by these authors is particularly fascinating in that they focus on memory processes in a group with presumed cognitive deficits—retarded children. In the course of challenging myths about memory in the retarded, the authors elucidate concepts and issues germane to the entire spectrum of memory training. Like several of the other authors in this volume, these contributors address the question of durability of learning.

In the final chapter, Alan Litrownik and Bradley Steinfeld pick up an important thread that has been notable throughout previous discussions of how social and/or intellectual skills are taught—namely, the question of self-regulation. Social and intellectual competencies are expected to be transsituational, enduring, and evolving into newer and better forms. The reason for these expectations is that the child is considered to be more than a passive responder to the demands of the external world; the child is expected to be active and self-directive. If the component skills of self-regulation can be taught to children with intellectual limitations (the trainable retarded), then psychology will have demonstrated the applied significance of an experimental paradigm. This will also pave the way for truly independent living in a population typically considered to be dependent and anatomically unable to control their own destinies. Of course, the studies described by Litrownik and Steinfeld cast light upon the normal processes of self-guidance as well.

In sum, this book should assist the reader to examine basic premises about children's competencies and to consider new and exciting possibilities for training. In all cases, the contributors have tied their assertions to data—so as to avoid substituting new armchairs for old.

Acknowledgments

The editors wish to thank each of the contributors for their diligence and patience and to acknowledge the outstanding efforts of the staff of Lexington Books, particularly Marjorie Glazer.

1 Conceptualizing Social Competence in Children

Martha Putallaz and
John Gottman

Given the pervasiveness of social interaction in human affairs, there is considerable advantage to the notion of one underlying attribute that both determines the quality of manifested social behavior and that also follows a predictable developmental progression (Bronson, forthcoming). Social competence also holds considerable practical utility for researchers by allowing the study of social interaction to become more manageable under one construct. While the popular trait-situation controversy has also raged in the study of social competence, it has been suggested that the concept of social competence provides a completer picture of social development than is possible through the study of more-isolated components such as empathy, locus of control, and self-esteem (O'Malley 1977). Thus, the construct of social competence has provided an air of conceptual integration.

This chapter explores the concept of social competence in children. A striking characteristic of the concept is the pervasive appeal that it has held for researchers in psychology, as evidenced by the vast amount of research the concept has generated (see Garmezy et al. 1979 for a partial review of the last fifty years of research, 1927–1977, done in the area).

The study of social competence has been stimulated by a growing disenchantment with the use of IQ as the major outcome measure of the success of educational-intervention programs like Head Start. Anderson and Messick, for example, stated, "After all that has gone before, it is not easy to see why in 1973 people are still using general IQ as the major yardstick of development and the principal criterion of the effectiveness of early education programs" (1974, p. 284). One critique of IQ testing, offered by McClelland (1973), argued that the validity of a successful ability measure should not be assessed by grades in school but by "grades in life." Similarly, Zigler and Trickett stated that although the IQ is an attractive evaluation measure, when taken alone it is not an adequate outcome measure. They believe that a high IQ score is not synonymous with the capacity to "behave admirably in the real world that exists beyond the confines of the psychologist's testing room" (1978, p. 791). Rather, they asserted that the IQ score's maximum efficiency as a predictor occurs when it is employed to predict school performance. Sundberg, Snowden, and Reynolds (1978) agreed that the global notion of intelligence may have passed its period of usefulness—with the possible exception of predicting generalized adaptation to traditional school or school-related environments.

It has thus been proposed that an index of social competence be employed as the major outcome measure for evaluating the effectiveness of early educational programs (Anderson and Messick 1974; Zigler 1970; 1973; Zigler and Trickett 1978). Even on purely educational grounds, the rationale for such a position has empirical support. O'Malley (1977) cited several studies that indicate that variables associated with social competence may improve the predictability of academic success beyond the information provided solely by cognitive variables. In addition, O'Malley pointed out that both teachers and parents have rated certain behaviors associated with social competence, such as social skills, goal directedness, and emotional stability, as more likely to lead to school and life success than variables such as IQ and aptitude. To summarize, part of the appeal of the notion of social competence derives from its perceived usefulness as a replacement for IQ as an outcome measure for evaluating educational-intervention programs.

In addition, the concept of social competence gains appeal from the extreme optimism it entails, particularly with respect to children's social behavior. As Asher, Oden, and Gottman (1977) pointed out, a number of personal characteristics influence children's relations with their peers, such as physical attractiveness, sex, and race. Similarly, Asher and his coworkers indicated that a variety of situational factors also affect the quality of children's peer relations (for example, size of classroom and school population or pupil turnover rate in a school). An attempt to alter some of these physical or situational factors in an effort to improve target children's interpersonal relations and to increase their levels of peer acceptance would be extremely difficult. The prospect of designing interventions would seem more optimistic, however, if research indicated that a knowledge or performance of certain behaviors or social or cognitive skills was the essential element required to attain minimal levels of acceptance by peers. A belief in the validity of the concept of social competence, then, allows one also to believe in the possibility of a correctional process to improve the quality of people's interpersonal relations and functioning.

Social competence has thus assumed the role of an individual-difference variable to be employed optimistically to help individuals who experience interpersonal difficulty to enjoy more-satisfying relationships. The concept's optimism has been captivating. For example, as Argyle wrote:

> Much research on social interaction is carried out in the hope that it may be possible to make social interaction more effective and more enjoyable. One of the main applications of this research is in training people to interact better. Many people are ineffective and unsuccessful in their jobs through lack of social competence. Candidates fail to get jobs and interviewers select the wrong people through lack of competence on either side. The "normal"

> human condition so far in the history of mankind has been that many people are lonely and unhappy or mentally ill, simply because they cannot establish and sustain social relationships with others. Conflicts between different social classes and cultural groups are partly due to difficulties of interaction. [1969, p. 294]

He added:

> The "normal" state of mankind in which there is so much loneliness, unhappiness, misunderstanding and conflict might be radically changed if education included training in social behavior among the other, probably less important, subjects in the curriculum. [p. 295]

Thus, the concept of social competence has led to the proposal of a hypothesis that poor interpersonal functioning may be remedied through the technological approach of social-competence training. In this respect, the notion of social-competence training assumes a democratic air. It brings to mind a Horatio Alger point of view—namely, that all individuals have an equal opportunity to succeed interpersonally if they so desire despite any accidental differences in social background. Any difficulty encountered can be remedied with social-competence training in the deficit areas, much as Mr. Higgins accomplished for his Pygmalion. Certainly, this aspect of social competence has made the notion especially appealing to the Western industrialized democracies.

A warning with respect to social-competence training, however, can be derived from Bereiter (1969), who criticized similar training attempts in the area of intellectual competence. Bereiter suggested that there is a basic fallacy in attempting to equate people with respect to their intellectual competence. He stated that training in intellectual tools and skills, given time, appears to act as an amplifier rather than as an equalizer of intelligence and, thus, that it functionally magnifies rather than nullifies individual differences in ability. For example, people differ considerably with respect to the complexity of mathematical problems they are capable of solving. With instruction in analytic geometry or calculus, the less-capable person would show little gain while the more-capable person would now be able to solve problems beyond the conception of the former. Bereiter further suggested that every tool requires certain minimum abilities of a person for it to be used at all. Accordingly, each new tool serves as a divider between those who can learn to use it and those who cannot. The more powerful the tool, the more noticeable this division becomes. With respect to social competence, then, training in social skills may comparably serve as a divider between those who can master the skill and those who cannot, functionally magnifying rather than eliminating differences in social competence.

Ubiquity of the Term

It is intriguing that, despite the wide usage of the term *social competence* and the vast amount of research the concept has generated in recent years, a consensus still has not been reached on an appropriate definition. Zigler and Trickett summarized the situation as follows:

> The construct seems to evaporate upon the application of the heat of even minimal debate. Social competence appears to be one of those constructs that is definable only in terms of other constructs whose own definitions are vague. Social competence theorists thus quickly find themselves adrift on a sea of words. [1978, p. 793]

Zigler and Trickett concluded that after reviewing the use of the term in four areas of research, they knew of "no rigorous or even mildly satisfying definition of the construct or term social competence" (p. 794).

In reviewing the social-competence literature, a great diversity of opinion obviously exists. To illustrate this point, we briefly review some of the ways the term has been used by researchers in the past. Argyle (1969) equated social competence with social skill and used both terms to convey the notion that some individuals are normally better at dealing with social situations than others. Rather than advocate that social competence is a general trait, Argyle suggested that it be viewed in terms of situationally specific abilities consisting of a number of trainable components that might include elements of motivation, perception, response patterns, self-confidence, and self-presentation.

O'Malley (1977) chose to deal with the varied definitions of social competence by limiting the focus of his review to include only those approaches that have dealt with preschool or early-school settings. He tentatively defined social competence as "productive and mutually satisfying interactions between a child and peers or adults. Productive interactions attain personal goals of the child, whether immediately or in the long run, which are adaptive in classroom settings. Interactions will be satisfying to the child when goals are attained, and to the others if actions in pursuit of the goals are received in either a benign or positive manner" (p. 29). However, there seems to be a flaw in the logic behind this definition. It does not seem intuitively correct to define social competence in terms of interactions. Productive or satisfying interactions may be indicative of competence or an outcome of competent behavior but cannot be considered competence themselves.

In her recent review of social competence, Bronson (forthcoming) initially adopted a dictionary definition of social competence "that the individual in question has the ability to relate effectively with other persons."

After expanding this notion, she concluded that much more conceptual and empirical work would be necessary to develop the definition of social competence so that it might achieve an adequate level of precision while at the same time allowing the concept to retain much of its theoretical interest and potential validity.

Meichenbaum, Butler, and Joseph (forthcoming) skirted the definitional issue of social competence by not attempting to define it. Rather, they proposed a three-component model of social competence that included overt behaviors, cognitive processes, and cognitive structures in order to clarify and integrate the various definitions and paradigms employed in the study of social competence. Meichenbaum and his co-workers concluded that only when the complexity of the nature of these processes is appreciated, social competence would be defined more adequately. While this may be a worthwhile strategy, it is frustrating to believe that one must wait for the nature of processes such as those mentioned by these authors to be understood before social competence may finally be explained. That task appears no easier to accomplish than defining social competence itself.

Thus, it is clear from the varied and numerous definitions that social competence has acquired in the literature that a great deal of confusion prevails as to precisely what is meant by the concept. In fact, the need for a resolution of this confusion and an adoption of a universal definition of social competence was so great that, in 1973, the Office of Child Development commissioned a panel of twelve experts jointly to agree on one definition of the term. The committee arrived at a total of twenty-nine statements believed to be important facets of social competence and that could additionally serve as goals of early-educational-intervention programs. The twenty-nine components of social competence included factors such as habits of personal maintenance and care, sensitivity and understanding in social relationships, morality and prosocial tendencies, fine motor dexterity, gross motor skills, language skills, general knowledge, and some positive attitudes toward learning and school experiences, to name but a few. The committee concluded their report by drawing attention to the need to operationalize the components of each of the twenty-nine statements into appropriate measurement terms and to the long-range importance of increasing the understanding of the basic mechanisms involved in learning and development (Anderson and Messick 1974).

Dissatisfaction with the committee's proposed definition of social competence was expressed recently by Zigler and Trickett (1978). They contended that the definition was problematic for at least three reasons. First, they charged that each of the twenty-nine components of social competence would require greater refinement as well as resolution of numerous difficulties to become useful. Second, even if all of the terms could be made adequately operational the task of evaluating any child on the twenty-nine items would be too time consuming to be feasible. Third, they believed the list was so filled with psychological jargon that it would be incomprehensible to many of its potential users.

Given the immediacy of the need for an acceptable definition of social competence, Zigler and Trickett responded by proposing "an arbitrary definition for social competence" (1978, p. 794). They suggested two major criteria that should be reflected by an adequate definition of the term. The first is that social competence should indicate that societal expectations have been successfully met. Second, the concept should reflect information concerning the self-actualization of personal development of the individual. To be included as components of a social-competence index, Zigler and Trickett proposed measures of physical health and well-being, a measure of formal cognitive ability, an achievement measure, and the measurement of motivational and emotional variables. While we concur with Zigler and Trickett that a definition of social competence may be useful, we do not agree that providing an arbitrary definition is either justified or useful. Further, their definition seems overly inclusive and no less vague that that proposed by Anderson and Messick (1974).

Toward a Definition of Social Competence

Thus, our field is in the awkward and embarrassing position of using widely a concept in both theoretical and research contexts without being able to define the term in a universally acceptable manner. Perhaps part of the blame for this problematic situation can be traced to the failure of researchers to employ some form of an organizing principle in their efforts to conceptualize social competence. Remarking on the many definitions of competence in the literature, Garmezy et al. wrote, "Most of these appear to have been constructed from that rather unsound piece of methodological software—the armchair" (1979, p. 35). Without a common organizing principle, researchers have had to resort to armchair speculation and their own individual plans for employing the term to guide them in arriving at a functional definition. Thus, as pointed out earlier, attempts to define social competence have resulted in many important discrepancies. Some of these definitions "are staunchly operational and down-to-earth, while still others seem to drift lazily skyward in the semantic wind" (Garmezy et al. 1979, p. 36).

We propose that one logical organizing principle for conceptualizing social competence would be to employ the criterion of psychological or physical risk. Further, we propose that, of the domain of factors demonstrated to predict psychological risk, only those related to social behavior be considered in defining social competence. Thus, social competence would be considered as aspects of social behavior that are important with respect to preventing physical illness or psychopathology in children and adults. The relationship between risk and incompetence has been expressed by White:

> Low degrees of social competence in children seem to be importantly related to psychopathology. Children thus handicapped need to acquire enough sense of competence to make true interaction possible and in this way allow social needs to be satisfied. This is where we can hope to accomplish something for prevention. [1979, p. 11]

Earlier we quoted Argyle (1969) as similarly stressing the importance of social-skills training in preventing psychopathology. We would suggest that the relationship between risk and incompetence be used in building a definition of competence. The identification of those factors that are social in nature and that satisfy a psychological-risk criterion would seem an eminently reasonable starting point for conceptualizing social competence.

The use of this criterion would further serve to eliminate many of the conjectured armchair correlates of social competence that have not been empirically demonstrated to predict psychological- or physical-health risks. As an example, we will review the old and venerable history of a social construct that has been fashionable in the United States for at least fifty years—assertiveness (or ascendance, as it was called in the 1930s). The design of instructional programs to train children in social skills reflects society's concern with this concept. One of the earliest studies in this line of social-skills training observed that a primary behavioral difference between ascendant and nonascendant children was the amount of self-confidence they displayed—the former group exhibiting more self-confidence than the latter. An intervention program was thus designed to increase the confidence level of the nonascendant children. As measured by the experimenters, the program did successfully result in increased manifestations of ascendance in the trained children (Jack 1934). In an extension of this study, Mummery (1947) further distinguished between "socially acceptable ascendant behavior" and "socially immature ascendant behavior." The results of a training program in self-confidence, similar to that used by Jack, indicated increases in socially acceptable ascendance by trained children that were significantly larger than the corresponding increases for the control-group children. These then represent two examples of investigators who successfully increased the level of assertiveness displayed by target children but without any empirical justification that their concern and subsequent interventions were warranted.

A third example from this line of assertiveness interventions was a program designed by Chittenden (1942) who believed assertiveness to be best defined as a concept comprised of two distinct components—domination and cooperation. Chittenden's hypothesis was that children used dominative strategies in attempting to obtain their goals because they were unable to generate any alternative cooperative strategies to employ. She thus designed a training program that centered upon two dolls involved in a variety of potential conflict situations that the experimenter and child used to discuss possible alternative courses of action for the dolls, the likely outcomes of these strategies, and the most successful strategy to employ in the situations. Postobservations of the children in a naturalistic play situation indicated that the trained children decreased significantly more than the control children with respect to the amount of dominative behavior they displayed and increased more—although not significantly more—than the control children in cooperative behavior.

This tradition of assertiveness training for children has continued in recent years. Using a social-skills-training procedure, consisting of instructions, feedback, behavior rehearsal, and modeling, Bornstein, Bellack, and Hersen (1977) attempted to increase the level of assertiveness of four children, aged eight to ten years. Specifically, the children were trained to increase the ratio of their eye contact to speech duration, the loudness of their speech, and their requests for new behavior. Results indicated that increases in each of these target behaviors occurred for all children. Furthermore, the treatment effects generalized from the children's role-play responses to six hypothetical situations in which they had received training to three situations in which the children had not been trained. These gains were maintained at two- and four-week follow-up sessions in the experimental setting. However, no naturalistic observations of the children were conducted, and so it is impossible to assess whether these treatment effects had generalized to the affect the children's interactions in their natural environment.

Thus, a great deal of attention has been devoted to intervention programs to increase the degree of assertiveness displayed by selected children. Yet curiously enough, there has been no empirical research to substantiate that this concern is warranted. In fact, Bornstein and his co-workers themselves stated, "However, there is a need to investigate the relationship between deficits in these components (of assertiveness) and children's level of interpersonal functioning in their natural environment" (1977, p. 191). Other than speculation, no evidence has suggested that nonassertive children are at psychological risk or that their lack of assertiveness represents a significant impairment in their interactions with other children. Gottman and Markman commented on this issue:

> Lack of care in selecting a target population may amount to a war on variance. The investigator may proceed by selecting that part of a population

> that is one or two standard deviations lower on some variable that seems to describe the target population. [1978, p. 39]

The use of a psychological-risk criterion, then, would eliminate assertiveness from serious consideration when conceptualizing social competence until some empirical research has indicated that children are at risk psychologically if a certain minimum level of assertiveness is not attained. This need not imply that one ought not to study assertiveness for its own sake; however, a construct should not be studied under the rubric of social competence until it has been shown to satisfy a high-risk criterion.

Another example of a target variable that has yet to be validated is represented by intervention programs that have focused upon attempts to increase the frequency of children's interactions with their peers; the rationale here is that extremely low rates of peer interaction are indicative of a child experiencing loneliness and peer-relationship problems. Shaping, which is characterized by the use of reinforcement in the form of social praise or tangible rewards, represents one form these interventions have taken. Studies have demonstrated that the use of such procedures can increase the frequency of children's peer interactions (Allen et al. 1964; O'Connor 1972), although it tends to return to baseline levels once the reinforcement has been terminated (O'Connor 1972). A second form of intervention program that attempts to increase specific children's low rates of peer interaction has utilized the principle of modeling. In the most well-known study of this type (O'Connor 1969), low-interacting children viewed a film consisting of eleven scenes of children receiving positive reactions following their approach and interaction with peers. After the film, the children showed a subsequent increase in their own rate of peer interaction that continued to be maintained at the time of a follow-up assessment several weeks later. Two studies have reported a maintenance of this increase four to six weeks later (Evers and Schwarz 1973; O'Connor 1972). However, a study by Gottman (1977) that replicated only the follow-up assessment of the O'Connor study with added controls failed to demonstrate an increase in peer-interaction rates.

Even if a successful intervention program were to be created, the issue is that again, we find a series of intervention programs designed to change children on a variable that has not to date been empirically demonstrated to predict any type of psychological risk. There is no evidence, other than intuitive, to indicate that children who interact less frequently with their peers suffer more social-adjustment problems than children who interact more frequently. An added problem in this literature, as Asher and Renshaw (forthcoming) pointed out, is that most of these intervention studies have selected children who interact with their peers at reasonably high rates. For example, one investigator used a selection criterion of 15 percent peer-interaction time (O'Connor 1969; 1972); in another study the criterion was 33 percent (Furman, Rahe, and Hartup 1979); while the investigators in a third study used a criterion of 50 percent interaction time (Keller and Carlson 1974). It is difficult to disagree with Asher and Renshaw's contention that it is implausible that all or even most of the children selected as targets for intervention in these studies can be regarded as at risk or in need of special attention. Further, according to Asher and Renshaw, when children are not interacting with their peers, they are usually engaged in constructive work or play activity rather than daydreaming or passively watching other children interacting. Thus, as was the case with assertiveness, the use of a psychological-risk criterion would eliminate rate of peer interaction from consideration when conceptualizing social competence until it has empirically demonstrated to predict psychological risk.

However, one aspect of social behavior that appears to be related to the prevention of psychopathology in children and adults is peer acceptance, as determined by sociometric tests. Note that this variable is best conceptualized as an indicator variable in the sense that it leads to the search for some other set of variables that explains its variation. It is not a variable like the amount of social interaction or the degree of assertiveness. However, some empirical evidence suggests that negative consequences result from low levels of peer acceptance (see Asher, Oden, and Gottman 1977). Although numerous methodological problems exist with this literature, the results are provocative and may suggest that measures of peer acceptance are good indexes of psychological risk. For example, with respect to academic endeavors, unpopular children are more likely to be low achievers in school (Bonney 1971; Buswell 1953); to experience more learning difficulties (Amidon and Hoffman 1965); and more apt to drop out of school (Kuhlen and Collister 1952; Ullman 1957) than their socially accepted peers. However, as Asher, Oden, and Gottman (1977) pointed out, the consequences of low peer acceptance may go beyond academic problems. Childhood unpopularity predicts the incidence of behavior problems like juvenile delinquency (Roff, Sells, and Golden 1972) and other selected indexes of behavior problems such as bad-conduct discharges from the military service (Roff 1961); the occurrence of emotional and mental-health problems in adulthood (Cowen et al. 1973); adult schizophrenia (Strain, Cooke, and Apollini 1976); neuroses (Roff 1963); and psychoses (Kohn and Clausen 1955; Roff 1963).

Similarly, other evidence suggests that the ability to establish at least one intimate relationship is also important with respect to both health psychological and physiological functioning (see Miller 1979). It appears, for example, from self-report data that hospitalized psychiatric patients have fewer good friends and intimate relationships within their social networks than matched normal controls (Henderson et al. 1978; Tolsdorf

1976). Similarly, Miller and Ingham (1976) reported a relationship between having a confidant and lower levels of fatigue, anxiety, and depression for both men and women. In addition, they found that women who lack a confidant reported higher levels of palpitations and breathlessness. Psychiatric illness as well as a higher incidence of tumors have been associated with self-reports of superficial relationships with both parents throughout childhood (Thomas and Duszynski 1974). Gove (1973) reported a higher incidence of psychiatric disorder and death attributed to diverse causes such as suicide, accidents, lung cancer, tuberculosis, diabetes, and homicide among unmarried individuals (that is, never married, widowed, or divorced) than among married individuals. Brown, Bhrolchain, and Harris (1975) have suggested that the presence of an intimate relationship may provide protection from the adverse effects of life stress, since they found that women who experienced a severe life event but who lacked a confidant were ten times more likely to be depressed than those who had been similarly stressed but who had a confidant. They proposed that an intimate relationship may function as a buffer of life stress by providing emotional support and increasing the individual's feeling of self-worth.

Therefore, both peer acceptance and having a close friend, as measured by sociometric tests, appear to satisfy the organizing principle we specified earlier in connection with the conceptualization of social competence. First, they satisfy a psychological-risk criterion since empirical evidence has suggested that they are associated with the incidence of later problems within the academic, behavioral, psychological, and mental-health domains. Second, they satisfy our additional criterion of being social in nature. To our knowledge, peer acceptance and having a close friend are the only variables that satisfy both of these criteria. Thus, they seem to represent legitimate manifestations of social competence.

Logically, then, it follows that factors empirically demonstrated to be related to establishing and maintaining a close friendship and good relations with peers should similarly be related to social competence. Therefore, once the factors required for a child to attain a close friendship and a high level of peer acceptance are identified, it would seem that we similarly have determined some of the factors associated with social competence. However, there is a problem with this strategy because sociometric data are indicator variables. While sociometric tests are useful for the clinical identification of problems like social isolation, they do not supply any information that would aid in the identification of the origin of the problem or in the detection of those factors currently maintaining the problems. By themselves they form an unsatisfactory basis for the construction of theory. Unfortunately, the factors primarily responsible for causing or contributing to a child's sociometric status or ability to establish a close friendship remain largely unidentified at this time. We now review what information is known concerning those factors associated with sociometric status and then review those factors associated with children's friendships.

Behavioral Correlates of Peer Acceptance

Several strategies have been employed by researchers in their efforts to determine those factors related to peer acceptance. One line of research in this area has been behavioral in orientation, searching for possible behavioral concomitants of sociometric status. Although this approach has had a long history, currently there are few known consistent behavioral concomitants of sociometric status. However, researchers usually support the conclusion that popular children tend to engage in a greater proportion of positive interactions with their peers as compared to unpopular children. Marshall and McCandless (1957) found that the observed degree of the preschool child's friendly social interactions was positively related to the child's sociometric status, while hostile play interactions were not. A study by Hartup, Glazer, and Charlesworth (1967) examined the relationship between positive and negative peer interaction and sociometric status in two nursery schools. They considered their study a revision and extension of the Marshall and McCandless work, and their results confirmed those of Marshall and McCandless—that is, social acceptance is significantly correlated with the frequency of being positive to peers but not by the frequency of being negative. Hartup and his associates (1967) also found that social rejection in one of the two schools was correlated with negative interactions with peers.

The detection of behavioral differences between popular and unpopular children is more difficult when studying elementary-school rather than preschool children (Asher and Hymel, forthcoming). Gottman, Gonso, and Rasmussen (1975) correlated peer acceptance of third and fourth graders with their social-interaction patterns in the classroom. Consistent with Hartup, Glazer, and Charlesworth (1967), they found that popular children initiated and received more frequent interactions with peers than unpopular children. A recent study by Butler (1979) also discovered this, despite using a different sociometric measure (the Bower Class Play; Bower 1960) to determine the sociometric status of the children studied. Gottman, Gonso, and Rasmussen further expanded the observational categories used by Hartup and his co-workers to include verbal and nonverbal behavior and examined behavioral differences between the children who were enrolled in a working-class school as opposed to those who were attending a middle-class school. The results indicated that peer acceptance in the middle-class school correlated with positive verbal interaction, while in the working-class school, peer acceptance was related to engagement in positive nonverbal interaction. Middle-class children who engaged in positive nonverbal behavior tended to be more disliked. A more-complicated picture of peer acceptance and its correlates is thus presented here than in the preschool literature. Apparently the environment affects what kinds of behavior will lead to acceptance or rejection.

A further complication emerges when the study by Oden and Asher (1977) is considered. The coaching intervention procedure used in this study was able to increase significantly the sociometric ratings of the coached children compared to the ratings of the two control groups, resulting in maintenance of these gains at the time of a one-year follow-up assessment. However, concomitant gains in the observed positive social behavior of the coached children were not found. More troublesome, behavioral differences were detected between popular and unpopular children prior to the intervention program. It is possible, as the authors suggested, that the particular coding categories were not specific enough for the frequency differences to emerge. It was also suggested that these observations should have been made in the classroom where behavior might more closely parallel the behavior upon which peer ratings were based, rather than out of the classroom as they were in the study. A replication attempt by Hymel and Asher (1977) included these suggestions and changed the behavior-observation technique employed accordingly. Again, behavioral differences were not found to discriminate between popular and unpopular children. A recent study by Ladd (1979) that used a modification of the coaching procedure and observational methods did find behavioral differences between coached and control children but did not involve observation of popular children.

Asher and Hymel (forthcoming) have recently offered some possible explanations for the more consistently obtained relationships between observed behavior and sociometric status for preschool rather than elementary-school children. First, they suggested that nonbehavioral characteristics such as sex, race, and physical attractiveness may play an increasingly important role in children's friendship choices as they become older. It appears, for example, that their friends' race becomes more important to children with age (Criswell 1939; Singleton and Asher 1977). Second, most of the naturalistic observations taken of elementary-school children contain fewer unstructured social-interaction situations than observations of preschool children. In fact, Asher and Hymel pointed out that the two studies of elementary-school children with the strongest results, that is, Benson and Gottman, reported in Putallaz and Gottman, (unpublished manuscript, 1979), and Gottman, Gonso, and Rasmussen (1975) included observations sampled from outside the classroom (for example, during recess). Third, while the behavioral coding systems employed may be sufficient to capture the more-personal and concrete constructs influencing the friendship choices of preschool children (for example, "he hits me," "he gives me things"), they may be too global to capture the more-abstract notions important to older children (for example, "he is intelligent," "he is kind"). Further, low-frequency events, which would probably not be detected by observation systems, may influence the friendship choices of older children more than those of younger children. Finally, Asher and Hymel suggested that the sequential order of the interaction (for example, whether one child hitting another was unprovoked or in response to being hit) should be taken into consideration as it may be more important to older children than younger ones.

Thus the overall picture of behavioral correlates is somewhat unclear. In addition to those points raised by Asher and Hymel (forthcoming), results have been further limited in several ways. First, the observational coding systems used have not been very detailed or descriptive, often ignoring language, for example. Second, these studies have not observed children in a wide variety of situations, thus possibly excluding potentially salient social situations (for example, a conflict situation and/or a situation requiring a child to initiate an interaction with a peer group). Further, as Asher and Hymel mentioned, only interaction rates have been used, and so the data have not been analyzed sequentially. This is particularly unfortunate, since interactions between children probably would be captured more accurately by specific interaction patterns rather than by the frequency of individual codes displayed. Using this approach, it would then be possible to study patterns and sequences of behavior over time that would enable us empirically and quantitatively to discover the implicit social rules in a type of interaction. (For a further discussion of sequential analysis, see Bakeman 1978; Gottman 1979; Gottman and Bakeman 1978; Gottman and Notarius 1978; Sackett 1977).

We recently conducted a study that examined behavioral differences between socially accepted and unaccepted children that corrected some of the methodological problems of previous studies in this area (see Putallaz and Gottman unpubl. ms. 1979, for a detailed report of this study). Second and third graders participated in the study. In all, twenty dyads of children were formed—ten popular pairs and ten unpopular pairs—homogeneous by sex and sociometric status. In addition, twenty children were selected to attempt entry into the dyads, thus creating four conditions. These conditions involved the entry of a popular child into either a popular or unpopular group and the entry of an unpopular child into similarly composed dyadic groups. Each dyad, playing a word-naming game in a research trailer for ten minutes, was videotaped. Fifteen minutes of additional videotaped data were the obtained on the attempts of a third child to enter the group. Verbatim transcripts were made from the videotapes and were coded using the interaction coding system developed by Gottman and Parkhurst (1980), with the addition of one entry code (bid for entry) and three group-response codes (accept, reject, and ignore) to facilitate the coding of the entry sequence.

First, we found that the dyadic interaction of popular and unpopular children did differ in several respects. Unpopular children were less agreeable and more disagreeable than popular children. Further, the use of sequential analysis revealed that when popular children disagreed, they would typically cite a general rule as the basis for their disagreement and then provide an acceptable alternative action for the other child. In contrast, unpopular children would typically express their disagreement by stating a prohibition very specific to the previous act of the other child without providing an alternative action for that child. Therefore, we summarized the dyadic social interaction of unpopular children as being disagreeable and bossy, while that of popular children was agreeable and positive. These interactional climates provided the contexts for the entry situation.

In the entry portion of the study, we found that unpopular children were less likely to be accepted and more likely to be ignored by the groups they attempted to enter than popular children. They also waited longer before making their first bid for entry, used more bids, and required more time for entry than popular children. Furthermore, there was no indication that unpopular children had an entry-skills deficit as they displayed all of the entry strategies used by popular children with moderately similar probabilities, although our coding system would not have detected any differences in timing or stylistic execution of the entry bids. It was still possible that the bids most preferred by the unpopular children were not those that would be most effective in terms of gaining them entry. To test this possibility, we computed a cost-benefit score for each entry behavior as used by popular and unpopular children by calculating the probability of the bid's leading to acceptance of the entering child by the group minus the probability of its leading to nonacceptance—that is, the entering child being either rejected or ignored by the group. Thus, a high positive score would be indicative of an entry bid that had a high probability of leading to acceptance and a low probability of leading to the group's rejecting or ignoring the user, while the converse would be true of a high negative score.

Next, the correlation between the probabilities of each entry bid and its cost-benefit score was computed. This correlation would allow us to ascertain whether the entry bids that had the highest probability of occurring corresponded to those that had the most favorable cost-benefit score. For popular children, this correlation was .74, $p < .025$ for entry into popular groups and .51, $p < .10$ for entry into unpopular groups. For unpopular children, this correlation was $-.06$ for entry into unpopular groups and $-.13$ for entry into popular groups; neither of the latter two correlations was significant. This result was remarkable. Popular children acted to maximize their benefits and minimize their costs, but this was not true of unpopular children. Popular children acted in accordance with the likelihood of being accepted rather than being rejected or ignored by the group, while this was not true of unpopular children. We are not implying that unpopular children were deliberately intending to be ignored or rejected when attempting to enter groups but, rather, that this was the net effect of their behavior.

To examine why unpopular children would not act in what appears to be their best interests, the correlations between the probabilities of each entry behavior and the separate likelihoods of the group's accepting, rejecting, or ignoring this bid for entry were studied. The purpose of these analyses was to determine empirically the criteria used by entering children in organizing their response hierarchy for entry, rather than relying on the cost-benefit score. To determine the criteria used by entering children in their response-hierarchy ordering, a procedure similar to stepwise multiple regression was followed. First, the correlations between the hierarchy (H) and each of the three consequences—accept (A), reject (R), and ignore (I)—were computed, and the highest of these correlations was taken as the first criterion. Second, the partial correlations were computed, and the highest of these was taken as the second criterion. In all cases, a statistical significance criterion of $p < .10$ was employed.

The results of this analysis showed that the entry-response hierarchies of popular children, regardless of the status of the group they attempted to enter, were ordered such that the probability of being accepted by the group was maximized, while the probability of being ignored or rejected was minimized. In contrast, unpopular children had their entry-response hierarchies ordered such that the probability of being ignored by the group they attempted to enter was maximized. An analysis of the specific entry bids showed that, during entry, unpopular children tended to disagree more than popular children; they also attempted to call attention to themselves by stating their feelings and opinions, making self-statements, and asking informational questions that, paradoxically, only resulted in their being ignored. It appeared that the most successful strategy for integration in this particular situation was for children to determine first the frame of reference common to the group members (for example, norms, values, activities) and then to establish themselves as sharing in this frame of reference, particularly by agreeing and imitating the words or actions of a child in the nucleus group.

To summarize the findings thus far from the behavioral-correlates literature, popular children apparently tend to initiate and receive more frequent positive interactions with their peers than unpopular children. Further, evidence shows that social rejection is related to negative peer interactions. Specifically, it appears that, compared to popular children, unpopular children are (1) less agreeable and more disagreeable and (2) less likely to provide a general reason for disagreeing or to suggest a constructive alternative when criticizing a peer. Thus, the interactive style of unpopular children might be summarized as disagreeable and bossy and that of popular children as agreeable and positive.

Cognitive Correlates of Sociometric Status

Social Knowledge

Rather than search for possible behavioral correlates of peer acceptance, a second research approach has concentrated upon identifying the cognitive concomitants of sociometric status. The goal of this strategy is to assess whether children's social knowledge is a determinant of peer acceptance and friendship. In the Gottman, Gonso, and Rasmussen (1975) study, third- and fourth-grade children of high and low sociometric status role-played how they would attempt to make friends with a new child in their school who was role played by the experimenter. The children's responses were scored differentially using the following friendship-making sequence: offering a greeting, asking for information, extending an offer of inclusion, and giving information to the new child. The results indicated that the popular and unpopular children differed in their demonstrated ability to make friends—the popular children being the more skillful. This study thus suggested that the children's social knowledge and peer acceptance are positively related.

This research approach has been employed also by Ladd and Oden (1979) in a study examining the relationship between peer acceptance and children's knowledge about helpfulness. In individual interviews, third- and fifth-grade children were asked to suggest behavioral solutions to three cartoon sets depicting situations in which a child was in need of help (for example, being teased by peers, being yelled at by a peer, and having a schoolwork problem). The children's responses were coded into thirteen mutually exclusive categories (for example, console/comfort, distract attention, instruct). The results showed that children who suggested many unique solutions—responses not given by other children—tended to receive low sociometric ratings, while children who suggested few unique responses tended to be those most liked by their peers. Ladd and Oden suggested that low-accepted children are less aware of peer norms and values for helpful social behavior than popular children who have shared knowledge regarding situationally appropriate helpful behavior. This is an especially interesting finding, as Ladd and Oden pointed out, in light of the previous research by Spivack and Shure (1974), indicating the ability to generate alternatives to be an important social problem-solving skill.

The most extensive research done in this area at present, building upon the work of Gottman and his associates (1975) and Ladd and Oden (1979), has been done by Asher and Renshaw (forthcoming). In this research, kindergarten children of high and low sociometric status were asked to suggest possible alternative strategies for the protagonist in nine drawings depicting hypothetical situations that required the protagonist to take some course of either behavioral or verbal action. The situations were of three types—initiating social relationships (for example, getting to know a new group of children, making a friend); social maintenance (for example, maintaining a conversation, helping a friend in need); and management of conflict (for example, responding when a child attempts to take away a toy). The majority of the responses given by the children did not discriminate between the children on the basis of sociometric status, as the responses most common to highly popular children were similarly the most common responses for the unpopular group. However, the strategies suggested exclusively by the unpopular group were often inappropriately negative (for example a strategy to join two peers playing a game was to take the game). In contast, the strategies unique to the popular group were described as quite prosocial and sophisticated (for example, waiting for a break in the game before asking to join).

Further differences between the two sociometric groups were evident when their responses to the three types of hypothetical situations were analyzed. With respect to the situations concerned with the initiation of social relationships, unpopular children were more likely to appeal to an authority figure for help or to suggest vague, uncodable strategies. Thus, Asher and Renshaw suggested independent resourcefulness as a possible deficit of unpopular children. In the conflict-management situations, unpopular children were more apt to employ aggressive strategies than popular children. For those situations dealing with the maintenance of social relationships, the suggestions made by unpopular children were again more likely to be vague, an appeal to adult intervention, or be of a negative quality despite the situation being rather neutral. Asher and Renshaw speculated that the responses of unpopular children reflected a lack of resourcefulness as well as an inability or desire to use normal social encounters in order to foster closer relationships with their peers.

Asher and Renshaw evaluated the strategies suggested by the children along three dimensions: (1) assertiveness, (2) relationship improvement, and (3) effectiveness. The responses of popular and unpopular children did not differ with respect to assertiveness but did differ on the effectiveness and relationship-improvement dimensions. Further analyses showed sociometric status to be significantly predicted only by the relationship-improvement dimension.

From the combination of evidence from previous studies and that of their own work, Asher and Renshaw concluded that children low in sociometric status are less socially skillful than their peers who are high in sociometric status. They further suggested that social skillfulness includes (1) knowledge of general interaction principles or concepts that could be used to guide behavior across a variety of situations; (2) knowledge of the specific behaviors or behavioral sequences that could be used to "operationalize" these general concepts or principles; (3) appropriate setting of goals (for example, goal of winning a game and having fun with one's opponent versus the goal of defeating one's opponent at all costs); and (4) ability to monitor one's impact on others. Unpopular children, then, would be expected to have deficits in one or more of these components.

Communication Accuracy

As the nature of children's verbal expression becomes more complex with age, it becomes increasingly important for children to be able to distinguish for their listeners between precisely what they are referring to (the referent) and what they are not referring to (the nonreferent). As Asher (1978) stated, the speaker's goal is to ensure that the listener will be able to identify the referent (for example, the particular object, location, idea) from alternatives that might be confused for the referent. This ability has been termed *referential communication* (Glucksberg and Krauss 1967). Asher (1979) has suggested that the development of such a skill is important for the facilitation of coordinated social interaction.

Given the proposed importance of referential-communication ability with respect to social interaction, it is not surprising that it has been found to be related to children's level of acceptance by their peers. Rubin (1971) found that the correlation between performance on Glucksberg and Krauss's (1967) referential-communication tasks and popularity, holding IQ constant, was .58 ($p < .01$) for both kindergarten and second-grade children. The correlations were not significant for children in the fourth and sixth grades. However, Gottman and co-workers (1975) found that the third and fourth graders who communicated more accurately on a referential-communication task also had more friends according to a sociometric measure ($F = 10.20$, $p < .01$). Therefore, the ability of children to communicate accurately appears to be related to their level of peer acceptance. Further, in a related study, socially accepted children were found to be more verbally fluent than unaccepted children on a doll-play task in which they had to complete stories, thus giving additional support that communicative ability is important with respect to obtained level of peer acceptance (Commoss 1962).

Some evidence suggests that unpopular children may also be less accurate in their nonverbal communication than their more socially accepted peers. Buck (1977) measured the tendency of twenty-four preschool children to communicate nonverbal messages accurately via their spontaneous facial expressions and gestures. The children individually viewed a series of sixteen emotionally loaded slides and rated their reactions to each slide along a pleasant/unpleasant continuum, while unknown to them, their mothers watched their televised spontaneous facial expressions for each slide and made similar pleasantness ratings as well as judgments of the nature of each slide. In this manner, two measures of nonverbal-communication accuracy were obtained: (1) the correlation between the ratings of pleasantness of each slide given by the children and their mothers and (2) the number of slides correctly categorized by the mothers. In addition, the children's teachers completed rating-scale assessments of them on a series of items related to an overall internal/external personality dimension. The results indicated that, for boys, teacher ratings of expressiveness were positively related to the accuracy of their nonverbal communication, whereas teacher ratings of the level of antagonism were related to the nonverbal-communication accuracy of girls.

Buck explained this apparent discrepancy by suggesting that boys and girls high in communication accuracy may be displaying similar behavior in the classroom but that the teachers rated these behaviors in girls as antagonistic while they considered them expressive in boys. What is important with respect to this discussion, however, is that the teacher ratings of the children's expressiveness were found to be positively correlated with teacher ratings of their overall level of popularity. Previous research has indicated that teachers' judgments of the popularity of their students are in fairly close agreement with their students' choices on a sociometric test (Gronlund 1959). Therefore, this study provides some support, albeit indirect, that children's expressiveness and thus their ability to communicate accurate nonverbal messages may be related to their obtained level of peer acceptance.

Buck's (1977) results are particularly intriguing when considered in light of the research done by Snyder (1974) on adults' self-monitoring of expressive behavior. Snyder defined self-monitoring as the extent to which individuals monitor—that is, both observe and control—their own expressive high on this dimension, then, would be an acute sensitivity to social-comparison information, stemming from their concern for social appropriateness. Indeed, Snyder found that the expression and self-presentation of others in social situations was attended to and used by these individuals to guide the monitoring and managing of their own self-presentation and expressive behavior more than by low-self-monitoring individuals. Further, Snyder found individuals scoring high on self-monitoring to be better able to express and communicate emotions accurately (both verbally and nonverbally) than individuals low on this dimension, as well as being better at judging emotions. Therefore, high-self-monitoring individuals apparently are both better senders and receivers of expressive behavior.

Thus, taken together, the Buck and Snyder studies would suggest that, although Snyder did not find a similar relationship in adults, Buck reported popular children to be both more expressive and more accurate in their spontaneous nonverbal communication than unpopular children. Further, Snyder found that individuals who were better senders of expressive behavior were also better receivers of both verbal and nonverbal communication. Thus, perhaps popular children are better able to interpret the verbal and nonverbal behavior of others in social situations and better able to send accurate and appropriate communications in those situations as well—that is, popular children may be better able to discern from the behavior of others in a given situation the prevailing norms or expectations in that situation, and thus to act in a socially appropriate manner. Following from this, it may also be the case that popular children are better able to respond to feedback from others and thus better able to modify their behavior so as to become more synchronized with the others in the situation.

This hypothesis gains support from the findings reported by Ladd and Oden (1979) and Putallaz and Gottman (unpub'l. ms, 1979). As may be recalled, Ladd and Oden suggested that unpopular children were less aware of peer norms and values for helpful social behavior and so suggested many unique solutions to such problems. However, popular children appeared to have knowledge concerning the norms of situationally appropriate helpful behavior and suggested few unique responses. Similarly, Putallaz and Gottman suggested that when attempting to enter peer groups, popular children seemed more adept than unpopular children at discerning the ongoing activity of the group and consequently better able to synchronize their behavior with that of the group members. Popular children entered groups in less time, used fewer bids than unpopular children, and were described as acting in accordance with a cost-benefit model because they used entry strategies that maximized the probability of their acceptance and minimized the probability of their being rejected or ignored by the group. In contrast, unpopular children did not appear as sensitive to the behavior of the groups they attempted to enter. Rather than join in the ongoing group activity, unpopular children attempted to influence the group by directing the group's attention to themselves that resulted in their being ignored by the group. In summary, then, there is some support for the hypothesis that popular children may be better able to determine the prevailing norms or expectations in a given situation and to act in accordance with those norms than unpopular children.

Self-Perception

Children's perceptions of themselves may be related to the kinds of cognitive self-statements they make (Meichenbaum 1972). Information assessing the possibility of differential self-statements made by popular children would appear to be important since such statements may be debilitating to children and the modification of cognitive self-statements has been demonstrated to be useful in other social-skills-training interventions—as with girl-shy boys (Glass, Gottman, and Shmurak 1976). The literature examining correlations betwen personality measures and peer acceptance may be taken as some index of cognitive self-statements children make about themselves. It does not appear that general measures of self-esteem and popularity are related, as findings have not been consistent from study to study (Berger 1974). However, more-specific self-assessments related to social relationships seem to correlate with sociometric measures of peer acceptance. Baron (1951) found that unpopular fifth- and sixth-grade girls feel that most of their friends do things better, find it difficult to make friends with people they like, worry that people do not like them as well as they should, feel that people hurt their feelings more than they do the feelings of others, and feel that people often say unfairly that they have many poor ideas. It is thus not surprising that Putallaz and Gottman (unpub,l. ms, 1979) found that unpopular children waited longer before making their first bid (that is, they hovered) when attempting to enter groups of their peers, given the negative nature of the cognitive self-statements Baron suggested that they make. More research is needed to directly assess the nature of the self-statements children may be making in specific social situations that they find problematic (see Schwartz and Gottman 1976, for a methodology used to address this problem with adults).

Summary of Cognitive Correlates

To summarize the literature concerning the cognitive correlates of peer acceptance, children apparently can be distinguished with respect to their level of social knowledge on the basis of their sociometric status. Usually, the strategies offered by unpopular children to hypothetical social situations are of a more-negative and unique variety than those of popular children that tend to be more prosocial and sophisticated. Further, unpopular children do not seem as knowledgable about the establishment or maintenance of social relationships with peers since their responses to these situations are likely to be negative and vague, including an appeal to an authority figure for help. Also, in response to conflict situations, unpopular children are more apt to suggest aggressive strategies than popular children. In addition, unpopular children appear to be less accurate in both their verbal and nonverbal communication and to have more negative self-perceptions than popular children. Thus, some additional, as well as some validating, information about peer relations needs to be learned through this channel of assessment.

Studies of Friendship

As may be recalled, in addition to peer acceptance, the other aspect of social behavior identified as satisfying a high-risk criterion was the ability to establish and maintain a close friendship. Rather than to attempt to discover those factors discriminating between popular and unpopular children, then the goal of this research approach is to determine empirically those skills necessary for friendship to develop—a subtle distinction.

The most comprehensive work in this area has been done by Gottman and Parkhurst (1980) who, based on their observational research of friendship and acquaintanceship, proposed a specific hierarchy of eight interactional events to describe the acquaintanceship process in children aged two to five years. The hypothesis that the lower events in the hierarchy, if successfully completed by the application of certain social skills, enable the children's interaction to progress to higher events that create greater intimacy and thereby increase the likelihood of developing friendship. What is especially important here, then, are the particular social skills identified as being necessary for a friendship between two children to develop. It is important to note that Gottman and Parkhurst did not suggest that this hierarchy was a lockstep description of acquaintanceship, but simply a probabilistic account of typical interaction between children of these ages.

This hierarchy and its relevant social skills were developed empirically from an intensive observational study of the conversations of dyads of children who were either best friends or strangers. Each dyad was audiotaped in the home of one of the children (the host child) in the room where that child usually played with friends. The children had available to them whatever toys were normally present. Further, the parents were asked to arrange that other children not be present and to leave the children alone as much as possible. The tapes were transcribed, using the children's interaction coding system developed by Gottman and Parkhurst (1980).

In the proposed first step in this hierarchical process, the host child attempts to interest the guest in something (for example, personal possessions, attributes), usually in a show-and-tell fashion. Two social skills are identified as being especially important at this initial point of the interaction—namely, connected discourse and communication clarity. Connected discourse is described as occurring when the two children are not talking on separate courses but rather when both are talking in a related fashion and are responding to one another. Gottman and Parkhurst provided the following example of two children engaged in connected conversation:

> Child 1: My mommy went to see my aunt cause she has a new baby.
>
> Child 2: Whoops, dropped the pencil. You know, my mom's getting a new baby soon too. [1980, p. 24].

As can be seen, the second child responded to the first child's comment with a related statement on the topic of their mothers having new babies, allowing the conversation to be connected. The other social skill, identified by Gottman and Parkhurst as important at this level, is communication clarity that they define as occurring when the children adequately clarify their messages upon request of the other child and appropriately answer informational questions the other child may ask.

Gottman and Parkhurst suggested that this step may lead to the second level in their proposed hierarchy that involves the two children in social-comparison activity. During this stage, the two children begin to compare their possessions and often their attributes (for example, age, number of siblings). One salient social skill at this level is that the two children are capable of establishing solidarity between them prior to exploring any contrasts. In other words, Gottman and Parkhurst suggested that the children discover their common ground prior to their differences in order to increase the probability that their interaction will progress to a higher level of acquaintanceship. An example of expressing solidarity would be the following sequence:

> Child 1: I'm doing mine green.
>
> Child 2: Me too. [p. 35]

Once a feeling of solidarity has been established, contrasts between the two children become interesting and pose less of a threat to the development of their friendship. In addition, it is helpful if the host is socially skillful enough during this social-comparison activity to begin to make offers to the guest (for example, "You can play with this"). In this way, an activity-play interaction, the next step in the hierarchy, may be initiated.

If an activity-play interaction is initiated (for example, coloring, glueing, dump trucks), there seems to be a high probability that the number of control attempts made by the host will subsequently increase. An important social skill identified at this level of the acquaintanceship process is that the guest comply with these requests, particularly with polite suggestions made by the host. In fact, Gottman and Parkhurst suggested that a measure of increased interpersonal comfort (or intimacy) at this level is compliance by the guest to the host's imperatives, demands, or expressed needs.

There appears to be an increased probability that conflict and disagreement between the two children will arise with the occurrence of control attempts, and thus the ability to resolve disagreements becomes an important skill in the fourth stage of the acquaintanceship process. It seems essential that the host child be capable of providing a rationale for any disagreement and that the guest follow any expression of disagreement by speaking in a fantasy role.

The remaining four levels of the proposed hierarchy concern the progression of the fantasy play that may develop between the two children. The first of these levels appears to be characterized by the initiation of stereotyped fantasy. The nature of stereotyped fantasy is such that the children are provided with a definite structure for their play with more or less clearly prescribed roles (for example, imitating well-known television characters, preparing food). The children's stereotyped fantasy then becomes developed and extended at the next step in the hierarchy, level six. At level seven, Gottman and Parkhurst propose that the stereotyped nature or quality of the children's fantasy decreases. Instead, they suggest that the children's fantasy begins to become less structured or ritualized and that, since the roles are not as established, more intervention and negotiation is required on the part of the children (for example, playing doctor, playing monsters). Finally, what seems to be important at the last level is how developed and extended the nonstereotyped fantasy of the children is. The prediction is that the less-stereotyped fantasy the children are able to sustain, the closer or more intimate their relationship will be. Gottman and Parkhurst identified the particularly salient social skills at this final level as the expression of important feelings by one child with subsequent support and solidarity provided by the other child (all occurring within the context of fantasy) as well as the resolution of conflict.

This, then, represents a summary of the acquaintanceship process proposed by Gottman and Parkhurst (1980) to characterize the interactions of preschool children, with certain specified social skills becoming particularly salient at different levels in the hierarchy. It is suggested that the likelihood of two strangers becoming friends depends upon their ability to progress through this acquaintanceship hierarchy. This acquaintanceship process, however, apparently becomes more difficult to specify for children beyond age five possibly because of their acquisition of a more-adult interactional style apparent particularly with strangers. The younger children appear to try to be good to their friends and to make friends with strangers, often attempting to engage their peers in activities that not only have a high potential for intimacy (like fantasy) but also a high risk of unclear communication, continued disagreement, or squabbling that can be disastrous. In contrast, older children are more moderate in their interactions with both friends and strangers, pursuing a low-risk, low-intimacy strategy of continuing in an activity-talk modality rather than attempting fantasy. Thus, the goals of the older children may have changed from those of the younger children. The older children seem to have become more skillful in their interaction with strangers, but apparently at the cost of less intimacy with fewer friends.

Conclusion

At this point, we are faced with what may seem to be an overwhelming number of individual social skills, from both a behavioral and cognitive realm, that have been shown to be related empirically to children's level of peer acceptance or their ability to establish a friendship and, consequently, their social competence. However, upon closer examination, it is apparent that several general dimensions might be selected that are common to both the peer-acceptance and children's friendship literatures and that can incorporate most of these separate skills. Specifically, these dimensions are overall positiveness, ability to resolve conflicts or disagreements, awareness of group norms or social rules, ability to communicate accurately, ability to establish a common bond between oneself and another, and positive self-perception (although less evidence exists for this last dimension than for the ones preceeding it).

It is possible to propose a profile of a child's social competence using these six dimensions. Socially competent children are usually positive and agreeable in their interactions with peers, in contrast to their less-competent peers who are disagreeable, bossy, and negative in their interactions with other children. Further, children high in social competence provide general reasons for their disagreements and suggest constructive alternatives when criticizing a peer, while children low in social competence are less able to keep their disagreements from continuing or escalating and are more apt to resort to aggressive solutions to conflict situations. Unlike their less-competent counterparts, socially competent children also seem more aware of group norms and social rules, or are more adept at discerning them, and thus appear to be better able, for example, to enter peer groups and are more knowledgeable about situationally appropriate behavior. They also seem to be more capable of establishing a feeling of solidarity between themselves and peers by exploring their commonalities prior to their differences and by conversing in a connected fashion. Moreover, children high in social competence also appear to be more accurate in both their verbal and nonverbal communication and to have less-negative self-perceptions than less-competent children.

We have thus far, then, through the use of high-risk criteria, identified six dimensions, consisting of behavioral and cognitive skills that are associated with social competence. We cannot say that taken together these six factors define social competence; we have only demonstrated that these dimensions are correlated with peer acceptance and the ability to establish a close friendship—not that they are causally related to them. However, we argue that presently these dimensions are the only ones empirically demonstrated to be associated with children's social competence. It is now possible to employ these dimensions to integrate and to understand future research findings and to provide a tentative research direction for the necessary transition from unguided hypothesis generation to systematic hypothesis testing.

At this point, the most immediate research question that needs to be addressed is to identify which of these dimensions are prerequisites for social competence and which are the results of being socially competent. Since we have proposed that a close friendship and the level of peer acceptance are good indexes of social competence, the research question is which of these dimensions is necessary or causes children to be able to establish a close friendship and to be accepted by their peers? Conversely, which of these dimensions follows after children have attained a high level of sociometric status and made a close friend? For example, it may be essential that children have the ability to perceive group norms and values to be accepted by their peers or make a friend, and so this ability would be considered necessary for social competence. In contrast, however, a positive self-perception may be a result of being accepted by one's peers or having a close friend and not a prerequisite for achieving such status. Therefore, research is essential to make this discrimination and thus to identify those factors causally related to social competence.

Identifying such causal factors may increase the effectiveness of intervention programs. The less than successful outcome of the majority of intervention programs previously attempted may be due, at least in part, to the lack of a solid descriptive-knowledge base from which the skills taught to target children were selected. Few of these previous intervention programs arrived at their choice of skills on the basis of empirically derived differences between socially accepted and unaccepted children or children with a friend versus those without. The majority of these interventions was designed on the basis of logic, intuition, and armchair speculation. If it can be determined which of these factors influences the degree to which children are accepted by their peers and make friends, then the prospects may improve for both adequate assessment and development of successful interventions aimed at remedying the identified deficits.

It would also be important to examine the developmental progression of these factors over time, because the form they assume may change as children grow older. For example, as mentioned previously, Gottman and Parkhurst (1980) proposed that preschool children (ages two–five years) progressed through a different acquaintanceship hierarchy with different goals than older children. Another example that illustrates this point is a study by Evans and Rubin (forthcoming). They examined both the verbal and nonverbal components of the game instructions that kindergartners and second and fourth graders related to a confederate listener. Specifically, the children's game explanations were scored for the number and type of hand gestures employed and also the number of rules correctly expressed either verbally, gesturally, or with both words and gestures. First, of a total of 162 rules expressed by the children, only 6 were found not to be accompanied by some form of hand gesture, thus highlighting the need to consider the nonverbal aspect of the children's communication. Second, kindergartners were found to express significantly more-inadequate rules than the two older groups when the verbal message alone was considered, but these became adequate when the accompanying gestures were taken into account. Further, older children were found to give more rules in which the verbal explanation alone was adequate than younger children. However, no significant age differences were found for the number of adequate rules expressed when both the gestural and verbal components of the communication were considered (Rubin 1979). Hence, this study provides an example of an empirical examination of the developmental progression of one of the previously identified factors. It appears that the form that an accurate communication assumes changes with age when gestures become compulsory accompaniments for the verbal messages of young children but extraneous for older children as their verbal expression alone is sufficient for accurate communication.

In addition to developmental changes in the form of these factors, it is also possible that the relative importance of these factors may change with age. For example, Rubin (1972) has suggested that communication accuracy may play a causal role in a child's attained level of peer acceptance through second grade but that it may then be replaced in importance by other factors by the time children reach fourth grade. Perhaps by determining the developmental progression of these factors and the relative weighting of their importance, the design and utility of preventive intervention programs would become more feasible. Presumably, a child's deficit or developmental lag in one or more of these factors could be detected early, thereby increasing the probability that that child might avoid the adverse effects of social isolation.

References

K.E. Allen, B. Hart, J.B. Buell, R.W. Haris, and M.M. Wolf, "Effects of Social Reinforcement of Isolate Behavior of a Nursery School Child," *Child Development* 35(1964):511–518.

E.J. Amidon, and C. Hoffman, "Can Teachers Help the Socially Rejected?" *Elementary School Journal* 66(1965):149–154.

S. Anderson and S. Messick, "Social Competency in Young Children," Developmental Psychology 10(1974):282–293.

M. Argyle, *Social Interaction* (Chicago: Aldine, 1969).

S.R. Asher, "Referential Communication," *The Functions of Language and Cognition,* eds. G.J. Whitehurst and B.J. Zimmerman (New York: Academic Press, 1978.

S.R. Asher, "Children's Peer Relations," in *Sociopersonality Development,* ed. M.E. Lamb (New York: Holt, Rinehart & Winston, 1979).

S.R. Asher and S. Hymel, "Children's Social Competence in Peer Relations: Sociometric and Behavioral Assessment," in *Social Competence,* eds. J.D. Wine and M.D. Smye (New York: Guilford Press, forthcoming).

S.R. Asher, S.L. Oden, and J.M. Gottman, "Children's Friendships in School Settings," *Current Topics in Early Childhood Education,* vol. 1, ed. L.G. Katz (Norwood, N.J.: Ablex, 1977).

S.R. Asher and P.D. Renshaw, "Children without Friends: Social Knowledge and Social Skill Training," In *The Development of Children's Friendships,* eds. S.R. Asher and J.M. Gottman (New York: Cambridge University Press, forthcoming).

F. Bakeman "Untangling Streams of Behavior: Sequential Analysis of Observational Data," In *Observing Behavior Data Collection and Analysis Methods,* vol. 2, ed. G.P. Sackett (Baltimore: University Park Press, 1978).

D. Baron, "Personal-Social Characteristics and Classroom Social Status: A Sociometric Study of Fifth and Sixth Grade Girls," *Sociometry* 14(1951):32–43.

C. Bereiter, "The Future of Individual Differences," *Harvard Educational Review* 39(1969):310–318.

B.N. Berger, "Children's Descriptions of Friends and Non-Friends: An Investigation of Peer Acceptance and Rejection" (Honors thesis, Indiana University, 1974).

M.R. Bonney, "Assessment of Efforts to Aid Socially Isolated Elementary School Pupils," *Journal of Educational Research* 64(1971):345–364.

M.R. Bornstein, A.S. Bellack, and M. Hersen, "Social Skills Training for Unassertive Children: A Multiple-Baseline Analysis," *Journal of Applied Behavior Analysis* 10(1977):183–195.

E.M. Bower, *Early Identification of Emotionally Handicapped Children in School* (Springfield, Ill.: Charles C Thomas, 1960).

W.C. Bronson, "The Measurement of Social Competence," In *Human Growth and Development: Physical and Behavioral Perspectives,* eds. A. Poche and J. Himes (Albuquerque: University of New Mexico Press, forthcoming).

G.W. Brown, M.N. Bhrolchain, and T. Harris, "Social Class and Psychiatric Disturbance among Women in an Urban Population," *Sociology* 9(1975):225–254.

R. Buck "Nonverbal Communication of Affect in Preschool Children: Relationships with Personality and Skin Conductance," *Journal of Personality and Social Psychology* 35(1977):225–236.

M.M. Buswell, "The Relationship between Social Structure of the Classroom and Academic Successes of the Pupils," *Journal of Experimental Education* 22(1953):37–52.

L.J. Butler, "Social Behavioral Correlates of Peer Reputation" Paper presented at the biennial meeting of the Society for Research in Child Development, San Francisco, 1979).

G.F. Chittenden, "An Experimental Study in Measuring and Modifying Assertive Behavior in Young Children," Serial No. 31 *Monographs of the Society for Research in Child Development* 7(1942).

H.H. Commoss, "Some Characteristics Related to Social Isolation of Second Grade Children," *Journal of Educational Psychology* 53(1962): 38–42.

E.L. Cowen, A. Pederson, H. Babijian, L.D. Izzo, and M.A. Trost, "Long-Term Follow-Up of Early Detected Vulnerable Children," *Journal of Consulting and Clinical Psychology* 41(1973):438–446.

J.M. Criswell, "A Sociometric Study of Race Cleavage in the Classroom," *Archives of Psychology,* no. 235(1939):1–82.

M.A. Evans and K.H. Rubin, "Hand Gestures as a Communicative Mode in School-Aged Children," *Journal of Genetic Psychology,* in press.

W.L. Evers, J.C. Schwarz, "Modifying Social Withdrawal in Preschoolers: The Effect of Filmed Modeling and Teacher Praise," *Journal of Abnormal Child Psychology* 1(1973):248–256.

W. Furman, D.F. Rahe, and W.W. Hartup, "Rehabilitation of Socially Withdrawn Preschool Children through Mixed-Age and Same-Age Socialization," *Child Development* 50(1979):915–922.

N. Garmezy, A. Masten, L. Nordstrom, and M. Ferrarese, "The Nature of Competence in Normal and Deviant Children," In *The Primary Prevention of Psychopathology: Promoting Social Competence and Coping in Children,* vol. 3, eds. M. Kent and J. Rolf (Hanover, N.H.: University Press of New England, 1979).

C.R. Glass, J.M. Gottman, and S.H. Shmurak, "Response Acquisition and Cognitive Self-Statement Modification Approaches to Dating Skills," *Journal of Counseling Psychology* 23(1976):520–526.

S. Glucksberg and R.M. Krauss, "What Do People Say after They Have Learned How to Talk? Studies of the Development Referential Communication," *Merrill-Palmer Quarterly* 13(1967):309–316.

J.M. Gottman, "The Effects of a Modeling Film on Social Isolation in Preschool Children: A Methodological Investigation," *Journal of*

Abnormal Child Psychology 5(1977):69–78.

J.M. Gottman, "Detecting Cyclicity in Social Interaction," *Psychological Bulletin* 86(1979):338–348.

J.M. Gottman and R. Bakeman, "The Sequential Analysis of Observational Data," In *Methodological Problems in the Study of Social Interaction,* eds. M. Lamb, S. Soumi, and G. Stephenson (Madison: University of Wisconsin Press, 1978).

J.M. Gottman, J. Gonso, and B. Rasmussen, "Social Interaction, Social Competence and Friendship in Children," *Child Development* 46 (1975):709–718.

J.M. Gottman and H.J. Markman, "Experimental Designs in Psychotherapy Research," in *Handbook of Psychotherapy and Behavior Change: An Empirical Analysis,* eds. S.L. Garfield and A.E. Bergin (New York: John Wiley & Sons, 1978).

J.M. Gottman and C. Notarius, "Sequential Analysis of Observational Data Using Markov Chains," in *Strategies to Evaluate Change in Single Subject Research,* ed. T. Kratochwill (New York: Academic Press, 1978).

J.M. Gottman and J. Parkhurst, "The Development of Friendship and Acquaintanceship Processes," in *Minnesota Symposia on Child Psychology,* vol 13, ed. A. Collins (Hillsdale, N.J. Lawrence Erlbaum, 1980).

W.R. Gove, "Sex, Marital Status and Mortality," *American Journal of Sociology* 79(1973):45–67.

N.E. Gronlund, *Sociometry in the Classroom* (New York: Harper & Brothers, 1959).

W.W. Hartup, J.A. Glazer, and R. Charlesworth, "Peer Reinforcement and Sociometric Status," *Child Development* 38(1967):1017–1024.

S. Henderson, P. Duncan-Jones, H. McAuley, and K. Ritchie, "The Patient's Primary Group," *British Journal of Psychiatry* 132(1978): 74–86.

S. Hymel and S.R. Asher, "Assessment and Training of Isolated Children's Social Skills" (Paper presented at the biennial meeting of the Society for Research in Child Development, New Orleans, 1977).

L. Jack, "An Experimental Study of Ascendant Behavior in Preschool Children," *University of Iowa Studies in Child Welfare* 9(1934):7–65.

M.F. Keller and P.M. Carlson, "The Use of Symbolic Modeling to Promote Social Skills in Children with Low Levels of Social Responsiveness," *Child Development* 45(1974):912–919.

M. Kohn and J. Clausen, "Social Isolation and Schizophrenia," *American Sociological Review* 20(1955):265–273.

R.G. Kuhlen and E.G. Collister, "Sociometric Status of Sixth- and Ninth-Graders Who Fail to Finish High School," *Educational and Psychological Measurement* 12(1952):632–637.

G.W. Ladd, "Social Skills and Peer Acceptance" (Paper presented at the biennial meeting of the Society for Research in Child Development, San Francisco, 1979).

G.W. Ladd and S.L. Oden, "The Relationship between Peer Acceptance and Children's Ideas about Helpfulness," *Child Development* 50(1979):402–408.

H.R. Marshall and B.R. McCandless, "Relationships between Dependence on Adults and Social Acceptance by Peers," *Child Development* 28(1957):413–419.

D.C. McClelland, "Testing for Competence Rather than for Intelligence," *American Psychologist* 28(1973):1–14.

D.H. Meichenbaum, "Cognitive Modification of Test-Anxious College Students," *Journal of Consulting and Clinical Psychology* 39(1972): 370 – 380.

D.H. Meichenbaum, L. Butler, and L.G. Joseph, "Toward a Conceptual Model of Social Competence," in *The Identification and Enhancement of Social Competence,* eds. J. Wine and M. Smye (Washington, D.C.: Hemisphere Press, in press).

P.M. Miller and J.G. Ingham, "Friends, Confidants and Symptoms," *Social Psychiatry* 11(1976):51–58.

R.S. Miller, "An Investigation of the Behavioral Correlates and Function of Interpersonal Intimacy" (Ph.D. dissertation, University of Waterloo, 1979).

D. Mummery "An Analytic Study of Ascendant Behavior of Preschool Children," *Child Development* 18(1947)40–81.

R.D. O'Connor, "Modification of Social Withdrawal through Symbolic Modeling," *Journal of Applied Behavior Analysis* 2(1969):15–22.

R.D. O'Connor, "Relative Efficacy of Modeling, Shaping, and the Combined Procedures for Modification of Social Withdrawal," *Journal of Abnormal Psychology* 79(1972):327–334.

S. Oden and S.R. Asher, "Coaching Children in Social Skills for Friendship Making," *Child Development* 48(1977):495–506.

J.M. O'Malley, "Research Perspective on Social Competence," *Merrill-Palmer Quarterly* 23(1977): 29–44.

M. Putallaz and J.M. Gottman, "Social Skills and Group Acceptance," in *The Development of Children's Friendships,* eds. S.R. Asher and J.M. Gottman (New York: Cambridge University Press, in press).

M. Putallaz and J.M. Gottman, "An Interactional Model of Children's Entry into Peer Groups, unpublished manuscript, University of Illinois, 1979.

M. Roff, "Childhood Social Interactions and Young Adult Bad Conduct," *Journal of Abnormal and Social Psychology* 63(1961):333–337.

M. Roff, "Childhood Social Interaction and Young Adult Psychosis," *Journal of Clinical Psychology* 19(1963):152–157.

M. Roff, S.B. Sells, and M.M. Golden, *Social Adjustment and Personal-*

ity Development in Children (Minneapolis: University of Minnesota Press, 1972).

K.H. Rubin, "Relationship between Egocentric Communication and Popularity among Peers," *Developmental Psychology* 7(1972):364.

K.H. Rubin, "Social Cognition and Communicative Development in Young Children (Invited address, S.R.C.D. Summer Institute on the Origins and Growth of Communication, University of Delaware, June 1979).

G.P. Sackett, "The Lag Sequential Analysis of Contingency and Cyclicity in Behavioral Interaction Research," in *Handbook of Infant Development,* ed. J. Osofsky (New York: John Wiley & Sons, 1977).

R.M. Schwartz and J.M. Gottman, "Toward a Task Analysis of Assertive Behavior," *Journal of Consulting and Clinical Psychology* 44(1976): 910–920.

L.C. Singleton and S.R. Asher, "Peer Preferences and Social Interaction among Third-Grade Children in an Integrated School District," *Journal of Educational Psychology* 69(1977):330–336.

M. Snyder, "Self-Monitoring of Expressive Behavior," *Journal of Personality and Social Psychology* 30(1974):526–537.

G. Spivack and M.B. Shure, *Social Adjustment of Young Children* (San Francisco: Jossey-Bass, 1974).

P.S. Strain, T.P. Cooke, and T. Apollini, *Teaching Exceptional Children* (New York: Academic Press, 1976).

N. Sundberg, L. Snowden, and W. Reynolds, "Toward Assessment of Personal Competence and Incompetence in Life Situations," *Annual Review of Psychology* 29(1978):179–222.

C.B. Thomas and K.R. Duszynski, "Closeness to Parents and the Family Constellation in a Prospective Study of Five Disease States," *Johns Hopkins Medical Journal* 134(1974):251–270.

C. Tolsdorf, "Social Networks, Support and Coping. An Exploratory Study," *Family Process* 15(1976):407–417.

C.A. Ullman, "Teachers, peers, and Tests as Predictors of Adjustment," *Journal of Educational Psychology* 48(1957):257–267.

B.L. White, "Social Competence," *The Primary Prevention of Psychopathology: Promoting Social Competence and Coping in Children,* vol. 3, eds. M. Kent and J. Rolf (Hanover, N.H. University Press of New England, 1979).

E. Zigler, "The Environmental Mystique: Training the Intellect versus Development of the Child," *Childhood Education* 46(1970):402–412.

E. Zigler, "Project Head Start: Success or Failure?" *Learning* 1(1973): 43–47.

E. Zigler and P.K. Trickett, "IQ, Social Competence, and Evaluation of Early Childhood Intervention Programs," *American Psychologist* 33 (1978):789–798.

Editors' Epilogue

The construct of social competence has been only vaguely defined by past investigators. Indeed, the common speculative method of definition has only led to increasing murkiness in recent attempts to clarify a concept essential to our understanding of how children succeed in adapting to their social worlds. A substantial contributor to this problem is our willingness to identify children as socially inadequate and in need of some form of social-skills training in the absence of any empirical determination of how the children are inadequate and what training methods should be used.

Putallaz and Gottman have made an excellent argument for an organizing principle to aid our conceptualization of social competence. Their use of the criterion of psychological or physical risk provides a greatly needed foundation for future investigators who wish to identify the constituents of social competence. Once such constituents have been isolated, methods of helping children who are found lacking in any of them will certainly be better informed. Their identification of two criteria of social competence—peer acceptance and the ability to form friendships—as well as the six general skill areas related to these criteria have been well documented by the literature cited in this chapter.

We believe, however, that two questions should be posed about social-competence research that have not been addressed here or by many other investigators in this field: What consideration can be given to the ecological validity of research on social competence in children? What is the meaningfulness of social competence as a construct across diverse cultures? Both questions are related to one regarding the generalizability or representativeness of studies on social competence but approach the question from different directions.

In questioning the ecological validity of social-competence research, we must examine the relations between the stimuli selected for study (for example, other children, social settings, behaviors displayed) and the universe of stimuli from which they have been selected. For example, most studies on social competence, when directly examining social behavior, use restricted-stimulus samples. The studied child is usually observed in interaction with one other child, in some standard setting, interacting along a narrow range of behaviors. Inferences regarding the target child's social competence and possession of valued social attributes are then drawn from such observations. We must ask, regarding this prototypical design, if the target child's behavior would be invariant across the universe of all other children or settings with whom or within which he or she might interact. If so, then we have indeed demonstrated a certain degree of representativeness regarding the selected stimuli. If not, then what have we proved through our investigation? To pose this question on a more-concrete level, we might choose to study the interactions between child A and child B and to determine that child A acts in a negative fashion and displays a limited knowledge of the social conventions of a five-year old. However, we could possibly observe an exchange between child A and child C that proceeds in a dramatically different fashion that might lead us to conclude that child A is a rather positive person who displays a sophisticated knowledge of social etiquette. Which observation is correct? Actually, both observations are correct in the sense that they demonstrate how child A interacts and permit a general inference regarding child A's social competence. The point we wish to make here is that investigators of social competence should understand that social competence (or any of its derivative components) is always a product of an interaction between at least two entities. Since social competence is, by our definition, interactional, what we determine it to be will always be a consequence of the actions, adjustments, and negotiations that occur between those entities. We could argue that there is no such thing as the social competence of an individual because it represents the unique, emerging, and unpredictable product of the encounter between two individuals and, therefore, can never be understood as something apart from the system within which it is found. At a lesser extreme, we must recommend that social-competence researchers make less-hasty inferences regarding the social actions of their subjects when they select a rather limited sample from the universe of available social stimuli.

The second question we posed earlier, regarding the cross-cultural meaningfulness of social competence, requires a step back from the question of stimulus representativeness to one of how universally meaningful is the construct of social competence. Is the socially competent child of one culture behaviorally and attitudinally similar to the socially competent child of another culture? If we assume that social competence, however it is construed, is essential for the healthy psychological and physical development of a child, does this assumption hold true across different and varied cultures? Freedman (1974), for example, has shown distinct temperamental differences between Caucasian (European-American) and Oriental (Chinese and Japanese-American) neonates in that Caucasians are more emotionally labile than their Oriental counterparts. These differences apparently persist at age six as shown by Caudill and Schooler (1973) in their study of Japanese and American children. American children were found to be more physically active and emotionally expressive (both positive and negative) than Japanese children. While some of the variance in their findings may be attributed to genetic differences among the samples, Werner (1979), among others, ascribes different patterns of caregiver/infant activity to a position of equal, if not greater, importance.

These findings and others from cross-cultural studies should demonstrate for us the incredible complexity of the construct of social competence. A well-grounded theory of social competence should not only include a major dimension of risk, as Putallaz and Gottman note, but also should recognize that both the interactional context and the participants' culture play essential roles as well.

References

W. Caudill and C. Schooler, C. "Child Behavior and Child Rearing in Japan and the United States: An Interim Report," *Journal of Nervous and Mental Distress* 157(1973):323–338.

D.G. Freedman, *Human Infancy: An Evolutionary Perspective* (Hillsdale, N.J.: Erlbaum, 1974).

E.A. Werner, *Cross-Cultural Child Development: A View from the Planet Earth* (Monterey, Calif.: Brooks/Cole, 1979).

2 Social-Skills Training for Socially Withdrawn/Isolate Children

Hyman Hops

The recent and mounting evidence that child-child interaction occurs among infants (Meighan and Birr 1979) stands in contrast to traditional beliefs (compare Lewis and Rosenblum 1975) and strongly suggests that the cultivation of such early relationships may be essential for healthy human development and their absence predictive of deleterious consequences later in life (Hartup 1979). Due in part to these findings and as an outgrowth of efforts to improve competent functioning in socially unskilled adults, social-skills training is now being directed at children with problematic social behaviors (Combs and Slaby 1977; Conger and Keane 1981; Hops and Greenwood 1981; Michelson and Wood 1980). Prime targets for much of this recent activity and the focus of this report are isolate children with low levels of peer popularity and withdrawn children with relatively lower levels of peer social interaction.[1] This chapter begins with a survey of the literature detailing the critical nature of peer relationships among young children. This is followed by evaluative reviews of interventions aimed at qualitatively and quantitatively improving social relationships among withdrawn/isolate children. Whether these treatments have the power to produce generalization and maintenance of effects across settings and over time is also examined. Finally, extrapolating from the available evidence, recommendations are made for improving the quality of further research with possible directions provided.

The Importance of Early Peer Social Interaction

Peer interaction in early childhood is becoming increasingly accepted as an essential prerequisite for successful development across a broad range of individual competencies. The specific skills learned through peer-group social involvement have been shown to be unique and independent of adult-

---

This chapter was prepared with assistance from NIH Biomedical Research Support Grant RR05612, Oregon Research Institute. The assistance of Susan Brewster and Katharine Wall in the typing of this manuscript is gratefully acknowledged. Thanks are also extended to Melissa Finch for her editorial contributions.

child interactions for children as young as toddlers (Mueller and Brenner 1977). Social play has been shown to stimulate toddlers toward maturer forms of object play (Rubenstein and Howes 1976). Also, fantasy play with peers facilitates divergent thinking (Johnson 1976). The positive effects of social play may be a consequence of its essential requisites. For example, play participants must discriminate between real and unreal situations, abstract general game rules, and practice shared imagination (Garvey 1976).

Both peer and adult-child interactions are basically reciprocal (Mueller 1972; Patterson and Reid 1970; Shores and Strain 1977; Greenwood et al. 1976). The probability of peers' response to child initiations increases markedly from infancy (12 percent) to toddlerhood (36 percent) (Finkelstein et al. 1978). At ages three to seven, these probabilities were found to be .97 with no differences between age groups (Greenwood et al. 1981). Qualitatively, the amount of positive reinforcement received from peers is positively and significantly related to the amount given (Charlesworth and Hartup 1967) and the level of social interaction related to social acceptance as measured by sociometrics (Hartup, Glazer, and Charlesworth 1967). Further, popular children are more rewarding of peers than less-popular ones (Hartup, Glazer, and Charlesworth 1967) and also more cooperative (Lipitt 1941), a behavior positively influenced by social interaction (Cook and Stingle 1974).

Social interaction tends to increase naturally from ages three to five (Raph et al. 1968; Reuter and Yunik 1973) before leveling off (Greenwood et al. 1981). With increasing age comes greater flexibility and variety, likely the result of increases in specific behaviors like the joint use of objects and conversation (Holmberg 1977). Garvey and Hogan (1973) noted that children aged 3½–5 adapted their utterances to the verbal or nonverbal behavior of their partners. They suggest that the more-spontaneous speech of older children serves as a vehicle for more-complex reciprocal interactions. Thus, young children have much to gain from social interaction within the peer group.

The Potentially Deleterious Consequences of Social Isolation

Investigators who seek to develop classificatory or descriptive instruments of childhood functioning have consistently identified a sociability dimension. Children at one extreme usually are described as shy, isolate, withdrawn, having few friends, and infrequently engaging in interactive behavior with peers. This factor has been isolated regardless of whether the data have been obtained from parents (Achenbach 1978a; Becker 1960; Gersten et al. 1976), teachers (Becker 1960; Kohn and Rosman 1972a), or peers (Pekarik et al. 1976). Similarly, instruments developed to screen and/or identify various childhood behavioral disorders have also delineated social withdrawal as an independent factor (Kohn and Rosman 1972a; Achenbach 1978a; Patterson 1964; Walker 1970). Social withdrawal has been estimated to be a major presenting problem in 15 percent or more cases of children referred for psychological treatment (Strain, Cooke, and Apolloni 1976a). It seems clear that childhood social withdrawal can be considered to be a unique clinical behavioral disorder.

Certainly, the classic work of Harlow and Suomi in the Wisconsin primate laboratories provides basic support for the significant contribution that peer interaction makes toward optimal development and the consequences of its absence. They found that monkeys reared in isolation from peers early in life failed to develop appropriate patterns of interactive behavior even with the availability of parents (Suomi and Harlow 1975). Such monkeys were usually contact shy and avoided most play interactions, but they were overly aggressive when they did interact with peers. Suomi and Harlow (1976) suggest that play serves two important functions: (1) it provides opportunities to practice behaviors leading to appropriate adult functioning, and (2) it acts to mitigate social aggression through less-aggressive behaviors exhibited in play. Support from human studies comes from Raph et al. (1968) who noted fewer negative interactions among preschoolers with greater school experience.

Stability

Some evidence indicates too that social behavior, and thus withdrawal, is relatively stable over time. In a follow-up study of two-year olds, observations obtained during the third trimester were predictive of an outgoing/withdrawn dimension at age 3½ (Bronson and Pankey 1977); specifically, the rate of initiations was one of the best predictors of a general social-approach behavioral pattern (Bronson 1981). Stability in overall social behavior was also reported in a longitudinal study of children from ages 2½ to 7½ (Waldrop and Halverson 1975). In a twelve-month follow-up of children referred to child-guidance clinics, parental responses on a behavioral checklist showed no differences from those of the original assessment (Achenbach 1978a). These data suggest that the pattern of withdrawn behavior may be established as early as age 3 to be predictable through childhood and even into adolescence (Bronson 1968).

Academic Effects of Social Withdrawal

A child's inability to interact with the peer group may have a profound impact on his or her academic standing and, subsequently, on later career choices. The impact of withdrawal has been noted as early as the preschool level. Children high on a factor of apathy/withdrawal while in preschool were found to be relatively low achievers from the onset of grade one to the end of grade two (Kohn and Rosman 1972b). Cobb (1970) noted that first graders who interacted more with their peers on academic materials tended to achieve at higher levels. Girls may be more greatly affected by withdrawn behavior than boys. In grades one to two, girls rated high on a facter indicative of withdrawal and tended to be low achievers on tests administered two years later (Victor and Halverson 1976). Similarly, sixth-grade girls who were overly concerned with peers' thoughts about them achieved less and withdrew more than those who were not (Lahaderne and Jackson 1970). Studies of peer status as measured by sociometrics have also shown popularity to be directly related to school marks at grade four and inversely predictive of school dropout (Roff, Sells, and Golden 1972). Thus, deficiencies in social skills that preclude contact with other children may interfere with academic functioning over the short and long term.

Taken together, these studies strongly suggest that the lack of responsiveness by and to the peer group may have profound implications for a child's later social, emotional, and academic adjustment. Some investigators consider children characterized by low levels of peer-group involvement to be at risk for later psychopathology (Rolf and Hasazi 1977).

The Lack of Treatment for Withdrawn Children

Notwithstanding the availability of instruments designed to screen socially withdrawn children and the mounting evidence indicating stability of the disorder, treatment of such children has been virtually ignored by researchers, educators, and clinicians alike. Several factors may have contributed to this apparent vacuum. Lewis and Rosenblum (1975) have clearly pinpointed the negative effects of Piagetian and psychoanalytical theory that established adult-child relations as more salient than child-child associations in their effect on child development overall. Accordingly, treatments designed to improve peer interactions directly may have been ignored in favor of the remediation of adult-child disturbances or parental psychopathology and their assumed effect on child sociability. This blind loyalty to the possibly overestimated importance of adults to child development has led to a meager literature on the etiology and/or treatment of social disorders in children for a significant period of time (Strain, Cooke, and Apolloni 1976a).

Achenbach (1978b) has noted also the negative influence of adult treatment models on the growth of effective treatment procedures for disturbances in children, especially the lack of emphasis on developmental processes. Many studies have likely been confounded because the effects attributed to experimental or predictor variables may have been partially accounted for by general development. Achenbach argues further that effective research on the treatment of childhood psychopathology must at least consider treatment effects in terms of their improvement over normal developmental change.

In some ways, withdrawn children themselves have contributed to their being virtually ignored. Such children, especially in contrast to aggressive, demanding, coercive, acting-out children, display behaviors that avoid rather than attract attention. These children rarely initiate interactions with peers (Greenwood et al. 1982); rather, they tend to extinguish or punish peer initiations to them. As a result, they systematically increase and maintain the probability of being ignored by a not very responsive social environment.

Additionally, it is clear that the focus of the great majority of parent and teacher training efforts in child behavioral management has been upon problematic child behavior that interferes with adult functioning. One can speculate that these services better serve the convenience and demands of adults as opposed to the developmental needs of children. In the author's experience, teachers have to be trained to locate withdrawn children in their classrooms. Given this context, it is easy to see why the withdrawn/isolate child has not been a primary target for intervention until recently.

The next section clearly shows that indeed the tide has changed and that the withdrawn/isolate child has become a target of intervention during the last decade. The effectiveness of the varied procedures that have been developed to improve the social skills and relationships of this population are presented and evaluated.

Interventions for Socially Withdrawn Children

Behavioral interventions aimed at increasing the social behavior and friendships of withdrawn and isolate children have shown dramatic increases in number and complexity over the last ten to fifteen years. In doing so, they largely reflect the advent of a behavioral approach to other social, educational, and clinical problems. Initially, studies tested the effects of adult social reinforcement and token reinforcement on social behavior. Subjects in these experiments were largely preschoolers. Later studies were more complex, involving film-mediated modeling that incorporated different sound tracks, the use of peers as therapeutic agents, desensitization plus shaping, and complex intervention packages that involved a number of different treatment components. In this section, studies examining the efficacy of each of these procedures are reviewed.

Reinforcement

Adult Social Attention. Adult attention has been well documented as an effective procedure for modifying a variety of social and academic deficits and excesses in children and adults. This procedure was first shown to be effective for changing social behavior in preschoolers in a series of studies emanating from the University of Washington in the early 1960s. Allen et al. (1964) demonstrated that teacher praise made contingent upon the social behavior of a 4-year old-interacting girl increased the amount of time she spent interacting with her peers from less than 20 percent to approximately 60 percent. In the final days of the study, the teachers gradually faded the reinforcement and found no drop in interaction levels. Postchecks up to one month later indicated persistence of the behavior at treatment levels. Hart et al. (1968) demonstrated that it is not simply adult attention that is effective but attention made contingent upon the desired response. Alternating teacher attention dispensed at random intervals with that made contingent upon social behavior, they noted increases in the cooperative play behavior of a 5-year old preschool child only under the latter condition. When praise was made contingent, the child's level of cooperative interaction increased from less than 5 percent of the day to approximately 20 percent.

Two studies found that social behavior may be influenced by teacher attention directed at collateral nonsocial behaviors. Crawling behavior in a 3½-year-old male preschooler was eliminated by praising all instances of on-feet behavior and ignoring off-feet behavior (Harris et al. 1964). The additional effect of this contingency was an increase in the amount of social interaction with his peer group. In the standing position, the child was more mobile and able to get around. Consequently, he appeared more like other children and less unusual, perhaps making him more attractive as a possible playmate. Similarly, a 3-year-old child, deficient in both motor and social play, was praised for playing with outdoor equipment (Buell et al. 1968). The related effect was a marked increase in social play with the peer group, partly as a result of his increased proximity to them; and unexpectedly, increases in touching, verbalizations, and cooperative play, none of which had been reinforced, maintained above-baseline levels even during reversal phases.

Not all side effects produced are necessarily desirable. In a study by Sajwaj, Twardosz, and Burke (1972), teachers were instructed to ignore the constant initiations to them by a 7-year-old retarded boy whose interaction level with the peer group was very low. Ignoring initiations to teachers did reduce the specific behavior but had concomitant effects on several others. On the positive side, social initiations to the peer group increased and play with girls' toys decreased during the free-time period. However, during circle time, the child's level of disruptive behavior increased, and a time-out procedure was necessary to completely suppress the inappropriate response.

Adult reinforcement, alone, may be an inefficient procedure for developing social responding in withdrawn children. Teacher praise directed contingently at the social behavior of withdrawn primary-grade children was slow to take effect and reached only minimal levels above baseline (Hops, Walker, and Greenwood 1979). Withdrawn children have, by definition, low rates of social responding, and the gradual shaping of increased behavior by adults is a slow and sometimes discouraging process. Other forms of adult manipulations in conjunction with praise may be necessary to facilitate the acquisition of social responses in isolate children. In most of the these studies, praise was usually combined with prompting and priming of both targets and peers' behavior to increase the likelihood that social interaction would occur and that praise could be delivered.

Priming can refer to getting other children to initiate to the target child (Hart et al. 1968) or to placing the child directly on the play equipment (Buell et al. 1968). Similarly, Baer and Wolf (1970) primed (asked other children to play with the target) and doubled primed (prompted others to initiate and the child to respond). Combined with more intense social reinforcement, the priming resulted in increased levels of social behavior, which maintained at desirable levels after three reinstatements of the total contingency.

Other investigators have added instructions, physical contact, and modeling to facilitate the training process. Praise and physical contact was delivered contingent upon initiating behavior to a behaviorally disordered preschool child and then to the child's peer in an ABAC design (Strain and Timm 1974). The social behavior of both children increased significantly under both conditions, although the initiation rate appeared to be more a function of the individual being reinforced. Unfortunately, the gains quickly extinguished upon the return to baseline. A combination of verbal and physical prompts plus verbal praise was provided contingent upon appropriate social behaviors with three behaviorally handicapped low-interacting preschoolers in a special-education class (Strain, Shores, and Kerr 1976). Physical prompts included moving the child closer to the other children and/or physically manipulating his body to respond. Verbal prompts included statements designed to elicit social behavior, "Let's play with your friends." The results were more notable for the two children with more-responsive but largely negative repertoires, one of whom responded positively even when the contingencies were directed at the other child. The one extremely isolated child with a low level of social behavior responded to the contingencies but returned to baseline levels when the conditions were terminated.

Four handicapped children in a classroom for the learning disabled were taught four social responses in cumulative fashion. The subjects were trained to smile, then to smile and share, after which positive physical contact was added and finally verbal compliments. Each condition involved the use of combinations of instructions, modeling, and praise (Cooke and Apolloni 1976) in multiple-baseline fashion across responses. Response generalization was noted for some subjects for sharing and physical contact when smiling was being trained. Three untrained subjects in the same setting increased their rates of the same social behaviors when contingencies and training were being applied to the experimentals. Verbal complimenting, a highly complex verbal behavior, was never seen to increase without specific training. All subjects demonstrated maintenance of the first three behaviors during postchecks up to one month later.

As part of a comprehensive preventative mental-health program in an elementary school, a study was conducted to increase the social behavior of third- and fourth-grade isolate children (Allen et al. 1976). A companionship program was designed to utilize college students who were carefully selected and then trained in six ninety-minute workshops in the intervention procedures. The students were trained in behavioral principles (contingent reinforcement, shaping, prompts, and so forth). Weekly supervisory meetings were also programmed during the four-month intervention program. The isolate targets were chosen based on teacher nomination and behavioral observations that indicated discrepancy between their levels of social behavior and their peer group. Ten observations conducted over a five-week baseline showed the experimental group to be functioning at 67 percent social behavior compared to a normal contrast group of ten socially skilled peers at 91 percent. Thirty subjects who were selected were placed in an experimental group of twenty and a matched control group of ten. The targets were first shown a modeling film depicting appropriate social behavior. Twice weekly the companions appeared during recess over the next four months, averaging twenty-two sessions, during which they attempted to get the child socially involved and get the peer group to accept the target. Implementation was aimed thus at the peer group and the subjects.

The results suggested a minimal treatment effect. Nineteen of the twenty experimental children improved, in contrast to only six of the ten controls. However, in controlling for baseline differences with an analysis of covariance using pretreatment scores as the covariate, the results were significantly at .09. No change was seen in any other behavioral scores, sociometrics, or teacher ratings.

Adult attention is potentially a pragmatic and cost-effective procedure. It is easily portable and available in all adults in treatment settings. It can be verbal and not require physical movement that may be awkward or inappropriate. However, the results summarized here suggest that it may not be the most effective procedure for all conditions. Failures or minimal effects were seen when implemented in classroom and recess settings in the elementary grades. Successes were noted usually at the preschool level and in special classes under rigorous experimental conditions. More-powerful procedures may be required for older children and less-well-controlled settings. As we will see later, adult attention and manipulation may be combined with other procedures more convincingly.

Token Reinforcement. A number of studies have investigated the effects of more-powerful reinforcement systems on the social behavior of withdrawn/isolate children. These have ranged from food and tokens with backups of various toys, candy, and trinkets, to toy components that could be combined to form toys.

Primary reinforcers like food were used to develop social responses in severely retarded but social children (Whitman, Mercurio, and Caponigri 1970). In a unique attempt to establish generalized control of the verbal behavior of a selectively mute child, seven therapists were faded into the treatment setting one at a time in sequence, taking over her feeding from her mother until the child was verbalizing under all conditions (Reid et al. 1967).

Token-reinforcement studies have also been carried out in a variety of settings. Clement and Milne (1967) used token reinforcement within a group-psychotherapy setting to increase the social behavior of third-grade boys referred because of shy, withdrawn behavior. The boys were seen weekly for fourteen weeks in typical fifty-minute sessions. The methodological problems in this study preclude clear indications of effects. However, reinforcement by the therapist, exchangeable for toy backups, appeared to increase the social behavior of the children. In contrast, a verbal group, simply praised for interaction by the therapist, actually decreased their level of social-play behavior during therapy. Only anecdotal data were available to indicate generalization to extratherapy settings. Clement, Roberts, and Lantz (1970) replicated this study with a group of second- to fourth-grade boys. Each group met for twenty-four weekly sessions. Again, only the group receiving social and token reinforcement from the therapist showed increases in the frequency of social play and proximity to one another during the therapy sessions. Other groups tended to decrease their frequency of social interaction and proximity. Modeling videotapes portraying the instances of prosocial appropriate behavior shown to two of the groups added nothing to the effects of token reinforcement and therapist praise.

Tokens were also used to increase the verbal behavior of two shy adolescent boys during a five-day camping trip (Hobbs and Radka 1976) and eight girls at a school for the emotionally disturbed (Simkins 1971). Strangely enough, few studies have been carried out at the preschool level using token reinforcement (Sacks, Moxley, and Walls 1975). Presumably, social praise, prompting, and other less-powerful procedures are sufficiently effective with this age group.

A series of three studies was carried out in an experimental classroom setting as the first step in the development of a standardized program for remedying socially withdrawn behavior of primary-grade children in the natural setting (Walker et al. 1979). The experiments were designed to investigate the effects of token reinforcement plus teacher praise on three topographic components of social interaction: (1) initiating positive interactions with others (STARTS), (2) responding to others' positive initiations (ANSWER), and (3) maintaining social interactions over time (CONTINUE). Three groups of six subjects each, evidencing low rates of social contact with their respective peer groups and enrolled in grades one to six, were assigned to an experimental classroom for three to four months of treatment, one group at a time in sequential fashion. Each group was involved in a different experiment. In experiment 1, the topographic components were reinforced in the following order during free-play-activity periods: START, ANSWER, and CONTINUE. Experiment 2 was an intersubject replication of experiment 1 with a different order of component reinforcement: CONTINUE, ANSWER, START, and CONTINUE. In experiment 3, all components were reinforced simultaneously within ongoing social behavior. The results showed that reinforcement of STARTS and ANSWERS actually suppressed overall interactive behavior as measured by amount of observed time spent in social interaction, although measurable increases were noted when CONTINUE was being reinforced with simultaneous decreases in STARTS and ANSWERS and interactions rate. Increasing the START and ANSWER components may have detrimental effects on the total amount of time spent in social interaction. First, the delivery of the token can be disruptive, occurring just after an interaction has occurred and preventing its continuity. Second, the contingencies may interfere with the natural interactive style of some of the subjects. For example, increasing STARTS or ANSWERS made the interactions somewhat artificial, especially when the latter were being reinforced. The most powerful and clear contingency was that used in experiment 3 when all interactive behavior was affected. No constraints were placed on individual styles, and this contingency seemed maximally to facilitate each subject's interactive behavior. It may be necessary in future research to examine the effect of reinforcing single responses on total interactive behavior before concluding that the experiment was a success. A more-effective strategy might be to provide specific social-skills instruction in a controlled setting prior to, or concomitant with, a procedure designed to increase overall social behavior in the natural setting (Greenwood et al. 1982; Paine et al. 1982; Hops et al. 1977).

In a series of related studies designed to extend token systems to the natural setting, points were provided to primary-grade socially withdrawn children contingent upon increases in their interaction rates or percentage of time spent interacting with their peers in the classroom (Hops, Walker, and

Greenwood 1979). Individual contingencies with individual backups for the target children were compared with individual contingencies with group backups shared by the entire class. Observation data showed that the group backup was clearly more powerful, motivating the peer group to help the child earn points. The peer group's overwhelming enthusiam had to be controlled to prevent the intimidation of the target child. In contrast, individual backups were extremely slow to take effect and did not produce the same levels of social behavior in the target child as the group reinforcement.

Another study in the series (Hops, Walker, and Greenwood 1979) examined the effects of different settings on social behavior. The individual contingency/group backup was applied to the same child in recess and in the classroom in a combination multiple-baseline reversal design. The subject, a 5-year-old kindergartner, was consistently lower than her peer group in time spent interacting. The group-backup procedure at recess produced greater social-behavior gains than those obtained in the classroom with the same intervention. Further, during recess these gains persisted for seven days after the nine-day treatment was terminated. In contrast, there was an immediate return to baseline levels in the academic setting.

To summarize, token reinforcement can be a powerful procedure for increasing social activity among withdrawn children. In a controlled setting, individual contingencies for individual backups are effective in producing social-behavior gains. In the natural setting, more-powerful group backups are clearly required. Furthermore, the results are more marked and persistent when the interventions are conducted during recess and when social behavior is reciprocated by the peer group. When the procedures are implemented in the classroom, the interaction rates are much lower during baseline, and the gains produced are much smaller and less likely to be maintained. In some cases, the regular classroom setting provides competing contingencies for incompatible nonsocial behavior—for example, academic. Evidently, the most powerful token-reinforcement procedure for withdrawn low-interacting children would consist of an individual contingency/group backup conducted during recess or other free-play period.

Modeling

The therapeutic effects of modeling have been demonstrated amply for a variety of children's problematic social behaviors (Bandura 1969). For example, symbolic modeling using films or videotape has been shown to aid in the reduction of children's dog phobias. Models are shown moving progressively toward increased contact with animals. Socially withdrawn children have also become prime targets for investigations of the impact of modeling procedures on social behavior. Live modeling with guided participation was used to modify the social behavior of an extremely withdrawn 6-year-old boy (Ross, Ross, and Evans 1971). A male undergraduate demonstrated social interactions, provided the boy with opportunity to practice, and participated with him in social situations. Finally, with the model nearby, the child played with a group of unfamiliar children in a nearby park. Each treatment component was composed of a series of graduated steps, successively approximating total participation in social interaction. Under these conditions, treatment was effective and generalized to other settings and over time. A two-month postcheck indicated that the child was functioning normally in the actual play setting.

Most modeling studies with withdrawn/isolate children have used film-mediated procedures. This complex technique is partially governed by variables such as the similarity between the subjects and the model's characteristics, the content of the soundtrack, and so forth. Each of these may account for a portion of the variance in the total effect on social behavior. However, of these variables, few have been examined for their unique contribution in studies of withdrawn children.

A study published in 1969 by O'Connor, demonstrating the positive effects of symbolic modeling on withdrawn children, has a major impact on the field. Teacher-nominated preschool children were selected after direct observations found them to be interacting at less than 15 percent of the time and below the level of nonisolates. The experimental children were taken individually from their classrooms and shown a twenty-three-minute color film that demonstrated progressively increasing social involvement of young models with their peers. In each of the eleven scenes, a child was shown first to observe one or more children at play before joining in. The scenes were designed to graduate systematically the number of peers involved and the intensity of the activity level.

The soundtrack that accompanied the film, described by O'Connor (1969) as a description of the play behavior of the children, actively induces the children to play by repeatedly emphasizing the pleasurable aspects of social participation. Gottman's (personal communication) analysis of the soundtrack found only 28 percent of the sentences to be purely descriptive. Six experimental children were shown to increase their levels of social interaction immediately following the viewing, from a mean of 5 percent to 38 percent. A control group of isolate children who watched a film of Marineland dophins showed no such behavior change. In a replication of this study, O'Connor (1972) demonstrated the effects of modeling for a similar group of children to persist over a three- and six-week follow-up. Furthermore, the children exposed to the modeling procedures alone were superior to a shaping (adult contingent praise) and a modeling-plus-shaping condition.

The O'Connor studies had an immediate effect on other researchers. In all likelihood the twenty-three-minute color film with the power to produce lasting behavioral gains in children was seen as highly relevant and desirable. Such cost-effective procedures are not frequently demonstrated in the behavioral literature. In two separate studies (Evers and Schwarz 1973; Evers-Pasquale and Sherman 1975) O'Connor's findings were replicated. The data further demonstrated that specific children identified as peer oriented as opposed to adult oriented, on the basis of an eleven-item questionnaire, were more likely to show improvement immediately following the film and four weeks later.

Other investigators, however, demonstrated more-equivocal results. For example, Gottman (1977) used the O'Connor film and soundtrack with isolate children; however, similar increases were noted for both the experimental and control children with no change in sociometric scores for either of the groups. Unfortunately, the pretreatment and posttreatment data were collected more than six weeks before and seven weeks after the treatment, respectively. Consequently, it was impossible to tell whether the subjects at treatment were at the same level during baseline or precisely when the effects for either group had occurred. Walker et al. (1975) showed the O'Connor film and soundtrack to a group of six withdrawn primary-grade children in an experimental classroom on three different occasions. Observational data collected each time during free play immediately following the film showed no appreciable increases in social behavior for the withdrawn children. The Walker et al. study differed from the O'Connor and Evers studies in at least two ways. The children were (1) older and (2) had no normal peer group to respond to them in the event they actually initiated social behavior. While these studies were not replications of previous ones, the data serve to indicate that the film and soundtrack are not effective under all conditions.

Keller and Carlson (1974) created their own set of videotapes depicting four social skills that they assumed to be related to social interaction: (1) imitation, (2) smiling and laughing, (3) token giving, and (4) physically affectionate behavior. Increases in social-behavior levels were noted immediately after the showing, but the effects disappeared at a three-week follow-up check. In a related study, Jakibchuk and Smeriglio (1976) found that videotapes with a narrative soundtrack depicting the same set of social skills produced minimal results. More-powerful effects were produced when the soundtrack used a self-speech condition—that is, social behavior described by a same-age child in the first person—and these persisted over the three-week follow-up.

The symbolic modeling studies reviewed here show that the effects of these procedures on the social behavior of withdrawn/isolate children are not entirely clear or consistent. The variable results may be in large part a function of the different subject-selection criteria used across studies (Hops and Greenwood 1981). Overall, subjects were nominated by their teachers and then observed directly in the play setting. However, the selection criterion of percentage of time spent interacting with peers ranged from 15 percent (O'Connor 1969; 1972; Gottman 1977) to 50 percent (Keller and Carlson 1974). As a consequence, the different criteria identified different proportions of the available population as isolate subjects; for instance, 5 percent in the O'Connor (1969) study and 28 percent in the Gottman (1977) investigation, averaging 25 percent across seven preschool studies. Selecting this large a proportion of the population suggests that most of the children were only mildly withdrawn and perhaps more easily affected by minimal treatments. In contrast, two studies conducted in the primary grades (Walker and Hops 1973; Walker et al. 1975) found that subjects meeting their criteria occurred at the lower rate of one in every two classrooms.

Another instance of differences across studies was in the level of social behavior found in nonisolate peers. This measure can be used as a standard for identifying experimental subjects and evaluating the effects of treatment (Walker and Hops 1976). In the preschool studies, the nonisolate level ranged from 22 percent (Gottman 1977) to 64 percent (Jakibchuk and Smeriglio 1976). Given these varying settings and selection criteria, it is not surprising that inconsistencies are found in results across studies of modeling.

More research appears to be necessary before the power of modeling alone can be accepted as a viable alternative to other forms of treatment for socially withdrawn children. The majority of the investigations reviewed here were conducted with preschool children. Extrapolation to older children awaits further research. Studies exploring the effects of other salient variables such as the settings, film content, soundtrack, lower-functioning children, and so on are also required. It may be important to assess the peer versus adult orientation of referred children as conducted by Evers-Pasquale and Sherman (1975) before subjecting them to a modeling procedure. Perhaps peer-oriented subjects who view a self-speech soundtrack (Jakibchuk and Smeriglio 1976) would demonstrate the most dramatic gains. As we shall see, symbolic modeling effects may be greater when combined with other treatment components.

Modeling plus Reinforcement

The effects of modeling alone were shown to be inconsistent, especially when examining their durability over the short and the long run. Let us see whether adding a powerful reinforcement component appreciably increases the power of modeling, as Bandura (1969) has suggested. Both O'Connor (1969; 1972) and Evers and Schwarz (1973) compared the addition of contingent social praise but found that condition no more effective than modeling alone. While the procedures were to some extent methodologically questionable, other data suggest that social praise, even with the addition of an individual token-reinforcement procedure, may not be the most effective technique for increasing the social behavior of primary-grade withdrawn children (Hops, Walker, and Greenwood 1979). Modeling and praise may have to be combined with more-powerful techniques to produce more-dramatic results.

A series of experiments by Walker and Hops (1973) demonstrated that symbolic modeling can be combined with token reinforcement to produce marked effects. Three primary-grade children were selected on the basis of teacher referral and observation data distinguishing them from their respective peer groups. Each child was assigned to a different experimental procedure in three single-subject reversal designs. In experiment 1, the subject was a girl whose mean rate of initiations to peers was significantly greater than their mean rate to her. After being shown the O'Connor film, she was awarded points toward an individual backup for any increases in the rate of peers' initiations to her. It was suggested to the child that she use some of the procedures demonstrated in the film to elicit initiations from her classmates. In experiment 2, the withdrawn subject's rate of initiations to her peers was significantly less than their rate to her. Consequently, the peers were the focus of the intervention. They were shown the film without the child's awareness and were told they would earn points toward a group backup for increases in the child's initiation rate to them. Experiment 3 was conducted with a markedly low-interacting child whose initiation rate to the peers and theirs to her was virtually zero. A double-interlocking contingency was established, combining the two procedures used in experiments 1 and 2. The entire classroom, including the target child, was shown the film and the two contingencies explained. The child earned points toward an individual backup for increased peer initiations to her; the group earned points toward a group backup contingent upon increases in the child's initiation rate to them. However, neither of the reinforcers was made available unless both the child and the peer group met specific predetermined criteria. All of the contingencies in the three experiments were effective in increasing initiation and interaction rates for both the target subjects and their respective peer groups. However, the combined interlocking procedure was shown to be the most powerful, producing immediate effects in contrast to the slower acquisition of gains noted in the first two studies. Interestingly, rates of social interaction during the reversal phases did not return to initial baseline levels even for the lowest interacting child. While the unique effects of each component were not determined, the combined effect of modeling and powerful token reinforcement appears to produce replicable effects that may persist over time.

In studies of modeling, specific social skills are assumed to be learned vicariously during the modeling sessions. These sessions are usually held in settings other than those in which the changed behavior is to occur. The training is also brief and the subjects do not get the opportunity to practice the new skills until they return to the natural setting. The next section covers more-elaborate training procedures. Many of them involve combinations of live modeling, didactic instruction, and the opportunity for the subjects to practice the behaviors.

Specific Social-Skills Training

A recent trend in the treatment of withdrawn children has been the development of interventions designed to provide training in specific social skills. The basic assumption herein is that these specific skills are directly related to social competence in children and, consequently, their successful social adjustment. Few studies, however, have examined such relationships. For example, Gottman, Gonso, and Rasmussen (1975) showed that popular and unpopular children, differentiated by peers' sociometric choices, differed in their knowledge of how to make friends and in their performance on a communication-skill task. In another study, low-rate social-interacting preschoolers compared to middle- and high-rate interactors were found to be deficient in social behaviors such as initiating to peers, responding to peers' initiations to them, and overall verbal output (Greenwood et al 1982). Tremblay et al. (1981) attempted to identify effective social skills by examining the power of specific behaviors to elicit positive social responding from the peer group. Using conditional probability analyses of normal preschoolers' social-interaction play, they found that motor/gestural antecedent initiations were more effective than vocal/verbal initiations in controlling positive peer responding. Although the results are somewhat confounded because group rather than individual data were used in the analyses, these procedures also merit further exploration. Such studies still require empirical validation via interventions directed at increasing the specifically identified skill areas to evaluate their impact on other more-global measures of social competence like sociometric popularity or interaction rate. In contrast, few treatment studies have selected specific targets based on more than face validity.

In this section, three recent trends in social-skills training are examined: coaching of specific skills and training in assertive and problem-solving behavior. In each case, the rationale for the selection of specific skills and their demonstrated relationship with other measures of social competence are also evaluated.

Coaching. Several studies emanating from the University of Illinois have tested the effects of coaching specific social skills on isolate children's social acceptance by the peer group. One of the most comprehensive of such studies was carried out by Oden and Asher (1977). A coaching procedure was compared with a peer-pairing arrangement and an untreated control group.

The coaching procedure was based on the early work of Chittenden (1942), who used modeling and verbal instruction with aggressive children, and McFall and Twentyman (1973), who taught assertive behavior to college students. Each coaching lesson occurred as follows. A target child was removed from the classroom and taken to an experimental room where direct instruction in a set of skills was provided by an adult instructor. This instruction was followed by the opportunity to practice the behaviors during a prearranged game setting with a classmate (a different peer was chosen for each lesson) and completed by the instructor's reviewing the child's behavior during the previous practice lesson. Six thirty-minute coaching lessons were provided over a four-week period. Based on reviews of the literature, Oden and Asher (1977) selected four categories of social skills that appeared to be related to social acceptance: (1) participation, (2) cooperation, (3) communication, and (4) validation/support—that is, being friendly and nice. Each lesson taught more-specific behaviors within each of the four categories. In the peer-pairing arrangement, the subjects were simply allowed to play the same games. The control group was also removed from the classroom but was involved in solitary play.

Sociometric play ratings provided the primary dependent measure. Differences between pre- and posttreatment-gain scores were significantly in favor of the coaching group. Observation data collected during the game setting revealed no differential treatment effects; all children showed significant increases most likely as a function of the peer-pairing or game procedure. Unfortunately, no observation data were collected in the subjects' own classrooms to indicate whether actual behavior change had occurred in the natural setting in addition to the increased social acceptance by their peers.

Follow-up sociometric data were obtained for twenty-two of the original thirty-three children during the subsequent academic year. To control for changes in peer raters, the scores at each phase were transformed to z scores; however, different effects were noted. Use of standardized scores for this sample reveals an increase in the control group mean scores at posttreatment to the level of the coaching group. Second, repeated-measures analysis of variance over the three phases produced only limited statistical significance ($p < .10$), although the gains produced by the coaching procedure were in the expected direction. Given that the twenty-two children in the follow-up were representative of the entire sample, the results—when statistically controlled for classroom differences—suggest only minimal efficacy of this coaching procedure for changing peer status in the long run.

Hymel and Asher (1977) attempted to replicate Oden and Asher's

(1977) work with third-, fourth-, and fifth-grade children similarly selected as social isolates. Three isolate children from each of the eight classrooms were randomly assigned to one of the three experimental conditions: (1) general coaching as in Oden and Asher, (2) individual coaching, and (3) peer-pairing. In the individualized-coaching procedure, instruction was provided based on the child's demonstrated deficits obtained from direct observation, interviews with teachers, and sociometric scores. In this study, direct observations of the children were made during regular classroom activities, prior to intervention and after termination. Long-term follow-up seven months later in the next academic year was conducted on twenty-one of the original twenty-four subjects. As in Oden and Asher (1977), the sociometric scores at each phase were transformed to z scores to control for differences in peer raters. The results were consistent across all sociometric measures, only the effect of time was significant. Neither coaching procedure was more effective than the peer-pairing arrangement alone. While one could argue that all treatments were effective in increasing peer ratings, an alternative plausible explanation is that the results simply indicate regression toward the mean. However, since no changes were noted in observed behavior in the classroom for any of the groups, little evidence supports the power of any of these procedures.

A third coaching study was conducted by Gottman, Gonso, and Schuler (1976). They compared social-skills training for two isolate children in a third-grade classroom with two untreated control children. The experimental children were seen individually by an adult for thirty minutes each day for one week and instructed in initiating interactions, making friends with others, and in referential communication skills. These behaviors had previously been shown to discriminate between popular and unpopular children (Gottman, Gonso, and Rasmussen 1975). The control children were seen for the same amount of time for general discussions about board games. The results were inconclusive.[2] On the sociometrics, one experimental child improved significantly; no significant improvement was noted for any of the other three children. The observation data showed increases in the frequency of positive interaction for the two experimental children and one of the two control subjects.

La Greca and Santogrossi (1980) combined coaching with modeling and behavioral rehearsal, within the format of a unique group-training procedure, and tested the effects of a four-week skills-training program on a sample of third, fourth, and fifth graders. Subjects with low sociometric acceptance scores were randomly assigned to a skills-training, attention-placebo, or waiting-list control group. The following specific skills were extracted from the literature for training: (1)smiling/laughing, (2) joining ongoing activities, (3) extending invitations, (4) conversational skills, (5) sharing and cooperating, (6) complimenting verbally, and (7) physical appearance/

grooming. This study also included a comprehensive set of dependent measures including a test of skill knowledge, a role-play test, sociometric ratings, and behavioral observations of initiation rate and positive social behavior in the natural setting.

The results proved to be quite interesting. Relative to the two control groups, the skills-training group demonstrated increases in skill knowledge, performance in the role-play situation, and the rate of initiations to peers during social interaction in situ. No group effects were noted for either total positive behavior or sociometric acceptance scores. The authors suggest that the absence of a significant change in sociometric ratings may have been due to the lack of sensitivity of this measure to the skills-training program. An alternative explanation suggests limited generalizability of the treatment effects. Changes were noted conceptually in increased skill knowledge, and behaviorally in the analogue situation, but generalization to the natural setting occurred for initiation rate only. This suggests that the overall power of the four-week, two-hour intervention may have been relatively weak and did not substantially influence peer ratings or the rate of positive social behavior. However, the two-category observation code did not allow for a full examination of whether the specific skills taught were actually demonstrated in the natural setting.

Gresham and Nagle (1980) also selected a sample of third and fourth graders with low sociometric ratings and randomly assigned them to a coaching, modeling, coaching-plus-modeling, or control group. The behaviors targeted for intervention were based on the work of Gottman, Gonso, and Rasmussen (1975); Hartup, Glazer, and Charlesworth (1967); and Oden and Asher (1977). Coaching involved behavioral rehearsal with feedback on performance. Children were also encouraged to perform their newly learned skills in the classroom after each session. Subjects in the modeling group watched a series of videotapes demonstrating the same skills and with a female narrator describing the events to highlight significant features. The modeling-plus-coaching condition provided a combination of abbreviated versions of the previous two. Each session consisted of a presentation of the videotape followed by coaching of the specific skills demonstrated. Subjects in the control condition were shown videotapes of "Wild Kingdom" with various peers to control for the effects of peer pairing, watching films, and being removed from the classroom. Each child was involved for two hours overall—six sessions of approximately twenty minutes each distributed over a three-week period.

The dependent measures consisted of sociometric ratings and nominations and a four-category behavioral-observation code. The Peer Preference Test was also administered to assess the effects of treatment on peer orientation as determined by Evers-Pasquale and Sherman (1975). Multivariate analyses of variance were computed on change scores for post- minus pretreatment, follow-up minus pretreatment, and follow-up minus posttreatment. Strangely enough, only one significant finding was noted for the pre- to posttreatment effect—namely, non-peer-oriented subjects showed larger changes on the play with sociometric ratings than peer-oriented subjects across all conditions.

Posttreatment to follow-up treatment effect was found to be significant for observational data only; the modeling group showed larger changes in positives received than any of the other groups. Additionally, the coaching and coaching-plus-modeling groups decreased significantly in negatives given compared to the modeling and control groups. Pretreatment to follow-up analyses revealed a significant decrease in negatives given and negatives received for the coaching group, while the coaching and modeling groups significantly increased their positives toward peers. All of the experimental groups also received significantly higher play-with ratings than the control group. It is interesting to speculate as to why no pre-/posttreatment effects were noted on either sociometric or observational data; only the follow-up assessment produced differential changes. How does one get maintenance without acquisition? As with La Greca and Santogrossi (1980), the length of treatment was relatively brief (two hours over a three-week period), and not enough time may have elapsed to affect the dependent variables. Less-sensitive sociometric data may require more-powerful and lengthier treatment effects as suggested by Gresham and Nagle (1980) to evidence such changes, but no such evidence had been noted by the more-sensitive posttreatment behavioral-observation data. The lack of a statistical effect may have been due to variability in the pretreatment data suggested by a closer inspection of the negatives given group means. Follow-up assessment in the La Greca and Santagrossi (1980) study may have shown similar effects.

One of the best designed studies was conducted recently by Ladd (1981) at the University of Rochester. He compared the effects of specific verbal-skill training with an attention-control and a no-treatment control group on both sociometric scores and on observational data collected in the classroom. Eighteen boys and eighteen girls from six third-grade classrooms in three schools served as subjects. The results clearly showed that the verbal-skill training conducted in the experimental setting was effective in producing generalized increases in two of the three specific targeted behaviors observed in free-play periods in the classroom and in peer-acceptance scores. These effects maintained four weeks after training had ceased. Several important factors differentiate Ladd's study from previous less-successful coaching attempts to increase behavioral and sociometric levels.

First, the selected subjects were ranked lowest on both peer acceptance and on the behaviors specifically targeted for treatment—that is, asking positive questions, offering suggestions or directions, and offering supportive statements. Second, the observations were conducted during prescribed free-play periods when social interaction was the modal behavior and was free to vary. Consequently, the significant increases noted in the first two targeted behaviors and in the children's peer ratings provide empirical support for the hypothesized relationship between specific classes of social behaviors and sociometric scores. The results also suggest that the relationship is more likely to occur when greater similarity exists between the sociometric referent situation and the setting in which the observations occur.

Third, the eight 45–50-minute sessions held on alternating days in Ladd's study provided more than twice the amount of training available in Oden and Asher (1977) and Gottman, Gonso, and Schuler (1976). Fourth, in previous work, each target child was seen individually by an adult trainer. Ladd trained his children in pairs. Behaviors practiced between peers may be more realistic and thus more effective than those conducted with an adult only.

Fifth, generalization of social behaviors to the normal peer group was sequentially programmed. Initially, social behavior was rehearsed under nonthreatening controlled conditions by the two subjects. This was followed in the last two sessions by interactions with two regular classmates in a structured game situation. Subsequent experimenter feedback was provided on the basis of actual behavior observed in the game setting rather than upon recalled self-report data. Finally, the skills-training subjects were taught to evaluate and correct, if necessary, their own social behavior, a specific skill that can be extremely useful when alone among the regular peer group.

The Ladd (1981) study suggests that well-programmed coaching of specific skills can be a viable procedure for increasing peer-acceptance scores and related targeted behaviors. More research is necessary to demonstrate such empirical relationships between other social behaviors and sociometric scores. The major weakness in the Ladd study is its limited relevance for more severely withdrawn/isolate children. Ladd's subjects included from 22 to 35 percent of the children in each classroom. As in the modeling and other coaching studies, this large a proportion of normal children may suggest less-powerful treatment effects than appear—mildly withdrawn/isolate children being more sensitive to these treatment procedures than more severely handicapped children. Certainly, more data and research are required to test this hypothesis. Thus, the results of the coaching studies, while suggestive of treatment effects, are still inconclusive and require further replication of the successful procedures with more attention paid to assessment.

Assertiveness Training. Studies in assertiveness have proliferated in recent years (Hersen and Bellack 1977; Hersen and Eisler 1976; Arkowitz 1977).

Training in assertive behavior is aimed at providing socially inadequate individuals with the specific social skills presumed to be prerequisite for socially competent functioning. An alternative explanation for inadequate social behavior hypothesizes inhibiting levels of anxiety that prevent individuals from utilizing adaptive behavior available in their repertoires. However, the high anxiety may be simply the consequences of skill deficits (Hersen and Bellack 1977).

Assessment and training are conducted typically in analogue or laboratory settings. Contrived real-life situations are presented in which the attainment of an individual's goal is being thwarted by another. The intervention involves pinpointing the problem and teaching the subject to be more assertive, using behavioral rehearsal, feedback, modeling, and instructions.

Assertiveness training has been directed primarily at adults; very few studies have been conducted with and designed specifically for children. Based upon their experience with adults, Bornstein, Bellack, and Hersen (1977) developed a set of procedures for assessing and training specific social skills in nonassertive children. Assessment procedures for establishing the baseline levels of assertive behavior were established. They created a set of social situations in which assertive responses were required for meeting specific goals. The subjects were instructed to respond naturally to each situation. Adult role models were present in the room with the child to serve as appropriate role-play interactors to create a more-realistic situation. Four of twelve children, referred by their teachers for difficulties in interpersonal situations, were selected as targets. Each of the target children was found to be consistently low in levels of eye contact, duration of speech, loudness of responding, and ability to make requests. Unfortunately, no normative data were available for assessing deficits, and only subjective clinical judgment was used.

Training was conducted in the same setting, using six of the nine scenes involved in the assessment procedure. The social-skills-training package consisted of instructions, feedback, behavioral rehearsal, and modeling and proceeded as follows. After the therapist presented a test scene, the adult model delivered the first prompt to initiate the interaction, then allowed the subject to respond. The therapist provided feedback and discussion about the specific target response to be trained. Next, appropriate responses were modeled, and specific instructions were given by the therapist, with subsequent responding by the subject. This procedure continued until the target behavior was acquired.

The results of the training procedure were conclusive. Increases in each of the responses occurred in multiple-baseline fashion across responses only when specific training was introduced. Generalization of the responses to the three untrained scenes was found to occur as well. Further, these increases in both trained and untrained responses persisted into follow-up probes taken two and four weeks after treatment. Ratings of overall assertiveness as judged by two independent raters from the videotapes created during each session also indicated improvement, especially after the third response had been acquired.

The Bornstein, Bellack, and Hersen (1977) study was a good first step in the development of effective assertiveness-training procedures for children. The authors noted a number of weaknesses that should be attended to in future investigations. First, no normative data were provided to indicate whether the specific skill deficits assessed in the target population were actually below the levels found in nonreferred children. Second, no evidence was provided via direct observations of generalization of treatment effects to the natural environment. Third, the models used in the study for assessment and treatment were all adults, and it is still questionable whether the subjects would respond to children similarly, either in the analogue or the natural setting.

Beck, Forehand, Wells, and Quante (1978) used the Bornstein, Bellack, and Hersen social-skills-training package and extended the assessment procedure for evidence of generalization to the natural environment. Observations were made of the subjects in school in four settings: during breakfast, at free play, in the classroom, and on the playground. Training occurred in two thirty-minute sessions per week for three weeks. Unfortunately, a major methodological weakness in the study limits its usefulness: Observations of the children compared with a selected socially skilled classmate show the targeted so-called deficient subjects to be usually higher on the targeted behaviors during baseline. Sociometric scores, in contrast, found the socially skilled classmates to be more popular initially. Further, the power of the intervention was noted for the specific behaviors only in the analogue setting; no generalization occurred in the natural setting or on sociometric scores.

A group assertiveness-training program (Michelson and Wood 1980) similar to the two described was tested on two groups of elementary-school children who were provided with eight and sixteen hours of treatment respectively. The primary evaluation instrument was a newly designed self-report rating scale Wood, Michelson, and Flynn (1978), purporting to measure assertive responses to various social situations. The internal consistency and test-retest reliability of the scale seem adequate. However, validity data were marginal; the correlation with behavioral observations in structured situations was only .38 and, with teachers' ratings of children's assertiveness, highly variable (.09–.82) with only low to moderate mean relationships. [A more-recent report indicates better discriminant validity; high- and low-assertive children based on scores on the rating scale were also significantly different on social-skill ratings by peers, teachers, and parents (Michelson, Foster, and Ritchey 1981)]. The subjects were selected from the general school population. No attempts were made to identify the effects of the treatment on children scoring low on the self-report scale. The results indicated significant treatment effects for both the eight- and sixteen-hour groups in contrast to the control groups. The only evidence of generalization to actual behavioral change in the natural setting, however, was provided by teacher ratings, but the authors did not indicate whether or not the teachers were aware of the purpose of the study.

The results of the few experiments on children's assertiveness training remain inconclusive, none having improved upon the deficits noted in the Bornstein and associates (1977) design. Normative data bases are required for each of the social skills from which to assess deficits and evaluate treatment. Evidence of generalization to the natural setting is also needed. Recent studies with adult normal and psychiatric populations (Bellack, Hersen, and Lamparski 1979; Bellack, Hersen, and Turner 1978; 1979) and adolescent male offenders (Spence and Marzillier 1978) typically demonstrate little relationship between role-play behavior in assessment or training settings and social behavior in the natural setting. There is reason to believe that similar results will be found for children (Van Hasselt, Hersen, and Bellack 1981). Also, as with other forms of treatment, an external criterion for social competence is required to establish the specific social skills for which training is provided as relevant for successful social adjustment.

Problem-Solving Training. A more-generalized approach to the treatment of social maladjustment may be seen in the development of programs designed to teach individuals a set of general problem-solving skills for interpersonal adjustment. It is posited that training a problem-solving-response set may help children cope with problems as they arise in the natural setting (Spivack and Shure 1974). In this sense, problem-solving skills establish self-control and independence (D'Zurilla and Goldfried 1971) and may be a truly powerful procedure for establishing long-term generalization and maintenance of effective responding across settings and over time.

The most comprehensive and long-term programmatic research to be carried out on interpersonal-relationship skills is that of Spivack, Shure, and their associates at the Hahnemann Medical School in Philadelphia (Shure and Spivack 1978; Spivack, Platt, and Shure 1976; Spivack and Shure 1974). Conceptually, their procedures are designed to provide children with a cognitive problem-solving style for coping with real-life problems. Children with these skills, they believe, will continue to generate their own ways of solving interpersonal problems—such a process manifesting itself in improved behavioral adjustment. On the face of it, the model clearly contains powerful preventative implications. Providing young children, and especially those at high risk, with skills enabling them to adjust more efficiently in the social environment might significantly reduce the incidence of later life difficulties.

Studies were conducted to examine the relationship between various problem-solving skills and behavioral adjustment (Shure and Spivack 1972; Shure, Spivack, and Jaeger 1971). The results consistently indicated that the ability to provide alternative solutions to specific interpersonal problem situations was the best predictor of teachers' ratings of social-emotional adjustment and differentiated between adjusted and aberrant children.

Two measurement instruments were developed to assess the relevant problem-solving skills and behavioral adjustment. The Preschool Interpersonal Problem Solving (PIPS) test (Shure and Spivack 1974) measures each child's ability to provide alternative solutions to problem situations. In addition to a total score, several other measures can be derived from the PIPS, such as a ratio of irrelevant to relevant talk and a force ratio indicating the probable use of coercive or aggressive solutions.

The Hahnemann Preschool Behavior Rating Scale (HPSB) (Shure and Spivack 1975) is a teacher rating scale used to assess the social-emotional behavior of preschool children. The main portion of the scale consists of seven items adapted from the Devereux Behavior Rating Scale (Spivack and Spotts 1966) to represent three independent factors: (1) inability to delay gratification, (2) proneness to emotional upset, and (3) social aggression. The scores on the seven items are used to group children into "adjusted," "impulsive," and "inhibited" categories; the latter two are sometimes combined to identify poorly adjusted, or aberrant, children. Both the PIPS and the HPSB have been shown to be highly related to one another, but convergent validation with other instruments has not been demonstrated.

To test experimentally the validity of the relationships between the PIPS and the HPSB, Spivack and Shure (1974) developed a highly structured program to teach young children to increase the number of alternative solutions they provide to hypothetical interpersonal problem situations. A series of studies was conducted over a four-year period to evaluate the program's ability to effect change in behavioral adjustment (Shure and Spivack 1975). The subjects consisted of several hundred 4- and 5-year-old children in Head Start classrooms. The procedures were implemented by teachers via group instruction in the classroom or by mothers working with single individuals or small groups of siblings at home.

Overall, the direct effects of training, as measured by the PIPS, were noted in (1) an increased number of alternative solutions to interpersonal problems, (2) decreased time spent in irrelevant talk during the test situation, and (3) a decreased number of forceful solutions. The indirect effect was seen in significant improvements in behavioral adjustment for the experimental children compared to the control children, regardless of whether the training occurred in the classroom or at home. Some of the effects were more marked for those children identified as shy and withdrawn. More important, increases in adjustment following teacher training were maintained in follow-up studies conducted up to two years later in the first grade as rated by teachers completely naive about the training program. Given the absence of generalizable effects noted in the behavioral literature, the power of this program's generalizability to new responses across settings and over time is indeed noteworthy. The authors concluded that verbal training in problem-solving skills was converted into improved behavioral adjustment that also generalized from the home to the school. Two-year maintenance effects were also noted following teacher training. Additionally, preventative effects were noted in the reduced number of previously adjusted experimental children who were later rated as aberrant compared to those in the control group.

The major deficiency in the Shure and Spivack program of research is its total dependence on a single unvalidated measure of behavioral adjustment. Researchers usually agree that a multimethod approach to program evaluation is necessary because of frequently occurring low to moderate relationships between different instruments purporting to measure the same event (Cone and Hawkins 1977; Hops and Greenwood 1981; Mash and Terdal 1976). Consequently, some of the effect may be due to the measurement instrument. For example, other studies have not found a significant relationship between behavioral adjustment and social-cognitive problem-solving skills either for upper-middle-socioeconomic-status children (Krasnor and Rubin 1981) or for third-grade inner-city, black, low-income subjects (Weissberg et al. 1981). Peery (1979) also noted that sociometric isolates were not deficient on tests of social comprehension.

Moreover, the adjustment/aberrant categories and subcategories of the HPSB have not been validated with other instruments or direct observation. The number of children classified as aberrant has varied in these studies from 40 to 77 percent; the inhibited group accounted for approximately 20 percent of the total population. This disproportionate number of high-risk children might also suggest that the inhibited children were only mildly deficient and likely to respond to less-intensive interventions.

Finally, without minimizing the potential power of the program, a second explanation of these results may be considered. A close examination of the highly structured and elaborate training procedures suggests to this writer that, in addition to teaching the children the problem-solving skills, the trainers inadvertently also taught them how to behave appropriately in the classroom setting. Such academic survival skills have been shown to be prerequisite for successful academic functioning, particularly at the lower primary grades (Cobb 1972; Greenwood, Hops, and Walker 1977a; 1977b; Greenwood et al. 1979; Hops and Cobb 1973; 1974). To benefit from an instructional program, children must learn to look at and listen to the teacher, respond to questions appropriately, and so forth. Children who display these behaviors are more likely to receive positive responses from teachers (Brophy and Good 1974). However, as Conger and Keane (1981) have noted, the HPSB is more a measure of classroom adjustment than interpersonal competence. Consequently, the teachers' higher ratings of the experimental children may simply represent more-appropriate academic-related classroom behavior rather than improved social-emotional adjustment with peers. Here too, the addition of direct observation and other instrumentation would have detailed more clearly the actual process of change.

In summary, a problem-solving approach toward improving the social-emotional adjustment of socially withdrawn children has much face validity. Unfortunately, the pioneering work of Spivack and Shure, while providing a major impetus for investigations in this area, has been methodologically weak. More work is presently required to test these procedures with children who are more severely withdrawn. Further replications should include a variety of process and outcome variables for a more-precise behavioral analysis of the effects.

The effectiveness of specific social-skills training has been shown to be powerful if the subjects are actually deficient in the specific skills being taught and if generalization to the natural environment is built into the procedures. Another variable that may be affecting the outcome but that has not been investigated is the involvement of peers in the training sessions. In the coaching studies, Ladd (1981) trained pairs of isolate children and involved normal peers with notably effective results. Shure and Spivack trained their children in problem-solving in groups of children selected from the regular classroom and with other siblings at home (Shure and Spivack 1978; Spivack and Shure 1974). It is possible that generalization over time and across settings was indeed partially due to the more-natural social conditions in the training setting. Generalization to peers is more likely to occur when peers are actually involved in the training procedures. In the next section, the involvement of peers as behavioral-change agents is examined more thoroughly.

Peers as Behavioral-Change Agents

Traditionally, peer-group assistance in the teaching of academic and social skills has been more widely accepted and advanced in cultures other than our own (Bronfenbrenner 1970). Recent evidence indicates that we too are increasing our use of peers as behavioral-change agents in remedying a wide range of problematic behaviors in children (Allen 1976; Apolloni and Cooke 1978; Strain 1981; Strain, Cooke, and Apolloni 1976b). Peers' attention was shown to be a powerful reinforcer for various social behaviors in the natural setting (Wahler 1967). More-competent or older peers can be used as instructors for tutoring less-skilled children (Willis, Crowder, and Morris 1972) and dispensing consequences (Greenwood, Sloane, and Baskin 1974). The peer group can be easily motivated to assist in the treatment of withdrawn or isolate children (Hops, Walker, and Greenwood 1979). Kirby and Toler (1970) increased an isolate child's low rate of interaction by having him pass out candy to his classmates. Others have used a group backup contingent upon the target child's increased social-interaction levels (Hops, Walker, and Greenwood 1979; Walker and Hops 1973). The power of the group backup for cases of withdrawn children is consistent with previous studies of aggressive acting-out children (Greenwood and Hops 1981; Hops et al. 1978; Patterson 1974; Walker and Buckley 1972; Walker, Hops, and Greenwood 1981).

Strain, Cooke, and Apolloni (1976b) have argued that involving peers rather than adults in treatment may be more practical because the intervention does not require the continuous presence of an adult, thereby improving its cost-effectiveness; adults who function primarily within a single setting cannot monitor cross-setting interventions, thereby creating procedural inconsistencies; many disordered children display specific deviant behaviors only in the presence of the peer group, thus precluding an effective adult intervention; and behavior changes brought about through adult involvement may not maintain in the absence of the adult change agent.

Peers more competent than target children can be trained to assist in the intervention. For example, Strain, Shores, and Timm (1977) and Strain (1977) used young intelligent preschoolers as confederates in two studies designed to increase the social behavior of developmentally delayed preschoolers with IQs ranging from 25–58. The confederates were trained in four sessions to initiate social behavior in the targeted children and were then instructed to do their best to involve those children in play during specific time periods outside the classroom. The confederates' increased initiations to the targeted children resulted in increases in the latter's initiating behavior and gains in social-behavior levels for both targets and trainers. Strain (1977) tested for generalization effects to the classroom setting and found positive indications for two of the three subjects even when probes were taken twenty-three hours after the training period. Similarly, Morris and Dolker (1974) used a high-interacting child as a trainer for a low-interacting one. Both were retarded, the target more severely than the trainer. The results provided further support for the practical utility of peer trainers who function at higher levels than the targeted subjects.

Children with more-extreme handicapping conditions may have to be taught to imitate before peer models become functionally useful. In a series of studies, Apolloni and Cooke and their associates (Cooke, Apolloni, and

Raver, in press; Peck et al. 1978; Peck, Cooke, and Apolloni 1981) developed the Peer Imitation Training (PIT) procedure for training developmentally delayed isolate children to imitate the social behavior of normal nondelayed models. Each day for three to four minutes, a trainer used instructions, verbal and physical prompts, and social reinforcement to establish imitative responding. The handicapped children not only learned to imitate the models but also the behavior generalized to untrained settings, providing some indications that a generalized imitative response had been acquired. The effect on overall social-behavior levels was not as dramatic, suggesting that more-specific training was required across a varied response repertoire. The data also indicated much less imitation of the delayed children by the peer models, who given the choice, preferred to interact with other normal children.

An important point made in the studies reviewed here is that simply placing handicapped and normal children in the same setting and expecting modeling to occur naturally is naive—especially when the targeted children are severely handicapped and do not have the imitative skills. At least some structure may be required to facilitate the usefulness of the peer group (Devoney, Guralnik, and Rubin 1974), although the type may vary considerably. Lilly (1971) placed low-achieving, low-sociometric-status children to work with high-status peers in making a movie for later presentation to the entire class. The sessions occurred twice weekly for five weeks. The results indicated that the intervention was successful, with the target children receiving increased scores on the measure of social acceptance. Unfortunately, the gains were short lived, disappearing at a six-week follow-up probe. Lilly (1971) suggested longer interventions may be necessary to increase and maintain the social acceptance of such children.

A similar procedure was used to improve the social status of mainstreamed retarded children in grades three to five (Ballard et al. 1977). Experimental children were assigned with their regular classmates to an activity group whose goal was to create a multimedia project such as a slide show or skit. The treatment procedure was relatively lengthy, forty minutes each day for eight weeks. The results of the treatment were assessed by a forced-choice sociometric procedure. Each child was rated by peers not involved in the same projects as being liked, disliked, or neutral. Both acceptance and rejection scores were produced for each subject. The experimental group showed significant increases in acceptance scores as compared to the control group. These gains were maintained in a posttest two weeks later. The success of the project was partially mitigated by the absence of change in the rejection-score data. In spite of an increase in the number of students rating the handicapped children as acceptable, the number of rejections remained fairly constant. These data indicate that the acceptance and rejection variables are likely to be orthogonal. Also, as the authors point out, it is difficult to know at what stage of acceptance-rejection the child becomes acceptable to the class of peers.

Another type of structure that has been tried successfully is a simple one-to-one pairing arrangement of the isolate child with other nonisolate children. For example, low-status handicapped children were paired with high-status nonhandicapped students for eight weeks in one of two experimental groups or two control groups (Fox 1978). The experimental groups were structured with tasks designed to promote mutual interest or tasks that were arbitrarily given academic assignments. The control groups were an attention control and a no-treatment control. Friendship ratings collected at pre- and posttreatment revealed that female subjects were more accepting of their partners only in the mutual-interest group. Boys, however, increased their preference for partners across both training groups. While success was noted for some pairs, no data were collected to indicate whether the effects generalized to the other class members.

In an unpublished study by Johnson et al. (1973), an isolate preschool girl was assigned to play on a cooperative task with one member of each of three distinct groups within her classroom. The play sessions occurred outside the classroom in an experimental room. Each cooperative response on the task was rewarded with a marble. The data were noteworthy. Initially, generalized increases in social behavior occurred in the classroom during free play with the first group's noninvolved members. Furthermore, as the child's involvement with the other group's representatives occurred, her social behavior in the classroom with their noninvolved members also increased. These gains maintained even when she was no longer being paired with the group representatives. The study lasted for almost fifty days, and its length of treatment may have partially accounted for the dramatic generalization of the child's social behavior from the laboratory to the three classroom groups.

Borrowing from the Johnson et al. concept, Hops, Walker, and Greenwood (1979) designed a series of studies to see if pairing a withdrawn child with a nonwithdrawn peer for a shorter period of time in the classroom (as opposed to removing them to a laboratory setting) would have a similar effect on the target child's social behavior. The joint task was constructed to ensure that interaction occurred, that much of it was verbal, and that both children's responses were interrelated.

An arithmetic-flash-card procedure clearly illustrates the structure. One child holds up a flash card with the problem (for example, 2 + 2 = ______) facing the other. The first child states the problem and then provides feedback to the second child's response (for example, "That's right"). During the sessions, they alternate roles. Other examples of the joint-task procedure include reading to one another, other card games, and so forth. Younger children, who are nonreaders, may play with mazes so that one child with eyes closed runs a pencil through a paper-and-pencil maze, while receiving corrective verbal feedback from the other.

Each day during the interventions, a different child was assigned to the task with the targeted child. The rate of interaction on each occasion soared dramatically for the withdrawn child and peer. Even the most withdrawn children responded positively to teacher directives. Unfortunately, reversals conducted as part of the experiments indicated that the results were short lived.[3] The absence of maintenance may have been partially due to the short intervention phases—that is, five to ten days—in contrast to Johnson et al.'s (1973) fifty days.

These studies all used tightly structured peer-pairing conditions to improve the social behavior of withdrawn children. In contrast, Furman, Rahe, and Hartup (1979) allowed the structure to vary but evaluated the impact of the peer's age on the acquisition of social skills by the target child. This study was based on the classic work of Suomi and Harlow (1972), who found that the social deficits of young monkeys who had been reared in isolation were eliminated after being paired with younger peer "therapists." Furman, Rahe, and Hartup (1979) paired withdrawn preschoolers with peers approximately the same age or fifteen months younger. Each pair was placed in a room for ten play sessions of twenty-minutes duration over a period of four to six weeks. The experimenter simply observed the children with minimal involvement. The results were highly impressive. Following treatment, the isolate children in the younger-aged therapist group increased their positive-interaction rates with their own age group in the regular classroom. Less-dramatic changes occurred in those isolates who were placed with same-aged therapists. The authors argued that the placement of isolates with younger children provided them the opportunity to learn and use leadership skills (that is, initiating and directing social activities), opportunities not available in the classroom with their own age mates. The results were also impressive in their cost-effectiveness since they required no more than three hours of intervention time to increase social interaction at least 50 percent beyond the pretreatment levels and to the levels of the normal population.

In summary, this section has illustrated how peers may be useful assistants in modifying the behavior of withdrawn/isolate children. More-skilled peers may be instructed in training less-skilled peers. Increases in initiations can result in increased social interaction because of the reciprocal nature of social behavior. Severely handicapped children first can be taught imitative responses so as to take greater advantage of the appropriate behavioral models provided by their competent peers. Skilled and unskilled peers can be paired in a variety of structured tasks to facilitate the interactive responding of low-interacting children. In such cases, lengthy treatment may be required before generalization and maintenance are established.

Finally, the pairing of younger-aged or developmentally equal peers as therapists may provide a potentially powerful cost-effective treatment for establishing social skills in isolate children. Certainly, further research is required to replicate this latter finding and to establish its power over the long run.

Programming Multiple Components

The early studies in the behavioral treatment of socially withdrawn children evaluated the effects of one or two simple independent variables over the short run. For example, in the preceding sections I reviewed studies that examined the effects of symbolic modeling alone and with social reinforcement, token reinforcement with adult and group backups, and contingent adult attention with verbal and physical prompting. Later studies evaluated more-complex treatment combinations. These included a variety of peer-pairing arrangements and direct instruction in social skills. As our knowledge base increases about the variables influencing children's social behavior generally and the behavior of withdrawn children specifically, more-powerful treatments that will persist over time and across settings are likely to result. In striving toward this goal, we may find that more-elaborate and heterogeneous combinations of treatment components previously found to be effective will have a more-powerful effect on the targeted behaviors and produce greater durability.

Weinrott, Corson, and Wilchesky (1979) evaluated the effects on classroom behavior of a combination of symbolic-modeling, behavioral-rehearsal, and individual- and group-reinforcement contingencies within a teacher-training program. Twenty teachers were trained to implement individualized programs for their children in their respective classrooms. Each of the teachers had referred a child who had also met stringent criteria indicating levels of social behavior below those of classroom peers. Five additional children who met the same criterion served as an untreated control group.

Teachers were trained in a series of eight weekly sessions over a ten-week period. They were given training on a variety of behavioral-management topics including writing behavioral objectives, social- and token-reinforcement procedures, and the effects of modeling. In the first five weeks, teachers established individual contingencies for the targeted children in their respective classrooms. The targets and several of their peers were also shown four fifteen-minute videotapes describing appropriate social behavior over a four-day period. Role playing of the appropriate behaviors followed the film session daily. Group rewards and the double-interlocking system, used by Walker and Hops (1973) and described earlier, were introduced during the last five weeks. Each of the child's peers was given a ticket with his name on it. The target child collected the ticket from each peer who initiated conversation with him or her. Group rewards were subsequently provided only to those peers whose tickets had been given to the target. Later on, to prevent misuse and easy access to the reward, the target children were told not to accept a peer's ticket unless the initiation had been meaningful (Weinrott, personal communication).

The results clearly showed that the intervention had a significant impact on the child's social behavior as measured by direct observations in the classroom and by teachers' ratings. Moreover, the group and interlocking contingencies were found to be the most powerful of the procedures used, increasing the children's behavior to normal peer levels. Follow-up data were collected in three weekly observations beginning two weeks after the intervention procedures had been terminated. They showed maintenance of subjects' behavior at peer levels.

These data indicate that a combined set of procedures may be useful for increasing and maintaining the social behavior of isolate children in the classroom. Although no data are available to shed light on the unique contribution of each, the teachers reported that they thought the crossover contingency with the group backup was the most powerful. Modeling and praise were felt to have had only minimal and temporary effects.

A five-year programmatic attack on the problem of social withdrawal in primary-grade children was conducted at the University of Oregon's former Center at Oregon for Research in the Behavioral Education of the Handicapped. The center was established to produce standardized intervention packages with cost-effective service delivery for subgroupings of behaviorally handicapped children. The programs are designed for use by regular school professionals directly in the school setting, who involve and train teachers and others as needed.

The PEERS (Hops et al. 1977) program for remedying socially withdrawn behavior of primary-grade children was the result of a series of studies on isolate children. The studies occurred within a three-stage research-and-development process, moving from investigations conducted under rigorous experimental conditions in an experimental classroom to interventions conducted in the natural setting involving regular school personnel as change agents. The results of many of the studies have been discussed in earlier sections (Hops, Walker, and Greenwood 1979).

The final packaged set of procedures incorporated into procedural manuals for the consultant and teacher consist of four major components. These are direct instruction in specific social skills, a peer-pairing arrangement, a token-reinforcement system with a group backup, and a verbal-correspondence procedure for establishing the persistence of social behaviors across settings and over time.

Social-Skills Tutoring. Results of early studies at the center indicated that not all children could benefit from a reinforcement procedure even when a group backup was used to involve the entire peer group. Some of the children appeared not previously to have acquired simple skills for initiating interactions with others or for responding to other initiations appropriately. Following the coaching study of Oden and Asher (1977), and based on the Direct Instruction model of Engelmann and Becker (1978), a social-skills-tutoring component was developed. This provides direct instruction in those specific skills that were isolated in previous studies in our experimental classroom (Walker et al. 1979): initiating interactions with others (STARTING), responding to peers' initiations (ANSWERING), and maintaining interactions already begun (KEEPING IT GOING). Additional lessons are also available to teach sharing and praising, but these have not been evaluated.

Joint Task. For ten minutes each day, a peer-pairing arrangement is set up in the classroom by the teacher. The child and a peer (a different one each day) are assigned to complete an academically related task. The tasks are designed to elicit alternate verbal responding to ensure that both the child and the peer interact. The structure of the task (arranged at three levels for controlling responding) is faded as the child demonstrates success at each level.

Token and Social Reinforcement with a Group Backup at Recess. The consultant awards points to the targeted child each day for all forms of social behavior during one preselected recess period. The child's level of social behavior over the previous three days determines the daily criterion for reinforcement, and the group backup motivates the child's peers to assist in the intervention. Each day prior to recess, the children select a reward from several provided by the teacher. Three or four special helpers are selected from volunteers and are also instructed in the behaviors required for assisting the child to earn points. At recess, the consultant prompts and praises both the child and special helpers for all forms of point-earning behavior. Terminology taught during the tutoring sessions is also used in recess to prompt and praise social behavior.

Verbal Correspondence. There is a growing interest in the relationship between verbal and nonverbal behavior. Some researchers have suggested the relationship is functional so that one exercises control over the other (Meichenbaum and Goodman 1969; 1971). A number of studies have demonstrated that this correspondence can indeed be trained in young children (Israel and O'Leary 1973; Karoly and Dirks 1977; Risley and Hart 1968; Rogers-Warren and Baer 1976), although it is not clear whether the verbal or nonverbal behavior is the controlling variable (Israel 1978). Initially, Risley and Hart (1968) demonstrated that children who are reinforced for reporting accurately about what they have done (DO-SAY) increase the rate of the nonverbal behavior. Israel and O'Leary (1973) contrasted the DO-SAY with the SAY-DO procedure. They found the latter to be more effective in training correspondence, suggesting that verbal mediation is more likely to act as the controlling mechanism that prompts the desired behavior in the appropriate setting. However, Israel (1978) concluded that, given the present state of knowledge, training with a SAY-DO-SAY procedure is more likely to ensure correspondence effects and increases in the targeted behavior.

Although not yet demonstrated, the verbal-correspondence studies have powerful implications for establishing the generalization and maintenance of behavior over time and across settings. During the development of PEERS, the addition of a verbal-correspondence procedure was conceptualized as a cost-effective component used primarily to establish cross-setting generalization of behavior. Initially, the child is taught by the consultant to report to the teacher on his social behavior following the point recess intervention. Then, subsequent to every other recess and free-play period, the teacher instructs the child to report after recess and assigns a peer to play with the child and corroborate his report. Reinforcement is delivered intermittently to the peer group for correct reporting. Data obtained on several subjects indicate that increased play behavior occurs during these other recess periods. This is partially due to the company of the assigned peer, but the behavior appears to maintain when peer corroboration ceases (Hops, Walker, and Greenwood 1979). Because the method has been used only as part of the total package, the results attributed to the procedure itself are confounded.

The individual components of the PEERS program are faded systematically after the child has reached the predetermined criterion levels of social behavior—one standard deviation above the mean for his or her grade level. The data are based on normative data collected on randomly selected peers during the course of the program development. The faded components include the daily setup in the classroom prior to each recess, the special helpers, the joint task, the consultant, and finally, the reinforcement. The minimum length of time required for the entire program is twenty-four days, averaging about thirty-five.

To date, a full test of the PEERS package has not been conducted. In an early study (Hops, Walker, and Greenwood 1979), seven children were involved in a test of only two of the components—(1) the token-reinforcement procedure with the group backup conducted during recess by the consultant and (2) the joint-task procedure arranged in the classroom by the teacher. The combined procedures were effective in increasing the social behavior of each child. Six of the original sample were observed in a six-month follow-up when all of the children were in different classrooms with different peers and teachers. Only two of the six demonstrated gains within the normative ranges for their age groups. In a subsequent test of the entire package (Hops, Walker, and Greenwood 1979), three targeted subjects all demonstrated gains during the intervention and maintained normal levels after all of the components had been removed. In a two-month follow-up of two of the three subjects, only one was still within the normal range. Thus, data regarding the durability of the program over the long run are still incomplete.

A third investigation was performed, using only the token-reinforcement-plus-praise and group-backup component during recess combined with the social-skills tutoring (Paine et al. 1982). These were delivered to nine children in a reversal design, alternating four baseline and three treatment phases. Five of the children had been involved previously in various studies of the PEERS program development; the other four had been referred but had not been treated. The purpose of this study was to see whether children would respond positively to booster on the maintenance of social behavior. As before, the procedures were effective in dramatically increasing the social behavior of all children during each treatment phase. The data for the final baseline phase showed that four of the five previously treated subjects were interacting within normal levels of social behavior following the booster sessions. However, only one of the four previously untreated subjects maintained at normal levels. Perhaps more-comprehensive and longer interventions are required before greater durability is obtained. Also, the previously untreated subjects were older and presumably had a longer history of reinforcement for withdrawn behavior.

Sociometric data collected as part of the study showed increases in peer status (as playmates) for four of the five previously treated subjects and for all of the previously untreated subjects. Needless to say, the sociometric scores did not agree with the behavioral observations. Increased acceptance scores were noted for one of the previously treated group who did not maintain social behavior in the final phase, and lower scores were noted for one who did. In the previously untreated group, three of the four subjects whose acceptance scores increased did not maintain normal rates of social behavior. Thus, peer status of these children may have increased after having been paired with the group backup; however, these increases were not reflected in durable social-behavior gains.

In the final study, five consultants in a school district were trained to implement the PEERS program in a two-day workshop. In previous research, we found that professional consultants can be trained effectively to use well-packaged standardized programs successfully in 2–4-day workshops (Hops et al. 1978; Greenwood et al. 1979). Of the five children on whom the program was implemented, all were shown to have significant increases in social-behavior levels during the intervention. This indicated that the workshop training and the manuals of procedure were used effectively by school personnel in changing the behavior of socially withdrawn children in the natural setting. Unfortunately, the school year ended prior to the program's termination. Only two children were able to move to the final phase in which the consultant had been faded from the program. However, both were maintaining above-baseline levels and were within the normative ranges for their respective grade levels.

Consequently, program conclusions are mixed. The program is effective in changing children's social behavior, even when implementation is conducted by consultants with minimal but sufficient training. The data indicating that the program has lasting benefits or is superior to the gains of an untreated control group are still lacking.

To summarize, combining program components whose efficacy has been demonstrated in previous work into a comprehensive package has much face validity. Weinrott, Corson, and Wilchesky (1979) combined several components into a ten-week teacher-training program. Gains in social behavior were produced in the classroom and maintenance noted up to five week later. Hops, and his co-workers (1979) combined four components into a comprehensive standardized intervention package that has been tested and replicated many times. However, follow-up data have been collected for only two subjects who were administered the entire package—one of whom maintained at normative levels two months later. Certainly, further research is required to test more fully the long-term effectiveness of such packaged procedures.

Generalization and Maintenance

It is becoming more evident that producing treatment effects with long-term durability or cross-setting generalization is exceedingly difficult and requires extensive programming efforts (Baer, Wolf, and Risley 1968). Following a recent and exhaustive review of the behavioral literature on generalization and maintenance, Stokes and Baer (1977) concluded that the present technological state is still "embryonic." "Train and hope" was how they referred to the most frequent experimental design for evaluating maintenance effects. Also, since the procedures are not designed specifically to establish maintenance, such studies are likely to provide minimal information for determining the relevant contributing variables, should maintenance effects occur. Thus far there exist more recommendations for, than demonstrations of, effective techniques for establishing long-term durability of treatment gains (see reviews by O'Leary and Drabman 1971; Kazdin and Bootzin 1972; O'Leary and O'Leary 1976; Stokes and Baer 1977).

Most of the procedures implemented or suggested for building persistence involve one of two basic strategies: (1) reprogramming the natural environment by changing the behavior of social agents in positions to support the child's newly acquired skills (for example, Patterson et al. 1967) or (2) "reprogramming the child" to survive in a nonsupportive environment (Graubard, Rosenberg, and Miller 1971). Environmental reprogramming has emphasized factors such as training parents or teachers to apply social consequences and subsequently fading discriminative stimuli [for example, gradual removal of points, tokens, experimenter, or other materials associated with the treatment procedures and not usually found in the child's normal environment (Greenwood et al. 1974)]. Programming the individual child has focused on teaching self-control (Drabman, Spitalnik, and O'Leary 1973), problem-solving (Spivack and Shure 1974), or how to change the environment to support appropriate child behavior (Graubard, Rosenberg, and Miller 1971; Seymour and Stokes (1976). However, the child's behavioral change and that of the social agents supporting the child's newly acquired skills are both subject to the same laws of behavior. They require systematic programming to be maintained. Such programming is likely to demand considerable effort, a factor that precludes its use by large numbers of behavioral change agents. For example, involving teachers, parents, and peers calls for systematic teaching and monitoring of each of these untrained agent groups. A major disadvantage in self-control procedures is that they are more difficult to use and less effective with younger children (Combs and Lahey 1981).

A third strategy, providing the child with specific behaviors that would likely be maintained by the natural environment without the need for systematic programming, has inexplicably remained virtually unexplored in spite of its initial recommendation some ten years ago (Ayllon and Azrin 1968). Transferring control of behavior from the clinician or teacher to stable natural contingencies that can be depended upon to operate within the child's normal environment has much to recommend it. Perhaps no other procedure is potentially as simple and effective.

Nevertheless, a prerequisite for naturally occurring maintenance may be the existence of a reciprocal relationship between the responding of the target and a social agent in the natural setting so that both control each other's behavior to some degree. Also, considerable evidence indicates that behavioral control may be one-sided in many cases. For example, ample demonstrations have shown that children's appropriate classroom behavior is controlled by teacher praise, attention, and feedback (Walker and Buckley 1973). Increases in children's classroom behavior can be maintained by concomitant increases in teacher-praise rates. Unfortunately, teacher behavior is not reciprocally under the control of appropriate child behavior. To begin with, most classroom behavior goes unrewarded (White 1975), and increases in appropriate child behavior alone is insufficient to maintain teachers' praising, without concomitant praise and feedback directed at the teacher from external sources (Brown, Montgomery, and Barclay 1969; Cossairt, Hall, and Hopkins 1973).

The nature of social behavior, however, clearly has been demonstrated to be reciprocal for child-child as well as child-adult relationships (Mueller 1972; Patterson and Reid 1970; Shores and Strain 1977). Initiations by one individual have an extremely high probability of being responded to by another. (Greenwood et al. 1981). Perhaps, then, it is not unrealistic to expect social-behavior gains to maintain over time with minimal programming requirements. As conceptualized by Baer and Wolf (1970), the social environment may be seen as a "behavioral trap." Children with efficient entry skills can enter the peer group and be trapped within it, there to be taught the skills that peers teach one another and to be involved in the teaching process itself. These investigators presented some illustrative data in support of their hypothesis. Using an ABAB design to increase the social behavior of a preschool isolate child, they found that repeated and more-intense deliveries of teacher attention plus prompting and priming in each successive treatment phase finally produced fewer and fewer reversal effects during return-to-baseline conditions. After the fourth treatment phase, the behavior maintained at treatment levels. They speculated that the child's behavior was now trapped by the social-reinforcement contingencies occurring naturally in the social environment. By increasing the child's social behaviors through an outside intervention, they argued, many potential reinforcers occurring naturally within the peer social community were now made available to him, which in turn maintained his own social interactive behavior. Several instances of similar limited reversal effects were also noted.

The entrapment hypothesis and evidence of the reciprocal nature of social interaction combine to suggest that interventions aimed at social responding may produce greater durability of behavior change than those designed to increase behaviors less likely to be reinforced naturally in the environment. Let us evaluate the literature again for evidence of generalization and attempt to extract from it the contributing procedures.

The evidence for the power of teacher praise and attention to produce short-term gains in the social behavior of withdrawn children is noted in occasional posttreatment checks (for example, Allen et al. 1964) and in limited reversal effects (for example, Baer and Wolf 1970; Buell et al. 1968; Walker and Hops 1973). Usually, this has not been the case, perhaps a function of the paradoxical reversal design that attempts to demonstrate both treatment effects with expected reversals in behavioral gains, as well as the maintenance of behavioral change following treatment with nonreversals (Hartmann and Atkinson 1973). An examination of the failures to achieve even short-term durability of effects suggests that failure is most likely to occur when the length of treatment has been relatively short—for example, from five to twelve days (Hart et al. 1968; Strain, Shores, and Kerr 1976; Strain and Timm 1974; Fleischman, Hops and Street 1976). Studies in which maintenance was achieved had lengthier interventions (for example, Cooke and Apolloni 1976). The Baer and Wolf (1970) study lasted over sixty days, with varying procedures in effect for over forty days before the behavior maintained at treatment levels.

The effects of modeling on the maintenance of social behaviors are somewhat equivocal. Gains were produced that lasted up to four months for children described as peer oriented (Evers-Pasquale and Sherman 1975) and for shorter periods when the modeling-film soundtrack was in the first person (Jakibchuk and Smeriglio 1976) or induced the children to interact (O'Connor 1972). However, maintenance was not always demonstrated (Gottman 1977; Keller and Carlson 1974). Moreover, the methodological deficiencies and variability in selection procedures in many of these studies suggest that further research is required to uncover the variables that may be facilitating social behavior and its persistence.

Long-term treatment effects were noted in several studies using token reinforcement in combination with symbolic modeling and other variables. For example, Weinrott and his associates (1979) found that appropriate academic interaction with peers maintained at peer levels up to five weeks after the eight-week-intervention procedures had terminated. In another study, withdrawn children subjected to an experimental classroom treatment for two months were followed up twice upon their return to the regular academic setting within the same year and twice again during the following academic year.

These children continued to make gains in social interaction relative to their peers throughout the follow-up period (Street et al. 1976). The results of both studies indicate that powerful treatments that operate daily for at least two months have enduring effects on social behavior.

A setting variable was noted to contribute to persistence of treatment gains in one study using a token economy and a group backup with a young kindergarten girl (Hops, Walker, and Greenwood 1979). Contrasting interventions in the classroom and on the playground at recess, social behavior was found to maintain longer at treatment levels during recess. In similar return-to-baseline conditions in the classroom, the behavior decelerated to near zero levels immediately after reinforcement was terminated. Levels of social behavior were usually higher during baseline conditions in recess, further indicating the greater density of reinforcement for social behavior occuring naturally within that setting.

When peers have been involved in the treatment of isolate behavior, the effects on maintenance have been inconsistent. On the one hand, pairing peers with the target child for brief periods in structured tasks eliciting high rates of interactive behavior had no persistent effects when return-to-baseline conditions were implemented (Hops, Walker, and Greenwood 1979). On the other hand, Johnston et al. (1973) found the effects of fifty days of peer pairing on a cooperative laboratory task to generalize to the classroom—gains that were also maintained after treatment had been terminated.

Strain (1977) trained peer confederates to initiate to behaviorally disabled children. The increases in social behavior generalized to the regular classroom from the training setting for two of the three subjects. Cooke, Apolloni, and Raver (in press) noted generalization of imitative behavior to untrained settings and new responses following involvement in a peer-imitation-training program for severely retarded children. In these studies, the closely controlled experimental setting and training may have had some effect on the persistence of child behavioral gains.

Some investigators have used elaborate peer-pairing arrangements for increasing the social status of low-achieving or retarded children as measured by sociometrics. Treatment gains were lost in a one-month follow-up when intervention occurred twice daily for five weeks (Lilly 1971). However, two-week maintenance was achieved in a similar study following a daily eight-week intervention (Ballard et al. 1977). Here, too, the length of the intervention may have been a significant factor.

Direct instruction in social, verbal, and problem-solving skills were evaluated for maintenance effects in several short- and long-term studies. Oden and Asher (1977) demonstrated that three hours of coaching in social skills over a four-week period produced significant increases in sociometric acceptance scores relative to simple peer-pairing and no-treatment control conditions. The gains were in the expected direction even in the next academic year. However, an attempted replication study was unable to produce sociometric or behavioral gains better than a simple peer-pairing arrangement (Hymel and Asher 1977). A more-recent investigation examined the effects of specific verbal-skills training in children with low sociometric acceptance and who were shown to be deficient in the targeted verbal behaviors (Ladd 1981). Significant generalized effects were noted in two of the three specific verbal skills and in sociometric ratings—gains that persisted into a four-week follow-up. Several factors differentiated Ladd's study from the previous coaching investigations. Ladd's intervention was twice as long, requiring eight 45–50-minute sessions on alternating days. Furthermore, he sequentially programmed generalization to the regular classroom by involving more than a single child in the intervention and members of the normal peer group in the final stages.

The Spivack and Shure (1974) program for teaching 4-year-old Head Start problem-solving skills also produced long-term gains in behavioral adjustment. In a second follow-up year, naive teachers rated the experimental children higher than the controls. This program was also lengthy, occurring daily for fifty sessions over a ten-week period.

The preceding review of the literature suggests that generalization and maintenance effects are more likely to occur under certain treatment conditions. In spite of methodological limitations in a number of studies, specific patterns appear across treatment modalities. For example, one major factor affecting the power of a program to produce durable gains over time and across settings is the length of treatment involved. Studies having the greatest impact over time, regardless of the type of treatment or measurement instrument used, were in effect daily for at least two months. Prime examples include the effect of adult contingent attention plus priming (Baer and Wolf 1970), the two-month intervention in an experimental classroom setting (Street et al. 1976), an eight-week teacher-mediated program involving symbolic modeling, group and individual token reinforcement, and behavioral rehearsal (Weinrott, Corson, and Wilchesky 1979), a ten-week primary-prevention program for preschool children (Shure and Spivack 1974), and an eight-week peer-pairing arrangement for mildly retarded children (Ballard et al. 1977).

Another factor to be considered important in producing persistent effects appears to be the degree of experimental control. Where small groups were treated in special classrooms under more-rigorous experimental procedures and involved peers in the interventions (Walker et al. 1979; Strain 1977), behavioral gains were found to generalize to other settings and to persist over time even when the subjects were severely retarded (Apolloni and Cooke 1978). When treatment was lengthy as well, gains were found to persist one year later in new classrooms with different peers (Street et al. 1976). Similarly, sequentially programming generalization to the peer group by involving peers in the treatment is also likely to produce desirable effects (Ladd 1981).

What is surprising is the durability of effects noted for interventions that were much shorter in length. Examples include the modeling studies consisting of no more than twenty to thirty minutes of filmed presentation on a single occasion (O'Connor 1972; Evers and Schwarz 1973) and the effects attributed to three hours of coaching over a four-week period (Oden and Asher 1977). Why was the power of these treatments so much greater than other studies using adult attention or token reinforcement? One likely answer may be found in the definition of social isolate used by the different experimenters. The modeling studies showing long-term gains usually involved from 10 percent (O'Connor 1972) to 25 percent (Evers-Pasquale and Sherman 1975) of the entire preschool population. Similarly, Oden and Asher (1977) selected three children from each classroom having the lowest sociometric scores. If an average classroom contains between twenty-five and thirty children, then 10–12 percent of each classroom are being defined as social isolates. It is likely that the children selected for treatment by Walker et al.(1979); Hops, Walker, and Greenwood (1979); and Weinrott, Corson, and Wilchesky (1979) are more severely withdrawn. They found only 2 percent of children in their classrooms who met their criteria. Thus, it may not be surprising that the effects noted for both modeling and brief coaching persisted for up to one year later.

How do these data fit the entrapment model for social behavior suggested by Baer and Wolf (1970)? The results of the literature reviewed here do not indicate that establishing durability of social behavior is any easier than programming maintenance of other behaviors. Admittedly, Bear and Wolf ascribed the behavioral-trap phenomenon to the preschool and not to social communities generally. Perhaps, at the preschool level, the degree of social withdrawal is not severe (compare Spivack and Shure 1974). Baer and Wolf provided no data to indicate the level of isolation of the target child in relation to his peer group. Withdrawn preschool children have limited histories of reinforcement. It may be that, as such children grow older, it becomes more difficult to establish the social skills required for entry into their respective peer communities. Paine et al. (1982) were unable to produce durable effects for their older, previously untreated group. Clearly, we have much to learn about the contingencies and variables controlling social behavior of withdrawn children so that we can plan effective interventions and program long-term maintenance of gains.

Conclusion

The preceding review has clearly demonstrated the ever-increasing emphasis in the behavioral literature on social-skills training of isolate/withdrawn children. Recent programs for the annual meetings of the American Psychological Association, the Association for the Advancement of Behavior Therapy, the Association for Behavioral Analysis, and the Society for Research in Child Development also reflect this trend. I have argued that social interaction with peers is necessary for health development, that children who are classified as withdrawn are less likely to succeed academically or socially, and that this association can be seen as early as the preschool years. Thus, the assault on the development of methods for treating the withdrawn child seems justified—perhaps overdue.

I have also shown that treatments have been designed to function in a variety of settings, may involve teachers and/or peers, and can include methods of broad ranging as training in general problem-solving skills or as simple as having the withdrawn child hand candy to a member of the normal peer group. The results so far have not been overly impressive in their demonstration of long-lasting gains over time and generalizability to other settings. Apparently we are just beginning to understand the nature of social interaction and its controlling stimuli.

One key to the problem of recurring limited and short-term effects across intervention models may lie in the reliance on nonspecific global measures for identifying target populations and evaluating outcomes. Global measures do not provide clear direction for the development of precise treatment techniques. For example, the two predominant methods used by researchers have been sociometric nominations and direct observations of social behavior in the natural setting. Usually, sociometric scores are estimates of trhe number of friendship choices or play choices by other members of a child's class. However, studies using sociometrics as dependent variables have been remiss by including among isolates those children who have been rejected (and likely to be aggressive), by relying heavily on research conducted with preschool populations for whom traditional nomination sociometrics are notoriously unreliable, and by not clearly specifying the goals of intervention necessary to increase a child's acceptance score.

Studies using direct observations have also been negligent in failing to pinpoint the specific behavioral skills required to increase the global observation measure (for example, rate of interaction or percentage of time spent interacting) and not defining the target group as one clearly below that of the normal population. Gottman (1977) and Asher and Hymel (1981) have criticized the use of such measures because research has not yet demonstrated their relation to inadequate functioning in children or their predictive validitiy for problematic behavior (as has been done with sociometrics).

Recent studies have not shown a relationship between global measures of observed interaction rate and sociometric play choices (Greenwood et al. 1979; Gottman 1977). Nevertheless, some investigators continue to use the predictive validity of sociometrics to justify the selection of withdrawn children on the basis of direct observation. The low relationship may be due to low test-retest reliabilities of sociometrics for preschool children, inadequate definitions of isolate or withdrawn children, or the absence of a linear relationship between peer popularity and interaction rate. Extremely low interactors may also be children with similar low scores on a peer-popularity instrument; but it does not follow that high interactors are socially more popular (they may indeed be aggressive and obnoxious) or that children who are highly popular interact more than average. In fact, it is possible for some children to have only one or two close friends (low friendship scores) yet spend more than the average amount of time interacting.

Some studies have focused on decreasing specific behavioral deficits in children. However, treatment components have been selected on the basis of adult research or simply because they appear to be relevant. While the effect of these deficits on overall functioning may be clear for extremely low-functioning children, it is not obvious (and it has not been demonstrated) that increasing specific targeted behaviors for isolates is related to improvement on some external criteria of social competence. One reason may be that we have not yet been able to reach consensus on a definition of social competence in young children (Anderson and Messick 1974; Zigler and Trickett 1978), thereby limiting specific directions for delineating treatment goals. Researchers are increasingly acknowledging that a multimethod approach may be necessary for defining precisely withdrawn/isolate children, such as sociometrics, direct observations, and teacher and parent ratings. Evans and Nelson (1977) and Hops and Greenwood (1981) make some cogent suggestions about how different data can determine the precise nature of the interventions required.

It is clear that future researchers investigating the development of treatment procedures for isolate children will have to consider these assessment issues. Definitions of social competence may require empirical derivations—that is, functionally demonstrating the behaviors that are causally related to skillful interpersonal responding. Some have suggested that social competence is situation specific and that precise targeting of social skills will have to be evaluated for different situations (Hersen and Bellack 1977; Combs and Slaby 1977). We may also find that some behaviors are cross situationally effective and tht acquiring these skills will lead to greater generalization of treatment effects across settings and/or people. Research will also have to focus on skill deficits other than social—for example, motor and language—as well as on the impact of parenting variables to account for a larger proportion of the variance in children's social competence (Hops and Finch 1981; Finch and Hops 1981).

Global measures may be useful as screening instruments to identify those children who may be lacking in specific social skills. More-detailed assessments would then provide indications of the specific deficits that require remediation. Outcomes would be reflected in improvements in both the specific targeted behaviors and the global variables (See Hops and Greenwood 1981). Hopefully, a different research focus will facilitate the development of more-efficient and -effective treatment strategies for children who for too long have been ignored by their social environment.

Notes

This chapter was prepared with assistance from NIH Biomedical Research Support Grant RR05612, Oregon Research Institute. The assistance of Susan Brewster and Katherine Wall in the typing of this manuscript is gratefully acknowledged. Thanks are also extended to Melissa Finch for her editorial contributions.

1. No distinction will be made between isolate and withdrawn children in the major portion of this chapter. However, the distinction between them is a critical variable that may be affecting research results and will be discussed in more detail in the conclusions section.

2. These conclusions were based on interpretation of the results using a p level of .05 and not the .10 used by the authors.

3. Some maintenance was achieved in one class whose teacher established the joint-task procedure for all members of the class as part of her academic lesson.

References

T.M. Achenbach, "The Child Behavior Profile: I. Boys Aged 6–11," *Journal of Consulting and Clinical Psychology* 46(1978a):478–488.

T.M. Achenbach, "Psychopathology of childhood: Research problems and issues," *Journal of Consulting and Clinical Psychology* 46(1978b): 759–776.

G.J. Allen, J.M. Chinsky, S.W. Larcen, J.E. Lochman, and H.V. Selinger, *Community Psychology and the Schools* (Hillsdale, N.J.: Lawrence Erlbaum Associates, 1976).

K.E. Allen, B. Hart, J.S. Buell, F.R. Harris, and M.M. Wolf, "Effects of Social Reinforcement on Isolate Behavior of a Nursery School Child," *Child Development* 35(1964):511–518.

V.L. Allen, *Children as Teachers* (New York: Academic Press, 1976).

S. Anderson and S. Messick, "Social Competency in Young Children," *Developmental Psychology* 10(1974):282–293.

T. Apolloni, and T.P. Cooke, "Integrated Programming at the Infant, Toddler, and Preschool Age Levels," in *Early Intervention and the Integration of Handicapped Children,"* ed. M. Guralnik (Chicago: University Park Press, 1978).

H. Arkowitz, "The Measurement and Modification of Minimal Dating Behavior," in *Progress in Behavior Modification,* eds. M. Hersen, R. Eisler, and P. Miller (New York: Academic Press, 1977).

S.R. Asher and S. Hymel, "Children's Social Competence in Peer Relations: Sociometric and Behavioral Assessment," in *Social Competence,* eds. J.D. Wine and M.D. Smye (New York: Guilford Press, 1981).

T. Ayllon and N.H. Azrin, *The Token Economy: A Motivational System for Therapy and Rehabilitation* (New York: Appleton-Century-Crofts, 1968).

D.M. Baer and M.M. Wolf, "The Entry into Natural Communities of

Reinforcement," in *Control of Human Behavior,* eds. R. Ulrich, T. Stachnik, and J. Mabry (Glenview, Ill.: Scott Foresman, 1970).

D.M. Baer, M.M. Wolf, and T.R. Risley, "Some Current Dimensions of Applied Behavior Analysis," *Journal of Applied Behavior Analysis* 1(1968):91–97.

M. Ballard, L. Corman, J. Gottlieb, and M.J. Kaufman, "Improving the Status of Mainstreamed Retarded Children," *Journal of Educational Psychology* 69(1977):605–611.

A. Bandura, *Principles of Behavior Modification* (New York: Holt, Rinehart & Winston, 1969).

S. Beck, R. Forehand, K.C. Wells, and A. Quante, "Social Skills Training with Children: An Examination of Generalization from Analogue to Natural Settings" (Paper presented at the annual meeting of the Association for Advancement of Behavior Therapy, Chicago, November 1978).

W.C. Becker, "The Relationship of Factors in Parental Ratings of Self and Each Other to the Behavior of Kindergarten Children as Rated by Mothers, Fathers, and Teachers," *Journal of Consulting Psychology* 24(1960):507–527.

A.S. Bellack M. Hersen, and D. Lamparski, "Roleplay Tests for Assessing Social Skills: Are They Valid? Are They Useful?" *Journal of Consulting and Clinical Psychology* 47(1979):335–342.

A.S. Bellack, M. Hersen, and S. Turner, "Roleplay Tests for Assessing Social Skills: Are They Valid?" *Behavior Therapy* 9(1978):448–461.

A.S. Bellack, M. Hersen, and S.M. Turner, "Relationship of Role Playing and Knowledge of Appropriate Behavior to Assertion in the Natural Environment," *Journal of Consulting and Clinical Psychology* 47(1979):670–678.

M.R. Bornstein, A.S. Bellack, and M. Hersen, "Social Skills Training for Unassertive Children: A Multiple Baseline Analysis," *Journal of Applied Behavior Analysis* 10(1977):183–195.

U. Bronfenbrenner, *Two Worlds of Childhood: U.S. and U.S.S.R.* (New York: Simon and Schuster, 1970).

W.C. Bronson, "Stable Patterns of Behavior: The Significance of Enduring Orientations for Personality Development," in *Minnesota Symposia on Child Psychology,* vol. 2, ed. J.P. Hill (Minneapolis: University of Minnesota Press, 1968).

W.C. Bronson, *Toddler's Behaviors with Agemates: Issues of Interaction, Cognition, and Affect* (Norwood, N.J.: Ablex Publishing, 1981).

W.C. Bronson, and W.B. Pankey, "The Evolution of Early Individual Differences in Orientation toward Peers" (Paper presented at the biennial meeting of the Society for Research in Child Development, New Orleans, March 1977).

J.E. Brophy, and T.L. Good, *Teacher-Student Relationships: Causes and Consequences* (New York: Holt, Rinehart & Winston, 1974).

J.C. Brown, R. Montgomery, and J.R. Barclay, "An Example of Psychologist Management of Teacher Reinforcement Procedures in the Elementary Classroom," *Psychology in the Schools* 4(1969): 336–340.

J. Buell, P. Stoddard, F.R. Harris, and D.M. Baer, "Collateral Social Development Accompanying Reinforcement of Outdoor Play in a Preschool Child," *Journal of Applied Behavioral Analysis* 1(1968): 167–173.

R. Charlesworth and W.W. Hartup, "Positive Social Reinforcement in the Nursery School Peer Group," *Child Development* 38(1967):993–1002.

G.F. Chittenden, "An Experimental Study in Measuring and Modifying Assertive Behavior in Young Children," *Monographs of the Society for Research in Child Development* 7(1942):1–87.

P.W. Clement and D.C. Milne, "Group Play Therapy and Tangible Reinforcers Used to Modify the Behavior of 8-Year-Old-Boys," *Behaviour Research Therapy* 5(1967)301–312.

P.W. Clement, P.V. Roberts, C.E. Lantz, "Social Models and Token Reinforcement in the Treatment of Shy, Withdrawn Boys," *Proceedings of the 78th Annual Convention of the American Psychological Association* 5(1970):515–516.

J.A. Cobb, "Survival Skills and First-Grade Achievement," Report No. 1 Eugene: Center at Oregon for Research in the Behavioral Education of the Handicapped, University of Oregon, 1970).

J.A. Cobb, "Relationship of Discrete Classroom Behaviors to Fourth-Grade Academic Achievement," *Journal of Educational Psychology* 63(1972):74–80.

M.L. Combs and B.B. Lahey, "A Cognitive Social Skills Training Program: Evaluation with Young Children," *Behavior Modification* 5 (1981): 39–60.

M.L. Combs and D.A. Slaby, "Social Skills Training with Children," in *Advances in Clinical Psychology,* vol. 1, eds. B. Lahey and A. Kazdin (New York: Plenum Press, 1977).

J.D. Cone and R.P. Hawkins, *Behavioral Assessment: New Directions in Clinical Psychology* (New York: Brunner/Mazel, 1977).

J.C. Conger and S.P. Keane, "Social Skills Intervention in the Treatment of Isolated or Withdrawn Children," *Psychological Bulletin* 90(1981): 478–495.

H. Cook and S. Stingle, "Cooperative Behavior in Children," *Psychological Bulletin* 81(1974):918–933.

T.P. Cooke and T. Apolloni, "Developing Positive Social-Emotional Behaviors: A Study of Training and Generalization Effects," *Journal of Applied Behavior Analysis* 9(1976):65–78.

T.P. Cooke, T. Apolloni, and S. Raver, "The Effects of a Second Nonretarded Playmate on the Free-Play Imitation and Interaction of Retarded and Nonretarded Children," *Mental Retardation,* in press.

A. Cossairt, R.V. Hall, and B.L. Hopkins, "The Effects of Experimenter's Instructions, Feedback, and Praise on Teacher Praise and Student Attending Behavior," *Journal of Applied Behavior Analysis* 6(1973): 89–100.

C. Devoney, M.J. Guralnik, and H. Rubin, "Integrating Handicapped and Nonhandicapped Children: Effects on Social Play," *Childhood Education* 50(1974):360–364.

R.S. Drabman, R. Spitalnik, and K.D. O'Leary, "Teaching Self-Control to Disruptive Children," *Journal of Abnormal Psychology* 82(1973): 10–16.

T.J. D'Zurilla and M.R. Goldfried, "Problem Solving and Behavior Modification," *Journal of Abnormal Psychology* 78(1971):107–126.

S. Engelmann and W.C. Becker, "The Direct Instruction Model," in *Encouraging Change in America's Schools: A Decade of Experimentation,* ed. R. Rhine (New York: Academic Press, 1978).

I.M. Evans and R.O. Nelson "Assessment of Child Behavior Problems," in *Handbook of Behavioral Assessment,* eds. A.R. Ciminero, K.S. Calhoun, and H.E. Adams (New York: Wiley, 1977).

W.L. Evers and J.C. Schwarz, "Modifying Social Withdrawal in Preschoolers: The Effects of Filmed Modeling and Teacher Praise," *Journal of Abnormal Child Psychology* 1(1973):248–256.

W. Evers-Pasquale and M. Sherman, "The Reward Value of Peers: A Variable Influencing the Efficacy of Filmed Modeling in Modifying Social Isolation in Preschoolers," *Journal of Abnormal Child Psychology* 3(1975):179–189.

M. Finch and H. Hops, "Childhood Social Competence and Parental Behavior: A Direct Observation Study" (Paper presented at the annual meeting of the Association for Advancement of Behavior Therapy, Toronto, November 1981).

N.W. Finkelstein, C. Dent, K. Gallacher, and C.T. Ramey, "Social Behavior of Infants and Toddlers in a Day-Care Environment," *Developmental Psychology* 14(1978):257–262.

D.H. Fleischman, H. Hops, and A. Street, "Increasing Interactive Behavior of Withdrawn Children in the Regular Classroom," in *Systematic Analysis of Social Interaction: Assessments and Interventions,* H. Hops, chair (Symposium presented at the Eighty-Fourth annual meeting of the American Psychological Association, Washington, D.C., 1976) (ERIC Document Reproduction Service No. ED 131 937).

C.L. Fox, "Peer Acceptance of Exceptional Children in the Regular Classroom" (Ph.D. diss., University of California, Los Angeles, 1978).

W. Furman, D.F. Rahe, and W.W. Hartup, "Rehabilitation of Socially

Withdrawn Preschool Children," *Child Development* 50(1979): 915–922.

C. Garvey "Some Properties of Social Play," in *Play—Its Role in Development and Evolution,* eds. J.S. Bruner, A. Jolly, and K. Sylva (New York: Basic Books, 1976).

C. Garvey and R. Hogan, "Social Speech and Social Interaction: Egocentrism Revisited," *Child Development* 44(1973):562–568.

J.C. Gersten, T.S. Langner, J.G. Eisenberg, O. Simcha-Fagan, and E.D. McCarthy, "Stability and Change in Types of Behavioral Disturbance of Children and Adolescents," *Journal of Abnormal Child Psychology* 4(1976):111–127.

J. Gottman, "The Effects of a Modeling Film on Social Isolation in Preschool Children: A Methodological Investigation," *Journal of Abnormal Child Psychology* 5(1977):69–78.

J. Gottman, J. Gonso, and B. Rasmussen, "Social Interaction, Social Competence, and Friendship in Children," *Child Development* 46(1975):709–718.

J. Gottman, J. Gonso, and P. Schuler, "Teaching Social Skills to Isolated Children," *Journal of Abnormal Child Psychology* 4(1976):179–197.

P.S. Graubard, H. Rosenberg, and M.B. Miller, "Student Applications of Behavior Modification to Teachers and Environments or Ecological Approaches to Social Deviance," in *A New Direction for Education: Behavior Analysis 1971,* vol. 1, eds. E.A. Ramp and B.L. Hopkins (Lawrence, Kansas: Support and Development Center for Follow Through, Department of Human Development, University of Kansas, 1971).

C.R. Greenwood, and H. Hops, "Group-Oriented Contingencies and Peer Behavior Change," in *The Utilization of Classroom Peers as Behavior Change Agents,* ed. P.S. Strain (New York: Plenum, 1981).

C.R. Greenwood, H. Hops, J. Delquadri, J. Guild, "Group Contingencies for Group Consequences in Classroom Management: A Further Analysis," *Journal of Applied Behavior Analysis* 7(1974):413–425.

C.R. Greenwood, H. Hops, H.M. Walker, J. Guild, J. Stokes, K.R. Young, K.S. Keleman, and M. Willardson, "A Standardized Intervention Program for Academic Related Behavior during Instruction (PASS): Field Test Evaluations in Utah and Oregon," *Journal of Applied Behavior Analysis* 12(1979):235–253.

C.R. Greenwood, H. Sloane, and A. Baskin, "Training Elementary Aged Peer-Behavior Managers to Control Small Group Programmed Mathematics," *Journal of Applied Behavior Analysis* 7(1974):103–114.

C.R. Greenwood, N.M. Todd, H. Hops, and H.M. Walker, "Behavior Change Targets in the Assessment and Treatment of Socially Withdrawn Preschool Children," *Behavioral Assessment* 4(1982).

C.R. Greenwood, H.M. Walker, N.M. Todd, and H. Hops, "Preschool Teachers' Assessments of Social Interaction: Predictive Success and Normative Data," Report No. 26 (Eugene: Center of Oregon for Research in the Behavioral Education of the Handicapped, University of Oregon, 1976).

C.R. Greenwood, H.M. Walker, N.M. Todd, and H. Hops, "Selecting a Cost-Effective Screening Device for the Assessment of Preschool Social Withdrawal," *Journal of Applied Behavior Analysis* 12(1979): 639–652.

C.R. Greenwood, H.M. Walker, N.M. Todd, and H. Hops, "Normative and Descriptive Analysis of Preschool Free-Play Social Interaction Rates," *Journal of Pediatric Psychology* 6(1981):343–367.

F.M. Gresham, and R.J. Nagle, "Social Skills Training with Children: Responsiveness to Modeling and Coaching as a Function of Peer Orientation," *Journal of Consulting and Clinical Psychology* 48(1980): 718–729.

F.R. Harris, M.D. Johnston, S. Kelley, and M.M. Wolf, "Effects of Positive Social Reinforcement on Regressed Crawling of a Nursery School Child," *Journal of Educational Psychology* 55(1964):35–41.

B.M. Hart, N.J. Reynolds, D.M. Baer, E.R. Brawley, and F.R. Harris, "Effect of Contingent and Non-Contingent Social Reinforcement on the Cooperative Play of a Preschool Child," *Journal of Applied Behavior Analysis* 1(1968):73–76.

D.P. Hartmann, and C. Atkinson, "Having Your Cake and Eating It Too: A Note of Some Apparent Contradictions between Therapeutic Achievements and Design Requirements in $N=1$ Studies," *Behavior Therapy* 4(1973):589–591.

W.W. Hartup, "Peer Relations and the Growth of Social Competence," in *Primary Prevention of Psychopathology: Social Competence in Children,* vol. 1, eds. M.W. Kent and J.E. Rolf (Hanover, N.H.: University Press of New England, 1979).

W.W. Hartup, J.A. Glazer, and R. Charlesworth, "Peer Reinforcement and Sociometric Status," *Child Development* 38(1967):1017–1024.

M. Hersen and A.S. Bellack, "Assessment of Social Skills," *Handbook of Behavioral Assessment,* eds. A.R. Ciminero, K.R. Calhoun, and H.E. Adams (New York: Wiley, 1977).

M. Hersen and R.M. Eisler, "Social Skills Training," in *Behavior Modification: Principles, Issues, and Applications,* eds. W.E. Craighead, A. Kazdin, and M.J. Mahoney (Boston: Houghton Mifflin, 1976).

T.R. Hobbs and J.E. Radka, "Modification of Verbal Productivity in Shy Adolescents during a Short-Term Camping Program," *Psychological Reports* 39(1976):735–739.

M.C. Holmberg, "The Development of Social Interchange Patterns from

12–42 Months: Cross-Sectional and Short-Term Longitudinal Analyses'' (Paper presented at the biennial meeting of the Society for Research in Child Development, New Orleans, March 1977).

H. Hops, and J.A. Cobbs, ''Survival Behaviors in the Educational Setting: Their Implications for Research and Intervention,'' in *Behavior Change: Methodology, Concepts, and Practice,* eds. L.A. Hamerlynck, L.C. Handy, and E.J. Mash (Champaign, Ill.: Research Press, 1973).

H. Hops and J.A. Cobb, ''Initial Investigations into Academic Survival Skill Training, Direct Instruction, and First-Grade Achievement,'' *Journal of Educational Psychology* 66(1974):548–553.

H. Hops, and M. Finch, ''A Skill Deficit View of Social Competence in Preschoolers (Invited address to the 8th annual convention of the Association for Behavior Analysis, Milwaukee, May 1981).

H. Hops, D.H. Fleischman, J. Guild, S. Paine, A. Street, H.M. Walker, and C.R. Greenwood, *A Program for Establishing Effective Relationship Skills (PEERS): Manual for Consultants* (Eugene: Center at Oregon for Research in the Behavioral Education of the Handicapped, University of Oregon, 1977).

H. Hops and C.R. Greenwood, ''Social Skills Deficits,'' in *Behavioral Assessment of Childhood Disorders,* eds. E.J. Mash and L.G. Terdal (New York: Guilford Press, 1981).

H. Hops, H.M. Walker, D.H. Fleischman, J.T. Nagoshi, R.T. Omura, K. Skindrud, and J. Taylor, ''CLASS: A Standardized In-Class Program for Acting-Out Children. II. Field Test Evaluations,'' *Journal of Educational Psychology* 70(1978):636–644.

H. Hops, H.M. Walker, and C.R. Greenwood, ''PEERS: A Program for Remediating Social Withdrawal in the School Setting: Aspects of a Research and Development Process,'' *The History and Future of the Developmentally Disabled: Programmatic and Methodological Issues,* ed. L.A. Hamerlynck (New York: Bruner/Mazel, 1979).

S. Hymel and S.R. Asher, ''Assessment and Training of Isolated Children's Social Skills'' (Paper presented at the biennial meeting of the Society for Research in Child Development, New Orleans, March 1977).

A.C. Israel, ''Some Thoughts on Correspondence between Saying and Doing,'' *Journal of Applied Behavioral Analysis* 11(1978):271–276.

A.C. Israel, and K.D. O'Leary, ''Developing Correspondence between Children's Words and Deeds,'' *Child Development* 44(1973):575–581.

Z. Jakibchuk and V. Smeriglio, ''The Influence of Symbolic Modeling on the Social Behavior or Preschool Children with Low Levels of Social Responsiveness,'' *Child Development* 47(1976):838–841.

J.E. Johnson, ''Relations of Divergent Thinking and Intelligence Test Scores with Social and Nonsocial Make-Believe Play of Preschool Children,'' *Child Development* 47(1976):1200–1203.

T.O. Johnson, E.M. Goetz, D.M. Baer, and D.R. Green, ''The Effects of an Experimental Game on the Classroom Cooperative Play of a Preschool Child" (Paper presented at the Fifth annual Southern California Conference on Behavior Modification, Los Angeles, October 1973).

P. Karoly and M.J. Dirks, "Developing Self-Control in Preschool children through Correspondence Training," *Behavior Therapy* 8(1977): 398–405.

A.E. Kazdin and R.R. Bootzin, "The Token Economy: An Evaluative Reveiw," *Journal of Applied Behavior Analysis* 5(1972):343–372.

M.F. Keller and P.M. Carlson, "The Use of Symbolic Modeling to Promote Social Skills in Preschool Children with Low Levels of Social Responsiveness," *Child Development* 45(1974):912–919.

F.D. Kirby and H.S. Toler, "Modification of Preschool Isolate Behavior: A Case Study," *Journal of Applied Behavior Analysis* 3(1970): 309–314.

M. Kohn and B.L. Rosman, "A Social Competence Scale and Symptom Checklist for the Preschool Child: Factor Dimensions, Their Cross-Instrument Generality, and Longitudinal Persistence," *Developmental Psychology* 6(1972a):430–444.

M. Kohn and B.L. Rosman "Relationship of Preschool Social-Emotional Functioning to Later Intellectual Achievement," *Developmental Psychology* 6(1972b):445–452

L.R. Krasnor and K.H. Rubin, "The Assessment of Social Problem-Solving Skills in Young Children," in *Cognitive Assessment,* eds. T. Merluzzi, C. Glass, and M. Genest (New York: Guilford Press, 1981).

G.W. Ladd, "Socials Skills and Peer Acceptance: Effects of a Social Learning Method for Training Social Skills," *Child Development* 52(1981):171–178.

A. La Greca and D. Santogrossi, "Social Skills Training with Elementary School Students: A Behavioral Group Approach," *Journal of Consulting and Clinical Psychology* 48(1980):220–228.

H.M. Lahaderne and P.W. Jackson, "Withdrawal in the Classroom: A Note on Some Educational Correlates of Social Desirability among School Children," *Journal of Educational Psychology* 61(1970): 97–101.

M. Lewis and L.A. Rosenblum, *Friendship and Peer Relations* (New York: Wiley, 1975).

M.S. Lilly, "Improving Social Acceptance of Low Sociometric Status, Low Achieving Students," *Exceptional Children* 37(1971):341–348.

R. Lipitt, "Popularity among Preschool Children," *Child Development* 12(1941):305–322.

E.J. Mash and L.G. Terdal, *Behavior Therapy Assessment: Diagnosis, Design, and Evaluation* (New York: Springer Publishing Company, 1976).

R.M. McFall and C.T. Twentyman, "Four Experiments on the Relative

Contributions of Rehearsal, Modeling, and Coaching to Assertion Training," *Journal of Abnormal Psychology* 81(1973):199–218.

D. Meichenbaum and J. Goodman, "The Development Control of Operant Motor Responding by Verbal Operants," *Journal of Experimental Child Psychology* 7(1969):553–565.

D. Meichenbaum and J. Goodman, "Training Impulsive Children to Talk to Themselves," *Journal of Abnormal Psychology* 77(1971):115–126.

M. Meighan and K. Birr, "The Infant and Its Peers" (Unpublished manuscript, University of Kansas Medical Center, 1979).

L. Michelson, S.L. Foster, and W.L. Ritchey, "Social-Skills Assessment of Children," in *Advances in Clinical Child Psychology,* vol. 4, eds. B. Lahey and A.E. Kazdin (New York: Plenum, 1981).

L. Michelson and R. Wood, "A Group Assertive Training Program for Elementary School Children," *Child Behavior Therapy* 2(1980):1–9.

R.J. Morris and M. Dolker, "Developing Cooperative Play in Socially Withdrawn Retarded Children," *Mental Retardation* 12(1974):24–27.

E. Mueller, "The Maintenance of Verbal Exchanges between Young Children," *Child Development* 43(1972):930–938.

E. Mueller and J. Brenner, "The Origins of Social Skills and Interaction Among Playgroup Toddlers," *Child Development* 48(1977):854–861.

R.D. O'Connor, "Modification of Social Withdrawal through Symbolic Modeling," *Journal of Applied Behavior Analysis* 2(1969):15–22.

R.D. O'Connor, "The Relative Efficacy of Modeling, Shaping, and the Combined Procedures for the Modification of Social Withdrawal," *Journal of Abnormal Psychology* 79(1972)327–334.

S. Oden and S.R. Asher, "Coaching Children in Social Skills for Friendship Making," *Child Development* 48(1977):495–506.

K.D. O'Leary and R. Drabman, "Token Reinforcement Programs in the Classroom," *Psychological Bulletin* 75(1971)379–398.

S.G. O'Leary and K.D. O'Leary, "Behavior Modification in the School," in *Handbook of Behavior Modification,* ed. H. Leitenberg (Englewood Cliffs, N.J.: Prentice—Hall, 1976).

S.C. Paine, H. Hops, H.M. Walker, C.R. Greenwood, D.H. Fleischman, and J.J. Guild, "Repeated Treatment Effects: A Study of Maintaining Behavior Change in Socially Withdrawn Children," *Behavior Modification* 6(1982).

G.R. Patterson, "An Empirical Approach to the Classification of Disturbed Children," *Journal of Clinical Psychology* 20(1964):326–337.

G.R. Patterson, "Interventions for Boys with Conduct Problems: Multiple Settings, Treatments, and Criteria," *Journal of Consulting and Clinical Psychology* 42(1974):471–481.

G.R. Patterson, S. McNeal, N. Hawkins, and R. Phelps, "Reprogramming the Social Environment," *Journal of Child Psychology and Psychiatry* 8(1967):181–195.

G.R. Patterson and J.B. Reid, "Reciprocity and Coercion: Two Facets of Social Systems," in *Behavior Modification in Clinical Psychology,* eds. C. Neuringer and J. Michael (New York: Appleton-Century-Crofts, 1970).

C.A. Peck, T. Apolloni, T.P. Cooke, and S.A. Raver, "Teaching Retarded Preschoolers to Imitate the Free-Play Behavior of Nonretarded Classmates: Trained and generalized Effects," *Journal of Special Education* 12(1978):195–207.

C.A. Peck, T.P. Cooke, and T. Apolloni, "Utilization of Peer Imitation in Therapeutic and Instructional Contexts," in *The Utilization of Classroom Peers as Behavior Change Agents,* ed. P.S. Strain (New York: Plenum, 1981).

J.C. Peery, "Popular, Amiable, Isolated, Rejected: A Reconceptualization of Sociometric Status in Preschool Children," *Child Development* 50(1979):1231–1234.

E.G. Pekarik, R.J. Prinz, D.E. Liebert, S. Weintraub, and J.M. Neale, "The Pupil Evaluation Inventory: A Sociometric Technique for Assessing Children's Social Behavior," *Journal of Abnormal Child Psychology* 4(1976):83–97.

J.B. Raph, A. Thomas, S. Chess, and S.J. Korn, "The Influence of Nursery School on Social Interactions," *American Journal of Orthopsychiatry* 38(1968):144–152.

J.B. Reid, N. Hawkins, C. Keutzer, S.A. McNeal, R.E. Phelps, K.M. Reid, and H.L. Mees, "A Marathon Behavior Modification of a Selectively Mute Child," *Journal of Child Psychology and Psychiatry* 8(1967): 27–30.

J. Reuter and G. Yunik, "Social Interaction in Nursery Schools," *Developmental Psychology* 9(1973):319–325.

T. Risley and B. Hart, "Developing Correspondence between Nonverbal and Verbal Behavior of Preschool Children," *Journal of Applied Behavioral Analysis* 1(1968):267–281.

M. Roff, S.B. Sells, and M.M. Golden, *Social Adjustment and Personality Development in Children* (Minneapolis: University of Minnesota Press, 1972).

A.R. Rogers-Warren and D.M. Baer, "Correspondence between Saying and Doing: Teaching Children to Share and Praise," *Journal of Applied Behavior Analysis* 9(1976):335–354.

J.E. Rolf and J.E. Hasazi, "Identification of Preschool Children at Risk and Some Guidelines for Primary Intervention," in *Primary Prevention of Psychopathology: The Issues,* vol. 1, eds. G.W. Albee and J.M. Joffe (Hanover, N.H.: University Press of New England, 1977).

D.M. Ross, S.A. Ross, and T.A. Evans, "The Modification of Extreme Social Withdrawal by Modeling with Guided Participation," *Journal of Behavior Therapy and Experimental Psychiatry* 2(1971):273–279.

J. Rubenstein and C. Howes, "The Effects of Peers on Toddler Interaction with Mother and Toys," *Child Development* 47(1976):597–605.

A.S. Sacks, R.A. Moxley, Jr., and R.T. Walls, "Increasing Social Interaction of Preschool Children with 'Mixies'." *Psychology in the Schools* 12(1975):74–79.

T. Sajwaj, S. Twardosz, and M. Burke, "Side Effects of Extinction Procedures in a Remedial Preschool," *Journal of Applied Behavior Analysis* 5(1972):163–175.

F.W. Seymour and T.F. Stokes, "Self-Recording in Training Girls to Increase Work and Evoke Staff Praise in an Institution for Offenders," *Journal of Applied Behavior Analysis* 9(1976):41–54.

R.E. Shores, and P.S. Strain, "Social Reciprocity: A Review of Research and Educational Implications," *Exceptional Children* 43(1977): 526–530.

M.B. Shure and G. Spivack, "Means-End Thinking, Adjustment, and Social Class among Elementary School-Aged Children," *Journal of Consulting and Clinical Psychology* 38(1972):348–353.

M.B. Shure and G. Spivack, *Preschool Interpersonal Problem-Solving (PIPS) Test: Manual* (Philadelphia: Department of Mental Health Sciences, Hahnemann Community Mental Health/Mental Retardation Center, 1974).

M.B. Shure and G. Spivack, "A Mental Health Program for Preschool and Kindergarten Children, and a Mental Health Program for Mothers of Young Children: An Interpersonal Problem-Solving Approach toward Social Adjustment," A comprehensive report of research and training, no. MH20372. (Washington, D.C.: National Institute of Mental Health, 1975) (available from Hahnemann Medical School and Hospital).

M.B. Shure and G. Spivack, *Problem-Solving Techniques in Childrearing* (San Francisco: Jossey-Bass, 1978).

M.B. Shure, G. Spivack, and M. Jaeger, "Problem-Solving Thinking and Adjustment among Disadvantaged Preschool Children," *Child Develment* 42(1971):1791–1803.

L.D. Simkins, "Modification of Duration of Peer Interactions in Emotionally Disturbed Children," *Journal of School Psychology* 84(1971): 287–299.

S.H. Spence and J.S. Marzillier, "Social Skills Training with Adolescent Male Offenders: I. Short-Term Effects," *Behavior Research and Therapy* 17(1979):7–16.

G. Spivack, J.J. Platt, and M.B. Shure, *The Problem-Solving Approach to Adjustment* (San Francisco: Jossey-Bass, 1976).

G. Spivack and M.B. Shure, *Social Adjustment of Young Children* (San

Francisco: Jossey-Bass, 1974).

G. Spivack and J. Spotts, *Devereux Child Behavior Rating Scale Manual* (Devon, Pa.: Devereux Foundation, 1966).

T.F. Stokes and D.M. Baer, "An Implicit Technology of Generalization," *Journal of Applied Behavior Analysis* 10(1977):349–367.

P.S. Strain, "An Experimental Analysis of Peer Social Initiations on the Behavior of Withdrawn Preschool Children: Some Training and Generalization Effects," *Journal of Abnormal Child Psychology* 5(1977): 445–455.

P.S. Strain, ed. *The Utilization of Classroom Peers as Behavior Change Agents* (New York: Plenum, 1981).

P.S. Strain, T.P. Cooke, and T. Apolloni, *Teaching Exceptional Children: Assessing and Modifying Social Behavior* (New York: Academic Press, 1976a).

P.S. Strain, T.P. Cooke, and T. Apolloni, "The Role of Peers in Modifying Classmates' Social Behavior," *Journal of Special Education* 10(1976b):351–356.

P.S. Strain, M.M. Kerr, and E.U. Ragland, "The Use of Peer Social Initiations in the Treatment of Social Withdrawal," in *The Utilization of Classroom Peers as Behavior Change Agents,* ed. Strain (New York: Plenum, 1981).

P.S. Strain, R.E. Shores, and M.A. Kerr, "An Experimental Analysis of Spillover Effects on the Social Interactions of Behaviorally Handicapped Preschool Children," *Journal of Applied Behavior Analysis* 9(1976):31–40.

P.S. Strain, R.E. Shores, and M.A. Timm, "Effects of Peer Social Initiations on the Behavior Analysis 10(1977):289–298.

P.S. Strain and M.A. Timm, "An Experimental Analysis of Social Interaction between a Behaviorally Disordered Preschool Child and Her Classroom Peers," *Journal of Applied Behavior Analysis* 7(1974):583–590.

A. Street, H.M. Walker, C.R. Greenwood, N.M. Todd, and H. Hops, "Normative Peer Interaction Rate as a Baseline for Followup Evaluation," *Systematic Analysis of Social Interaction: Assessments and Interventions,* H. Hops, chair (Symposium presented at the Eighty-Fourth annual meeting of the American Psychological Association, Washington, D.C., 1976) (ERIC Document Reproduction Service No. ED 131 937).

S.J. Suomi and H.F. Harlow, "Social Rehabilitation of Isolate-Reared Monkeys," *Developmental Psychology* 6(1972):487–496.

S. Suomi and H.F. Harlow, "Effects of Differential Removal from Group on Social Development of Rhesus Monkeys," *Journal of Child Psychology and Psychiatry* 16(1975):149–164.

S. Suomi and H.F. Harlow, "Monkeys without Play," in *Play: Its Role in Development and Evolution,* eds. J.S. Bruner, A. Jolly, and K. Sylva (New York: Basic Books, 1976).

A. Tremblay, P.S. Strain, J.M. Hendrickson, and R.E. Shores, "Social Interactions of Normal Preschool Children: Using Normative Data for Subject and Target Behavior Selection," *Behavior Modification* 5(1981):237-253.

V.B. Van Hasselt, M. Hersen, and A.S. Bellack, "The Validity of Role Play Tests for Assessing Social Skills in Children," *Behavior Therapy* (1981):202-216.

J.B. Victor, and C.F. Halverson, Jr., "Behavior Problems in Elementary School Children: A Follow-up Study," *Journal of Abnormal Child Psychology* 4(1976):17-29.

R.G. Wahler, "Child-Child Interactions in Free Field Settings: Some Experimental Analysis, *Journal of Experimental Child Psychology* 5(1967):278-293.

M.G. Waldrop and C.F. Halverson, "Intensive and Extensive Peer Behavior: Longitudinal and Cross-Sectional Analyses," *Child Development* 46(1975):19-26.

H.M. Walker, *The Walker Problem Behavior Identification Checklist. Test and Manual* (Los Angeles: Western Psychological Services, 1970).

H.M. Walker and N.K. Buckley, "Programming Generalization and Maintenance of Treatment Effects across Time and across Settings," *Journal of Applied Behavior Analysis* 5(1972):209-224.

H.M. Walker and N.K. Buckley, "Teacher Attention to Appropriate and Inappropriate Classroom Behavior: An Individual Case Study," *Focus on Exceptional Children* 5(1973):5-11.

H.M. Walker, C.R. Greenwood, H. Hops, and N.M. Todd, "Differential Effects of Reinforcing Topographic Components of Social Interaction: Analysis and Systematic Replication," *Behavior Modification* 3(1979):291-321.

H.M. Walker and H. Hops, "The Use of Group and Individual Reinforcement Contingencies in the Modification of Social Withdrawal," in *Behavior Change: Methodology, Concepts, and Practice,* eds. L.A. Hamerlynck, L.C. Handy, and E.J. Mash (Champaign, Ill.: Research Press, 1973), pp. 269-307.

H.M. Walker and H. Hops, "Use of Normative Peer Data as a Standard for Evaluating Classroom Treatment Effects," *Journal of Applied Behavior Analysis* 9(1976):159-168.

H.M. Walker, H. Hops, and C.R. Greenwood, "RECESS: Research and Development of a Behavior Management Package for Remediating Social Aggression in the School Setting," in *The Utilization of Classroom Peers as Behavior Change Agents,* ed. P.S. Strain (New York: Plenum, 1981).

H.M. Walker, H. Hops, C.R. Greenwood, and N.M. Todd, "Social Interaction: Effects of Symbolic Modeling, Individual and Group Reinforcement Contingencies, and Setting on the Behavior of Withdrawn Children," Report No. 15 (Eugene: Center at Oregon for Research in the Behavioral Education of the Handicapped, University of Oregon, 1975).

M.G. Weinrott, J.A. Corson, and M. Wilchesky,- "Teacher Mediated Treatment of Social Withdrawal," *Behavior Therapy* 10(1979): 281-294.

R.P. Weissberg, E.L. Gesten, B.C. Rapkin, E.L. Cowen, E. Davidson, R. Flores de Apodaca, and B.J. McKim, "Evaluation of a Social-Problem-Solving Training Program for Suburban and Inner-City Third-Grade Children," *Journal of Consulting and Clinical Psychology* 49(1981):251-261.

M.A. White, "Natural Rates of Teacher Approval and Disapproval in the Classroom," *Journal of Applied Behavior Analysis* 8(1975):367-372.

T.L. Whitman, J.R. Mercurio, and V. Caponigri, "Development of Social Responses in Two Severely Retarded Children," *Journal of Applied Behavior Analysis* 3(1970):133-138.

J.W. Willis, J. Crowder, and B. Morris, "A Behavioral Approach to Remedial Reading Using Students as Behavioral Engineers," in *Behavior Analysis and Education,* eds. G. Semb, D.R. Green, R.P. Hawkins, J. Michael, E.L. Phillips, J.A. Sherman, H. Sloane, and D.R. Thomas (Lawrence: University of Kansas Follow Through Program, 1972).

R. Wood, L. Michelson, and J.M. Flynn, "Assessment of Assertive Behavior in Elementary School Children" (Paper presented at the annual meeting of the Association for the Advancement of Behavior Therapy, Chicago, November 1978).

E. Zigler and P.K. Trickett, "IQ, Social Competence, and Evaluation of Early Childhood Intervention Programs," *American Psychologist* 33(1978):789-798.

Editors' Epilogue

Most species, from the moment of birth, require some form of social contact and interaction—first for the organism to thrive and later to become a succesfully adapting member of its community. Humans are certainly no exception to this requirement for social contact. The essential role of social contact as the primary mechanism for physical survival and growth is undeniable. Equally compelling is the necessity of contact for successful social and emotional development (see Bowlby 1969; Suomi and Harlow 1972). It should be no surprise, then, that clinicians and researchers have shown considerable interest in the remediation of social inadequacy in children and adults (Bellack and Hersen 1979; Phillips 1978; Turner and Hersen 1981).

In this chapter, Hops provides us with a thought-provoking and critical review of social-skills training with socially withdrawn and isolated children. Like Putallaz and Gottman (chapter 1), he acknowledges the conceptual confusion surrounding the definition of social competence, but he also reviews some of the more-recent attempts to treat the socially inadequate child. Most important, Hops addresses two of the most nagging problems that confront clinicians who work with children: the frequently limited generalization of treatment effects beyond the clinic and the often short-lived nature of this change.

Limited generalization, in this instance, refers to the frequently noticed fact that children may display dramatic gains in their sociability in treatment settings with little or no change shown elsewhere. Obviously this is a nettlesome problem for researchers and clinicians since the usual goal of treatment is to foster change in those real-life settings where the child's problem occurs.

As Hops notes, the nature and structure of the treatment program may be the major contributor to this problem. The length of treatment, for example, may be too brief fo allow the withdrawn child the opportunity to develop skills that are useful outside of the consulting norm. Readers should make careful note of Hops's recommendations and analyses in this regard if they wish their treatment programs to have an impact in settings other than the one within which training occurs.

The second problem, the shortlived effects of change, has only recently come under close scrutiny by clinicians and researchers (Goldstein and Kanfer 1979; Karoly and Steffen 1980). The major difficulty, in this case, involves the failure of many programs to instigate behavioral change that extends beyond the termination of treatment. Quite often, a training program may show powerful effects while treatment is underway, only to have those effects fade when the program is terminated. Again, Hops's discussion of this difficulty should be heeded carefully by those who might plan for the longterm maintenance of change.

A concern of ours that cuts across these two problems regards the relative absence in the social-skills-training literature of references to work done within social psychology, anthropology, and sociology; all are fields of inquiry that can inform and augment what we have learned about social skills from clinical research. Argyle (1967) was one of the first social psychologists to suggest that individuals could be directly trained to improve their social performances. More recently, Trower (1979) has reveiwed some newer research in social psychology that could be fruitfully applied to social-skills training. Just a few relevant areas within this field are attribution theory, interpersonal attraction, nonverbal communication, relationship formation, and social cognition. Brehm and McAllister (1980), for example, have formulated an analysis of the maintenance of therapeutic change that draws heavily from attribution theory and psychological reactance. Such a synthesis, we feel, is essential if social-skills training is to move beyond its current limitation.

References

M. Argyle, *The Psychology of Interpersonal Behavior* (London: Penguin, 1967).

A.S. Bellack and M. Hersen, eds., *Research and Practice in Social Skills Training* (New York: Plenum, 1979).

J. Bowlby, *Attachment and Loss,* vol. 1 (New York: Basic Books, 1969).

S. Brehm and D.A. McAllister, "Social Psychological Perspective on the Maintenance of Therapeutic Change," in *Improving the Long Term Effects of Psychotherapy: Models of Durable Outcome,* eds. P. Karoly and J.J. Steffen (New York: Gardner Press, 1980).

A. Goldstein and F.H. Kanfer, *Maximizing Treatment Gains* (New York: Academic Press, 1979).

P. Karoly and J.J. Steffen, *Improving the Long-Term Effects of Psychotherapy: Models of Durable Outcome* (New York: Gardner Press, 1980).

E.L. Phillips, *The Social Skills Basis of Psychopathology: Alternatives to Abnormal Psychology and Psychiatry* (New York: Grune & Stratton, 1978).

S.J. Suomi and H.F. Harlow, "Social Rehabilitation of Isolate-Reared Monkeys," *Developmental Psychology* 6(1972):487–496.

P. Trower, "Fundamentals of Interpersonal Behavior: A Social Psychological Perspective,'' in *Research and Practice in Social Skills Training,* eds. A.S. Bellack and M. Hersen (New York: Plenum, 1979).

S.M. Turner and M. Hersen, ''Disorders of Social Behavior: A Behavioral Approach to Personality Disorders,'' in *Handbook of Clinical Behavior Therapy,* eds. S.M. Turner, K.S. Calhoun, and H.E. Adams (New York: Wiley, 1980).

3 Community-Based Interventions for the Developmentally Disabled

Michael F. Cataldo,
Brian A. Iwata, and
Eric M. Ward

A number of factors, past and present, have resulted in a movement toward community rather than institutional/residential settings for the retarded. Exposés on conditions in institutional settings (Blatt and Kaplan 1966; Rivera 1972), class-action suits on the right to treatment (*Ricci* v. *Greenblatt* 1972; *Wyatt* v. *Stickney* 1971), studies on the debilitating effects of total institutions (Goffman 1961; King, Raines, and Tizard 1971; Klaber 1969; Rosenham 1973; Wolfensberger 1969a; 1969b), and models for alternative programs for the retarded, particularly from Scandinavia (Grunewald 1969; Nirje 1969; Perske 1969), have all contributed to the present shift in emphasis toward treatment of the developmentally disabled.

While this chapter is about community programs for the developmentally disabled, we approach it with two biases: first, we are biased toward data-based considerations for programs, and second, we present topics that should be included in community living for all individuals—of which the developmentally disabled are only one subgroup.

An Act of Faith

The reliance on a sufficient data base as a prerequisite for initiation or continuation of community programs is a reasonable yet unprecedented consideration in the case of the developmentally disabled. Our modern society has approached the problem of the retarded from a practice rather than research orientation (Begab 1977). This is directly reflected in the funding distributions in the United States for programs for the developmentally disabled. Over $5 billion is spent annually on service and income maintenance, and three-fourths of this is for residential care and education. Only 1.5 percent of the $5 billion has been allotted for research purposes.

The current movement toward deinstitutionalization and the placement and maintenance of the handicapped in the community makes eminently good sense. It is the sort of innovative, rational, and humanistic movement that should proceed from an empirical foundation. Yet, it has not. The dangers that result from not establishing this data base threaten the continuation of this community movement as evidence by the following excerpts from opening remarks at the Congress of the International Association for the Scientific Study of Mental Deficiency in April 1976. The meeting honored the bicentennial of the United States, and also the centennial of the American Association on Mental Deficiency at which approximately 500 speakers addressed 1,152 registrants representing 63 countries.

> We cannot say with scientific certitude at this time that the move to mainstream retarded children will be more harmful or beneficial. It is clear, however, that we need more empirical data than is currently available before committing ourselves on a national scale to the abandonment of the special education system. Normalization and deinstitutionalization are other areas in which further research is urgently needed. Here, too, past investigations plagued by methodological weaknesses offer little direction to patterns of care and training . . . . [D]espite the establishment of halfway houses, group-care homes, and an increased use of foster family care, there has been no systematic effort to determine what factors within these various settings are most contributory to successful placement . . . . [P]hilosophical dictates and grave concern with the quality of *existing* forms of care have precipitated massive programs to relocate retarded persons . . . . [T]here is always the danger that the alternatives may prove little better than current practice. [Begab 1977, pp. A23–A24]

> For almost 15 years now, the predominant thrust of social policy in the mental retardation area has been a movement away from large central institutions to a community-based regionalization model in which the retarded are treated in the community in small residential settings. This social policy has evolved almost completely without an empirical base. If policymakers cannot demonstrate that regional centers or group homes are cost-effective, it may well be that large central institutions will be rediscovered. [Zigler and Balla 1977, pp. 267–268]

Thousands of individuals are now mandated to be in the community rather than in an institution—not because we have researched the benefits of this strategy, not because we have determined how to identify a good as opposed to a poor community program, not because we have empirically documented procedures for operating and improving community programs but because the community was thought to be a better environment for the developmentally disabled than institutions. It is unclear whether this is because the community is particularly good (well suited, receptive, responsive to needs) as much as institutions were judged particularly bad places for the developmentally disabled. In the absence of empirical evidence on which to base our judgments about the adequacy of community residence, we can only accept these judgments as we would common sense or an act of faith.

Thus, the movement toward deinstitutionalization—and all it implies—is based upon factors other than those that result from systematic empirical investigation. We do not suggest that this movement is ill advised or that sweeping change must always proceed from research. Rather, the fact that the movement toward community programs for the developmentally disabled lacks a strong empirical basis is important to note primarily so that the resulting limitations can be recognized. Such limitations would include no clearly specified empirical analyses defining the effective components of quality programs. This limitation will likely result in many unnecessary components being perpetuated and, thus, perpetuating unnecessarily higher costs. Another limitation has to do with replication of effective programs. While such replication is desirable, it is often difficult. Systematic research often results in an increased probability of replication. Without structure and program analysis from research activities, replicability will likely suffer. Perhaps the most notable limitation is research on assessment. No accepted procedures for examining the adequacy of community programs have been adopted. Thus, even with a clear technology for program implementation and remedial help, we could not proceed with the task of determining, in an unbiased and empirical fashion, which programs were in need of such assistance.

Defining Characteristics of Community Living

Since the genesis of this movement toward community living was not data based, perhaps continuation and expansion will not be empirically based either. However, accepting the course taken to date, what should the future course be? Which activities and skills are requisite or necessary parts of a community program for the developmentally disabled, regardless of whether they have been generated from a data base?

Certainly, we must begin the assessment and component analyses necessary to identify quality community programs and to justify their continuation. In addition, community programs should be expanded to include those components that characterize a community-living situation common to most individuals—normal as well as developmentally disabled. A somewhat entertaining yet germane comparison by Woodford (1977) exemplifies such a consideration. In a nondata discussion paper, Woodford analyzed the similarities between the nineteenth-century leisure class and the multihandicapped. He suggested that the level of activity, particularly of the women of the nineteenth-century leisure class, was comparable to those limitations imposed upon the multihandicapped. Thus, the cultural and financial restrictions placed on this leisure class engendered specific daily activities to occupy and satisfy their lives, and these types of activities might well be applicable to today's handicapped. As he points out in describing these people of the leisure class, "They, like the severely handicapped, were born into a life of obligatory leisure that could easily develop into a torment but that could, by careful management, be moulded into a thing of purpose and pleasure" (pp. 53–54). While sheltered workshops or industrial therapy may more closely approximate normalization, they are not synonymous with what nonhandicapped people do with all of their time or even aspire to do with their time—and certainly they are no panacea for boredom. The ladies of leisure began their day being assisted through dressing, toileting, and breakfasting, like the handicapped. After that, they would read over, discuss, and reply to correspondence of the day. Then came aspects of household management, ordering meals, doing or examining household accounts, and choosing materials for decorating the house. Next would come an hour or so for creative activities such as sketching or painting in watercolor and then a visit from neighbors or a trip to the village to make a small purchase or to look over newly arrived merchandise. Clearly, none of these activities—reading, writing, organizing, making music, painting, visiting, shopping, and arranging for personal adornment—is beyond the scope of capabilities of the handicapped and have well served generations of the much envied upper class in the United Kingdom, Europe, and the United States. Providing a similar living situation for the physically limited is an intriguing notion. The specifics are perhaps less important than the notion of basing programs for the mentally and physically handicapped on what otherwise normal people in similar limiting situations would prefer to, or in fact, do.

Unfortunately, no such extensive analysis exists for normal adults or children upon which we can base comprehensive community-living plans. We would, however, advocate considering such an approach for extending present community programs. Additionally, activities could be planned that promote and develop key skills, or skills on which many other activities depend. Thus, in the analogy to the nineteenth-century leisure class, activities that initiate and maintain contact with friends and acquaintances, such as letter writing, visits, and shopping, would be key behaviors for decreasing boredom and inceasing contact outside of the physical confines of one's immediate environment.

We have identified what we believe are some important characteristics of community living—compliance, behavioral engineering, interpersonal skills, and community-survival skills—that are particularly important for the developmentally disabled child. The following sections elaborate on these characteristics.

Compliance

One of the primary criteria for inclusion in many, if not all, community-related activities is an individual's ability to follow the rules and instructions for a given situation. Instruction following, or compliance, is, therefore, a key behavior for community living and has been identified as a significant childhood-behavior problem. Noncompliance is one of the most frequent presenting problems reported by parents about their children's behavior (Forehand et al. 1975). Of the range of deviant childhood behaviors, noncompliance accounts for at least one-third (Johansson et al. 1973). Child noncompliance represents an even greater problem with developmentally disabled children and others who are sometimes classified as deviant. Studies of deviant children show noncompliance to be as high as 57 to 80 percent (for example, Forehand and King 1977), with one study indicating that the problem was reported by 96 percent of parents with deviant children (Taplin and Reid 1977).

When encountered in the home setting, childhood noncompliance is most typically considered to be a problem related to parental interactions. This behavior by definition is the result of interaction between the parent and child. In a typical situation a request is made by the parent to which a specific child behavior would be appropriate. If that behavior occurs, the parent's response—that is, reinforcing, punishing, or ignoring—to the behavior is important as to whether the same or similar responses are made to future requests by the parent. Instructing parents in the use of behavior-analysis and modification procedures has been shown to be effective in increasing children's compliance to the parents' requests (Bernhardt and Forehand 1975; Budd, Green, and Baer 1976; Eyberg and Johnson 1974; Hobbs and Forehand 1975; Patterson 1974; Peed, Roberts, and Forehand 1977; Scarboro and Forehand 1975; Wahler 1969; Hanf 1968; 1969; 1970; Hanf and Kling 1973). Further, compliance has been investigated as an interaction between parent and child in which modification of parental behavior is often critical (Forehand, Cheney, and Yoder 1974; Forehand and King 1974; 1977; Forehand et al. 1975). Research on compliance has resulted in the development of excellent behavioral parent-training programs to modify child noncompliance (Forehand et al. 1979).

Variables Affecting Compliance

In assessing the parent-child dyad in a compliance situation, a number of important features have been identified. Adapted from Peed, Roberts, and Forehand (1977) these are:

> Potentially reinforcing parental behaviors including rewards and attention. Rewards could be considered as praise, approval, or positive physical attention that refers to the child or the child's activity; verbal rewards include both specific (labeled) and nonspecific (unlabeled) reference to praiseworthy behavior. Attention as opposed to rewards

refers to descriptive phrases by the parent that follow and refer to the child's ongoing behavior, objects directly related to his play, his spatial position, or his appearance;

Questions by the parent to which the only appropriate response is a verbal reply by the child;

Commands by the parent that are, at least, of two types. Commands to which a motoric response is appropriate and possible (termed *alpha commands* by Peed and associates) and commands to which the child has no opportunity to demonstrate compliance because the commands are too vague or interrupted by further parental verbal behavior or carried out by the parent before the child has an opportunity to comply (termed *beta commands*);

Criticisms by the parent such as negative evaluations and disaprovals of the child or his activities;

Warnings including statements that describe aversive consequences to be delivered by the parent if the child fails to comply;

Time-out during which a child is removed from the opportunity to engage in positive reinforcing events because of inappropriate or noncompliant behavior.

The contingent nature of parental behavior in relation to the child's behavior; particularly contingent parental rewards or attention to child compliance.

Methods for increasing children's compliance include the use of parental rewards and attention contingent upon compliance and time-out for noncompliance. For example, parents whose children have been referred to a child-management clinic because of noncompliance show that they attend or reward on the average only 7 percent of compliant responses. With a behavioral parent-training program this can be increased to 30 percent (Peed, Roberts, and Forehand 1977), which is comparable with the amount of contingent attention and reward by nonclinic children's parents (Forehand, Gardner, and Roberts 1976). Other parent-child interactions involving questions, criticisms, and warnings are probably, at best, nonfunctional in improving compliance. One obvious important feature about which parents nonetheless consistently err is the type of commands they give their children. Mothers whose children are referred to a clinic for noncompliance issue a considerably greater number of commands to which there is no opportunity to respond (beta commands) than parents of nonclinic children (Forehand et al. 1975; Lobitz and Johnson 1977). In a behavioral parent-training program, this inappropriate command behavior can be greatly reduced—by as much as 45 percent (Forehand et al. 1979). Thus, while noncompliance is a major problem of children, particularly those who are developmentally disabled, and can be a major impediment for entrance into community situations, critical features for analysis of the problem and means for remediation of noncompliance have been identified.

Similar to noncompliance with parents, recent studies on noncompliance in the classroom have also demonstrated remedial techniques. For example, Shutte and Hopkins (1970) showed that teachers could increase student's compliance with the use of contingent praise. These results on the use of contingent praise were replicated in a later study comparing control conditions (Goetz, Holmberg, and LeBlanc 1975). Similarly, access to preferred activities can also be used to increase compliance behavior if access is contingent upon compliance with teacher's requests (Baer, Rowbury, and Baer 1973). Over the past decade such studies have demonstrated clearly the effectiveness of reinforcement principles in improving classroom compliance (Zimmerman, Zimmerman, and Russell 1969; Whitman, Zakaras, and Chardos 1971), especially with the developmentally disabled child, and are now routinely recommended for classroom behavioral-management programs.

Compliance as a Response Class

Another reason why compliance may be considered a key behavior is the degree to which it has been shown to function as a response class. Bijou and Baer define a response class as "a group of responses which develop together. All grow strong or weak, even though the environment may be acting directly on only some of them" (1967, p. 78). With children's behavior, response classes have been studied in regard to diverse behaviors such as imitation (for example, Baer and Sherman 1964; Metz 1965; Waxler and Yarrow 1970); reading comprehension (Rosenbaum and Breiling 1976); and social interaction (Petersen, Austin, and Lang 1979). In a compliance-training situation, reinforcement of compliance to specific requests has been shown to result in increased compliance to both reinforced and other different nonreinforced requests (Bucher 1973; Doleys et al. 1976). The importance of this finding for children who are noncompliant should be clear: Compliance could be increased to many different types of requests by reinforcing compliance of only selected requests. The fact that compliance may be considered a response class offers the possibility for great economy of procedures for correcting noncompliance. However, with very retarded individuals, additional training techniques such as physical guidance and fading may need to be used in combination with reinforcement of compliance, since generalization to nonreinforced requests does not always occur (Striefel and Wetherby 1973).

Compliance and Behavioral Covariation

The most intriguing aspect of compliance training and the modification of deviant behavior has to do with covariation of behavior. In a preliminary study of behavioral covariation, Sajwaj, Twardosz, and Burke (1972) applied behavioral procedures to selected problems of a 7-year-old child while measuring other behaviors. The results indicated that "a response class may have member behaviors that covary directly and/or inversely. Some covariations may be socially desirable, others undesirable." Wahler (1975) has elegantly shown, in an extensive three-year study of two children's deviant behavior, that each subject's behavior repertoire contained responses that covaried predictably, that the behavior clusters differed with the environmental setting the child was in, and that planned changes in behavior in one setting were accompanied by unplanned changes in behavior in another setting. Determining behavioral covariation can have dramatic therapeutic implications. When behaviors covary, employing procedures to change one behavior can indirectly change other behaviors that are presumably of the same response class. For example, using reinforcement procedures to improve minor behavioral problems has been shown to decrease stuttering (Wahler et al. 1970), and reinforcement of academic behavior has resulted in decreased rates of disruptive behavior (Ayllon and Roberts 1974). Similarly, procedures that increase compliance have been shown to result in a reduction in nocturnal enuresis (Nordquist 1971), a decrease in hyperactive-type behavior, and an increase in some social behaviors (Zimmerman, Zimmerman, and Russell 1969).

Results like these suggest the possibility that deviant behaviors of developmentally disabled children may be modified by employing standard behavior-change procedures (like reinforcing compliance) that affect not only the target behavior but also other behaviors that covary. This generalization of effects from target to other behaviors could offer great economy of treatment and avoid some of the ethical difficulties facing the field of behavior modification. For example, if reinforcement of compliance could be shown to decrease aggressive and self-injurious behavior, the ethical problems of employing aversive techniques to suppress these undesirable behaviors could be avoided. Recent literature has demonstrated effective techniques for the treatment of disruptive behavior (Bostow and Bailey 1969; Twardosz and Sajwaj 1972) and self-injurious behavior (Bucher and Lovaas 1968; Corte, Wolf, and Locke 1971; Frankel and Simmons 1976;

Romanczyk and Goren 1975) to name only two. However, such programs are characterized by providing direct consequences for the occurrence of problem behaviors and thus offer several drawbacks including the facts that they usually program change for one response at a time, increase the possibility of emotional side effects, and do not teach or increase any specific positive behavior. In addition, behaviorally oriented investigators have advocated for renewed efforts to find alternatives to aversive techniques (Carr, Newsom, and Binkoff 1976).

To address these problems, we recently conducted a study to assess decreases in responses such as self-injurious behavior, aggression, and tantrums as the result of compliance training (Cataldo and Russo 1979). Three retarded children, aged three to six years, with documented noncompliance and additional behavioral problems, served as subjects. During all phases of the program, continuous measurements of both compliance and the occurrence of other behaviors were made.

Figure 3–1 shows the data from one of these children. As can be seen in the figure, a multiple-baseline design across three therapists was used to assess the effects of compliance training on rate of compliance and on the two untreated corollary responses of hair pulling and thumb sucking. Each of these behaviors was mildly self-injurious, and the frequency was sufficient to warrant individual modification.

As figure 3–1 indicates, baseline levels of compliance were low across all three therapists. With the beginning of treatment, compliance to each therapist's requests (a series of five standard commands) increased. In the reinforce-compliance 1 condition, social praise and small bits of food were used as reinforcers. As compliance dropped in the later sessions of this condition, a second treatment (reinforce-compliance 2) was instituted in which the child received pennies for appropriate compliance that could later be used during a trip to a nearby store. For all three therapists, this produced immediate and stable increases in compliance.

Perhaps the most interesting aspect of these data, however, is the behavior of the untreated corollary responses of thumb sucking and hair pulling over the course of compliance treatment. Visual inspection of the data shows the correlated changes in these behaviors with respect to compliance, even though no specific contingencies were operative. Additionally, the protocol was designed such that corollary responses were compatible with compliance and that reinforcement of compliance could occur during instances of the nontreated corollary behaviors (for example, the child was reinforced while sucking her thumb because she had complied with the therapist's request to sit down). Data for the two other children showed similar effects.

We suggest that compliance training may be both an economical and effective procedure to produce multiple behavior changes in children. Fur-

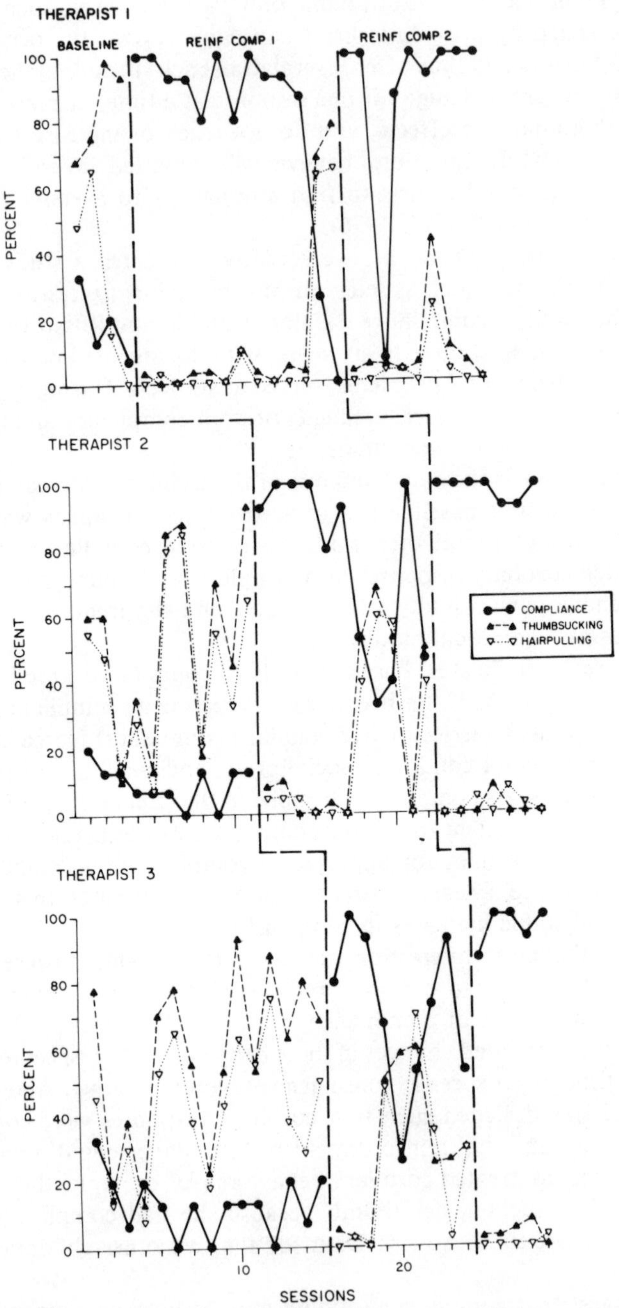

Figure 3–1. Percent Occurrence of Compliance and Untreated Corollary Behaviors of Thumb Sucking and Hair Pulling across Therapists and Experimental Conditions

ther studies are necessary for an empirical evaluation and implementation of such procedures for community treatment.

Implications of Compliance-Training Programs

To conclude the issue of compliance training, reinforcement of compliance may offer a solution to children's behavioral problems that is considerably broader than the one that has been traditionally considered. Because compliance and noncompliance may tend to come under environmental control with other important positive and deviant childhood behaviors, they may form direct and inversely related response classes. Thus, manipulating one behavior may provide treatment generalization across deviant behaviors. Currently, child-management programs can be said to involve two approaches to the generalization of treatment. One is the usual program in which a target behavioral problem is dealt with immediately and directly by providing parents with a specific behavioral procedure for that target problem. However, generalization of treatment procedures across problem behaviors, as instituted by the parents, rarely occurs; the parents thus seek additional behavioral programs with each succeeding problem. A second type of program is one in which the target, or referring, problem is not dealt with immediately but rather where the parents are trained in general behavioral principles. Later these principles are to be applied to specific presenting-behavior problems. Because the parents are presumably well versed in the principles, generalization of techniques to successive behavioral problems is supposed to be increased.

Training in compliance offers a third possibility. Parents can be taught to reinforce compliance using a standard, specific set of techniques. Since almost any behavioral problem can be defined as a compliance problem, an immediate solution is provided for the target problem. Generalization of effects to covarying behaviors can be expected to occur. Further, treatment techniques can be generalized to subsequent behavioral problems to the extent that these (as most behaviors) may be defined as a failure to comply. Generalization is then inherent in the procedure rather than being a process that the parents must extrapolate from successive behavioral programs or from being taught general principles.

To summarize, because compliance is necessary for interaction in the community, is a behavior readily generalized to nonreinforced requests, has been noted to covary importantly with other behaviors, and sets the occasion for other important behaviors and events to occur, we consider it a key to community living. Fortunately, through behavioral procedures, compliance can be taught, increased, and shown to be a member of a class of important behaviors.

Children as Behavioral Engineers

Another set of skills that may be key to successful adjustment is the child's ability to change the behaviors of others and him- or herself. While the other sections in this chapter emphasize skills necessary to meet the demands of adults (compliance) or the community at large (community survival), this section considers skills that enable children to analyze their own behavior, to create conditions to change it, and constructively to induce adults or peers to behave in ways the child finds more reinforcing.

The child's first experience in influencing adult behavior is reflexive. The infant's earliest crying, smiling, vocalizations, and eye contact all appear to exert powerful control over adult behavior (Bell 1971). While there are ample demonstrations (Gewirtz 1977) that these behaviors may, in a matter of weeks, come under the operant control of parental attention, influence is probably bidirectional as parents and children strengthen and weaken each other's behaviors in an interactional paradigm (Bell 1968; Mash 1973; Patterson 1977). Children and their caregivers or peers thus learn to interact in ways that produce desirable or undesirable effects for one or both parties (Patterson 1976).

Rationale

While reciprocal arrangements may obtain results in which child and care giver or peer exchange reinforcing events and mutually negotiate desired changes in behavior, frequently one party controls the behavior of the other by coercive means (Patterson and Reid 1970). Patterson's research on families of deviant children (Patterson 1976; 1977; Patterson and Fleischmann 1979) provides examples in which parents give fewer reinforcement for appropriate behavior and more punishment for disruptive behavior than for the behavior of the child's nondeviant siblings. In the face of parental punishment, however, these children may dramatically accelerate disruptive behaviors in an apparent attempt to terminate aversive demands. Other studies (Buehler, Patterson, and Furness 1966; Patterson and Brodsky 1966; Solomon and Wahler 1973) showed that children frequently try to control their peers' inappropriate behavior by providing negative consequences but rarely provide consequences for appropriate behavior. Shy, withdrawn, or behaviorally deficient and disturbed children are unable to exert either positive or negative control over the behavior of others (Van Hasselt et al. 1979) or themselves.

While strong and consistent patterns may develop, interactional behavior appears to remain unplanned. Recent systematic attempts to teach children the skills necessary to engineer changes in the behavior of others and themselves were motivated by several factors. Some relationships between the child and others are so reciprocally aversive that both parties may need to make simultaneous attempts to engineer change in the other. While programs in which adult members of disturbed dyads are taught to instigate behavior change have been demonstrably effective, the reasoning was that the child's reciprocal influence on the adult should not be left to chance (Sherman and Cormier 1974).

Child-instigated programs may also be necessary because teachers or other adult mediators of child behavior have failed previously or refused to change mutually aversive interactions (Seymour and Stokes 1976). Even if adult-instigated programs are successful, the child may have to be taught to engineer changes in the behavior of others to ensure that improvements maintain in different settings where mediators are not available. This is particularly true of children who have been labeled as retarded, maladjusted, or otherwise deviant. Despite improvements in controlled settings, such children may require skills to reshape contingencies actively on their own behavior when they return to more-natural settings (Polirstok and Greer 1977). Seymour and Stokes (1976) reported an example in which improvements in the behavior of delinquent adolescents was not noted by care givers until the youths were taught to engineer recognition from adults. Isolated and withdrawn children may require similar skills to gain access to "communities of reinforcement" (Stokes, Fowler, and Baer 1978) by learning how to induce others to attend to their behavior.

In some settings, significant others may be too numerous to make training cost-effective or feasible (Polirstok and Greer 1977; Seymour and Stokes 1976). Walker and Buckley (1972) concluded that it would take less time to teach a disruptive child to use positive behavior-change methods with his several teachers than to train the teachers themselves. In addition, children who engineer desired academic and social behavior in their peers would thus free teachers for more-specialized academic activities.

Children as Behavioral Engineers of Other Children's Behavior

Not surprisingly, behavioral analysts, in considering what children needed to engineer changes in others, turned to the same skills that had enabled adults to establish unidirectional control of child behavior. They reasoned that such skills including observing and recording behavior, defining behaviorally specific goals, and consistently using antecedent and consequent events could be taught to children as well. While it is beyond the scope of this section to analyze extensively findings in the rapidly expanding and much debated area of self-management (Bandura 1971; Goldiamond 1976;

Graziano 1975; Mahoney, 1974; 1976), most would probably agree that, at a minimum, these same behaviors directed by the child toward his own behavior (self-observation, self-recording, and so forth) are key components of effective child self-management (Wahler, Berland, and Coe 1979).

Analyses of children's ability to observe and record behavior in classrooms revealed that students reliably could record the inappropriate (McLaughlin and Malaby 1971; 1972b) and academic (McLaughlin and Malaby 1975) behavior of their peers as well as their own story writing (Ballard and Glynn 1975), on-task behavior (Glynn, Thomas, and Shee 1973), and completion of homework and classroom assignments (McLaughlin and Malaby 1971; 1972a; Broden, Hall, and Mitts 1971). Some researchers have noted that sixth-grade students required no more training than college students to learn similar recording skills (McLaughlin and Malaby 1972b). In residential programs, self-recording led to an increase in delinquent girls' work output (Seymour and Stokes 1976) and predelinquent boys' room cleaning (Fixsen, Phillips, and Wolf 1972).

Children were also taught to dispense reinforcers contingent on appropriate peer behavior. Preschool children learned to praise reliably the play of their peers (Rogers-Warren and Baer 1976; Warren, Baer, and Rogers-Warren 1979). Warren, Baer, and Rogers-Warren (1979) used modeling and reinforcement to teach children to use more-descriptive praise when the use of previously trained open-ended praise ("I like what you are making") became stereotypic and was found not to generalize. Older, elementary-age students in a "behavior problem" classroom (Greenwood, Sloane, and Baskin 1974) learned to deliver praise and points for their peers' work on programmed mathematics.

Other studies examined whether reliably delivered reinforcers actually changed peer behavior. A fifth-grade student's use of a desk light to signal appropriate behavior to a group of fourth graders (Surratt, Ulrich, and Hawkins 1969) and 5-year-old preschoolers' use of social reinforcers with 3-year-olds (Long and Madsen 1975) reliably decreased out-of-seat, disruptive, and off-task behavior. Socially isolated children who were drawn out by trained confederates not only increased their interaction skills with confederates but also began to initiate social contacts with others as well (Strain, Shores, and Timm 1977).

Studies of peer tutoring indicated that children could effectively present academic materials to their peers. As an example, Ayllon and Garber (1977) showed that while regressed students required one-to-one tutoring, average students could be taught by peers in more-cost-effective groups with up to one-to-five ratios.

In each of these studies, the participation of the child agent of reinforcement was motivated by more-immediate and desirable external reinforcers than the hoped-for change in their peer's target behaviors. Adults continuously monitored and reinforced the behavior of 5-year olds who observed, recorded, and reinforced the on-task behavior of 3-year-old peers in the study by Long and Madsen (1975). Performance monitoring and reinforcement was less frequent with older children (McLaughlin and Malaby 1975), but only in the study by Warren, Baer, and Rogers-Warren (1979) were children successfully prompted to generalize their praising to new environments in which external reinforcers were unavailable. In addition, none of the studies provided more than anecdotal follow-up evidence of treatment maintenance over time.

While one of the stated purposes of self-management programs is to promote generalization to settings and times in which adult mediators of behavioral change are unavailable, the evidence is not strong. In a review of generalization of child-behavior change, Wahler, Berland, and Coe (1979) point out that while limited generalization of the effects of self-management over time (Drabman, Spitalnik, and O'Leary 1973) and settings (Turkewitz, O'Leary, and Ironsmith 1975) has been documented, the results are not striking. They concluded that evidence for generalization of self-management procedures was as weak as for traditional operant interventions. The self-regulated changes in the disruptive behavior of special students that lasted only a few days following training in a study by Santogrossi et al. (1973) was cited as an example. Clearly, the selection of targets more likely to maintain and the use of strategies that promote maintenance over time and setting are necessary. In one study by McLaughlin and Malaby (1975), a sixth-grade student with a previous knowledge of behavioral principles was able to design and carry out a program to control successfully a peer's classroom littering with minimal adult assistance.

Children as Behavioral Engineers of Adults' Behavior

Parent and teacher behaviors have also been targets for child behavioral engineering. Elementary-age children, taught to look and smile, talk enthusiastically, and ask for feedback (Cantor and Gelfand 1977) were found to receive more-positive interactions from their teachers. Mentally retarded children taught to give eye contact, compliments, and to ask for help (Graubarb, Rosenberg, and Miller 1971) and disruptive students who used decreases in their own problem behavior as consequences produced reliable improvements in a variety of teacher behaviors (Sherman and Cormier 1974; Polirstok and Greer 1977). Delinquent girls were successful in prompting praise from their care givers in an institutional setting when increased work output failed to do so (Seymour and Stokes 1976). Children have been taught to reinforce socially the smiling and laughing of their parents as well (Patterson and Reid 1970).

The effects of child behavioral engineering on others are well documented. Less frequently measured are the positive effects of behavioral engineering on the child. A review of such effects should highlight the status of these skills as key behaviors.

Other Benefits

The child who is successful in self-management, of course, benefits from improvements in the target behavior. Self-regulated improvements in disruptive behavior (Drabman, Spitalnik, and O'Leary 1973) and a variety of academic behaviors (Felixbrod and O'Leary 1973; Lovitt and Curtiss 1969) including story writing (Ballard and Glynn 1975) have been documented. As with externally mediated change, collateral behaviors that are covariant with the self-modified target may also improve (Wahler, Berland, and Coe 1979).

Three subtler types of positive outcomes appear to accrue to children as engineers of the behaviors of others. First, children may receive reciprocal reinforcement from peers or adults. Children taught to be more responsive to adults by smiling, talking enthusiastically, and asking for feedback on their play received more attention and assistance than their peers (Cantor and Gelfand 1977). In addition, they were rated more intelligent, likeable, adept, and natural in their interactions. Children who praised their peers during free-play periods were rated maturer by supervising adults (Warren et al. 1979). Children's reductions in problem behavior (negatively) reinforced similar improved ratings by their teachers, who also changed their rates of approval and disapproval (Polirstok and Greer 1977). Admiration apparently became mutual as children rated their teachers "nicer" at the conclusion of the intervention. It is interesting that, in the study by Warren, Baer, and Rogers-Warren (1979), rates of reciprocal praise from peers actually decreased. The authors suggested that peers may have felt their free play was not praiseworthy and thus rejected peer praise.

Children who earned reinforcers from their peers (Walker and Buckley 1972) did so ostensibly to motivate more strongly their own academic and social behavior. In addition, they benefited their peers through the reinforcers earned, their teachers via reductions in disruptive and off-task behavior, and themselves indirectly by receiving additional encouragement and attention from interested peers.

A second class of benefits accrues when children learn more about the behaviors they observe, record, and reinforce in others. Improvements in the children's performance of behaviors they change in others may be expected. Tutors with average intellectual ability simultaneously increased their own knowledge of vocabulary words taught to peers (Ayllon and Garber 1977), and peer reinforcement of alternatives to disruptive classroom behavior produced similar improvements in the agent of peer reinforcement as well (Siegel and Steinman 1975).

Finally, collateral behaviors may also improve. In a curious reversal of historical trends concerning animal and human studies, one child self-initiated a program to successfully shape a pet's behavior following an experience as the agent of peer reinforcement. More socially relevant, a withdrawn child interacted more frequently following her reinforcement of peer on-task behavior in school (Long and Madsen 1975).

Thus, by-products for the child include increases in reciprocal reinforcement, reductions in aversive interactions, and improvements in target and nontarget behavior. While not empirically documented yet, Long and Madsen (1975) suggest that the child behavioral engineer may develop increased sensitivity and self-awareness as a result of a growing knowledge of functional relationships in human behavior.

If a key behavior is one that maximizes reinforcement and/or is a precursor to several other adaptive skills, behavioral engineering appears to qualify. These skills may take a place at the top of the list of behaviors described in that their direct function is to produce desired reinforcement and to promote more-adaptive behaviors. While research on the applicability and generality of these skills across several dimensions is clearly necessary, the skills may nonetheless represent powerful yet flexible tools for children to reshape their environment.

Interpersonal Behavior

While the defining characteristics of behavioral-engineering skills and more broadly defined interpersonal or social skills overlap somewhat, the latter is treated as a separate set of key behaviors. Used less deliberately to modify the behavior of others, interpersonal skills such as sharing, initiating social contact, resolving conflict without aggression, conversational skills, and cooperating in work and play may nevertheless have pervasive indirect effects on the child's peers, parents, and teachers.

Child behavioral-engineering skills (observing, recording, and arranging antecedent and consequent events) are employed contingent on prespecified behaviors of others. While the goals of maximizing reinforcement and inducing others to change their behavior are the same for both parties, interpersonal skills can be used as a general strategy without moment-to-moment evaluation of the behavior of another. As an example, a child taught to increase his or her rate of smiling, sharing, and praising in interactions with peers could do so without respect to the behavior of peers. The hope in recommending such a strategy, which may be easier to teach, is that the risk of unwittingly reinforcing inappropriate peer behavior is low.

The Problem of Deficits in Interpersonal Skills

In a review of child social-skill assessment and training procedures, Van Hasselt et al. (1979) provide the disturbing demographics of childhood social-skill deficits. With regard to social isolation and withdrawal, 11 percent of children were found to have no friends (Hymel and Asher 1977) while 12 percent have only a single friend (Gronlund 1959). In studies of socially withdrawn children, clusters of behavior were identified, including shyness, passivity, slow speech, and reactions (Patterson 1964) and inability to communicate feelings of anger, conformity, and failure to stand up for legitimate rights (Ross, Lacey, and Parton 1965).

Social isolation also appears to be a key to a host of long-term adjustment problems including juvenile delinquency, dropping out of school, and mental-health referrals, while "high social status" as a child correlates highly with improved academic achievement and interpersonal adjustment in later life (Van Hasselt et al. 1979).

Aggressive children represent a second class of youths with social-skill deficits. A variety of behaviors also covary with this behavior, including teasing, threatening, and arguing (Patterson 1964; Ross, Lacey, and Parton 1965); quarrelsomeness, tantrums, and ignoring the rights of others (Quay 1972); and embarrassing others, using a negative tone of voice, and demanding excessively (Patterson 1976). Unpopularity, school failure, and physical retaliation often result, and increased rates of alcoholism and psychotic or antisocial behaviors in later life are cited as more likely outcomes for these children (Van Hasselt et al. 1979).

The social-skill deficits of withdrawn/isolated or aggressive children are thus likely to covary with a large number of other problem behaviors and are associated with both short- and long-term negative outcomes. Effective treatment of social-skill deficits might logically, if not empirically, be expected not only to prevent several long-term harmful consequences but also to correct current deficiencies in a variety of non-target-problem behaviors. Conversely, intervention on one or other of the behaviors that reliably occur with a social-skill deficit might indirectly alter that deficit as well (Wahler 1975; Wahler, Berland, and Coe 1979).

Based on the interrelations described here, conceptualization of the function of interpersonal behavior and accompanying taxonomies of presumed requisite skills have been developed for several types of social-skill deficits. The conceptual base, suggested component skills, and assessment and treatment methods for each of several social-skill deficits are discussed later.

Establishing and Strengthening Interpersonal Behaviors

Isolated and withdrawn children are thought to suffer from a deficit in skills that can be used to elicit reciprocal reinforcement from others (Bellack and Hersen 1978). With the lack of reinforcement, frustration and anxiety are thought to accompany isolation. Findings of a significant relation between children's giving and receiving potential reinforcers (Charlesworth and Hartup 1967; Keller and Carlson 1974) led to the logical conclusion that children trained to increase delivery of potential reinforcers to peers, parents, and teachers are likely to gain reinforcers themselves. The smiling, sharing, and physical contact of selected handicapped children were found to increase these same behaviors in untrained peers (Cooke and Apolloni 1976). Similar behaviors, modeled by selected children from videotaped examples, led target children to give and receive these behaviors in interactions with untrained peers. Giving and receiving were correlated highly ($r = .78$).

Conversational skills such as answering questions of peers after shorter latencies and with longer replies, more-appropriate affect, and follow-up questions were also hypothesized as means to elicit positive social attention from peers. In a recent study by Kelly et al. (1979), modeling, coaching, and behavior rehearsal were used with two moderately mentally retarded adolescents to train them to answer questions fully, to ask questions, and to extend social invitations in conversations with normally intelligent peers. Improvements generalized to conversations with other normally intelligent and nonretarded peers.

Programs that actually shape new skills, like the one used by Kelly et al. (1979), can be contrasted with those that strengthen already existing skills (Van Hasselt et al. 1979). The cooperative play of young isolated children has been reinforced with teacher attention in studies by Allen et al. (1964), Buell et al. (1968), and Hart et al. (1968). In a recent analysis of the components of older children's deficient social interactions (Walker et al. 1979), the investigators found that the reinforcement of social initiation with peers and answering peer questions actually reduced overall social interactions. Reinforcers delivered contingent on the continuation of already initiated social interactions increased these children's overall interactive behavior. The authors concluded that increases in the former targets were probably perceived as artificial by the target child and his or her peers and thus inhibited social interaction. A thorough behavioral analysis of the child's skill deficit and a careful matching of socially validated treatments to each child was recommended.

Vicarious reinforcement was apparently responsible for the increase in social interactions of isolated children who observed nonisolate peers receiving reinforcement for their social interaction (Strain and Timm 1974). The use of nonisolate peers to initiate social interaction with withdrawn children led to increased initiating by the withdrawn children (Strain 1977; Strain, Shores, and Timm 1977). Film observations by withdrawn children of peers receiving positive consequences for their social interactions were responsible for improvements in subsequent classroom test periods in which isolate children were indistinguishable from their peers.

In these and other studies, results may vary depending on which of several assessment measures is used. Behavioral observations in natural settings or during more-structured role playing of standard interpersonal scenes can be contrasted with a variety of ratings by the child's teachers or peers. While the issues are discussed fully in the review by Van Hasselt et al. (1979), these authors contend that the more-developmental approach inherent in the ratings of peer acceptance or rejections should be contrasted with the behavioral approach to objective measures of child interactions with peers. They conclude that the measures probably do not assess the same phenomena and argue for both types of assessment.

An area of social-skill deficit related to, but not separate from, social isolation and withdrawal is childhood unassertiveness. Skills in this area can be conceptualized as those that enable children to influence the behavior of others or to make legitimate demands on them without the use of coercion. While only structured role-play tests of assertiveness in interpersonal-conflict situations were used, Bornstein, Bellack, and Hersen (1977) found that instructions, behavioral rehearsal, modeling, and feedback on several component skills of assertiveness led to improvements that were maintained at one-month follow-up assessments. These findings were replicated, but no changes were found in auxiliary assessments using peer ratings (Beck et al. 1978) or observations of assertive behavior in the child's natural environment (Panepinto 1976). While the difficulty in sampling interpersonal conflict that presumably occurs at low frequency during naturalistic observations is recognized (Johnson, Bolstad, and Lobitz 1976; Patterson and Fleischman 1979), expanded assessments and treatments both may be required if generalized treatment effectiveness is to be documented.

Research on the modification of childhood aggression has a longer history than that on other social-skill deficits. There are several accounts of the effectiveness of operant-intervention programs in which parents or other care givers are taught to arrange alternative or no consequences such as extinction (Pinkston et al. 1973), time-out (Burchard and Tyler 1965), and token fines for the aggression of their children (Phillips 1968). In a recent review by Patterson and Fleischman (1979), the relative efficacy of a standard parent-training program (Patterson and Reid 1973), as compared to traditional treatment modalities, was discussed. High percentages of families who, after completing the program, maintained treatment gains at one-year follow-up assessments was also documented. While procedures to strengthen alternative behaviors such as compliance with instructions

(Wahler 1969) and household chores (Phillips 1968) have been included in such treatment programs for aggressive children, the recent emphasis has been more on the development of social skills as more-direct alternatives to aggression (Elder, Edelstein, and Narick 1979; Gittleman 1965; Goodwin and Mahoney 1975; Wallace et al. 1973). For example, Elder and coworkers (1979) taught four adolescent psychiatric inpatients more-appropriate methods of interrupting others, requesting behavior change, and responding to negative communication. Not only was role playing in trained and untrained conflict exercises improved but also rates of token fines and seclusion for these behaviors in the daily residential program were significantly reduced. Nine-month follow-up data indicated that three of four subjects had been discharged and remained in community settings for at least six months.

To summarize, a variety of interpersonal behaviors have been taught to isolated/withdrawn, unassertive, and aggressive children. Findings were described as "highly promising" in a review of this research (Van Hasselt et al. 1979) in documenting that social skills can be taught and strengthened, particularly in role-play situations. Several measurement problems exist in the form of difficulties in adequately sampling behavior during conflict events with low rates of occurrence in the natural environment and the probably separate skills measured by peer/teacher ratings and behavioral-observation codes used in natural settings. Despite these difficulties, some generalization across peers and settings (Kelly et al. 1979) and time (Elder, Edelstein, and Narick 1979) has been well documented.

This chapter is particularly concerned with the generalization of treatment gains across behaviors. Since social isolation and aggression may be implicated in placing the child at risk for a host of covariant behavior problems, it is reasonable to expect that the strengthening of prosocial alternatives might be accompanied by several positive effects. Of course, effects other than those listed here are likely to be documented only if investigators predefine and measure a variety of potential collateral behaviors before treatments are begun. As with other proposed key behaviors, effects can be measured on the child or others as either personally or mutually beneficial (Combs and Slaby 1977). For example, peers increased their social behavior when targeted children were trained to use a variety of emotional and interactive social skills (Cooke and Apolloni 1976; Strain, Shores, and Kerr 1976; Strain and Timm 1974). In treating a child's aggressive behavior with time-out, researchers found that vicarious effects occurred on the aggressive behavior of peers (Wilson et al. 1979). As might be expected, interpersonal behaviors appear to be maximally influenced by interventions that stress modeling.

Kelly et al. (1979) found that conversational-skills training with mentally retarded individuals not only improved conversation with both mentally retarded and normally intelligent peers but also improved cooperative play. The importance of conversation as a potential reinforcer or a behavioral precursor for cooperative play deserves more research attention—perhaps at several developmental levels. Kelly and his associates questioned whether improved communication with normally intelligent peers might serve as a training model to help fill the social gap between handicapped and nonhandicapped students in mainstreamed education.

Finally, and more generally, the reciprocity that occurs when children who socially reinforce the behavior of their peers are highly likely to receive potential reinforcers in return (Keller and Carlson 1974) parallels effects with other key behaviors described previously. As with those behaviors, interpersonal skills appear to offer the child an efficient means of eliciting potentially reinforcing events from his or her social environment. The correlation at .78 between giving and receiving is high enough so that a potent reinforcement trap for the child's long-term giving almost certainly exists.

Community-Survival-Skills Training

The current national emphasis on community preparation for handicapped persons has highlighted the need for effective methods of developing and maintaining community-survival skills that are necessary for independent functioning. Deinstitutionalization efforts are proceeding at a rapid pace, yet outcome data suggest that handicapped individuals are not receiving adequate training prior to community placement (Nihira and Nihira 1975a; 1975b; Perske and Marquiss 1973). Moreover, technologies for promoting adaptive community behaviors are not widely available at the present time. Although much behavioral research has been conducted over the past fifteen years in the area of basic self-care skills, programmatic investigations that focus on more-complex repertoires are a relatively recent phenomenon in the literature. Already, however, the results of these investigations are encouraging, and a model for program development and evaluation apparently is beginning to emerge.

The purpose of this section is to describe the major elements of community-survival-skills training, with an emphasis on general methodology and procedures rather than specific content or skill areas. Since the inclusion of all research on adaptive behavior would be well beyond the scope of this discussion, we limit coverage primarily to those studies focusing upon skills that appear to have some obvious value outside of the institution, classroom, and work environments and that emphasize empirical approaches to experimental design and outcome evaluation.

Assessment

Although the functions and methods of conducting assessment may vary widely, attempts to measure behavior serve at least three purposes with respect to community-skills training. First, assessment is essential in determining an individual's ability to function in environments whose behavioral requirements are known and in identifying areas of deficit. Second, if pre- and posttraining assessment of trainee behavior is performed in a controlled manner, the resulting data provide evidence of program effectiveness. Finally, the most elegant forms of assessment should assist not only in the evaluation of individuals and programs but also throughout the entire process of program development and revision.

Standardized, norm-referenced methods of assessment (for example, IQ, personality, or interest measures) are useful in making certain general predictions and placement decisions. However, these methods are inadequate from the standpoint of both individual and program evaluation in the area of community skills. Such techniques provide only the most general information regarding level of functioning. For example, IQ scores, reflecting educational history and intellectual ability, are poor indicators of whether or not an individual either has learned or has the ability to learn how to behave appropriately in one or more noninstitutionalized environments. In addition, since the goal of community-oriented treatment programs is to impart specific skills rather than to increase overall intellectual ability, results obtained from most standardized instruments have little bearing on program evaluation.

A second approach to assessment makes use of formal rating scales (for example, Balthazar 1973; Halpern et al. 1975). These instruments contain listings of adaptive behaviors (for example, independent toileting, self-dressing), many of which are relevant to community functioning. Thus, baseline data reflect the extent to which individuals can perform certain criterion tasks; in addition, posttraining scores tend to be a good indicator of overall program effectiveness. The major disadvantage of rating scales is that they are not designed to provide detailed information within a given skill area. For example, if clients remain unable to order meals following the completion of training in a restaurant-skills program, a dichotomous rating of either pass or fail does not identify those responses that clients either can or cannot perform. In order to determine whether or not additional or different training is needed, the development of instruments that are more sensitive to relatively small changes in performance becomes necessary.

Behavioral-research methods have always been noted for their emphasis on the precise definition and measurement of behavior. Thus, it is not surprising to find that observation techniques derived from applied behavioral analysis have had a major impact on both the assessment and training of community skills. The most widely used model in experimental research on community skills has been task analysis (Resnick, Wang, and Kaplan 1973). A task analysis consists of a sequential breakdown of skill components that comprise a behavioral chain. Although task analyses are often too detailed to administer acrss a wide range of skills at a single point in time, their ability to discriminate performance differences within a task improves their utility in assessing the strengths and weaknesses of individuals and in designing the content of treatment programs. Recent studies have demonstrated the use of task analyses in teaching a number of skills such as street crossing (Matson, in press a), bus riding (Neef, Iwata, and Page 1978), clothing care (Cronin and Cuvo 1979), home first aid (Matson, in press b), and restaurant skills (Marholin et al. 1979; van den Pol et al., in press). An example of a particularly detailed task analysis is presented in table 3-1. Taken from a study by Page, Iwata, and Neef (1976), it is important to note that the analysis includes not only descriptions of components of pedestrian skills (listed in terms of both correct and incorrect responses) but also a specification of the stimulus condition in which the behavior is to be observed.

The design of task analyses has been achieved primarily through informal means. However, since the predefined steps of a task analysis represent the ultimate criterion for successful performance, several issues appear to warrant more-systematic investigation. First, individual items in a task analysis should possess a high degree of necessity in that components of component clusters should consist of essential rather than arbitrary responses. Second, the complete task analysis should represent sufficient performance in that it defines functional success in one or more naturalistic settings. Third, the order of sequencing skills within a task analysis may constitute a variable important to both performance and training. Cronin and Cuvo (1979) recently described a thorough process in which experts assisted in the development of task analyses by observing correct technique demonstrated by a model, listing response sequences, and later performing the target activities in accordance with the listed sequence. However, no data were presented on the extent to which these procedures resulted in noticeable improvements in the task analysis, and to our knowledge, no studies on community skills have attempted to examine empirically methods of identifying, defining, and validating skill sequences. Although the importance of research on these aspects of assessment is seen perhaps as secondary to a demonstration of behavioral change, it is doubtful that we will progress from the training of discrete repertoires to the development of subtler modes of behavior (for example, complex social interaction) without careful attention to potentially important characteristics of task analysis.

Table 3–1
Generalization of Pedestrian Skills: Correct and Incorrect Response Definitions for the Five Areas of Street Crossing

Situation	*Correct Response*	*Incorrect Response*
Intersection	Subject (S) goes to intersection to cross street.	S crosses street anywhere not at intersection.
Pedestrian light	S stops upon arrival at intersection.	S crosses street without first stopping at intersection.
	S starts across street within 5 seconds of light changing to walk condition.	(1) S starts across street before light has changed to walk condition, or (2) S does not start across street within 5 seconds of light changing to walk condition.
	S turns head at least 45° to left and right at least once while in the street.	S fails to turn head at least 45° to left and right at least once while in the street.
	S does not stop walking until completely across the street.	S stops before getting completely across the street.
Traffic light	S stops upon arrival at intersection.	S crosses street without first stopping at intersection.
	S starts across street within 5 seconds of light changing to green condition.	(1) S starts across street before light has changed to green condition, or (2) S does not cross street within 5 seconds of light changing to green condition.
	S turns head at least 45° to left and right at least once while in the street.	S fails to turn head at least 45° to left and right at least once while in the street.
	S does not stop walking until completely across the street.	S stops before getting completely across the street.
Stop sign (for cars going across the pedestrian's path)	S stops upon arrival at intersection and turns head at least 45° to left and right at least once.	S crosses street without first stopping at intersection.
	S starts across street within 5 seconds of intersection being clear of traffic.	(1) S starts across street while cars going across his path are in the intersection , or (2) S does not start across street within 5 seconds of intersection being clear of traffic.
	S turns head at least 45° to left and right at least once while in the street.	S fails to turn head at least 45° to left and right at least once while in the street.
	S does not stop walking until completely across the street.	S stops before getting completely across the street.
	S stops stops upon arrival at intersection and turns head at least 45° to left and right at least once.	S crosses street without first stopping at intersection.

Table 3–1 continued

Situation	*Correct Response*	*Incorrect Response*
Stop sign (facing cars going in the same direction as pedestrian)	S stops upon arrival at intersection and turns head at least 45° to left and right at least once.	S crosses street without first stopping at intersection.
	S starts across street within 5 seconds of street being clear of moving cars for at least one block in both directions.	(1) S starts across street before street is clear of traffic for one block in both directions, or (2) S does not start across street within 5 seconds of street being clear of traffic for one block in both directions.
	S turns head at least 45° to left and right at least once while in the street.	S fails to turn head at least 45° to left and right at least once while in the street.
	S does not stop walking until completely across the street.	S stops before getting completely across the street.

Training Methods

The criterion most often applied to community-skills-training research has been whether or not client performance improves as a function of treatment. Thus, in an effort to maximize positive outcome, interventions have been characterized by what might be called a package approach to problem solving in which the independent variable consists of a series of treatments. The inclusion of verbal instructions and modeling by the trainer, client practice accompanied by verbal and (if necessary) physical prompts for correct responses, feedback and remediation of incorrect responses, and social reinforcement have been utilized extensively in almost all published studies on community-skills training. Although some studies have emphasized the use of one or more of these, none has seriously attempted to undertake a component analysis of instructional processes. This apparent lack of concern with subtle differences in treatment technique may reflect the fact that community research is still in an early developmental stage and that the search for effective technique has not progressed to the point where relative effectiveness is an important consideration. However, the use of modeling, prompting, and so forth might be seen as relatively low-cost and benign interventions, in which case most component analyses, although theoretically interesting, would be of dubious pragmatic value. Although it is doubtful that major advances will be realized through initiation of studies aimed at teasing out the effects of minor procedural variations, there appear to be several potentially important differences in the way that community-skills training can be approached, none of which has been adequately addressed.

Initial interest in preparing handicapped persons for community living was based, in part, on the general philosophy of normalizaton (Nirje 1969; Wolfensberger 1972). Normalization refers not only to a therapeutic outcome (for example, deinstitutionalization, access to community services) but also to a process (the use of less-restrictive treatments). Although normalized methods of teaching community skills have never been defined, it is assumed that nonhandicapped children residing in the community receive instruction in a casual and often unsystematic manner. Thus, behavioral methods of instruction are in marked contrast to techniques commonly employed in the home. In order to justify the use of highly structured formats, comparative data on the effects of informal versus formal training would seem beneficial. In addition, since most community-residence staff are relatively unskilled in behavioral techniques, it would seem important that staff-training efforts result in more-rapid gains on the part of clients.

Although no studies have compared behavioral training with other approaches, some work has recently examined the role played by the training environment. In several studies, training has been conducted directly in the natural environment (Marholin et al. 1979; Yeaton and Bailey 1978) in an attempt to ensure that learned skills would actually occur under appropriate stimulus conditions. Other studies have proceeded on the assumption that at least some types of classroom-based instruction generalize to other settings (for example, Neef, Iwata, and Page 1978; Page, Iwata, and Neef 1976). Two experiments have included a comparison of natural-environment versus classroom instruction. Matson (in press a) used a group design to study the acquisition of pedestrian skills in retarded institutionalized adults. One group received classroom training, similar to that developed by Page, Iwata, and Neef (1976), in which subjects controlled the actions of a doll in response to trainer instructions and stimuli presented by a tabletop model of an intersection. A second group also received classroom instruction but, in addition, was exposed to training trials conducted on a lifesized model of an intersection located on the hospital grounds. Statistical analysis of the data revealed that both types of training led to significant improvements in performance on a posttest conducted at a city intersection and that the combined program of instruction was more effective than classroom training only (posttest scores on the task analysis differed by approximately 20 percent).

Neef and his associates (1978) attempted to teach bus-riding skills to five retarded adolescents in a classroom using the following components: a miniature model similar to that of Page, Iwata, and Neef (1976); visual slide sequences depicting stimulus conditions found in the natural environment, as well as examples of correct and incorrect responses; and a larger, simplified model of a bus on which subjects practiced some but not all of the target skills. Two additional subjects received daily instruction, using procedures equivalent to those employed in the classroom, on the city buses. Both types of training were evaluated by way of multiple-baseline designs. Results showed no performance differences in that all subjects demonstrated the ability to take a bus to and from a designated location following the completion of training. However, data taken on the time and costs associated with training revealed that, on the average, instruction in the natural environment was approximately four times as expensive and time consuming as classroom training.

Results of the Matson (in press a and b) and Neef, Iwata, and Page (1978) studies exemplify differences that may be attributed to a number of variables associated with training, including subject characteristics, the extent to which role-played situations approximate naturalistic conditions, response contingencies, and methods for assessing behavior in the criterion situation. Clearly, more research needs to be done to identify those aspects critical to the success of training before widescale application of techniques can be achieved with large groups of clients.

Generalization and Maintenance

It has been noted previously that the major goal of community-skills-training research is the development of repertoires that improve functioning outside of the institutional setting. By definition, then, successful interventions should demonstrate behavioral change not just immediately following the completion of training or only in the training setting. Rather, a technology of community-skills training exists only to the extent that behavioral change is both durable over time and generalizable to new situations. With very few exceptions, research to date has not adequately addressed the questions of maintenance and generalization through empirical investigation. Typical research strategy has included the use of a more or less artificial situation for assessment that has little resemblance to the setting in which the behavior(s) will ultimately be expected to occur. Moreover, attempts to measure maintenance and generalization usually consist of additional assessments conducted in the artificial environment for a brief period following the termination of training.

Several studies are noteworthy in their efforts to establish procedures for assessing the by-products of treatment. Research conducted by Neef, Iwata, and Page (1978), van den Pol, et al. (in press), and Yeaton and Bailey (1978) has included the collection of follow-up data for periods up to one year after training has been completed. In addition, the Neef, Iwata, and Page and van den Pol et al. studies assessed clients' ability to exhibit target skills in more than one situation, using unknown observers to reduce the possibility that demand characteristics were mainly responsible for the finding of generalized behavioral change.

None of these studies, however, has attempted to identify variables responsible for either maintenance or generalization. Stokes and Baer (1977) have proposed a number of strategies that are available to increase generalization, and several of these have been incorporated into the design of community-skills research. Additonal studies are ow needed to demonstrate relationships between specific generalization-programming techniques and therapeutic outcome.

Toward Empirical Program Evaluation

As pointed out in the beginning of this chapter, evaluation of community programs may be critical to the continuation of the movement toward community living for the developmentally disabled. While empirical analysis of community programs is not extensive, some work has, of course, been done in this area. Edgarton (1977) has pointed out that "most of the published research about the community adaptation of retarded persons has serious flaws . . . the body of literature rests primarily on second order data, not directly on observation," and a prospective longitudinal study of 100 persons is offered as an example. Other examples of program evaluation related to community living and normalization include the follow-up analysis of persons discharged from the Pacific State Hospital (Edgerton 1967), a survey of 120 graduates of the California public-school programs for trainable mentally retarded students (Stanfield 1973), and an analysis and follow-up on a program to train moderately retarded adults from community living (Parnicky 1977). The findings of such empirical studies can provide important guidelines for the future. For example, in the face of popularized programs on early-childhood intervention, Bronfenbrenner's (1974) review of twenty-one studies indicates that intervention in the home is likely to be more successful than in preschool.

Perhaps equally important for the future of program evaluation is the approach and methodology that should be employed so that accurate conclusions can be made about program effectiveness. This opens a new area for research with the handicapped and allows us to extend the best of what we have learned about program evaluation in other areas. For example, Butterfield (1967) summarizes some of the major problems that must be taken into account when evaluating interrelationships between various factors in community-care facilities. One of the most cogent and complete descriptions of steps for program evaluation has been offered in a paper by Van Biervliet (1979). The significant aspects of this recommendation are abstracted in outline form:

I. Determine the program's goals
- A. Groups with a stake in the outcome
  1. Persons directly receiving the treatment
  2. Persons whose complaints are being alleviated by the program
  3. Persons who provide tangible and intangible support for the program
  4. Persons conducting the program
- B. Techniques for determining goals
  1. Ask potential consumers for a list of goals
  2. Administer tests
  3. Conduct interviews and surveys
  4. Elicit goal statements from various government agents and agencies
  5. Examine current laws and policy statements
  6. Consult knowledgeable experts
  7. Examine the extent to which apparently successful individuals engage in the behavior
  8. Assess the participants' needs in relation to the goals

II. Specify the program's objectives—objectives are short-term, more-tangible statements of purpose that are used to evaluate progress toward the goals. Frequently, a task analysis of the behavior specified in the goal must be conducted to develop the objectives.
- A. Components
  1. The behavior: Each objective requires the careful description of the target behavior; the target behavior must be described in a manner that can be accurately recorded
  2. The context: The important conditions under which the behavior occurs
  3. The criteria: The level of responding that will enable the participant to function better in his or her environment or the level of response the participant needs in order to progress in the program
  4. The measurement: How, when, and who will measure the behavior

III. Design an experimental or quasi-experimental strategy that can be incorporated into the program; the purpose of the research strategy is to examine the functional relationship between the program procedures (independent variable) and the desired effect on behavior (dependent variable).
- A. Basic design process
  1. What information should be collected?
  2. What comparisons should be made?
  3. How are conclusions reached?
- B. Factors to consider
  1. Types of information needed to evaluate the program

2. Data-collection system
3. Effects on the participants
4. Effects on the program itself

C. Data should enable the program planners to accurately describe three points of reference

1. Important characteristics of the target behaviors before treatment
2. Important characteristics of the target behaviors during treatment
3. Important characteristics of the target behaviors after treatment

D. Bases for selecting data system

1. Comprehensiveness
   a. Select aspects to measure that are relevant to the objectives (list plausible and undesired outcomes as a starting point, and from this list develop comprehensive measures)
   b. Consider a measure of the independent variable
   c. Consider a measure of permanence of effects
   d. Consider a measure of generality of effects

Data should be collected on the independent and the dependent variables over time, in a variety of relevant environments, and across a variety of related behaviors. The data may provide support and general endorsement of the program and may point out problems with the program not detectable by other means. Measures can also put the social effects of the program into proper perspective.

2. Reliability: Without some minimum degree of reliability, the relevance of a measure is doubtful; the reliability of the measurements is critical if others are to use the same program in a similar situation; without reliable measures, evaluators cannot determine what produced an observable change in behavior; an unreliable measure may not be able to detect a change in behavior
3. Fesibility: Certain measures may not be feasible because of considerations that are technical; humanitarian; cost related (manpower, supplies, money); or disruptive to the program

E. Possible sources of evaluative information

1. Tangible products of the participants' behavior
2. Observations of and reports from the participants
3. Observations of and reports from the program implementors
4. Observations of and reports from those in a position to observe or be affected by the behavior of the participants

IV. Additional purposes for evaluation—provide feedback information to the program

A. To make knowledgeable decisions concerning modifications to achieve the program's desired outcomes better

B. To protect the participants and others from harmful situations that may develop

V. Data Analysis
  A. General considerations
    1. Making comparisons
    2. Breaking the data into manageable groups
    3. Graphing the data
    4. Looking for interesting relationships among the variables
  B. Issues of Concern
    1. Effectiveness of the program in achieving its goals and objectives
    2. Impact of the program upon the people and the environment
    3. Manner in which the program achieves its impact
    4. Efficiency of the program
    5. Cost-benefit ratio of the program
  C. Involving persons outside the program with the analysis may help to strengthen and improve the analysis since they tend to be less likely to be biased

VI. Communication of results and conclusions
  A. Must be done in an objective, intelligible manner
  B. Targeted for persons in the program and directly involved in similar programs and to outside interested persons and agencies
  C. Such information can serve as rational starting point for the design of future programs

While such an extensive evaluation is not likely considering the current precedents and the almost certain financial restraints, an approximation toward this model outline would certainly be a move forward for program evaluation. With the increasing pressures on the nation's economy and the decrease in discretionary monies, program planning and evaluation for the developmentally disabled in the community cannot be expanded too soon.

Summary

This chapter has argued that the shift toward community as opposed to institutional life for the developmentally disabled has occurred on a humanistic, not empirical, basis. We have also pointed out that unless an empirical rationale for the importance, superiority, and cost-effectiveness of a community emphasis is established, we may shift back to an institutional model. this notion would dictate that methods of evaluation be adopted from other areas. In considering evaluation of programs for delinquent youth, Kirigin et al. (1979) distinguish between *component evalua-*

tion, in which different intervention components are assessed, and *program evaluation,* in which the overall program outcome is assessed. With rare exception, evaluation of the developmentally disabled in the community has been characterized by component rather than program evaluation.

Accepting the current programmatic-evaluation limitations, some components may be key to community life. We have considered as key behaviors those that are necessary for other behaviors to develop that set the occasion for individuals to make contact with a wide range of environmental reinforcers and learning opportunities. This chapter has reviewed four such key behaviors: (1) compliance, (2) behavioral engineering, (3) interpersonal skills, and (4) community-survival skills. Each has great relevance to community life and considerable component research has been conducted, albeit often with populations other than the developmentally disabled. In addition, generalization and the occurrence of collateral behavior change have been noted with these key behaviors. For example, overall compliance clearly has been shown to increase with reinforcement of only some specific requests. Corollary decreases in hyperactive behavior, crying, self-injurious behavior, and enuresis have occurred with increases in compliance. When children are trained to act as engineers of other's behavior, positive outcomes in addition to the targeted behavior change have included reciprocal reinforcement from peers and adults, reductions in aversive interactions, and improvements in nontarget behaviors of both the child acting as the behavioral engineer and others. Similar changes in nontarget behaviors have been noted when interpersonal skills were targeted, including an increase in cooperative play when conversational skills were taught and a decrease in aggressive behavior of peers when one individual's aggressive behavior was reduced by behavioral procedures.

Accordingly, we strongly advocate that a key behavioral concept be used in choosing programmatic targets for community programs and that research be extended from component to program evaluation. Community programs for the developmentally disabled are an intrinsically noble idea and one whose time has certainly come. The form that community programs take in the future, as well as their eventual fate, is still in question.

References

K.E. Allen, B. Hart, J.S. Buell, F.R. Harris, and M.M. Wolf, "Effects of Social Reinforcement on Isolate Behavior of a Nursery School Child," *Child Development* 35(1964):511–518.

T. Ayllon and S. Garber, "Teaching Reading through a Student-Administered Point System," in *New Developments in Behavioral Research: Theory, Method, and Application In honor of Sidney W. Bijou,* eds. B.C. Etzel, J.M. LeBlanc, and D.M. Baer (Hillsdale, New Jersey:

Lawrence Erlbaum Associates, 1977).

T. Ayllon and M.D. Roberts, "Eliminating Discipline Problems by Strengthening Academic Performance," *Journal of Applied Behavior Analysis* 7(1974):71–76.

A.M. Baer, T. Rowbury, and D.M. Baer, "The Development of Instructional Control over Classroom Activities of Deviant Preschool Children," *Journal of Applied Behavior Analysis* 6(1973):289–298.

D.M. Baer and J.A. Sherman, "Reinforcement Control of Generalized Imitation in Young Children," *Journal of Experimental Child Psychology* 1 (1964):37–49.

K.D. Ballard and T. Glynn, "Behavioral Self-Management in Story Writing with Elementary School Children," *Journal of Applied Behavior Analysis* 4(1975):387–398.

A. Bandura, "Vicarious and Self-Reinforcement Processes," in *The Nature of Reinforcement,* ed. R. Glaser (New York: Academic Press, 1971). pp. 228–278.

E.E. Balthazar, *The Balthazar Scales of Adaptive Behavior, II: The Scales for Social Adaptation* (Palo Alto, Calif.: Consulting Psychologists Press, 1973).

S. Beck, R. Forehand, K.C. Wells, and A. Quante, "Social Skills Training with Children: An Examination of Generalization from Analogue to Natural Settings" (Unpublished manuscript, University of Georgia, 1978).

M.J. Begab, "Barriers to the Application of Knowledge," in *Research to Practice in Mental Retardation: Care and Intervention,* vol. 1, ed. P. Mittler (Baltimore: University Park Press, 1977), pp. A21–A25, A21–A24.

R.Q. Bell, "A Reinterpretation of the Direction of Effects in Studies of Socialization," *Psychological Review* 75(1968):81–95.

R.Q. Bell, "Stimulus Control of Parent or Caretaker Behavior by Offspring," *Developmental Psychology* 4(1971):63–72.

A.S. Bellack and M. Hersen "Chronic Psychiatric Patients: Social Skills Training," in *Behavior Therapy in the Psychiatric Setting,* eds. Hersen and Bellack (Baltimore: Williams and Wilkins, 1978).

A.J. Bernhardt and R. Forehand, "The Effects of Labeled and Unlabeled Praise upon Lower and Middle Class Children," *Journal of Experimental Child Psychology* (1975):536–545.

S.W. Bijou and D.M. Baer, "Editors' Comments for D.M. Baer, and J.A. Sherman. Reinforcement Control of Generalized Imitation in Young Children," in *Child Development: Readings in Experimental Analysis* (New York: Appleton-Century-Crofts, 1967), pp. 68–79.

B. Blatt and F. Kaplan, *Christmas in Purgatory: A Photographic Essay in Mental Retardation* (Boston: Allyn and Bacon, 1966).

M.R. Bornstein, A.S. Bellack, and M. Hersen, "Social-Skills Training for Unassertive Children: A Multiple-Baseline Analysis," *Journal of Applied Behavior Analysis* 10(1977):183–195.

D.E. Bostow and J.B. Bailey, "Modification of Severe Disruptive and Aggressive Behavior Using Brief Timeout and Reinforcement Procedures," *Journal of Applied Behavior Analysis* 2(1969):31–37.

M. Broden, R.V. Hall, and B. Mitts, "The Effect of Self-Recording on the Classroom Behavior of Two Eighth Grade Students," *Journal of Applied Behavior Analysis* 4(1971):191–200.

V. Bronfenbrenner, "A Report on Longitudinal Evaluations of Pre-School Programs, Vol. 2.: Is Early Intervention Effective?" (Washington, D.C.: DHEW Pub. No. (OHD) 74–25, 1974).

B. Bucher, "Some Variables Affecting Children's Compliance with Instructions," *Journal of Experimental Child Psychology* 15(1973):10–21.

B. Bucher and O.I. Lovaas, "Use of Aversive Stimulation in Behavior Modification," in *Miami Symposium on the Prediction of Behavior, 1967: Aversive Stimulation,* ed. M.Jones (Coral Gables, Fl.: University of Miami Press, 1968).

K.S. Budd, D.R. Green, and D.M. Baer, "An Analysis of Multiple Misplaced Parental Social Contingencies," *Journal of Applied Behavior Analysis* 9(1976):459–470.

R.E. Buehler, G.R. Patterson, and R.M. Furness "The Reinforcement of Behavior in Institutional Settings," *Behaviour Research and Therapy* 4(1966):157–167.

J. Buell, P. Stoddard, F.R. Harris, and D.M. Baer, "Collateral Social Development Accompanying Reinforcement of Outdoor Play in a Preschool Child," *Journal of Applied Behavior Analysis* 1(1968): 167–174.

J.D. Burchard and V.O. Tyler, "Modification of Delinquent Behavior through Operant Conditioning," *Behaviour Research and Therapy* 2(1965):245–250.

E.C. Butterfield, "The Role of Environmental Factors in the Treatment of Institutionalized Mental Retardates," in *Mental Retardation: Appraisal, Education and Rehabilitation,* ed. A.A. Baumeister (Chicago: Aldine, 1967).

E.G. Carr, C.D. Newsom, and J.A. Binkoff, "Stimulus and Control of Self-Destructive Behavior in a Psychotic Child," *Journal of Abnormal Child Psychology* 4(1976):139–153.

N.L. Cantor and D.M. Gelfand, "Effects of Responsiveness and Sex of Children on Adult's Behavior," *Child Development* 48(1977): 232–238.

M.F. Cataldo and D.C. Russo, "Developmentally Disabled in the Community: Behavioral/Medical Considerations," in *Behavioral Systems for the Developmentally Disabled II. Institutional, Clinic, and Community Environments,* ed. L.A. Hamerlynck (New York: Brunner/Mazel, 1979).

R. Charlesworth and W.W. Hartup, "Positive Social Reinforcement in the Nursery School Peer Group," *Child Development* 38(1967):993-1002.

M.L. Combs and D.A. Slaby, Social-Skills Training with Children," in *Advances in Clinical Child Psychology,* vol 1, eds. B.B. Lahey and A.E. Kazdin (New York: Plenum Press, 1977).

T.P. Cooke and T. Apolloni, "Developing Positive Social-Emotional Behaviors: A Study of Training and Generalization Effects," *Journal of Applied Behavior Analysis* 9(1976):65-78.

H.E. Corte, M.M. Wolf, and B.J. Locke, "A Comparison of Procedures for Eliminating Self-Injurious Behavior for Retarded Adolescents," *Journal of Applied Behavior Analysis* 4(1971):201-213.

K. Cronin and A.J. Cuvo, "Teaching Mending Skills to Retarded Adolescents," *Journal of Applied Behavior Analysis* 12(1979):401-406.

D.M. Doleys, K.C. Wells, S.A. Hobbs, M.W. Roberts, and L.M. Cartelli, The Effects of Social Punishment on Noncompliance: A Comparison with Time Out and Positive Practice," *Journal of Applied Behavior Analysis* 9(1976):471-482.

R.S. Drabman, R. Spitalnik, and K.D. O'Leary, "Teaching Self-Control to Disruptive Children," *Journal of Abnormal Psychology* 82(1973): 10-16.

J.P. Elder, B.A. Edelstein, and M.M. Narick, "Adolescent Psychiatric Patients: Modifying Aggressive Behavior with Social Skills Training," *Behavior Modification* 3(1979):161-178.

R.B. Edgerton, *The Cloak of Competence: Stigma in the Lives of the Mentally Retarded* (Berkeley: University of California Press, 1967).

R.B. Edgarton, "The Study of Community Adaptation: Toward an Understanding of Lives in Progress," in *Research to Practice in Mental Retardation: Care and Intervention,* vol. 1, ed. P. Mittler (Baltimore: University Park Press, 1977), pp. 371-376.

S.M. Eyberg, and S.M. Johnson, "Multiple Assessment of Behavior Modification with Families: Effects of Contingency Contracting and Order of Treated Problems," *Journal of Consulting and Clinical Psychology* 42(1974):594-606.

J.F. Felixbrod and K.D. O'Leary, "Effects of Reinforcement on Children's Academic Behavior as a Function of Self-determined and Externally Imposed Contingencies," *Journal of Applied Behavior Analysis* 6(1973):241-250.

D.L. Fixsen, E.L. Phillips, and M.M. Wolf, "Achievement Place: The Reliability of Self-Reporting and Peer-Reporting and Their Effects on Behavior," *Journal of Applied Behavior Analysis* 5(1972):19-32.

R. Forehand, T. Cheney, and P. Yoder, "Parent Behavior Training: Effects on the Non-Compliance of a Deaf Child," *Journal of Behavior Therapy and Experimental Psychiatry* 5(1974):281–283.

R. Forehand, H.L. Gardner, and M. Roberts, "Maternal Response to Child Compliance and Noncompliance: Some Normative Data" (Unpublished manuscript, University of Georgia, 1976).

R. Forehand and H.E. King, "Pre-School Children's Non-Compliance: Effects of Short Term Behavior Therapy," *Journal of Community Psychology* 2(1974):42–44.

R. Forehand and H.E. King, "Noncompliant Children: Effects of Parent Training on Behavior and Attitude Change," *Behavior Modification* 1(1977):93–108.

R. Forehand, H.E. King, S. Peed, and P. Yoder, "Mother-Child Interactions: A Comparison of a Noncompliant Clinic Group and a Nonclinic Group," *Behaviour Research and Therapy* 13(1975):79–84.

R. Forehand, E.T. Sturgis, R.J. McMahon, D. Agur, K. Green, K.C. Wells, and J. Breiner, "Parent Behavioral Training to Modify Child Noncompliance," *Behavior Modification* 3(1979):3–25.

F. Frankel and J.Q. Simmons, "Self-Injurious Behavior in Schizophrenic and Retarded Children," *American Journal of Mental Deficiency* 80(1976):512–522.

J.L. Gewirtz, "Maternal Responding and the Conditioning of Infant Crying: Directions of Influence within the Attachment-Acquisition Process," in *New Developments in Behavioral Research: Theory, Method, and Application. In Honor of Sidney W. Bijou* eds. B.C. Etzel, J.M. LeBlanc, and D.M. Baer (Hillsdale, N.J.: Lawrence Erlbaum Associates, 1977).

M. Gittleman, "Behavior Rehearsal as a Technique in Child Treatment," *Journal of Child Psychology and Psychiatry* 6(1965):251–255.

E.L. Glynn, J.D. Thomas, and S.M. Shee, "Behavioral Self-Control of On-Task Behavior in an Elementary Classroom," *Journal of Applied Behavior Analysis* 6(1973):105–113.

E.M. Goetz, M.C. Holmberg, and J.M. LeBlanc, "Differential Reinforcement of Other Behavior and Noncontingent Reinforcement as Control Procedures during the Modification of a Preschooler's Compliance," *Journal of Applied Behavior Analysis* 8(1975):77–82.

E. Goffman, *Asylums: Essays on the Social Situation of Mental Patients and Other Inmates* (New York: Doubleday, 1961).

I. Goldiamond, "Self-Reinforcement," *Journal of Applied Behavior Analysis* 9(1976):509–514.

S.E. Goodwin and M.J. Mahoney, "Modification of Aggression through Modeling: An Experimental Probe," *Journal of Behavior Therapy and Experimental Psychiatry* 6(1975):200–202.

P.S. Graubard, H. Rosenberg, and M.B. Miller, "Student Applications of Behavior Modification to Teachers and Environments on Ecological Approaches to Social Deviancy," in *A New Direction for Education: Behavior Analysis,* eds. E.A. Ramp and B.L. Hopkins (Lawrence, Ks. Support and Development Center for Follow Through, 1971).

A.M. Graziano, ed., *Behavior Therapy with Children,* vol. 2 (Chicago: Aldine, 1975), p. 531.

C.L. Greenwood, H.N. Sloane, Jr., and A. Baskin, "Training Elementary Aged Peer-Behavior Managers to Control Small Group Programmed Mathematics," *Journal of Applied Behavior Analysis* 7(1974):103–114.

N.E. Gronlund, *Sociometry in the Classroom* (New York: Harper & Row, 1959).

K. Grunewald, "A Rural Country in Sweden, in *Changing Patterns in Residential Services for the Mentally Retarded,* eds. R. Kugel and W. Wolfensberger (Washington, D.C.: President's Committee on Mental Retardation, 1969).

A. Halpern, P. Raffeld, L. Irvin, and R. Link, *The Social and Prevocational Information Battery* (Monterey, Calif.: CTB/McGraw-Hill, 1975).

C. Hanf, "Modifying Problem Behaviors in Mother-Child Interactions: Standardized Laboratory Situations" (Paper presented at the meeting of the Association of Behavior Therapies, Olympia, Washington, 1968).

C. Hanf, "A Two-Stage Program for Modifying Maternal Controlling during Mother-Child (M-C) Interaction" (Paper presented at the Western Psychological Association Meeting, Vancouver, B.C. 1969).

C. Hanf, "Shaping Mothers to Shape their Children's Behavior" (Unpublished manuscript, University of Oregon Medical School, 1970).

C. Hanf and J. Kling, "Facilitating Parent-Child Interaction. A Two-Stage Training Model" (Unpublished manuscript, University of Oregon Medical School, 1973).

B.M. Hart, N.J. Reynolds, D.M. Baer, E.R. Brawley, and F.R. Harris, "Effect of contingent and Non-Contingent Social Reinforcement on the Cooperative Play of a Pre-School Child," *Journal of Applied Behavior Analysis* 2(1968):73–76.

S.M. Hobbs and R. Forehand, "Effects of Differential Release from Time-Out on Children's Behavior," *Journal of Behavior Therapy and Experimental Psychiatry* 6(1975):256–257.

S. Hymel and S.R. Asher, "Assessment and Training of Isolated Children's Social Skills" (Paper presented at the biennial meeting of the Society for Research in Child Development, New Orleans, March 1977).

S.M. Johnson, O.C. Bolstad, and G. Lobitz, "Generalization and Contrast Phenomena in Behavior Modification with Children," in *Behavior Modification and Families,* eds. E.J. Mash, L.C. Handy, and L.A. Hamerlynck (New York: Brunner/Mazel, 1976).

S.M. Johnson, G. Wahl, S. Martin, and S. Johansson, "How Deviant Is the Normal Child? A Behavioral Analysis of the preschool Child and His Family," in *Advances in Behavior Therapy,* vol 4, eds. R.D. Rubin, J.P. Brady, and J.D. Henderson (New York: Academic Press, 1973).

M.F. Keller and P.M. Carlson, "The Use of Symbolic Modeling to Promote Social Skills in Preschool Children with Low Levels of Social Responsiveness," *Child Development* 45(1974):912–919.

J.A. Kelly, W. Furman, J. Phillips, S. Hathorn, and T. Wilson, "Teaching Conversational Skills to Retarded Adolescents," *Child Behavior Therapy* 1(1979):85–98.

R.D. King, N.V. Raynes, and J. Tizard, *Patterns of Residential Care: Sociological Studies in Institutions for Handicapped Children* (London: Routledge & Kegan Paul, 1971).

K.A. Kirigin, M.M. Wolf, C.J. Braukmann, D.L. Fixsen, and E.L. Phillips, "Achievement Place: A Preliminary Outcome Evaluation," in *Progress in Behavior Therapy with Delinquents,* ed. J.S. Stumphauzer (Springfield, Ill.: Charles C Thomas, 1979).

M. Klaber, "The Retarded and Institutions for the Retarded: A Preliminary Research Report," in *Psychological Problems in Mental Deficiency,* eds. S. Sarason and J. Doris (New York: Harper & Row, 1969).

G.K. Lobitz, and S.M. Johnson, "Normal vs. Deviant Children: A Multimethod Comparison," *Journal of Abnormal Child Psychology* 3(1975):353–374.

J. Long and C.H. Madsen, "Five-Year-Olds as Behavioral Engineers for Younger Students in a Day-Care Center," in *Behavior Analysis: Areas of Research and Application,* eds. E.A. Ramp and G. Semb (Englewood Cliffs, N.J.: Prentice-Hall, 1975).

T.C. Lovitt and K.A. Curtiss, "Academic Response Rates as a Function of Teacher- and Self-Imposed Contingencies," *Journal of Applied Behavior Analysis* 2(1969):49–53.

T.F. McLaughlin and J.E. Malaby, "Development of Procedures for Classroom Token Economies," in *A New Direction for Education: Behavior Analysis, 1971,* eds. E.A. Ramp and B.L. Hopkins (Lawrence, Ks.: Support and Development Center for Follow Through, Department of Human Development, University of Kansas, 1971).

T.F. McLaughlin and J.E. Malaby, "Intrinsic Reinforcers in a Classroom Token Economy," *Journal of Applied Behavior Analysis* 5(1972a): 263–270.

T.F. McLaughlin and J.E. Malaby, "Reducing and Measuring Inappropriate Verbalizations in a Token Economy," *Journal of Applied Behavior Analysis* 5(1972b):329–333.

T.F. McLaughlin and J.E. Malaby, "Elementary School Children as Behavioral Engineers," in *Behavior Analysis: Areas of Research and Application,* eds. E.A. Ramp and G. Semb (Englewood Cliffs, N.J.: Prentice Hall, 1975).

M.J. Mahoney, *Cognition and Behavior Modification* (Cambridge, Mass.: Ballinger, 1974).

M.J. Mahoney, "Terminal Terminology: A Self-Regulated Response to Goldiamond," *Journal of Applied Behavior Analysis* 9(1976):515–517.

D. Marholin, II, K.M. O'Toole, P.E. Touchette, P.J. Berger and D.A. Doyle, "I'll Have a Bid Mac, Large Fries, Large Coke, Apple Pie, . . . or Teaching Adaptive Community Skills," *Behavior Therapy* 10(1979): 236–248.

E. Mash, L. Terdal, and K. Anderson, "The Response Class Matrix: A Procedure for Recording Parent-Child Interactions," *Journal of Consulting and Clinical Psychology* 40(1973):163–164.

J.L. Matson, "Preventing Home Accidents: A Training Program for the Retarded," *Behavior Modification,* in press a.

J.L. Matson, "A Controlled Group Study of Pedestrian Skill Training for the Mentally Retarded," *Behaviour Research and Therapy,* in press b.

J.R. Metz, "Conditioning Generalized Imitation in Autistic Children," *Journal of Experimental Child Psychology* 2(1965):389–399.

N.A. Neef, B.A. Iwata, and T.J. Page, "Public Transportation Training: In vivo versus Classroom Instruction," *Journal of Applied Behavior Analysis* 9(1978):433–444.

L. Nihira and K. Nihira, "Normalized Behavior in Community Placement," *Mental Retardation* 13(1975a):9–13.

L. Nihira and K. Nihira, "Jeopardy in Community Placement," *American Journal of Mental Deficiency* 79(1975b):538–544.

B. Nirje, 'The Normalization Principle and Its Human Management Implications," in *Changing Patterns of Residential Services for the Mentally Retarded,* eds. R. Kugel and W. Wolfensberger (Washington, D.C.: President's Committee on Mental Retardation, 1969).

V.M. Nordquist, "The Modification of a Child's Enuresis: Some Response-Response Relationships," *Journal of Applied Behavior Analysis* 4(1971):241–247.

T.J. Page, B.A. Iwata, and N.A. Neef, "Teaching Pedestrian Skills to Retarded Persons: Generalization from the Classroom to the Natural Environment," *Journal of Applied Behavior Analysis* 11(1976): 331–344.

R.A. Panepinto, "Social Skills Training for Verbally Aggressive Children," (Unpublished master's thesis, West Virginia University, 1976).

J.J. Parnicky, "Pathways toward Independence for Institutionalized Moderately Retarded Adults," in *Research to Practice in Mental Retardation: Care and Intervention,* vol. 1, ed. P. Mittler (Baltimore: University Park Press, 1977), pp. 295–304.

G.R. Patterson, "An Empirical Approach to the Classification of Disturbed Children," *Journal of Clinical Psychology* 20(1964):326–337.

G.R. Patterson, "Intervention for Boys with Conduct Problems: Multiple Settings, Treatments, and Criteria," *Journal of Consulting and Clinical Psychology* 42(1974):471–481.

G.R. Patterson, "The Aggressive Child: Victim and Architect of a Coercive System," in *Behavior Modification and Families,* eds. E.J. Mash, L.A. Hamerlynck, and L.C. Handy (New York: Brunner/Mazel, 1976), pp. 267–316.

G.R. Patterson, "A Three Stage Functional Analysis for Children's Coercive Behaviors: A Tactic for Developing a Performance Theory," in *New Developments in Behavioral Research: Theory, Method, and Application. In Honor of Sidney W. Bijou,* eds. B.C. Etzel, J.M. LeBlanc, and D.M. Baer (Hillsdale, N.J.: Lawrence Erlbaum Associates, 1977).

G.R. Patterson and G. Brodsky, "A Behavior Modification Program for a Boy with Multiple Problems," *Journal of Child Psychology and Psychiatry* 7(1966):277–295.

G.R. Patterson and M.J. Fleischman, "Maintenance of Treatment Effects: Some Considerations Concerning Family Systems and Follow-up Data," *Behavior Therapy* 10(1979):168–185.

G.R. Patterson and J.B. Reid, "Reciprocity and Coercion: Two Facets of Social Systems," in *Behavior Modification in Clinical Psychology,* eds. C. Neuringer and J.L. Michael (New York: Appleton-Century-Crofts, 1970).

G.R. Patterson and J.B. Reid, "Family Intervention in the Homes of Aggressive Boys: A Replication," *Behaviour Research and Therapy,* 11 (1973):383–394.

S. Peed, M. Roberts, and R. Forehand, "Evaluation of the Effectiveness of a Standardized Parent Training Program in Altering the Interaction of Mothers and Their Noncompliant Children," *Behavior Modification* 3(1977):323–350.

R. Perske, "Diary of Travel to Scandinavia," mimeographed, 1969.

R. Perske and J. Marquiss, "Learning to Live in an Apartment: Retarded Adults from Institutions and Dedicated Citizens," *Mental Retardation* 11(1973):18–19.

G.A. Petersen, G.J. Austin, and R.P. Lang, "Use of Teacher Prompts to Increase Social Behavior: Generalization Effects with Severely and Profoundly Retarded Adolescents," *American Journal of Mental Deficiency* 84(1979):82–86.

E.L. Phillips, "Achievement Place: Token Reinforcement Procedures in a Homestyle Rehabilitation Setting for Pre-delinquent Boys," *Journal of Applied Behavior Analysis* 1(1968):213–223.

E.M. Pinkston, N.M. Reese, J.M. LeBlanc, and D.M. Baer, "Independent Control of a Preschool Child's Aggression and Peer Interaction by

Contingent Teacher Attention," *Journal of Applied Behavior Analysis* 6(1973):115–124.

S.R. Polirstok, and R.D. Greer, "Remediation of Mutually Aversive Interactions between a Problem Student and Four Teachers by Training the Student in Reinforcement Techniques," *Journal of Applied Behavior Analysis* 10(1977):707–716.

H. Quay, "Patterns of Aggression, Withdrawal, and Immaturity, in *Psychopathological Disorders of Childhood,* eds. Quay and J. Werry (New York: Wiley, 1972), pp. 1–29.

L.B. Resnick, M.C. Wang, and J. Kaplan, "Task Analysis in Curriculum Design: A Hierarchically Sequenced Introductory Mathematics Curriculum," *Journal of Applied Behavior Analysis* 6(1973):679–710.

Ricci v. *Greenblatt,* C.A. No. 72–469F (D. Mass filed March 1972).

G. Rivera, *Willowbrook: A Repont on How It Is and Why It Doesn't Have to Be that Way* (New York: Vintage Books, 1972).

A. Rogers-Warren and D.M. Baer, "Correspondence between Saying and Doing: Teaching Children to Share and Praise," *Journal of Applied Behavior Analysis* 9(1976):335–354.

R.G. Romanczyk and E. Goren, "Severe Self-Injurious Behavior: The Problem of Clinical Control," *Journal of Consulting and Clinical Psychology* 43(1975):730–738.

M.S. Rosenbaum and J. Breiling, "The Development and Functional Control of Reading-Comprehension Behavior," *Journal of Applied Behavior Analysis* 9(1976):323–333.

D.L. Rosenham, "On Being Sane in Insane Places," *Science* 17(1973):250.

A.O. Ross, H.M. Lacey, and D.A. Parton, "The Development of a Behavior Checklist for Boys," *Child Development* 36(1965):1013–1027.

T. Sajwaj, S. Twardosz, and M. Burke, "Side Effects of Extinction Proceures in a Remedial Preschool," *Journal of Applied Behavior Analysis* 5(1972):163–175.

D.A. Santogrossi, K.D. O'Leary, R.G. Romanczyk, and K.F. Kaufman, "Self-Evaluation by Adolescents in a Psychiatric Hospital School Token Program," *Journal of Applied Behavior Analysis* 6(1973): 277–287.

M.E. Scarboro and R. Forehand, "Effects of Two Types of Response-Contingent Time-Out on Compliance and Oppositional Behavior of children," *Journal of Experimental Child Psychology* 19(1975): 252–264.

R.W. Seymour and T.R. Stokes, "Self-Recording in Training Girls to Increase Work and Evoke Staff Praise in an Institution for Offenders," *Journal of Applied Behavior Analysis* 9(1976):41–54.

T.M. Sherman and W.H. Cormier, "An Investigation of the Influence of Student Behavior on Teacher Behavior," *Journal of Applied Behavior*

Analysis 7(1974):11–21.

R.C. Shutte and B.L. Hopkins, "The Effects of Teacher Attention on Following Instructions in a Kindergarten Class," *Journal of Applied Behavior Analysis* 3(1970):117–122.

L.J. Siegel and W.M. Steinman, "The Modification of a Peer-Observer's Classroom Behavior as a Function of His Serving as a Reinforcing Agent," in *Behavior Analysis: Areas of Research and Application,* eds. E. Ramp and G. Semb (Englewood Cliffs, N.J.: Prentice-Hall, 1975).

R.W. Solomon and R.G. Wahler, "Peer Reinforcement Control of Classroom Problem Behavior," *Journal of Applied Behavior Analysis* 6(1973):49–56.

J.S. Stanfield, "Graduation: What Happens to the Retarded Child when He Grows Up?" *Exceptional Children* (1973):540.

T.F. Stokes, and D.M. Baer, "An Implicit Technology of Generalization," *Journal of Applied Behavior Analysis* 7(1977):599–610.

T.F. Stokes, S.A. Fowler, and D.M. Baer, "Training Preschool Children to Recruit Natural Communities for Reinforcement," *Journal of Applied Behavior Analysis* 11(1978):285–303.

P.S. Strain, "An Experimental Analysis of Peer Social Initiations on the Behavior of Withdrawn Preschool Children: Some Training and Generalization Effects," *Journal of Abnormal Child Psychology* 5(1977): 445–455.

P.S. Strain, R.E. Shores, and M.M. Kerr, "An Experimental Analysis of Spillover Effects on the Social Interaction of Behaviorally Handicapped Preschool Children," *Journal of Applied Behavior Analysis* 9(1976):31–40.

P.S. Strain, R.E. Shores, and M.A. Timm, "Effects of Peer Social Invitations on the Behavior of Withdrawn Preschool Children," *Journal of Applied Behavior Analysis* 10(1977):289–298.

P.S. Strain and M.A. Timm, "An Experimental Analysis of Social Interaction between a Behaviorally Disordered Preschool Child and Her Classroom Peers," *Journal of Applied Behavior Analysis* 7(1974): 583–590.

S. Striefel and B. Wetherby, "Instruction-Following Behavior of a Retarded Child and Its Controlling Stimuli," *Journal of Applied Behavior Analysis* 6(1973):663–670.

P.R. Surratt, R.E. Ulrich, and R.P. Hawkins, "An Elementary Student as a Behavioral Engineer," *Journal of Applied Behavior Analysis* 2(1969):85–92.

P.S. Taplin and J.B. Reid, "Changes in Parent Consequation as a Function of Family Intervention," *Journal of Consulting and Clinical Psychology* 45(1977):973–981.

H. Turkewitz, K.D. O'Leary, and M. Ironsmith, "Producing Generalization and Maintenance and Appropriate Behavior through Self-Control," *Journal of Consulting and Clinical Psychology* 43(1975): 577–583.

S. Twardosz and T. Sajwaj, "Multiple Effects of a Procedure to Increase Sitting in a Hyperactive Retarded Boy," *Journal of Applied Behavior Analysis* 5(1972):73–78.

A. Van Biervliet, "Program Evaluation Research: Its Importance for Applied Behavior Analysis and Its Basic Components," *The Behavior Therapist* 2(1979):3–7.

R.A. van den Pol, B.A. Iwata, M.T. Ivancic, T.J. Page, N.A. Neef and F.P. Whitley, "Teaching the Handicapped to Eat in Public Places: Acquisition, Generalization, and Maintenance of Restauranting Skills," *Journal of Applied Behavior Analysis,* in press.

V.B. Van Hasselt, M. Hersen, M.B. Whitehill, and A.S. Bellack, "Social Skill Assessment and Training for Children: An Evaluative Review," *Behaviour Research and Therapy* 17(1979):413–437.

R.G. Wahler, "Oppositional Children: A Quest for Parental Reinforcement Control," *Journal of Applied Behavior Analysis* 2(1969): 159–170.

R.G. Wahler, "Some Structural Aspects of Deviant Child Behavior," *Journal of Applied Behavior Analysis* 8(1975):27–42.

R.G. Wahler, R.M. Berland, and T.D. Coe, "Generalization Processes In Child Behavior Change," in *Advances in Clinical Child Psychology,* vol. 2, eds. B.B. Lahey and A.E. Kazdin (New York: Plenum Press, 1979), pp. 35–69.

R.G. Wahler, K.A. Sperling, M.R. Thomas, N.C. Teeter, and H.L. Luper, "The Modification of Childhood Stuttering: Some Response-Response Relationships," *Journal of Experimental Child Psychology* 9(1970): 411–428.

H.M. Walker and N.K. Buckley, "Programming Generalization and Maintenance of Treatment Effects across Time and Settings," *Journal of Applied Behavior Analysis* 5(1972):209–224.

H.M. Walker, C. Greenwood, H. Hops, and N.M. Todd, "Differential Interaction: Analysis and Direct Replication," *Behavior Modification* 1(1979):291–321.

C.J. Wallace, J.R. Teigen, R. Liberman, and V. Ballsen, "Destructive Behavior Treated by Contingency Contracts and Assertive Training: A Case Study," *Journal of Behavior Therapy and Experimental Psychiatry* 4(1973):274–284.

S. Warren, D. Baer, and Rogers-Warren, "Teaching Children to Praise: A Problem in Stimulus and Response Generalization," *Child Behavior Therapy* 1(1979):123–137.

C.Z. Waxler and Yarrow, M.R. "Factors Influencing Imitative Learning in Preschool Children," *Journal of Experimental Child Psychology* 9(1970):115-130.

T.L. Whitman, M. Zakaras, and S. Chardos, "Effects of Reinforcement and Guidance Procedures on Intruction-Following Behavior of Severely Retarded Children," *Journal of Applied Behavior Analysis* 4(1971): 283-290.

C.C. Wilson, S.J. Robertson, L.H. Herlong, and S.N. Haynes, "Vicarious Effects of Time-Out in the Modification of Aggression in the Classroom," *Behavior Modification* 1(1979):97-111.

W. Wolfensberger, *Normalization* (Toronto: National Institute on Mental Retardation, 1972).

W. Wolfensberger, "The Origin and Nature of our Institutional Models," in *Changing Patterns in Residential Services for the Mentally Retarded,* eds. R. Kugel and W. Wolfensberger (Washington, D.C.: President's Committee on Mental-Retardation, 1969a).

W. Wolfensberger, "Twenty Predictions about the Future of Residential Services in Mental Retardation," *Mental Retardation* 7(1969b):51.

F.P. Woodford, "A Theory of the New Leisure Class: Some Philosophical Reflections on Residential Life for the Multipli-Handicapped Adult," in *Research to Practice in Mental Retardation: Care and Intervention,* vol. 1, ed. P. Mittler (Baltimore: University Park Press, 1977), p. 53-58.

Wyatt v. *Stickney,* 325 F.Supp. 781 (M.D. ALA.); and 334 Supp. 1341 (M.D. ALA.), 1971.

W.H. Yeaton and J.S. Bailey, "Teaching Pedestrian Safety Skills to Young Children: An Analysis and One-Year Followup," *Journal of Applied Behavior Analysis* 11(1978):315-329.

E. Zigler and D. Balla, "The Social Policy Implications of a Research Program on the Effects of Institutionalization on Retarded Persons," in *Research to Practice in Mental Retardation: Care and Intervention,* vol. 1, ed. P. Mittler (Baltimore: University Park Press, 1977), pp. 267-274.

E.H. Zimmerman, J. Zimmerman, and C.D. Russell, "Differential Effects of Token Reinforcement on Instruction-Following Behavior in Retarded Students Instructed as a Group," *Journal of Applied Behavior Analysis* 2(1969):101-112.

Editors' Epilogue

Consider the following three scenes: In the first scene a visitor travels many miles from a large urban center to a small rural community that looks like one Normal Rockwell might have painted. A few miles further from the center of the town, rising from the midst of its surrounding fields, is a huge, gray stone cluster of buildings. Upon entering the building and passing through many locked doors, the visitor is greeted with a vision that weds the worst excesses of a Fellini movie with the torment of Dante's *Inferno*. The visitor has now entered the maximum-security ward of a large state mental hospital. In one corner of the ward, a childlike man is standing rigid as if he were a plumbing fixture; in another, a man is rocking mindlessly to the crackled disco beat coming from the flickering black-and-white television set in the center of the room. Babbling voices and animal-like grunts compete with a sweet, stale stench to overcome the visitor's senses.

In the second scene, a visitor boards an uptown bus, leaving steel and concrete towers for smaller ones of crumbling stone and rotting wood. The visitor departs the bus at an intersection busy with cars racing through red lights. Down one street the visitor sees the decaying carcases of several abandoned automobiles, down another are half-standing buildings that are home to rats and week-old garbage. The visitor approaches one intact building and enters an unlocked front door, stepping over fallen plaster and passing through a dirty gray unlit hallway. Through an open door the visitor sees a room decorated with peeling wallpaper. The room is small and serves as the bedroom, kitchen, and bathroom for the gray-haired woman sho is sitting on her cot watching the wallpaper peel.

In the final scene, the visitor leaves the urban center for the tree-lined, quiet, wide avenues of a suburb. Well-kept homes bordered by lush green lawns line the streets. Stopping, the visitor notices several smartly, yet casually, dressed people gathered in front of one home. These people are carrying placards that decry the presence in their family community of other people who best belong elsewhere. Faint murmurs of molested children and lowered property values run through the group.

Each scene depicts the possible fate of those individuals who run seriously afoul of the standards for being a normally adjusted member of society. In the first scene, the individuals were victims of the institution to which they had been relegated, perhaps forever. In the second and third scenes, the individuals were, again, victims. This time, however, they ran afoul of the process of deinstitutionalization rather than that of institutionalization.

As Cataldo, Iwata, and Ward note, mental-health professionals must do more than simply promote the entry of formerly hospitalized patients into the community. A major and potentially fatal drawback, they observe, is the relative absence of systematic and thorough evaluations of the efficacy of community-based treatment programs. In opening up the gates of the mental hospitals, reformers were certainly never envisioning the second and third scenes as products of their humanitarian efforts. Yet thousands of former patients do find themselves in substandard living conditions outside the hospital, and numerous others have been greeted with something less than community warmth and goodwill when they have sought more-residential living environments.

Much of their credit, the authors of this chapter have identified several important types of intervention that should well serve the community-based patient. They have also reiterated the necessity for a firmly grounded, empirical evalutation of any form of intervention applied to the deinstitutionalized.

Mental-health professionals, clinicians, and researchers who are seriously considering an excursion into the world of program evaluation should acquaint themselves with the rapidly expanding literature in this area. The almost dated, but still important, volumes on evaluation research by Elmer Struening and the late Marcia Guttentag (Guttentag and Streuning 1975; Streuning and Guttentag 1975) should be among the first reference sources consulted. Other, more-recent and programmatic works include those by Fink and Kosecoff (1980a; 1980b; 1980c) and Morell (1979) from among many others that are now available. Familiarity with program-evaluation methods as well as its application in field settings will go a long way to help up to assess more accurately the success or failure of our efforts at developing community-based interventions.

References

A. Fink and J. Kosecoff, An Evaluation Primer (Beverly Hills, Calif.: Sage, 1980a).

———. *An Evaluation Primer Workbook: Practical Exercises for Health Professionals* (Beverly Hills, Calif.: Sage, 1980b).

———. *An Evaluation Primer Workbook: Practical Exercises for Educators* (Beverly Hills, Calif.: Sage, 1980c).

M. Guttentag and E.L. Streuning, eds., *Handbook of Evaluation Research,* vol. 2 (Beverly Hills, Calif.: Sage, 1975).

J.A. Morrell, *Program Evaluation in Social Research* (New York: Pergamon, 1979).

E.L. Struening and M. Guttentag, eds., *Handbook of Evaluation Research,* vol. 1 (Beverly Hills, Calif.: Sage, 1975).

4 Direct Instruction Technology: Making Learning Happen

Wesley C. Becker, Siegfried Engelmann, Douglas W. Carnine, and *Alex Maggs*

Skill deficiencies represent a major presenting problem for children brought to clinics. Labels such as retarded, autistic, brain injured, minimal brain injured, dyslexic, and learning disabled imply skill deficiencies. In fact, in most cases, one would find no need for the label if procedures for overcoming the skill deficiencies could be applied. In this chapter we examine the assumptions, underlying principles, methods, and research relating to an approach to preventing and remedying skills deficiencies called Direct Instruction.

Direct Instruction is based on carefully scripted programs designed by Siegfried Engelmann and colleagues. The most well known of these programs are the nine DISTAR programs published by Science Research Associates (SRA) (three levels each in reading, arithmetic, and language).[1] Other programs include SRA *Corrective Reading* (comprehension and decoding skills at three levels each), *Morphographic Spelling* (Dixon 1977), and a math series (Engelmann and Steeley 1978; 1979) that covers fractions and equations. Under development are programs in expository writing, cursive writing, a basal spelling series based on morphographs, a telephone-book-based program to teach library and reference skills, and a basic vocabulary program.

Parts of this chapter are summarized from the book in preparation by S. Engelmann and W.C. Becker, "*Forward from Basics—The Case for Direct Instruction.*"

The University of Oregon Follow Through Project was supported by funds from the U.S. Office of Education, Department of School Systems, Division of Compensatory Education, Follow Through Branch, under Grants OEG-070-4157 (286) and GOO-750-7234. Views expressed in this chapter are the sole responsibility of the authors.

The authors are indebted to their many co-workers in this endeavor—office staff, data staff, project managers, project directors, supervisors, teachers, aides, parents, and children—who made this work possible.

Origins

Direct Instruction had its origins in the Bereiter-Engelmann Preschool at the University of Illinois in the 1960s, and became more fully developed as a teaching system under the auspices of the U.S. Office of Education's (USOE) Follow Through Program (Follow Through being a USOE-funded program for the economically disadvantaged in kindergarten to third grade). In his studies of intellectual development with young children in Illinois, Carl A. Bereiter found that whatever skills he tried to teach could be taught. He concluded that (1) no magic could quickly make retarded or disadvantaged children brighter and (2) if you wanted to help children who were behind to catch up, it was necessary to find a way to teach them at a faster rate than average children. These deductions led to the Bereiter-Engelmann preschool program that was an attempt to provide a systematic curriculum two hours a day for disadvantaged four- and five-year olds. Intensive, carefully sequenced, teacher-directed, small-group, verbal instruction was used as the modus operandi. The evaluation of two successive groups produced promising results (Bereiter and Engelmann 1966; Engelmann 1968; Bereiter 1967).

Siegfried Engelmann and Wesley C. Becker began working together in 1967 after Bereiter left Illinois for the Ontario Institute for Studies in Education. On the basis of the promising outcomes in the preschool studies, the USOE in 1967 invited Engelmann and Becker to develop a model program that could be applied in kindergarten through third grade within Project Follow Through, a follow-through on Head Start. The evidence suggests that Direct Instruction was the most successful Follow Through approach (USOE 1977; Abt Associates 1977; Becker and Engelmann 1978; Becker 1978).

Becker, a child-clinical psychologist became dissatisfied with traditional clinical procedures and explored behavioral-based approaches. He and his associates performed a number of functional studies of child behavior (Becker, Zipse, and Madsen 1967; O'Leary, O'Leary, and Becker 1967) and eventually moved to the classroom to study ways to eliminate problem behaviors and to improve on-task performance of children (O'Leary and Becker 1967; Becker et al. 1967; Becker et al. 1968; Thomas, Becker, and Armstrong 1968; Becker 1973). These studies revealed a variety of procedures that teachers could use to reduce and eliminate problem behaviors without sending the children out of the classroom to a therapist. They also brought to Becker's attention the great amount of downtime present in elementary classrooms and the need for better instruction systems. After some work with Sidney Bijou and Dave Phillip in developing a behavioral-oriented elementary school, using individually prescribed instruction (IPI), Becker teamed up with Engelmann in an effort to design, implement, and evaluate a school instructional system based on teacher-directed instruction (Becker, Engelmann, and Thomas 1971; 1975).

Engelmann brought to this venture unique expertise in the analysis of curriculum contents and the design of task sequences to teach complex behaviors step by step. Engelmann also brought the skills required to teach his programs and to train others to do likewise (Engelmann 1968). The venture represented a merger of an empirically based behavioral scientist with a logically oriented educational pragmatist. At the beginning, there were communication problems, but when they got to talking about what teachers were to do to facilitate child learning, they were in complete agreement. In keeping with B.F. Skinner's advice, "Let the pigeon teach you," Engelmann let the children teach him whether his teaching sequences were adequate or not. At the level of the children, arguments about logical analyses and behavioral principles were readily settled. Procedures worked or they did not. If they did not, they were redesigned and field tested.

The third author of this chapter, Douglas W. Carnine, first worked with Becker ad Engelmann as an undergraduate at the University of Illinois. As a college senior he became co-author with Engelmann of DISTAR Arithmetic I, and he continued to work with Engelmann on the next two DISTAR arithmetic programs and their later revisions. He has served as a field supervisor and teacher trainer in Follow Through. He has directed an experimental Direct Instruction teacher-training program at the University of Oregon since 1970 when the authors moved there from Illinois. He has also directed a research program aimed at validating or refuting, through experimental analysis, the critical assumptions and principles in our teaching and programming strategies. When Becker left Follow Through to take on an associate deanship in 1978, Carnine became the director of the University of Oregon Direct Instruction Follow Through Model. He is also authoring college method texts on Direct Instruction in reading and math (Carnine and Silbert 1979; Carnine, Silbert, and Stein, forthcoming).

The fourth author, Alex Maggs, has been actively involved in Direct Instruction research since working on his doctorate at Macquarie University in 1972.

Direct Instruction

The careful program-development and field-testing work of the past fifteen years has led to the emergence of Direct Instruction as a technologically based approach to remedying and preventing skill deficiencies. Studies using this basic technology have been carried out with retarded (including severely retarded), autistic, non-English-speaking, bilingual, deaf, disadvantaged, and perfectly normal children in all parts of the United States,

Canada, Australia, and many Pacific Island groups. We review the more-salient aspects of this research later.

Assumptions and Principles

The Direct Instruction approach is built upon the following premises that derive from empirical behavioral theory and logical analyses of knowledge systems:

Operant (voluntary) behavior is learned.

Learning is a function of environmental events.

The teacher can control environmental events to make learning happen.

Intelligent behavior is operant behavior; therefore, it is learned and can be taught.

Learning rate is largely a function of teaching technology. If you can find ways to teach more in less time, the children will gain relative to those taught less.

Thinking and related covert cognitive processes can be taught first as overt (usually verbal) processes.

Program sequences derive logically from the nature of the skills and knowledge to be taught—not the individual. This implies that it is possible to teach all children with the same program sequence, although several different sequences could work equally well.

Task sequences to teach concepts and operations should be designed to permit only one interpretation wherever possible. If the sequence permits only one interpretation consistently, only that interpretation can be learned.

Transfer of skills to related (but different) tasks and situations must be planned for in the teaching program. There is no magic in learning.

Generalization to new examples not used in the teaching will occur only where there are specific cues (discriminative stimuli) present in the new examples that were the essential features of the examples already taught. Again, there is no magic.

Instructional processes require careful monitoring and feedback systems to insure quality control.

If the student fails, do not blame the student; diagnose the teaching history. The teaching sequences control what can be learned.

Basic Features

Common to the various Direct Instruction programs developed under Engelmann's direction are (1) pretested scripted lessons; (2) teacher-directed group instruction for part of each lesson; (3) specified teaching, motivating, and training procedures; (4) built-in systems for monitoring student progress; and (5) a common logic in selecting teaching materials, examples, and program sequences.

The DISTAR programs are used widely in special and regular education for the first three or four years of basic skill instruction. For the past ten years, they have played a central role in the Direct Instruction Follow Through Model. The Direct Instruction classroom in Follow Through had a teacher and one or two aides. Usually, each specialized in one area—either reading, arithmetic, or language.

The Corrective Reading programs are used in upper-elementary and higher grades. They are sometimes taught as a full-class developmental program (particularly comprehension) but most often are taught in special classes or learning centers. Group size might range up to twenty-five, although fifteen is a preferred maximum. Morphographic Spelling is used in a similar way to Corrective Reading. In each case, the class involves a teacher-directed activity, student practice in prepared materials, and checkouts on student performance.

The writing and math programs are most often used as teacher-directed full-class presentations with much student-practice activity.

Scripted Presentations. A program is a series of tasks to be taught. To ensure that what is intended is delivered, daily lessons are designed in script form, showing the teacher what to do and what to say. This feature makes it possible, where necessary, to implement effective instruction, using aides as teachers after only one or two weeks of preservice training. The use of scripted lesson plans has been criticized as restricting the teacher's initiative. However, some important values derive from the use of scripts. We are concerned with designing disseminable procedures for improving instruction. Scripts permit the use of explicitly pretested examples and sequences. The teacher knows that, if the student has the prerequisite skills, the teaching sequence will work. The teacher does not have to spend time experimenting with various possible illustrations, choosing appropriate language, and analyzing possible teaching sequences. The scripts also make explicit the teacher behaviors that are required to follow them. Thus, the training requirements for a given program can be formalized in detail and executed. Next, note that a supervisor of a scripted program can walk into any room and within a few seconds be explicitly oriented as to what should be going on and thus can evaluate what is going on and provide appropriate help. Finally, because the teaching sequence is standardized, it is easier to monitor the progress of the children with program-based tests. Scripts make possible what Lessinger (1976) has called "the missing link in education"—namely, quality control. While scripted presentations are not necessary or even desirable in all areas or levels of education, they most certainly can serve an important role when dealing with competencies that all children should have. They may also play an important role in teacher training (Clark et al. 1976).

Small Groups. Small groups have many advantages. They are more efficient than one-on-one instruction and provide for more adult direction, prompting, reinforcement, correction, and individualization than found in large group instruction. They also permit an emphasis on oral communication, which is frequently a problem for children from non-English-speaking and economically disadvantaged backgrounds. Finally, small groups provide a setting where repetitious practice on important building blocks can be made fun and where other students can be used as models. While we have most often worked with groups of five to fifteen students, at advanced levels and with less-disadvantaged students larger groups have been used effectively.

Specified Teaching Procedures. Teaching procedures change with the level of student skill development. Some of the more-distinctive features of Direct Instruction (choral responding on signal with rapid pacing in small-group instruction) occur primarily in the early levels of basic learnings in the DISTAR programs. Group responses keep all the children actively involved in learning (Durling and Schick 1976; Abramson and Kagan 1975; Frase and Schwartz 1975). Signals facilitate attention (Cowart, Carnine, and Becker 1973) and keep some children from cuing on what the others say. Rapid pacing keeps the students interested and allows more material to be covered in a fixed time (Carnine 1976b). As the students develop skills, more independent activities are built into the programs. By tying workbook or other seat-work activities closely to what has been taught (so that the students can do them) and by carefully monitoring their work with checkouts, the commonly observed low productivity of seat-work time can be avoided. With careful programming, it is also possible to anticipate the kinds of errors students will make and to prepare the teacher to correct them with effective procedures.

Motivating Procedures. It is common knowledge that where you have skill deficiencies, you will find students who tend to avoid school-work activities. It is therefore important to build strong motivational procedures into teaching programs for basic instruction with children who are behind and for remedial programs. Within the DISTAR series, a variety of strategies are aimed at facilitating motivation. These include (1) rapid confirmation of correct responses; (2) frequent use of praise; (3) use of races against the teacher to help to consolidate skills; (4) use of intentional teacher mistakes to teach students to think for themselves, to learn they are smart, and to challenge authority; (5) use of storylines that introduce humor, plots, and absurdities that catch the student's attention; (6) giving of points for good learning performances that lead to a grade and/or special activities or treats; and (7) use of goals and charts of progress. The advanced programs use charting of student progress and point-contract systems tied to grades to aid motivation.

Training Procedures. With scripted programs, it is possible to train teachers to deliver them in much the same way as actors learn to deliver their lines. Directed practice is given using the general strategy of model, lead, and test (Carnine and Fink 1978). The supervisor shows the teachers what to do by pretending the teachers are students and the supervisor is the teacher. Then the teachers do the task with the supervisor. Finally, the teachers do it on their own, with pairs of teachers taking turns being teacher and student. Preservice workshops are usually followed by actual classroom observations, classroom demonstrations, and in-service workshops. The training requirements for various programs vary from one to five full days of training. This may be followed up by several hours of in-service training each month for a year.

Monitoring. Criterion-referenced tests to monitor student (and teacher) progress are built into (or available for) each Direct Instruction program. These tests permit an assessment of student performance every two to six weeks. With the results of the tests, it is possible for the teacher to detect student problems in need of correction—as well as teaching problems. They make possible doing something about problems before it is too late. They permit the quality control spoken of by Lessinger.

Rosenshine's Direct Instruction: Support for the Engelmann-Becker Approach

The Direct Instruction goal of teaching more in less time can be accomplished by better utilization of the total school time available as well as by better teaching techniques. Better outcomes should be associated with more available time or more content covered in a given area, and with better student engagement during that time (Rosenshine 1976). More available time is similar to Carroll's (1963) concept of opportunity to learn. In a review of "content-covered" studies, Rosenshine (1976) reported that in fifteen or sixteen studies, significant positive relations were found between amount of content covered and student achievement gain. In a review of studies of engaged time, Bloom (1976) reported that correlations of engaged time with student gain were about .40 when the student was the unit of analysis and .52 when the class was the unit.

Rosenshine (1976) has used the term *direct instruction* to summarize a converging set of studies relating teaching strategies to student outcomes in reading and mathematics achievement. Rosenshine's direct instruction refers to teaching activities that focus on academic matters where goals are clear to the students, time allocated for instruction is sufficient and continuous, content covered is extensive, student performance is monitored, questions are at a low cognitive level and produce many correct responses, and feedback to students is immediate and academically oriented. The teacher controls the instructional goals, choose material appropriate for the student's level, and paces the teaching. Interaction is structured, but lively and fun, not authoritarian.

The studies covered in Rosenshine's (1976; Rosenshine and Berliner 1978) reviews include classroom-observation studies by Soar (1973) and by Stallings and Kaskowitz (1974), using Follow Through classrooms for a variety of major sponsors; studies by Brophy and Evertson (1974) from the Texas Teacher Effectiveness Study; studies by Good (Good and Grouws 1975; Good and Beckerman, in press; Good, Grouws, and Beckerman, in press); studies from the Far West Lab (Gall et al. 1975; Marliave et al. 1977; Tikunoff, Berliner, and Rist 1975); and studies from the Stanford Center for Research and Development in Teaching (Clark et al. 1976).

These studies give independent support to many of the teaching strategies adopted by Engelmann and Becker in building Direct Instruction programs.

Design of Instructional Materials

Just as the procedures discussed previously are designed to maximize the likelihood of student success, so are the curriculum-design procedures. The design procedures deal with many issues central to learning research: attention, generalization, meaningfulness, interference, memory, readiness, and cognitive structures. However, the goal in program design is not internally consistent hypothetical systems but rather the development of procedures that teachers can use to maximize attention, appropriate generalization, meaningfulness, retention, and the development of functional cognitive structures. The goal is one of external validity rather than internal validity. Each of these areas is discussed as it applies to the design of Direct Instruction programs.

Generalization

Generalization to new examples is a form of stimulus control in which the learner responds only to examples that contain the essential features of a particular concept (Becker, Engelmann, and Thomas 1975, p. 68). A stimulus-control analysis does not predict correct generalization to situations with dramatically different stimulus characteristics than those found in training—for example, one would not expect generalization of red-white-discrimination training to red-pink-orange-discrimination testing. The generalization of red responses to pink or orange examples would show an absence of discrimination training between red and pink-orange. Generalization occurs only with examples comparable to those used in training—for example, we would expect appropriate generalization (interpolation) of red-white-discrimination training to red-white testing with values of red and white within the range used in training. This view of generalization provides a basis for an analysis of instructional sequences.

The analysis involves an answer to the question: Is the instructional sequence consistent with more than one interpretation? This question is a starting point because whenever a presentation is consistent with more than one interpretation, a student may learn an interpretation other than that intended by the teacher. For example, when a young, educationally high-risk student is shown an apple and told, "This is red," some of the interpretations are that red has to do with apple, food, round, small, or smooth. If the teacher presented an orange and asked, "Is this red?" a yes response would indicate an absence of control by redness. The student might have learned that red is round, food, or something held in the hand.

Adults often have difficulty appreciating the importance of designing presentations that convey a single interpretation—that is, a presentation with a high probability of establishing stimulus control. This appreciation is more likely when adults are in a position similar to that of a younger student—that is, learning the meaning of a new concept. For example, a teacher draws this form on the board and says, "This is a concave region."

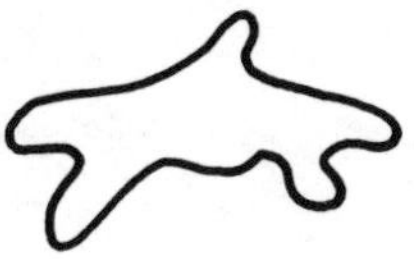

Indicate which of the following regions are concave:

Adults typically find this exercise difficult; the interpretations they generate are often incorrect. The difficulty is understandable because to teach a new concept with one example is often impossible. At this point some people might object that concave region could be better taught through a definition. While this objection might hold for teaching concave region to adults, concepts such as red or dog cannot be taught with a definition to younger students. For example, consider what verbal definition could meaningfully explain red or under to a four-year old? Obviously, many concepts must be taught through examples to students who have limited language skills.

When examples are used as the primary instructional device, they must be selected so that the example set is consistent with only one interpretation—the one the teacher intends to convey. To do this, the teacher often must use negative examples and a range of positive examples to illustrate irrelevant and relevant features. When less than a full range of positives is presented, some learners will form a misinterpretation. For example, Carnine (n.d.) taught college students a nonsense concept defined as a geometric form with 1, 2, or 3 points.

One group received a restricted-range set of positive examples in which all positive examples contained irrelevant dots.

Negative examples did not have dots. As might be expected, most of the students learned that the concept was defined as forms with dots. In contrast, another group received a full range of positive examples where the irrelevant dots were varied; some 1-, 2-, or 3-pointed forms had dots and others did not.

These students learned that the concept was defined as forms with 1, 2, or 3 points (correct transfer responses were 99 percent for the full range of positive examples group and 49 percent for the narrow range). In short, the range of positive examples can determine what concept students learn.

Two other studies demonstrate the applied significance of presenting a full range of positive examples. Flanders, Carnine, and Maggs (1979) taught a limited-language student receptive plural usage according to a widely used procedure (Guess et al. 1968). The procedure involved a restricted range of positive examples (plural labels were elicited only in the presence of two objects, never three or more objects). After training the student to criterion according to the Guess et al. procedure, the experimenter tested him on a full range of examples and found he had several misinterpretations, one of which was that plural labels were used with any two objects—for example, he called a cat and a dog "cats." Training with a full range of positive examples was then introduced, and the misinterpretations were eradicated. In the second applied study (Carnine 1978), students were taught to transform fractions with the denominator of 100 into a decimal. The examples in the full range of positive examples treatment included 1-, 2-, and 3-digit numerators: 7/100 = .07, 77/100 = .77, 777/100 = 7.77. In contrast, the examples in the restricted-range set included only 2-digit numerators: 77/100 = .77. When students were tested on a full range of new examples, students in the restricted-range group consistently placed the decimal point in front of the first numeral in the numerator: 7/100 = .7, 77/100 = .77, 777/100 = .777.

Misinterpretations can also be conveyed if unsuitable negative examples are selected or if negative examples are not presented at al. The important aspect of negative examples is that they clearly define the boundary of the positive range. For example, in figure 4–1, the five pairs of examples illustrate five example sets that could be used to teach "on." The boundary is most clearly defined by a set *a*. When an object ceases to be in contact with another object's surface, it is no longer on. In set *d*, the negative example is very dissimilar from the positive, which means the boundary is not clearly defined. Students receiving a set-*d* presentation might learn that on means not in the hand, within a foot of the table, horizontally oriented, a block, and so forth. The absence of negative examples in set *e* makes the boundary even less clear. Carnine (1977d) presented sets of examples similar to those in figure 4–1 and found a significant linear trend between the quality of negative examples and performance on a transfer test (set *a*, mean = 10.2; set *b*, mean = 7.8; set *c*, mean = 7.8; set *d*, mean = 5; set *e*, mean = 4.3). Other studies have replicated the effect of excluding negative examples (Williams and Carnine 1979a) and have found that a misinterpretation can also be learned when a restricted range of negative examples is presented (Carnine 1976a).

In short, if an example set is comprised of a restricted set of positive and/or negative examples that do not define the boundary of positive-concept features and vary irrelevant features, students might learn an interpretation that is consistent with that set but that is not the one the teacher intended to teach. The result is inappropriate generalization.

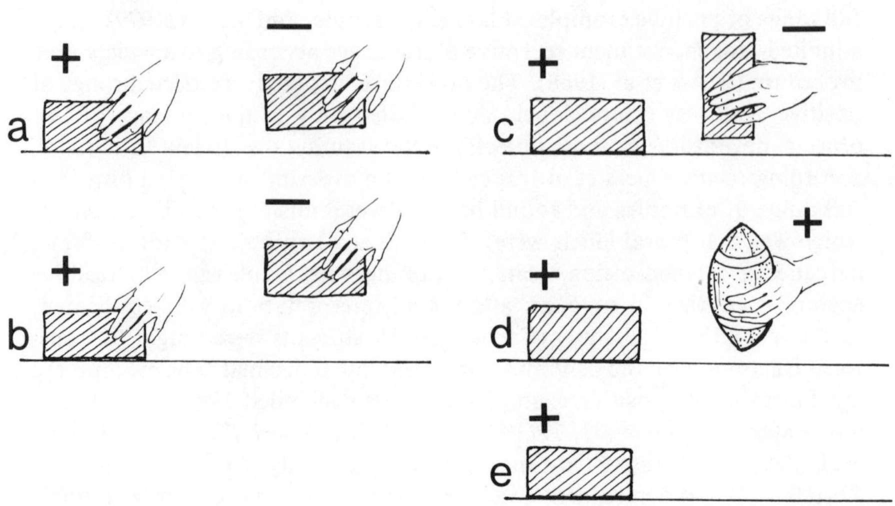

Figure 4–1. An Example of the "Only One" Principle for Training the Discrimination of *On*

Attention

Direct Instruction sequences are designed to maximize the saliency of relevant-concept features. Increasing the saliency of relevant features increases efficiency by decreasing teaching time. Efficiency is a critical aspect of Direct Instruction because educationally high-risk students must be taught as quickly as possible if they are to overcome their educational deficits. Procedures for increasing the saliency of relevant features range from familiar ones such as stimulus prompting to more-unique ones involving the isolation of relevant features through continuous conversion of examples. Traditional stimulus prompting involves drawing attention to a critical attribute by exaggerating the value of the attribute (making the loop larger and darker in the letter *b* than in *d*), by adding an emphasizer (coloring the loop in *b* red), or by using verbal prompts ("If you see a bat hit a ball, then it is *b*"). The potential effectiveness of stimulus prompting has been fairly well documented (Trabasso and Bower 1968). However, problems can occur with stimulus prompting when the prompts are faded (Warren 1953; Restle 1959). For example, when the red loop in *b* is faded to black, students might begin confusing *b* and *d*. Another concern is that the addition of emphasizers to complex stimuli can in fact result in students requiring more trials to reach a training criterion (Carnine 1976c). The problems with fading prompts, especially emphasizers, suggests that exaggeration of relevant features or verbal prompts be used rather than emphasizers. Exaggeration of a value of an attribute is more likely to draw student attention to that value rather than to an extraneous feature, which can occur when an emphasizer is added. The advantage of verbal prompts is that they can be reintroduced easily whenever students begin making errors.

The other procedures relating to attention have been less well researched—namely, uniform instructions and isolation of relevant-attribute features. Uniform instructions during initial concept teaching require the same type of response in every task. The learner can focus his attention upon the examples themselves with less concern over the form of the response. For example, Williams and Carnine (1979) compared two types of instruction for teaching "diagonal" (called blurp): uniform and variable. In the uniform-instruction treatment, the teacher presented examples and always asked, "Is this blurp?" Preschoolers in the variable treatment were presented the same examples but with a variety of instructions—for example, "Is this blurp? Tell me blurp or not blurp. Touch blurp. Hold your hand to show me blurp." The uniform-instruction group reached the training criterion in half as many trials.

Several procedures can be used to isolate relevant-attribute features: minimum differences, continuous conversions, and physical isolation. In the minimal-difference procedure, the teacher simultaneously presents positive- and negative-example pairs that differ only in terms of the relevant-attribute value. Granzin and Carnine (1977) presented the same examples on conjunctive and exclusive-disjunctive concepts in two studies with first and second graders. The treatments differed in the sequence of examples. In the minimal-difference group, juxtaposed positive and negative examples differed only in terms of a single relevant-attribute value—that is, minimally different positive and negative examples were presented. Students in the minimal-difference treatment in study 1 required only 56 percent as many trials to reach criterion as did the students presented with randomly sequenced examples (mean = 17.4 versus 29) and scored significantly higher on a transfer test. In study 2, students in the minimal-difference treatment made fewer errors on both the conjunctive (mean = 8.1 versus 19.1) and disjunctive tasks (mean = 21.1 versus 37.1).

The second procedure for isolating relevant-attribute values is continuous conversion. In continuous conversion, a single object or set of objects is manipulated to generate positive and negative examples. For example, a black line segment drawn in a white dial is rotated to generate positive and negative examples of diagonal. Carnine (1978d) compared a continuous conversion with a noncontinuous-conversion treatment in which examples were drawn on individual cards. In one study, the concept was diagonal; in another, convex. In both studies, trials to criterion measures were significantly fewer for the continuous-conversion treatment (mean = 46.4 versus

10.6 for diagonal; mean = 5.8 versus .1 for convex). Since the noncontinuous-conversion treatment employed minimum differences (as did the continuous-conversion treatment), continuous conversion is a procedure that can be used in conjunction with minimal-difference juxtapositions.

Another study was conducted to evaluate them with Tennyson's "matched-divergent" procedure (Tennyson, Woolley, and Merrill 1972) in which differences are minimal within pairs but maximal between pairs. Preschoolers in the minimal-difference, continuous-conversion group reached criterion in the fewest trials (mean = 7.6), the noncontinuous-conversion, minimal-difference group required an intermediate number of trials (mean = 12.8), and the matched divergent group required the most trials (mean = 26).

The final procedure for isolating a relevant-attribute value involves physical isolation. In a number of reading decoding studies (Stein, Carnine, and Maggs 1979), an unknown letter-sound correspondence was taught in two ways. In the isolation procedure, the letter combination (for example, *oi*) was first presented in isolation. For example, the teacher pointed to *oi* and said, "These letters usually say 'oi'." Next students read lists of words, several of which contain *oi*—for example, *coil, cat, point, was, jump, soil,* and so on. Finally, students read a passage that contained several *oi* words. In the nonisolation treatment, students just practiced reading passages containing *oi* words. When given a transfer passage, which contained *oi* words not presented in training, students in the isolation treatment read significantly more *oi* words.

In summary, teachers can increase learner attention to relevant-attribute values by selecting carefully and sequencing examples. Stimulus prompting can be achieved by exaggerating the relevant-attribute value, adding an emphasizer, or using verbal prompts. Uniform instructions across tasks that involve new learning increase attention to relevant-attribute values by minimizing attention demands for responding. Procedures for increasing attribute salience through isolation include juxtaposing minimally different positive and negative examples, continuous conversions in which a single set of objects is manipulated to create positive and negative examples, and physical isolation in which critical aspects of examples are presented apart from the context in which they ultimately appear.

Meaningfulness

A common adage of psychology and education is that meaningful learning occurs more quickly and is remembered longer than meaningless learning (Cronbach 1970). Becker and Engelmann (1976) have suggested that these data can be interpreted to say that meaningful learning takes advantage of prior learning so that there is actually less to learn. To capitalize on this phenomenon, Direct Instruction design procedures build on prior learning whenever possible. This is done by showing a systematic relationship between new knowledge and familiar knowledge and by incorporating familiar knowledge into more-complex tasks. In one study (Carnine 1977e), three groups of preschoolers who knew how to make statements about a picture (the familiar knowledge) were taught to make commands (the new knowledge). For a picture of a boy washing his face, the statement was "The boy is washing his face"; the command was "wash your face." The treatments differed according to how systematically they portrayed the relationship between the new and familar knowledge. Least systematic was the treatment that received seven random pairs of statement and command instructions; intermediate was the treatment that received all statements, then all commands; most systematic was the treatment that started out with small blocks of statement and command items and progressed to a more-random sequence. A significant linear trend was found between the three degrees of systematization and transfer performance (means = 41 percent, 61 percent, and 69 percent).

Similar results were found in another study (Carnine 1978a) in which the subject matter was addition facts. In the high-meaningfulness treatment, the facts were presented and recited in related sets before the memorization drill began: for example, $6 + 1 = 7$, $6 + 2 = 8$, $6 + 3 = 9$. The relatedness of the groupings was based on counting: 1, 2, 3 for the second addend in each problem and 7, 8, 9 for the answers. The low-meaningfulness treatment consisted of fact drill on the same facts but in random order. The mean number of facts remembered on a one-week delayed twenty-four-item test was significantly higher for the high-meaningfulness treatment (mean = 13.8 versus 6); training time was also higher but not significantly (mean = 74 versus 50). A recently completed study in which time was held constant for both treatments found that the high-meaningfulness treatment still produced higher maintenance scores.

Meaningfulness can also be increased by incorporating previously taught skills into more-complex applications. For example, almost all students will have been taught single-digit multiplication (4×2) and place value before encountering multiplication involving two digits (43×5). A high-meaningfulness approach might teach the students to multiply 43×5 by multiplying 3×5, then 40×5, which would maintain the place value of the 3 and the 40:

$$\begin{array}{r} 43 \\ \times 5 \\ \hline 15 \\ 200 \\ \hline 215 \end{array}$$

In contrast, a low-meaningfulness approach might follow the more-traditional algorithm of multiplying 3 × 5 and carrying the one:

$$\begin{array}{r} 1 \\ 43 \\ \times 5 \\ \hline 215 \end{array}$$

this latter method is computationally quicker for adults, it may be more difficult for educationally high-risk students to learn and possibly no faster for them to use. A study comparing these two methods (Paine, Falco, and Carnine 1979) found that the low-meaningfulness (or traditional) approach required significantly more trials for students to reach the training criterion; and even with the extra training, those students did not show higher maintenance scores.

Interference and Memory

The Direct Instruction design procedures associated with interference and memory are to sequence examples to reduce confusion and to provide adequate practice and review of critical discriminations as related sets of concepts are expanded. The two procedures are presented together because of the way they interrelate. If confusions are not minimized, extensive practice can be detrimental. Similarly, if confusions are minimized yet practice is minimal, learning and retention will be poor. Potentially confusing elements can be identified through descriptive studies. For example, Carnine and Carnine (in press) measured the relative decoding difficulty for begining readers of various word types, and Carnine (1978b) did the same for various letter-sound correspondences. Once the potential confusion of a set of elements has been identified, an order of introduction that separates similar elements can be established to minimize confusion errors. For example, Carnine (1976d) compared a similar separated sequence for the similar letter-sound correspondences *e* and *i* (*e, c, m, u, s, i*) with a similar-together sequence (*e, i, u, c, m, s*). First graders made fewer errors (33 percent versus 51 percent), and preschoolers reached criterion in fewer trials (178 versus 293) when similar letters were separated from each other in the order of introduction.

In another study (Carnine 1977f), the guidelines of separating similar stimuli were investigated in a visual-discrimination task. Preschoolers who received a similar-separated sequence reached criterion on a later letter-matching task in significantly fewer trials than preschoolers in a similar-together treatment: a mean of thirty-one versus sixty-nine trials. Moreover, Carnine (1977b) found that when a new member is added to a previously taught set that contains a similar member, the learner should not be required to label the new member in a discrimination task involving just those two members. Rather, the new member should first be discriminated from less-similar members, or initial discrimination training on the two similar members should call for yes/no rather than labeling responses. Students required to discriminate the two similar members by labeling them required thirty trials to reach criterion. Three other treatments that separated the similar members resulted in an average of about fifteen trials each.

Procedures for adequate practice involve the principles of spaced presentation and cumulative introduction. In a spaced presentation, examples of a new concept are separated from each other by examples of familiar concepts. Kryzanowski and Carnine (1978) compared a spaced presentation with a massed presentation in which examples of the new concept were clustered. They taught two relatively new, difficult correspondences (*i* and *e*) to preschoolers. For one group, *e* was massed and *i* was spaced. In the other group, *i* was massed and *e* was spaced. Since students could repeat the same answer to several examples in the massed group, training errors were fewer for the massed group (mean = 56 percent versus 73 percent). However, in the posttest, examples appeared randomly. Since the massed group received less discrimination practice during training, they tended to make more errors on the posttest (mean = 72 percent versus 38 percent).

The second procedure for providing practice is cumulative introduction—that is, a discrimination is introduced and practiced until it is mastered (in the context of previously introduced, related discriminations) before a new discrimination is introduced. A set is built cumulatively. Carnine (1976d) reported that preschoolers mastered six letter-sound correspondences in fewer trials when the letters were introduced cumulatively rather than simultaneously. Preschoolers in the cumulative group required an average of 178 trials, whereas the simultaneous group required 261 trials. The learning rate was not only faster for the cumulative group but also retention was better—an average of 84 percent correct for the cumulative group on a posttest in contrast to 66 percent for the simultaneous group. A similar study was conducted with addition facts rather than letter-sound correspondences (Carnine 1978c). Preschoolers in the cumulative group required 197 trials on the average, whereas preschoolers in the simultaneous group required an average of 342 trials. Posttest differences were not significant. Another study on cumulative introduction (Fink and Bryce, in press) involved training of moderately and severely handicapped preschoolers on a word-matching task. The cumulative group reached criterion in an average of 173 trials, whereas a successive-pairs treatment took 208 trials. Posttest differences were also significant: 90 percent versus 48 percent. Positive results from cumulative programming have also been reported by Cheyne (1966), Gruenenfelder and Borokowski (1975), and Ferster and Hammer (1966).

Readiness

Although readiness is usually treated as a developmental concept, we consider it to be a state of preparedness for complex learning. The preparedness can result from instruction on component skills of the complex-learning task. (Readiness can also occur through incidental learning or maturation, but these topics are not central to Direct Instruction). Instruction in multiplication can serve as an example of developing readiness by preteaching the component skills of a complex task. Carnine (1977c) found that primary-grade children who were pretaught the component skills of the single-digit-multiplication operation required less training time (a mean of 105 versus 137 minutes) and had higher transfer scores (an average of 81 percent versus 61 percent correct) than students who learned the component skills as part of the operation at the same time.

Although identification and teaching of component skills can result in more-rapid learning of complex tasks, research shows that some such preteaching is not necessary while in other cases the need for preteaching is overlooked. For example, visual-discrimination training, in part involving letter-matching tasks, is usually a recommended activity for early reading instruction. After students can discriminate letter forms, they will supposedly be better prepared to learn the alphabet or letter sounds. Zoref and Carnine (1979) found that sound-symbol-correspondence training alone was more effective than visual-discrimination training followed by sound-symbol-correspondence training. Two groups of preschoolers received seventeen training sessions on nine letter-sound correspondences. The visual-discrimination group received match-to-sample training for one day on each letter and then two days on each letter-sound correspondence. The other group began letter-sound-correspondence training on the first session and received three training sessions on each correspondence. Each child was tested individually after the last training session for each letter. Students who received visual-discrimination training made significantly more errors (2.2 versus .2), indicating that the time might be better spent on letter-sound-correspondence training.

In other cases, research suggests that preteaching is unnecessary. For example, Goodman (1965) emphasizes the importance of reading for meaning—that reading is the application of language. More specifically, he discusses how students apply their knowledge of semantics and syntax when reading. Students would not read the sentence, *Dan put an apple in the bag* as "Dan put an apple in the bug" because they know that people do not put apples in bugs. The often overlooked assumption in the emphasis on reading for meaning is that students, in fact, have the language skills needed to assist them in their reading. Keith, Carnine, and Maggs (1979) compared good and poor beginning readers in their application of language skills to reading. A greater percentage of decoding errors that rendered sentences meaningless revealed an inadequate application of language skills on the part of the poor readers (mean = 40 percent versus 13 percent). In addition, their relative inability to recognize orally presented meaningless sentences (with manipulated semantics or syntax) indicated that they lacked some of the language skills they are expected to apply when reading (mean = 20 versus 16.3). In other words, the application of language to print (reading for meaning) will not be possible if students do not have the language skills to apply. Preteaching oral-language skills may be necessary for some students to develop readiness so that they can apply language skills while reading.

Cognitive Structures

Cognitive structures might be thought of as ways of organizing information (Anderson 1977) or strategies for solving problems. We restrict our discussion to strategies students can learn to apply to a wide range of related problems. For example, in beginning reading, the reading-for-meaning strategy just discussed can be compared to a decoding strategy where the learner is taught to say a sound for each letter, to blend the sounds in a word, and then to identify the word. Carnine (1977a) compared this sound strategy with a whole-word strategy used in "meaning approaches." Preschoolers in both groups responded to a list of eighteen training words until they identified them all correctly. (The sounds group was first taught the sounds for the letters that appeared in the training words and how to blend them.) Training time was comparable for both groups, but the sounds group correctly read more transfer words (mean = 8 versus 4.7 for regular words and mean = .6 versus 0 for irregular words).

Direct Instruction strategies for a variety of cognitive tasks have been studied—for example, sequencing and literal comprehension; subtraction; comprehension of complex syntactic structures; rule applications involving protein's passage along a food ladder; the reading of words with vowel-consonant-final-*e* patterns; and the use of context cues to determine the meaning of unknown words, fractions, and column multiplication. In each study, a Direct Instruction strategy that makes explicit a set of problem-solving steps is compared with a conventional instructional procedure. Some of the strategies are quite obvious. For example, to use context cues, students are taught to scan the surrounding text to determine the meaning of an unknown word. For subtraction, students draw the number of lines indicated by the first numeral, cross out the number of lines specified by the second numeral, and then make the sides equal by writing the answer—for example, 6 − 2 = 4.

Although these strategies are relatively simple, they are not directly taught in most commercial programs. For simple subtraction, students are taught to look at pictures representing subtraction or to use manipulatives to solve problems. However, they are not taught a strategy to use when the manipulatives are taken away. When this happens, higher-performing students intuitively know to use lines or fingers until them memorize their subtraction facts; many other students do not make the transfer and become frustrated and discouraged. Stein and Carnine (1979) compared a Direct Instruction strategy with a strategy from a widely used basal program. They found that students taught the Direct Instruction subtraction strategy worked significantly more problems on delayed tests taken from the basal program that was used with the comparison group (mean = 92 percent versus 47 percent on the last training-day test; 89 percent versus 73 percent on the five-day unit test; and 55 percent versus 18 percent on the one-week cumulative test).

Other Direct Instruction strategies are less obvious. For dealing with sentences containing a clause, students are taught to generate two simple, equivalent sentences. For example, a student reads "John, who ran two miles with Mary, was tired and sore the next day" and then mistakenly answers "Mary" to the question: Who got tired and sore? To avoid such errors, students would be taught to translate the complex sentence into two simpler sentences: the word before *who* would appear in both sentences. The two single sentences for this example would be "John ran two miles" and "John was tired and sore the next day." Kameenui, Carnine, and Maggs (1979) evaluated this strategy by comparing it with a practice-only treatment in a multiple-baseline design. Subjects were students who performed at a chance level on comprehension questions about complex sentences. All three students were presented the same items each session; strategy training was introduced to one student at a time. Percentage correct increased dramatically for each student after training commenced (44 percent versus 90 percent for student 1; 38 percent versus 85 percent for student 2; and 44 percent versus 91 percent for student 3).

Another example of a more-complex strategy involves drawing inferences based on rules (Kameenui, Carnine, and Ludlow 1978). Rules are taught in three stages of decreasing structure: rule repetition, simple applications, and complex applications. For the rule, "The lower you eat on a food ladder, the more protein goes directly to you,'' the learner first repeats the rule to ensure information retention. The simple applications follow the wording of the rule: ''A pound of beans is lower on the food ladder than a pound of hamburger. Which food gives more protein directly to you?'' The students indicate that beans would provide more direct protein. Complex applications do not use the words from the rule—that is, the item would not state that beans are lower on the food ladder. The student must use the information in the application item to draw an inference about whether beans are lower on the food ladder and then draw a second inference that beans provide more direct protein than hamburgers. (If students are to perform on complex applications, they must have previously learned key concepts from the rule—that is, food ladder.) The teacher asks, ''Which food gives more protein directly to you, peanuts or fried chicken?'' The student answers, ''Peanuts.'' The teacher asks, ''How do you know?,'' and the learner answers, ''Peanuts are lower on the food ladder.'' The last question tests whether the learner applied the rule in arriving at an answer.

One important aspect of strategies that we have not yet discussed is the transition from teacher-structured presentations to independent student application. We refer to this transition as a ''covertization'' process. The steps made overt by the teacher become covertized when the students apply them on their own. The covertization process can be described in four steps. For column multiplication, the first step would be structured board presentations. The teacher would write a problem on the board, demonstrate the steps, and then present additional problems about which students are asked questions. The second step might be a structured worksheet presentation. Rather than the teacher writing each part of the problem, the students are required to do this as the teacher asks questions. Third is the less-structured step. Students continue to write each part of the problem, but the teacher provides less structure by asking fewer and more-inclusive questions. Finally, the strategy is fully covertized; the students apply the strategy independently.

Paine and Carnine (1979) found that some students' performance on independent work did not improve until the steps in the covertization process were carried out. These students were provided with a highly structured board presentation on multiplication each day. However, their independent performance did not improve until steps two and three were introduced (mean = 20.52 during structured board presentation versus 46.69 during structured worksheet and less-structured worksheet). These results were obtained with one-digit multiplicands; comparable results were found in a replication with the same students when two-digit multiplicands were used (mean = 29.50 versus 73.52). These findings suggest that a carefully designed strategy and demonstration are not necessarily sufficient. In addition, many students will need to be guided through the covertization process.

Summary

The Direct Instruction programs are basically instructional systems, engineered to induce certain desired kinds of basic learning if the systems are implemented. The engineering is concerned with the fine details of each task presented to the student and with the transportability of program to new settings—with ease of training and fidelity of implementation in the field. The engineering is also concerned with efficiency in the use of time and tasks to accomplish important educational goals. In the section that follows we review some of the studies that provide evidence for the adequacy of our engineering strategies.

Evaluation Studies

The evaluation studies of Direct Instruction programs range from the national Follow Through Project for the disadvantaged to studies of learning-disabled and severely retarded children in Australia. We begin with an overview of the national evaluation of Follow Through, a six-year study of thirteen different approaches to teaching the economically disadvantaged in kindergarten through third grade.

Follow Through

In Follow Through, the developers of a variety of promising programs for teaching the disadvantaged in the primary grades (K–3) were invited to propose model programs. The models were to have an educational program at the core but also to include comprehensive services and maximum involvement of the communities being served. Follow Through came to serve 75,000 low-income children annually, from 170 communities, under the guidance of 20 model sponsors. Several of the models had their theoretical base in behavioral theory—especially the University of Kansas Behavior Analysis Model and the University of Oregon Direct Instruction Model. The national evaluation compared the performance of 13 model sponsors in the Cohort II Study and 16 model sponsors in the Cohort III Study.[2]

The basic data for the national evaluation were collected by the Stanford Research Institute and analyzed by Abt Associates Inc. The main reports of the evaluation were published by Abt Associates (1976; 1977).

A critique of the Abt reports was published by House et al. (1978) and rebutted by several groups in the same issue of *Harvard Educational Review* (we would be the first to join in many points of the critique). However, the major findings of the national evaluation of Follow Through summarized in the next section stand in spite of the critique (see also Bereiter and Kurland 1978).

The Educational Models

This summary is restricted to the nine major sponsors for whom at least eight control-group comparisons were made in the Abt study. These sponsor groups covered a broad range of educational philosophies, ranging from open education to carefully programmed models based on behavioral-analysis principles. Five of the major sponsors have programs oriented toward use of the unique motivations each individual brings to school. They derive their practices from the subjective theories of Piaget, Freud, and Dewey. They have in common (1) individualized approaches to instruction, (2) goals that focus upon the whole person, and (3) encouragement of child-initiated activities.

Open Education Model. Sponsored by the Education Development Center (EDC), this model is derived from the British Infant School revolution that focused upon building the child's responsibility for his own learning. Reading and writing are not taught directly but through stimulating a desire to communicate. Flexible schedules, child-directed choices, and a focus upon intense personal involvement characterize this model.

Tucson Early Education Model (TEEM). Sponsored by the University of Arizona, this model was developed by Marie Hughes and uses a language-experience approach. The teaching attempts to elaborate on the child's present experience and interest. A goal is to teach intellectual processes such as comparing, recalling, looking, and relating. The content itself is not so important. Researchers believe that children have different styles of learning that must be provided for. Child-directed choices are important to the model.

Cognitively Oriented Curriculum. Sponsored by the High/Scope Educational Research Foundation and directed by David Weikart, this model builds on Piagetian concern with underlying cognitive processes that allow one to learn on one's own. As in the aforementioned models, the children are encouraged to schedule their own activities, develop plans, choose whom to work with, and so forth. The teacher fosters the development of a positive self-concept by the way the student is provided choices. The teacher demonstrates language by the use of language in labeling what is going on, making interpretations, and explaining causes. The schedule for the cognitive-curriculum model places greater emphasis than the other models on the student's working out a sequence of events for the day and then following that sequence.

Responsive Education Model. Sponsored by the Far West Laboratory and originated by Glenn Nimnict (who left the program in 1971), this model is eclectic, drawing on a variety of source including O.K. Moore's "talking typewriter" and materials and procedures developed by Maria Montessori and Martin Deutsch. The model operates through learning centers that concentrate on a variety of contents. The child's own interest determines where and when he works. The goal is to build an environment that is responsive to the child and that will thereby teach. Researchers feel that the development of self-esteem is essential to the acquisition of academic skills.

Bank Street College Model. The Bank Street College of Education has long advocated the early-childhood-education philosophy adopted by Head Start that underlies traditional middle-class nursery schools. The model incorporates strands of philosophy from Dewey, Piaget, and Freud. The goal is to help children to become confident, inventive, responsive, and productive human beings. The program begins with a language-experience approach to reading. Many options for learning are provided in the classroom, such as blocks, games, counting materials, painting tables, quiet areas, and comfortable chairs for reading. The major responsibility for program implementation rests with the teacher, who must be able to take advantage of learning situations as they arise and to structure the classroom to increase the opportunities for learning experiences.

In contrast to these five models that are oriented to the individual's unique motivation are two models oriented directly to student-skill development. These models have their theoretical base in the objective principles of behavioral analysis as developed by B.F. Skinner. Their concern is with procedures that will work and will provide skill-deficient children with the skills they will need to get the most out of schooling and life. The Direct Instruction model has already been discussed.

Behavior Analysis Model. Sponsored by the University of Kansas and developed under the direction of the behavioral sociologist, Donald Bushell, the model focuses on the systematic and precise use of positive reinforcement to enduce mastery in reading, arithmetic, handwriting, and spelling. Social praise and tokens, which can be traded for desired activities, are explicitly used. A technology of teaching is used to sequence and present tasks in small steps, where successful performance can occur and be reinforced. Procedures for carefully monitoring the progress of the students are followed so that corrective actions can be taken before the children fall too far behind in their progress through the program. Training and supervision strategies are also carefully derived from an objective behavioral technology.

The remaining two models have some common features with the two previous major groupings, yet they stand apart.

Florida Parent Education Model. Sponsored by the University of Florida, this model is based on the work of Ira Gordon (1969) who demonstrated lasting effects of instructing parents of disadvantaged children how to teach their children. While the model professes philosophical allegiance to Piaget, it differs radically from those previously discussed. The classroom programs of the children remain as they were. Parent educators spend part of their time in the classroom getting to know the children and part of the their time working with parents. The parent educators train parents to teach a variety of tasks that focus upon language development and provide for cognitive, affective, and psychomotor-skill instruction.

Language Development (Bilingual) Model. This model is sponsored by the Southwest Educational Development Laboratory (SEDL). Like the behavioral models, the SEDL model is curriculum oriented and has built systematic programs in English and Spanish. However, the theoretical background is clearly not behavioral but eclectic. The primary concentration of the model is on language development. Where appropriate, language material is first presented orally in Spanish and then in printed form for reading. Later, similar materials are covered in English.

Method

The major sponsors were evaluated in four to eight sites with kindergartens. A smaller sample of first-grade starting sites was included where available. The children were tested at entry and each spring until the third grade was completed. In each site (school district) that implemented a Follow Through model, a non-Follow Through comparison group was identified. Each site was analyzed separately against its control group. The analytic sample included a total of 9,255 Follow Through children and 6,485 non-Follow Through children. Major sponsors represented 111 of the 139 sites studied.

One problem with the study was that the non-Follow Through children were often less disadvantaged (economically) than the Follow Through children. For this reason, covariant analysis was used to adjust outcomes for initial differences. As Campbell and Erlebacher (1970) point out, the covariant adjustment will underestimate the effects for the initially lower group.

Another problem with the study was that the outcomes confounded model adequacy with implementation adequacy. No provision was made in the analysis for evaluating model implementation at each site. The failure to examine implementation of control groups also poses a problem. In many sites, special programs were being used for the control groups, and occasionally they were effective.

Tests. The test battery included the Elementary Level, Form F, of the Metropolitan Achievement Test (MAT) (1970), Raven's Coloured Progressive Matrices (1956), the Coopersmith Self-Esteem Inventory (1967), and the Intellectual Achievement Responsibility Scale (IARS + and IARS −) (Crandall, Katkowsky, and Crandall 1965). The Coopersmith was designed to assess children's feelings about themselves, about the way they think other people feel about them, and about school. The IARS measures the extent to which children attribute their success (+) or failures (−) to themselves or to outside forces.

The Children. The Direct Instruction Model has provided services to students from low-income homes in ten communities. Our communities included a cross section of poor America—rural and inner-city blacks, rural whites, Mexican-Americans in Texas, Spanish-Americans in New Mexico, native-Americans in South Dakota and North Carolina, and a variety of ethnically mixed communities. Approximately 8,000 low-income students were in the program at one time. More than 27,000 names have entered our computer file. Other sponsors have usually served a similar range of communities.

Results: Significant Outcomes

The major findings of the Abt report are given in a series of tables, one for each sponsor. For each variable, a covariance-adjusted comparison was made with a local comparison group and with a pooled national comparison group. When Follow Through exceeded non–Follow Through by at least one-fourth standard deviation on a given variable and when the difference was statistically significant, this was considered an educationally significant outcome and a plus (+) was placed in the table. When non–Follow Through exceeded Follow Through by the same criteria, this was considered to be a significant negative outcome and a minus (−) was placed in the table. When the results were in between these limits, the difference was considered null and the table left blank. At the third-grade level, the one-fourth-standard-deviation criterion corresponds to about two-months difference in grade-norm terms.

To summarize model effects in table 4–1, the number of pluses for a

Table 4–1
Index of Significant Outcomes

Models	*Number of Sites*	*Word Knowledge*	*Spelling*	*Math Computation*	*Language*	*Reading*	*Math Concepts*	*Math Problem Solving*	*Coopersmith Self-Esteem*	*IARS+*	*IARS−*
Direct Instruction	16	+065	−065	+656	+562	+219	+312	+479	+156	+188	+188
Southwest Lab	8	−250	000	+250	+062	+062	+250	+062	+231	−077	+231
Parent Education	12	+125	−042	−167	+042	000	−083	000	+042	+125	+125
Behavior Analysis	13	−038	−269	−115	+385	−094	−188	−156	+188	000	000
Bank Street	12	−208	−500	000	−125	+042	−167	−083	−056	−056	−111
TEEM (Arizona)	15	−367	−500	−200	+033	−300	−333	−167	−031	−094	−188
Responsive Education	16	−250	−406	−188	−062	−154	−077	−115	+042	−083	−125
Open Education (EDC)	10	−300	−400	−250	−300	−400	−300	−300	000	−250	−250
Cognitive Curriculum	9	−389	−333	−500	−222	−222	−389	−222	−167	−267	−233

given sponsor on a given measure is counted, then the number of minuses is subtracted, and the result is divided by the number of comparisons. Both local and pooled comparisons are included. To eliminate decimals, we have multiplied by 1,000. For a given effect, if a sponsor is more positive than negative, the index is positive. If the average effect is more negative than positive, the index is negative.

In other reports (Becker 1978; Becker and Carnine 1978; Becker and Engelmann, forthcoming), we have presented the Abt summary results and with different data-inclusion rules. Since all the methods of analysis produce the same conclusion, we have presented here indexes based on all the data in the Abt analyses, except that results for the Raven's Progressive Matrices are excluded because the Raven's is not an academic measure.

The sponsors are ordered in table 4-1 according to overall rank on the outcomes index. The first four programs are the only programs with more positive than negative outcomes on some measures. Direct Instruction is the only model to show the most consistently positive outcomes across measures. The more-open-ended, child-centered programs show consistently negative outcomes.

Results: Normative Performance

The Abt reports provide median grade-equivalent scores by site and by sponsor for four MAT measures: Total Reading, Total Math, Spelling, and Language. The means for these data by model (converted to percentiles) are presented in figures 4-2 through 4-5. The tables display percentiles on a one-fourth-standard-deviation scale. With this display, differences between sponsors of one-fourth standard deviation or more are easily detected and a norm reference is provided. The 20th percentile, which represents the average expectation for disadvantaged children without special help, was chosen for a baseline in drawing the graphs in the figures.[3]

The Direct Instruction Model is clearly the highest in normative performance and is close to or at national norms on all measures. Four sponsors have reading programs that are making some headway toward average reading performance by the end of third grade (Direct Instruction, Behavior Analysis, Bank Street College, and Responsive Education). On Total Math, Direct Instruction is at least one-half standard deviation ahead of the others. On Spelling, the Behavior Analysis program is the only program other than Direct Instruction approaching national norms. On Language (usage, punctuation, and sentence types), the Direct Instruction program is three-fourths of a standard deviation ahead of all other programs.

The normative-performance data add much to the interpretation of the statistical comparisons. The Direct Instruction program is apparently able

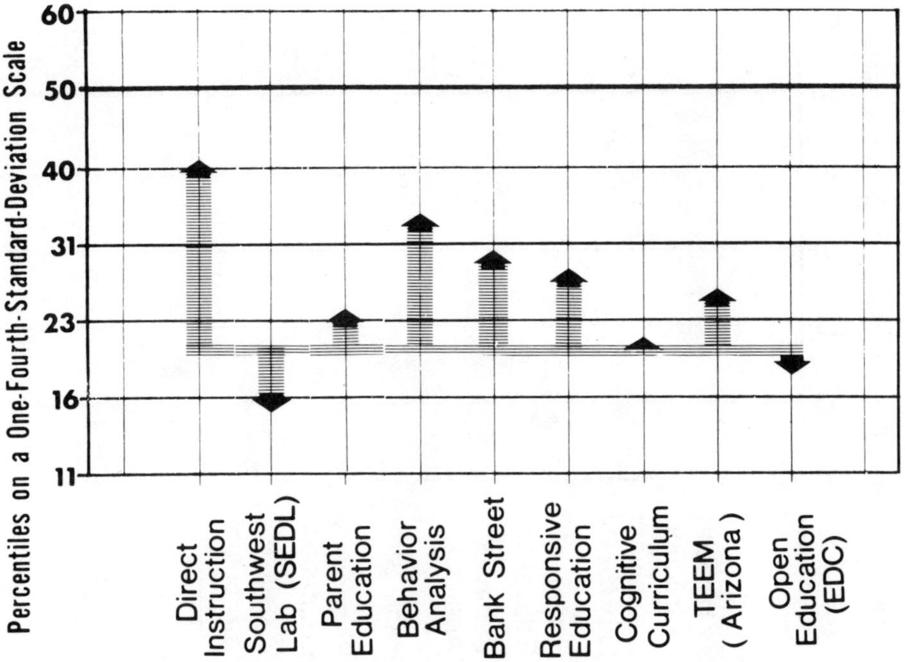

	Direct Instruction	Southwest Lab (SEDL)	Parent Education	Behavior Analysis	Bank Street	Responsive Education	Cognitive Curriculum	TEEM (Arizona)	Open Education (EDC)
%-tile	41	15	24	34	30	28	21	26	18
S. S.	58.3	49.6	52.8	55.8	55.1	53.8	51.5	53.7	50.6
G. E.	3.23	2.43	2.68	2.98	2.91	2.78	2.55	2.77	2.48

Grade equivalent for 50th percentile is 3.5

Figure 4–2. MAT Total Reading

to make effective use of teaching time in most areas of skill development so as to show a superior outcome nearly across the board.

Results: Sponsor-Collected Data

Detailed findings from the sponsor-collected data are presented by Becker and Engelmann (1978). We have attempted to test every child in the Direct Instruction program at entry, from 1969 to 1973, and each spring thereafter through third grade. Financial cutbacks led us to omit second-grade testing in one year. From 1969 until 1971, all children were tested with the Wide

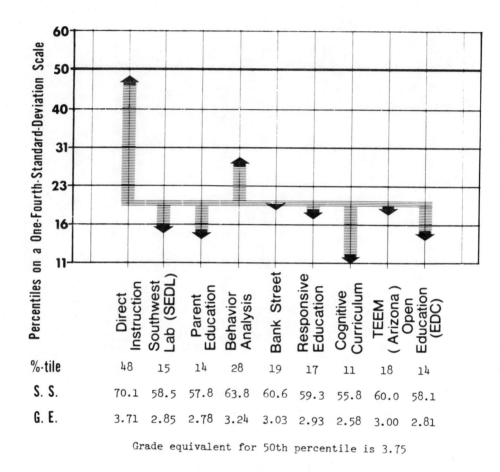

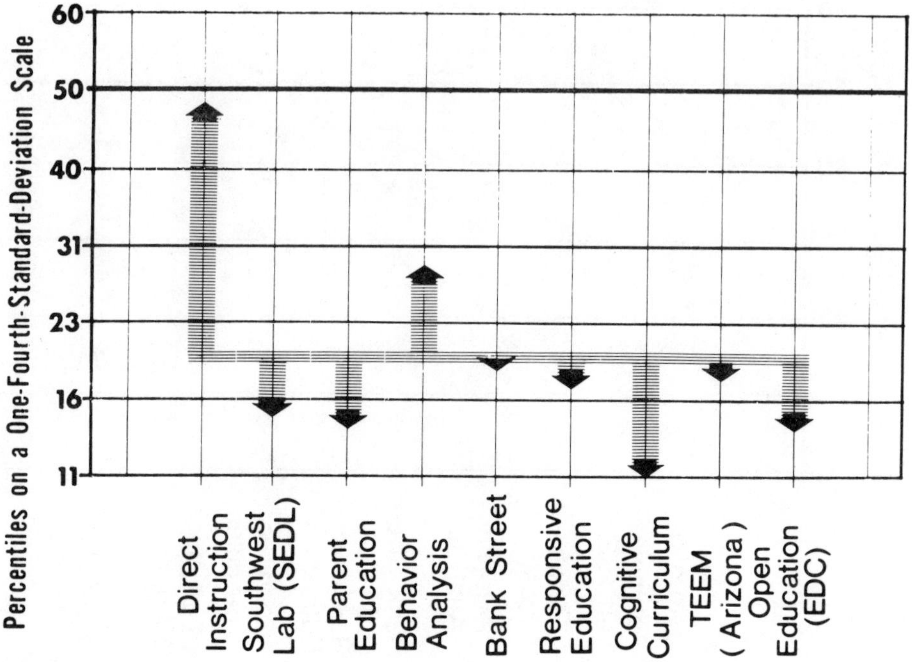

%-tile	48	15	14	28	19	17	11	18	14
S. S.	70.1	58.5	57.8	63.8	60.6	59.3	55.8	60.0	58.1
G. E.	3.71	2.85	2.78	3.24	3.03	2.93	2.58	3.00	2.81

Grade equivalent for 50th percentile is 3.75

Figure 4–3. MAT Total Math

Range Achievement Test (WRAT) and the Slossen Intelligence Test (SIT). The SIT was used to measure general language competence. Beginnig in 1972, the MAT was used at the end of first, second, and third grades.

Norm-Referenced Gains. Figure 4–6 shows the sponsor-collected norm-referenced data on low-income children from thirteen kindergarten sites for six entry years. Students are included in this analysis if they met the OEO (Office of Economic Opportunity) poverty guideline (low income), if they started the program at its earliest grade level, and if tests are available at more than one point in time. The MAT results from this broader sample of sites and entry years are nearly identical to those found in the national eval-

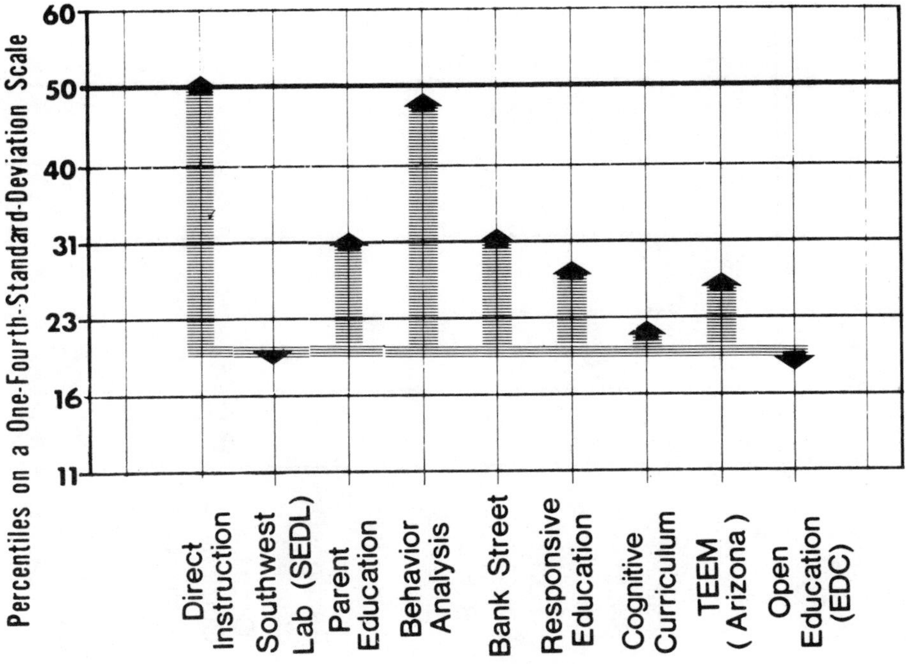

	Direct Instruction	Southwest Lab (SEDL)	Parent Education	Behavior Analysis	Bank Street	Responsive Education	Cognitive Curriculum	TEEM (Arizona)	Open Education (EDC)
%-tile	51	19	32	49	32	28	22	27	18
S. S.	64.3	52.6	58.0	63.6	58.0	56.6	54.1	56.4	51.8
G. E.	3.63	2.53	2.95	3.56	2.95	2.86	2.61	2.84	2.48

Grade equivalent for 50th percentile is 3.6

Figure 4-4. MAT Spelling

uation. The WRAT results in Arithmetic and Spelling confirm those from the MAT. In all cases but MAT Reading, where they place at the 40th percentile, our students are performing at the national average. On WRAT Reading, the Direct Instruction students perform at the 82nd percentile, a full standard deviation above the national norm. WRAT Reading measures decoding skills, while MAT Reading measures comprehension skills. This difference in performance levels is to be expected, given the tasks to be taught and the children being taught. (This issue is discussed in more detail in the implications section.)

Other Findings. Sponsor-collected findings (Becker and Engelmann 1978) also support these conclusions:

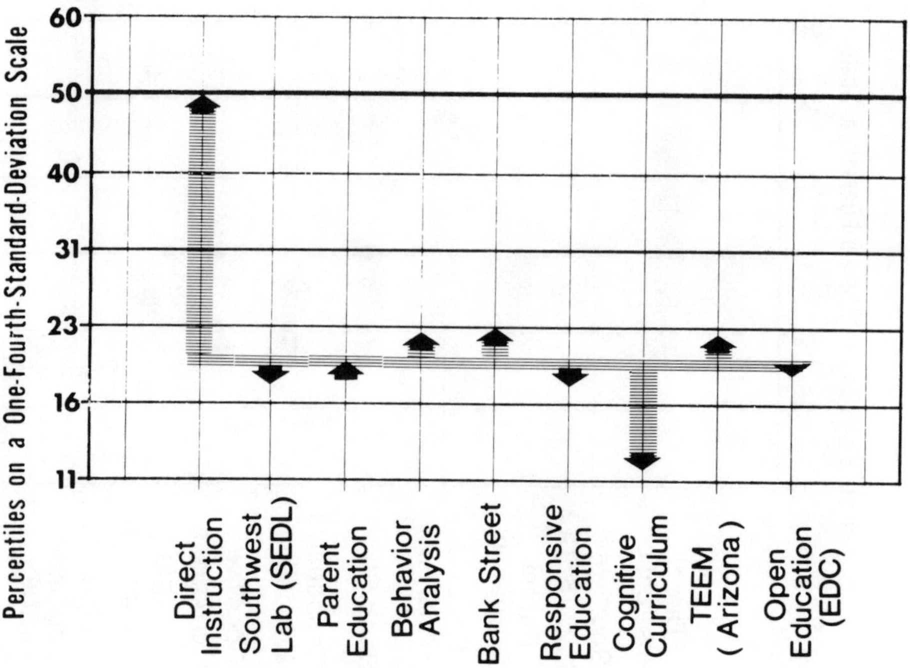

%-tile	50	18	20	22	23	18	12	22	19
S. S.	70.0	56.0	57.2	58.0	58.6	56.1	54.1	58.5	56.6
G. E.	4.00	2.60	2.72	2.80	2.86	2.61	2.41	2.85	2.66

Grade equivalent for 50th percentile is 4.0

Figure 4-5. MAT Language

There is a measurable and educationally significant benefit present at the end of third grade for those who began Direct Instruction in kindergarten as opposed to first grade.

Significant gains in IQ are found that are largely maintained through third grade. These average seven points for all K-starting children and eighteen points for those starting with IQ under 80 (regression adjusted).

Follow-up studies at fifth and sixth grade show significantly better performance by Direct Instruction Follow Through children than by comparison groups. These findings exist in spite of evidence that the schools

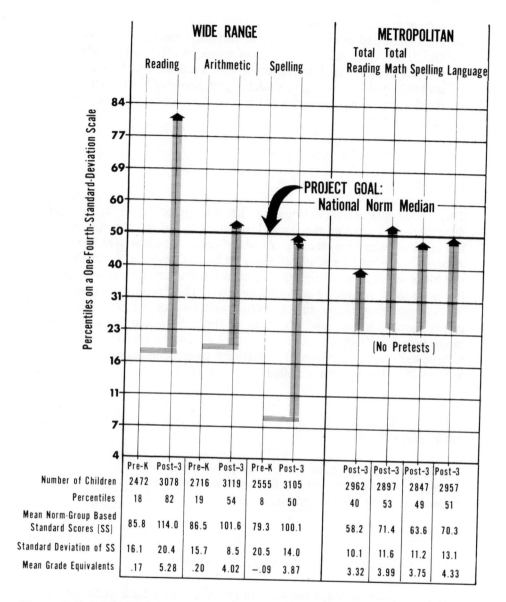

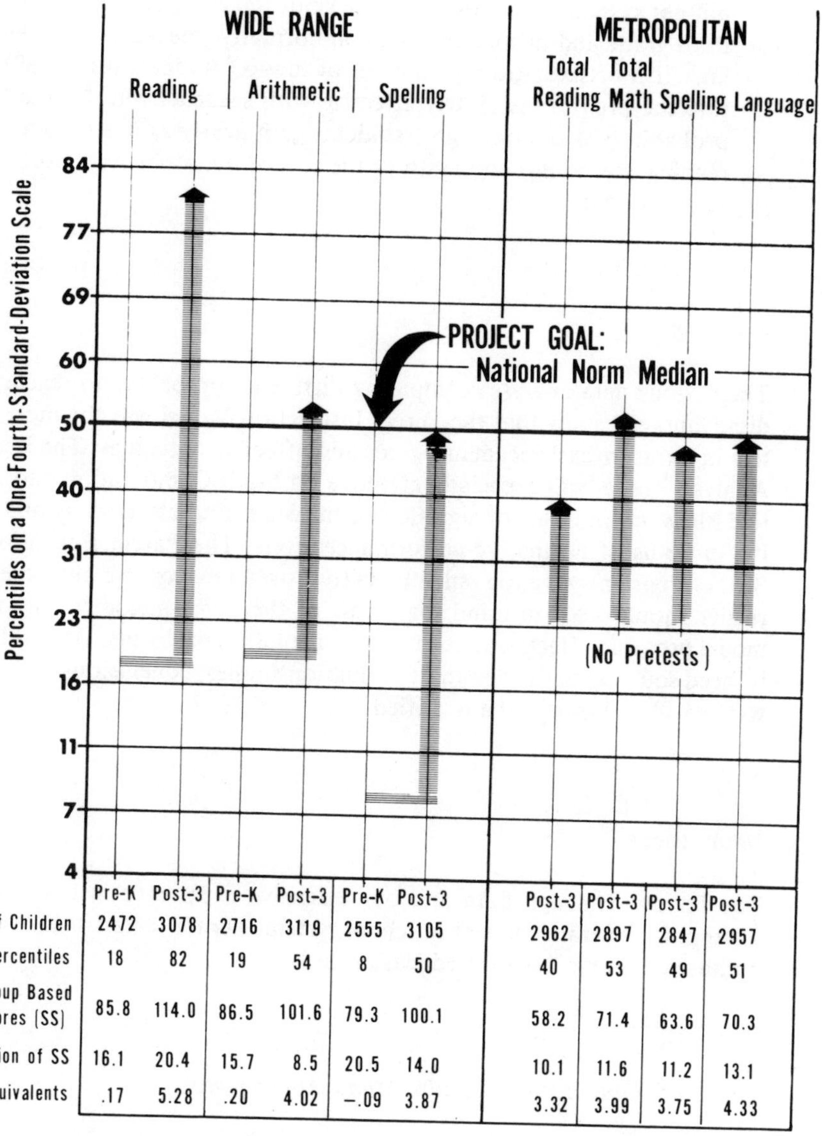

	Pre-K	Post-3	Pre-K	Post-3	Pre-K	Post-3	Post-3	Post-3	Post-3	Post-3
Number of Children	2472	3078	2716	3119	2555	3105	2962	2897	2847	2957
Percentiles	18	82	19	54	8	50	40	53	49	51
Mean Norm-Group Based Standard Scores (SS)	85.8	114.0	86.5	101.6	79.3	100.1	58.2	71.4	63.6	70.3
Standard Deviation of SS	16.1	20.4	15.7	8.5	20.5	14.0	10.1	11.6	11.2	13.1
Mean Grade Equivalents	.17	5.28	.20	4.02	–.09	3.87	3.32	3.99	3.75	4.33

Figure 4–6. Norm-Referenced Gains on the Wide-Range (Pre-K to Post-3) and Post-3 Performance on the Metropolitan for K-Starting, Low-Income, E-B Model Follow Through Students

did not systematically build on the skills the children had at the end of third grade and in spite of losses on normative measures between third and fifth or sixth grades.[4] Studies of low-IQ students (under 80) show that the program is clearly effective with students who have a higher probability of failure. These students gain nearly as much each year in reading (decoding) and math as the rest of our students—more than a year per year.

Summary

The various data analyses comparing different approaches to teaching the disadvantaged show that the Direct Instruction Model was the most effective in terms of basic academic goals and affective outcomes. The Behavior Analysis Model was especially effective on Math Computation and Affective Measures in terms of significance measures and on Reading and Spelling in terms of normative-performance levels. The Parent Education and SEDL programs were the only others to show a few positive outcomes. The reader should keep in mind that some of the poor outcomes may not be model program effects but due to implementation problems. Until this issue is faced squarely in the design of evaluation studies, conclusions about what works will continue to be qualified.

Implications

The Follow Through data and our extensive experience in the field that attempt to generate changes in school systems permit tentative answers to a number of major issues in education today.

Does Individualization Require Many Approaches?

The programs that failed the most in terms of educational achievements were those oriented to individual needs in instruction. The popular belief that it is necessary to teach different students in different ways is, for the most part, fiction. The requirements for sequencing an instructional program are determined by what is to be taught, not who. In the DISTAR programs used by the Direct Instruction Model, each child faces the same sequence of tasks and the same teaching strategies. What is individualized is entry level, when corrections are used, reinforcement procedures, and number of practice trials to mastery.

Is Self-Directed Learning Best?

A common assumption arising from dominant subjective educational philosophies is that self-directed learning is the only meaningful learning. Direct attempts to teach are said to produce isolate rote learning, not meaningful learning. The Follow Through results obviously demonstrate that such an assumption is false. The student who performed best on all measures of higher cognitive processes were taught by the Direct Instruction Model. The assumption about the value of self-directed learning probably arises from observing young children (as Piaget did) interacting with the physical environment. The physical environment will directly reinforce and punish different responses. The child does learn, without directed teaching, how to get around without bumping things and falling—and how to get to reinforcers. However, a child cannot learn the arbitrary conventions of a language system without learning from someone who provides systematic teaching (including modeling of appropriate language usage). In addition, there is no question that intelligent adults can organize experiences and their sequence that will teach concepts and problem-solving skills better than children can.

Does Curriculum Make a Difference?

The Kansas Behavioral Analysis Model and the Oregon Direct Instruction Model both relied upon behavioral principles. In fact, we trained our first group of teachers together at Lawrence, Kansas in summer 1968. The models differed in choice of curricula. Engelmann designed new curricula for the Direct Instructional Model (DISTAR), whereas Bushell adopted available curricula (McGraw-Hill Sullivan Reading, Singer Math, SRA Reading Labs), except for a phonics preprogram, modeled after the DISTAR phonic program and a writing program devised by the Kansas group. The mode of instruction also differed, with the Direct Instruction Model emphasizing more small-group verbal instruction. The Direct Instruction Model did better on all significant comparisons, but especially on cognitive skills. On grade-norm data, the Kansas program was comparable to Direct Instruction on Spelling, was close on Total Reading, but fell behind on Math and Language. These differences suggest a superiority of the DISTAR programming strategies but also may be due to the additional verbal practice provided by the small-group method.

Why Is Improvement in Reading Comprehension Hard to Achieve?

The Abt report (1977) notes that successful outcomes were harder to come by in reading comprehension than in other skill areas. Only the Direct Instruction program made significant and sustained gains (over grades K-3) in this area. Even then, we only reached the 40th percentile on MAT Reading. Becker (1977) has previously analyzed the Follow Through data and other data on reading and concluded that schools are not currently designed to teach the English language to "poor kids" (for example, to children whose parents, on the average, are less well versed in knowledge of standard English). Schools are basically designed for white middle-class children and leave largely to parents the teaching of a most basic building block for intelligent behavior—namely, words and their referents.

In brief, the major arguments for this conclusion are (1) that empirical facts show that other skills can be readily taught and that reading comprehension is high as long as vocabulary is controlled, but drops rapidly at the end of third-grade tests that move to an uncontrolled adult vocabulary and (2) that our logical analysis reveals the massive requirements for effective instruction in word forms, word meanings, and usage. Vocabulary instruction to achieve an average-adult competency is a major task that involves at least 7,000 basic words with twice as many meanings, an additional 15,000 related words, and about 1,000 proper nouns. Basic words (Dupuy 1974) are words that have a unique meaning in English and are not proper nouns, derivatives, inflections, compounds, archaic, foreign, or technical terms. They do not represent a teaching objective that can be accomplished by teaching some members of a set and getting generalization to the rest. Basic words, on the one hand, constitute what Becker and Engelmann (1976) have called a "linear additive set" that each member must be taught. Related words, on the other hand, can sometimes be taught as general cases by affixing basic words.

We are currently attempting to identify and define a basic adult vocabulary that will make possible the development of various programs to teach systematically language where the home does not provide adequate instruction (Dixon and Becker 1977). Our analysis has two major components. On the form side, we are attempting to identify the minimum set of morphographs contained in an average-adult vocabulary. Morphographs can be thought of roughly as roots and affixes. On the semantic side, we are attempting to identify a set of initial concepts (A) to be taught by demonstrations, which can be used to define a larger set of words (B). Then A and B would be used to define a larger set and so forth. The goals will be prescriptions for vocabulary growth by grade level based on an analysis of the language and instructional requirements—not just frequency in print. One can, for example, imagine a dictionary where higher-level words are always defined in terms of lower-level words. The system might also be used to control vocabulary usage in textbooks through computer analysis. Finally, the system could be used to develop systematic programs for the initial teaching of vocabulary and practice in its use. We see these developments as making possible systematic procedures for preventing skill-development failures for a high proportion of children who now become clinical referrals.

The Australian Studies

During the past eight years, Alex Maggs has carried out a series of studies with his colleagues on a wide range of problem learners in Australia (Maggs and Maggs, in press).

These studies involved the use of DISTAR, Corrective Reading, and Morphographic Spelling programs with children in regular classes, special classes, pull-out groups, and special schools at the elementary and junior-high levels. Retarded, migrant, aboriginal, learning disabled, and socially disadvantaged children have participated in these investigations. These findings demonstrate that the Direct Instruction programs were effective across settings and populations when independently evaluated against norm-referenced and criterion-referenced dependent measures.

The Maggs study found that Direct Instruction provided programs across such a wide range of skills that both the brightest children in regular classes could be extended, while the lowest children in the class could develop in the same programs.

Over a period of several years a research program (Maggs 1978) was carried out to establish the viability of Direct Instruction in the regular Australian classroom. Because children who failed in the regular classroom are routinely placed in special classes, the program was first tried in those special classes. Two teachers implemented the DISTAR Language, Reading, and Arithmetic programs with ten normal but severely learning-disabled children in two classes. Ages ranged from nine to thirteen years. A token economy was used where small toys could be traded for points earned. Results showed an average of fifteen month's gain in the ten weeks of instruction in all skill areas, which generalized to significantly higher scores on tests such as the Wechsler Intelligence Scale for Children (WISC) and Illinois Test of Psycholinguistic Abilities (ITPA) that were usually used to make the special-school placements.

The same program was then tried in a rural school where six children of normal intelligence, but with severe academic deficits and some with behavioral problems, were taken out of third- and fourth-grade classes and placed in a special class in the regular school. The children ranged from eight to ten years of age. There was one teacher for the six children. Again a token economy used small toys as reinforcers. The results replicated the dramatic improvement shown in the city unit where the children had been pulled out of their usual schools. In fact, the children in the special class at their regular school did significantly better on some of the results. Both groups had shown progress across all skill areas that were from three to eight times greater than would be expected from the average school child in the same period of time. The reaction of teachers to the findings were along the lines of, "That's amazing, but you had one teacher to every five or six children; I've got to cope with thirty-five to forty kids." The next step in their research project was to discover whether an intensive remediation program that normally required a high teacher-pupil ratio could be effectively integrated into the depleted resources of the regular classroom.

The research was carried out in a regular Australian third-grade classroom (Maggs 1978). As in most regular classes there was little homogeneity. The children were aged from seven to nine years with WISC IQs ranging from borderline defective to very superior and with basic skill differences covering a span of six years. The class of thirty-five children had one teacher with no aide, no parental help, and no other help. The children were placed in three groups: severe, mild, and no skill deficits. All three groups were put on appropriate levels of the DISTAR programs.

A token economy (points traded for a few sweets) was used to allow the teacher to take different groups of from ten to twelve children while teaching the rest of the class to work productively on their own. The program worked very effectively. The token economy maintained excellent work and good behavior from those children not working with the teacher. Statistical treatment of the data showed (in complete contrast to usual findings) that each of the three groups showed dramatically improved skills at the year's end, with no significant difference in the rate of learning among the three groups.

The potential of the Direct Instruction Model for teaching moderately to severely retarded children was first researched by Maggs in 1972. The significance of the findings was seen in the results two years later (Maggs and Morath 1976a). Twenty-eight institutionalized moderately to severely retarded children, most with Binet IQs in the 20s to low 30s, aged from 6 to 14 years, were randomly assigned to the experimental and control groups. The experimental groups were given intensive direct verbal instruction in language using the DISTAR Language I program and behavioral teaching techniques for one hour per school day over the two-year period. The control groups continued lessons with the classes' standard curricula (for example, Peabody Language Kit and related materials). They had less-intensive language programs, and their teachers did not apply systematic behavioral teaching techniques.

The results indicated that the experimental group could demonstrate knowledge of a significantly higher number of concepts than the control group on posttesting. They also showed significantly greater improvement in verbal comprehension. The Piaget-Bruner tests were included to answer two questions: (1) Were these children simply rote learning verbal concepts, or could they apply their newly learned skills and principles to different conceptual situations? (2) Would concepts learned purely by verbal instruction transfer to a nonverbal situation in which the concepts had to be demonstrated by manipulating concrete objects?

The results showed a significantly better posttest performance by the experimental subjects, indicating that their skill went beyond mere rote learning and that concepts taught verbally, with only two-dimensional visual material, could be applied readily to three-dimensional concrete objects. Most significantly, while retardation and normality are discriminated by IQ tests, there was a significantly greater increase in mental age for the experimental groups than for the control groups over the same period of time. The experimental group gained 22.5 mental-age months on the Stanford-Binet Intelligence Test in the 24 months of the program. In other words, these severely to moderately retarded children were progressing at approximately the rate of a normal child. The control group, however, gained only 7.5 mental-age months in the 24 months of the program, showing the continual intellectual deterioration usually observed in institutional settings and pointing up graphically the ever-widening gap between retarded and normal.

In another study, the DISTAR Arithmetic program was used together with behavioral techniques to teach arithmetic skills to a group of six institutionalized moderately mentally retarded children (IQs 35 to 50). The aim of the study was to determine if the children made significant gains in four types of arithmetical skills: (1) object counting, (2) making lines from numerals, (3) the meaning of plus, and (4) increment additions. The results showed significant improvement in each of the skill areas under consideration (Bracey, Maggs, and Morath 1975a).

A group of moderately retarded children (IQs 30 to 40) were also given the direct phonic approach of DISTAR Reading I. Tangible reinforcers were paired with social praise, with the children earning money they could spend in the institution's shop or on outside trips. The study found that moderately mentally retarded children could be taught to read, using a task-analyzed, structured phonic approach, coupled with positive-reinforcement techniques. The importance of reading for the mentally retarded should not be underestimated. Being able to read, these children can function more effectively in the community, have greater vocational opportunity, and have a useful leisure-time activity at their disposal (Bracey, Maggs, and Morath 1975b).

A further study of 130 moderately and severely mentally retarded children aged 6 to 16 years used DISTAR Reading, Language, and Arithmetic programs to improve their problem-solving skills. The children were either in long-term institutions or special schools. Most children showed significant improvement on tests designed to check their problem-solving skills, and the specific concepts and operations that were taught generalized to significant improvement on the IQ test that classified these children as retarded. The variations in results related to the duration of the study (from 6 months in one school up to 2.5 years in another) and the amount of time the schools allowed in their weekly schedule for the program [from ½ to 2.5 hours daily (Maggs and Morath 1975b)].

A special-school research program began eight years ago (1974) using some of the DISTAR programs. The study involved thirty-three children with IQs in the upper levels of moderate retardation. Twelve of these original children remained in the greatly expanded Direct Instruction programming five years later. The average age of the children who participated in the study in 1974 was 10 years. They already had massive deficiencies in all academic areas. Looking at statistical data for the DISTAR Language and Reading programs that these children have been doing for five years, it has been found that they have the basic language and literacy skills that were thought to be beyond the potential of such children. At the beginning of the program they were learning at the development rate of two months for each five calendar months. At the five-year point they had made an average gain of thirty-four language-age months in the actual thirty-two school months of instruction. In the same thirty-two instructional months they had moved from nonexistent reading skills to performing at a third- to fourth-grade reading level (Booth et al. 1979).

A special school for the mildly retarded has now been involved in Direct Instruction research for several years. Significant gains have continued to be made across all areas of the programming. With these children there has also been an assessment of the transfer of the skills taught to a range of other situations. It was found that the children on Direct Instruction could generalize their classroom skills into outside situations in a way the control group could not (Maggs and Morath 1976c).

Research into Direct Instruction with disadvantaged children has been carried out over a three-year period at two schools made up of disadvantaged (socially, economically, and linguistically) aboriginal and white children. In the larger school, 130 children aged 5 to 13 years are on the DISTAR programs. Kindergarten and grades one to three now have all children on DISTAR as a class program. Grades four to six cluster those children who most need remediation on a morning withdrawal basis. The aim is that all children should receive thirty minutes of daily instruction in language, reading, and arithmetic. The three-year study has shown that the number of aboriginal and nonaboriginal children who have learning difficulties can be markedly reduced by Direct Instruction methods. In addition, the implementation of Direct Instruction as basal programs in kindergarten demonstrated that these disadvantaged children can begin first grade with reading, language, and arithmetic skills in keeping with their chronological age. Furthermore, those children who have been taught DISTAR reading-skills for two to three years have begun to demonstrate reading-comprehension skills in excess of their chronological age. The study has also clearly shown that the aboriginal children have achieved as well as nonaboriginal children on the tested tasks (Hawke, Maggs, and Moore 1978).

The first trial of the Direct Instruction–based Corrective Reading Program took place in 1978 in a withdrawal class comprising fourteen upper-primary and early-secondary students with marked reading deficits. The secondary students were selected on the basis of failure to learn to read during their lower-primary years. However, the upper-primary pupils were selected on the basis on consistent deficits when reading skills were compared with other areas of academic achievement. There was an average gain of ten months' comprehension in seven months of instruction by the primary students, with the more severely reading-deficient secondary students gaining twenty-five months in reading comprehension in seven months of instruction. In reading accuracy the primary students showed twelve months' gain in seven months of instruction (Maggs and Murdock, 1979).

The same school has also been involved in research into the new Direct Instruction–based Morphographic Spelling program, in conjunction with the school for the disadvantaged discussed earlier. Forty-four children from grades two to six, whose spelling age was behind their chronological age, have to date participated an average of fourteen weeks in the program. In this time they have covered an average of 48 of the 140 lessons in the program. Current statistical data indicate that one-third of the children now have a spelling age higher than their chronological age, while all but two of the other children have significantly closed the gap. The mean gain in spelling age was 8.5 months in the 3-month instructional period (Hawke, Maggs, and Murdock 1979).

In all of these studies, Maggs and his associates have used independent assessors and carried out their programs in existing Australian schools. This has ensured that their results are likely to be replicable in other existing school settings.

The Direct Instruction Model has now been shown to be effective in the Australian school system for:

Normal children in the regular classroom,

Children in the regular classroom with mild skill deficits,

Children in the regular classroom with moderate to severe skill deficits,

Children going out to so-called resource-rooms or withdrawal classes in a regular school,

Children in a special class within a regular school,

Children in schools for the disadvantaged, including aboriginal and migrant children,

Children in schools for the mildly retarded,

Children in schools for the moderately to severely retarded.

As the children in the research programs were grouped on the basis of instructional need (and not the traditional classification), there was a mixture of children with behavioral or emotional problems across all these groups. The schools for the retarded had in addition the usual mixture of Downs Syndrome, phenylketonuric, epileptic, spastic, and other children. The only children not yet tried on Direct Instruction are those in schools for the blind and for the deaf. Maggs and Maggs (in press) conclude that reaction to the Direct Instruction program, not only from the teachers but also from the children and their parents, was remarkably favorable.

Other Studies

A large number of studies, add further support to these findings. In this final section, we briefly mention some of the more-important ones.

Preschool Studies

Findings from the original Bereiter-Engelmann preschool were reported by Engelmann (1968). The study compared twelve disadvantaged four-year olds who were given Direct Instruction for two years with twelve disadvantaged control children who received a traditional preschool education that followed a child-development model. On the Stanford-Binet, the mean IQ of the experimental group changed from 95.3 at pretest to 121 at posttest. The disadvantaged control group changed from 94.5 to 99.6. The WRAT was given to the experimental group only (the control group did not have the skills). Mean performance in reading (decoding) was 2.6 grade equivalents, and in arithmetic, 2.5 grade equivalents.

A second experimental group of middle-class children who received one year of Direct Instruction was compared to a middle-class control group who had one year of Montessori preschool. The middle-class children in Direct Instruction reached the same levels of performance in one year as the disadvantaged children had in two years.

In the Planned Variation Head Start study, nine Follow Through sponsors used their models with the Head Start programs within their Follow Through sites. Weisberg (1973) reported the findings for the third (and final) year of this study. The Direct Instruction students in this study consisted of five-year olds in Tupelo, Mississippi, and East Las Vegas, New Mexico. Twelve of the seventeen significant outcomes were produced by the academic-focused models from Oregon (five out of eight), Kansas (four out of eight), and Pittsburg (three out of eight). No negative outcomes were found for these models.

Preschool-Early-Grade Studies

Richards (1970) studied the use of DISTAR programs for one year in six classes of disadvantaged children (one four-year-old preschool class, three kindergarten classes, and two first-grade classes). Five control classes of less-disadvantaged children were used (1 preschool, 2 kindergarten, and 2 firstgrade, respectively). The results showed that the experimental groups did significantly better

Tests of Basic Experience (Language) in kindergarten and first grade;

WRAT Spelling and Reading in preschool (four-year olds);

WRAT Spelling, Arithmetic, and Reading in kindergarten and first grade.

Richards concluded that the disadvantaged can catch up with middle-class children with proper instruction.

Callahan, Erickson, and Bonnell (n.d.) reported the results comparing children at the end of first grade who had three years (N = 15), two years (N = 13), one year (N = 12), and no years (N = 12) of Direct Instruction. The tests used were the Stanford-Binet and the Stanford Achievement Test (SAT). They found that disadvantaged students with three years of Direct Instruction were nearly one full year above national norms on measured intelligence. Those with one or two years of Direct Instruction were at national norms on the averages, and the controls (no years) were one year below national norms. On the SAT, the disadvantaged students with three years of Direct Instruction performed 1.5 to 1.6 grade equivalents on the six SAT subtests.

James and Stier (n.d.) studied students who were in a parent-operated DISTAR preschool for economically disadvantaged children (CAMPI Satellite School) and who were then fed into DISTAR programs in kindergarten and first and second grades. Their performance was compared with that of children in the Head Start and Follow Through Cognitively-Oriented Model developed by Weikart. In each program, 10 percent of the children were not disadvantaged.

The Metropolitan Readiness test (MRT) was given to beginning first graders. The MAT (Primary I) was given to beginning second graders. On the MRT, Test, the DISTAR group ($N = 53$) scored at or above the overall mean on Word Meanings and Numbers subtests. The Weikart groups all scored below the mean. On MAT Primary I, the DISTAR groups were significantly higher than the Weikart groups. The mean for the DISTAR group ($N = 72$) on MAT Total Reading was 2 grade equivalents, and on Math, 1.8.

Cafarella (1973) compared DISTAR and non-DISTAR groups in kindergarten and first and second grades. Only the Reading and Language programs were used. The DISTAR students were significantly higher on reading measures at each grade level. The first graders also showed a significant gain in Kuhlmann Anderson IQ scores. DISTAR second graders had a median score of 2.5 on Word Knowledge and 2.4 on Reading (MAT Primary I). The non-DISTAR classes had a median score of 1.9 on Word Knowledge and 2 on Reading.

Special Education

In Edmonton, Canada, M. Crozier and Youngberg (1974) showed that low-achieving third and fourth graders gained between 1.2 and 2 grade levels during one year of DISTAR Reading and Arithmetic instruction. Parents were extremely high in their evaluation of the program effects on their children. R. Crozier (1974) studied use of DISTAR programs with educable junior-high mentally retarded students. These students showed gains at a better-than-average rate on reading and math measures.

Conclusion

Direct Instruction offers considerable promise as an approach to the alleviation of skill deficiencies. The approach is based on principles derived from empirical behavioral theory and logical analysis of knowledge systems. The goal is a sophisticated application of available technology to learning problems. Common to Direct Instruction programs are the use of pretested scripted lessons; teacher-directed group instruction; specified teaching, motivating, and training procedures; and built-in systems for monitoring student progress.

The most widely known Direct Instruction Programs are the nine DISTAR programs published by SRA. Other programs involve Corrective

Reading (six programs, Engelmann et al. 1977; 1978; 1979), Morphographic Spelling (Dixon 1977), and a math series covering fractions and equations (Engelmann and Steeley, 1978; 1979). Programs are being developed in cursive writing, basal spelling, creative writing, reference skills, and vocabulary.

The principles underlying the design of Direct Instruction programs were overviewed. Most central to good design is the preanalysis of what is to be taught to identify general-case building blocks. The designer is seeking small sets of component skills that can generate a wide set of applications. The goal is to teach more in less time. Once a potential analysis is completed, the problem becomes one of designing and sequencing tasks that are subject o only one interpretation so that students learn what they are expected to learn. Examples of programming strategies were given.

The evaluation studies show the Direct Instruction programs to be consistently effective in a wide range of settings, with a wide range of problems. In Follow Through, Direct Instruction brought disadvantage children near grade level (on the average) on most measures of academic progress. The Direct Instruction students also were significantly higher than control of children on measures of self-esteem and locus of control. Some issues important to the future design of educational systems for children from disadvantaged backgrounds were discussed.

The Australian studies by Maggs show that the successful application of the techniques is not restricted to the originator. Retarded, migrant, aboriginal, learning-disabled, socially disadvantaged, and normal children all greatly benefited from Direct Instruction programs.

A final group of studies extends the application of the programs to preschools and a variety of school settings in the United States and Canada.

A major obstacle to overcome ignorance is the belief that it cannot be done. The evidence on Direct Instruction technology is showing that ignorance can be conquered. We may need to actively re-examine our assumption about who can learn what.

Notes

1. DISTAR, a registered trademark, is an acronym for Direct Instruction Systems for Teaching and Remediation.

2. Cohort II children entered kindergarten or first grade in fall 1970; Cohort III children entered the program in fall 1971.

3. An Office of Education report (1976) substantiates this approach: "Analysis of all test scores showed that the typical student who received compensatory assistance in reading was at the 20th percentile for grade 2 and the 22nd percentile for grades 4 and 6" (p. 88). Moreover, in a footnote

to page 88, this additional information is given: "In conjunction with the Emergency School Aid Act evaluation, children in grades 3, 4, and 5 of a nationally representative sample of minority isolated schools (50% or more non-white) performed at the 23rd, 18th and 19th percentiles, respectively, on reading achievement in the Spring 1973; similar results were obtained for mathematics achievement" The educational requirement for Title I eligibility (one year or more below grade level) is the 20th percentile for Metropolitan Total Reading.

4. Weber and Fuhrmann (1978) followed up the first Follow Through students in East Saint Louis to complete the ninth grade (six years after leaving the program). One-hundred-and-twenty Follow Through students were compared with 1,524 non–Follow Through students on the California Achievement Tests. All mean differences favored Follow Through except in Spelling. A greater percentage of Follow Through students tested above norm average in each case except Spelling (Reading, 16 percent versus 11 percent; Math, 10 percent versus 6 percent; Language, 23 percent versus 13 percent; and Spelling, 18 percent versus 29 percent). As in our own follow-up studies at fifth and sixth grades, it is apparent that the children (without special programs for six years) are losing relative to national norms. There is still a need for a continuous Follow Through to facilitate continuous language development (see the implications section).

References

T. Abramson and E. Kagan, "Familiarization of Content and Differential Response Modes in Programmed Instruction," *Journal of Educational Psychology* 67(1975):83–88.

Abt Associates, Inc., *Education as Experimentation: A Planned Variation Model,* vol. 3 (Cambridge, Mass., 1976).

Abt Associates, Inc., *Education as Experimentation: A Planned Variation Model,* vol. 4 (Cambridge, Mass., 1977).

R.C. Anderson, "The Notion of Schemata and the Educational Enterprise," in *Schooling and the Acquisition of Knowledge,* eds. R.C. Anderson, R.J. Spiro, and W.E. Montague (Hillsdale: N.J.: Lawrence Erlbaum Associates, 1977).

W.C. Becker, "Application of Behavior Principles in Typical Classrooms," in NSSE Yearbook, 1973, *Behavior Modification in Education,* ed. C. Thoresen (Chicago: University of Chicago Press, 1973).

W.C. Becker, "Teaching Reading and Language to the Disadvantaged; What We Have Learned from Field Research," *Harvard Education Review* 47 (1977):518–543.

W.C. Becker, "The National Evaluation of Follow Through: Behavior-Theory-Based Programs Come out on Top," *Education and Urban Society,* 1978.

W.C. Becker, C. Carlson, C.R. Arnold, and C.H. Madsen, Jr., "The Elimination of Tantrum Behavior of a Child in an Elementary Classroom," *Behavior Research and Therapy* 6(1968):117–119.

W.C. Becker and D.W. Carnine, "Direct Instruction: A Behavior Therapy Model for Comprehensive Educational Intervention with the Disadvantaged" (Paper presented at the Eighth Symposium on Behavior Modification, Caracus, Venezuela, February 1978).

W.C. Becker and S. Engelmann, "The Direct Instruction Model," in *Encouraging Change in America's Schools: A Decade of Experimentation,* ed. R. Rhine (New York: Academic Press, in press).

W.C. Becker and S. Engelmann, *Teaching 3: Evaluation of Instruction* (Chicago: Science Research Associates, 1976).

W.C. Becker and S. Engelmann, "Analysis of Achievement data on Six Cohorts of Low Income Children from 20 School Districts in the University of Oregon Direct Instruction Follow Through Model," Follow Through Project, Technical Report #78-1 (Eugene, University of Oregon, 1978).

W.C. Becker S. Engelmann, and D.R. Thomas, *Teaching: A Course in Applied Psychology* (Chicago: Science Research Associates, 1971).

W.C. Becker, S. Engelmann, and D.R. Thomas, *Teaching 2: Cognitive Learning and Instruction* (Chicago: Science Research Associates, 1975).

W.C. Becker, C.H. Madsen, Jr., C.R. Arnold, and D.R. Thomas, "The Contingent Use of Teacher Attention and Praise in Reducing Classroom Behavior Problems," *Journal of Special Education* 1(1967): 287–307.

W.C. Becker, D. Zipse, and C.H. Madsen, Jr., "Effects of Exposure to an Aggressive Model and Frustration on Children's Aggressive Behavior," *Child Development* 38(1967):739–745.

C. Bereiter, "Acceleration of Intellectual Development in Early Childhood," Final Report Project No. 2129, Contract No. OE 4-10-008 (Urbana, Ill.: College of Education, University of Illinois, June 1967).

C. Bereiter, and S. Engelmann, *Teaching Disadvantaged Children in the Preschool* (Englewood Cliffs, N.J.: Prentice-Hall, 1966).

C. Bereiter and M. Kurland, "Were some Follow Through Models More Effective than Others?" (Paper presented at AERA, Toronto, 30 March 1978).

B.S. Bloom, *Human Characteristics and School Learning* (New York: McGraw-Hill, 1976).

A. Booth, D. Hewitt, W. Jenkins, and A. Maggs, "Making Retarded Children Literate: A Five Year Study," *Australian Journal of Mental Retardation,* 1979.

S. Bracey, A. Maggs, and P. Morath, "Teaching Arithmetic Skills to Moderately Mentally Retarded Children Using Direct Verbal Instruction: Counting and Symbol Identification," *Australian Journal of Mental Retardation* 3(1975a):200–204.

S. Bracey, A. Maggs, and P. Morath, "The Effects of a Direct Phonic Approach in Teaching Reading with Six Moderately Retarded Children: Acquisition and Mastery Learning Stages," *The Slow Learning Child* 22(1975b):83–90.

J.E. Brophy, and C.M. Evertson, *Process-Product Correlations in the Texas Teacher Effectiveness Study: Final Report* (Austin: University of Texas, 1974).

Ruth L. Cafarella, "DISTAR Report: 1972–1973" Mount Vernon, N.Y.: Mount Vernon School District, 1973.

O.D. Callahan, E.L. Erickson, and J.A. Bonnell, "Final Report: Third Year Results in Experiments in Early Education," (Grand Rapids Public School Testing and Evaluation Division, Grand Rapids, Michigan, n.d.).

D.T. Campbell and A. Erlebacher, "How Regression Artifacts in Quasi-Experimental Evaluations in Compensatory Education Tend to Underestimate Effects," in *Disadvantaged Child. Compensatory Education: A National Debate,* vol. 3, ed. J. Hellmuth (New York: Brunner/Mazel, 1970), pp. 185–225.

D.W. Carnine, "Conditions under which Children Learn the Relevant Attribute of Negative Instances Rather than the Essential Characteristic of Positive Instances" (Unpublished manuscript, Follow Through Project, University of Oregon, 1976).

D.W. Carnine, "Similar Sound Separation and Cumulative Introduction in Learning Letter-Sound Correspondences," *Journal of Educational Research* 69(1976d):368–372.

D.W. Carnine, "Effects of Two Teacher Presentation Rates on Off-Task Behavior, Answering Correctly, and Participation," *Journal of Applied Behavioral Analysis* 9(1976b):199–206.

D.W. Carnine, "Emphasizer Effects on Children's and Adults' Acquisition Rate and Transfer Scores on Simple and Complex Tasks," in Technical Report 76–1, Appendix B: Formative Research Studies (Eugene: Follow Through Project, University of Oregon, 1976c).

D.W. Carnine, "A Comparison of Two Beginning Reading Approaches with Regard to Training Time, Sounds Learned, and Transfer Scores on Regular and Irregular Words," *Reading Teacher* 30(1977a): 636–640.

D.W. Carnine, "Four Procedures for Introducing Similar Discriminations'' (Unpublished manuscript, Follow Through Project, University of Oregon, 1977b).

D.W. Carnine, ''Preteaching versus Concurrent Teaching of the Component Skills of a Multiplication Problem-Solving Strategy'' (Unpublished manuscript, University of Oregon, 1977c).

D.W. Carnine, ''Stimulus Variation between Positive and Negative Examples and Generalization in Concept Acquisition'' (Unpublished manuscript, Follow Through Project, University of Oregon, 1977d).

D.W. Carnine, ''Three Procedures for Teaching Relational Concepts'' (Unpublished manuscript, Follow Through Project, University of Oregon, 1977e).

D.W. Carnine, ''Two Letter Discrimination Sequences: High Confusion Alternatives First versus Low Confusion Alternatives First'' (Unpublished manuscript, Follow Through Project, University of Oregon, 1977f).

D.W. Carnine, ''Application of Cumulative Introduction and Relational Learning Procedures to Teaching Math Facts'' (Unpublished manuscript Follow Through Project, University of Oregon, 1978a).

D.W. Carnine, ''The Relative Difficulty of Identifying Three Consonants and Three Vowels,'' in *Formative Research Studies on Direct Instruction* (Eugene: Follow Through Project, University of Oregon, 1978b).

D.W. Carnine, ''Simultaneous versus Cumulative Introduction of Addition Facts,'' in *Formative Research Studies on Direct Instruction* (Eugene: Follow Through Project, University of Oregon, 1978c).

D.W. Carnine, ''Two Procedures for Sequencing Instances in Discrimination Learning Tasks: Simultaneously Presenting Minimally Different Instance Pairs and Changing a Single Stimulus to Generate Successive Instances,'' in *Formative Research Studies on Direct Instruction* (Eugene: Follow Through Project, University of Oregon, 1978d).

D.W. Carnine, ''Undergeneralization as a Function of Examples Used in Training,'' in *Formative Research Studies on Direct Instruction* (Eugene: Follow Through Project, University of Oregon, 1978e).

D.W. Carnine, ''Establishing a Discriminative Stimulus by Distributing Attributes of a Compound Stimuli between Positive and Negative Instances (Unpublished manuscript, Follow Through Project, University of Oregon, n.d.).

L. Carnine and D.W. Carnine, ''Determining the Relative Decoding Difficulty of Three Types of Simple Regular Words,'' *Journal of Reading Behavior,* in press.

D.W. Carnine, and W.T. Fink, ''Increasing the Rate of Presentation and the Use of Signals in Elementary Classroom Teachers,'' *Journal of Applied Behavioral Analysis* 11(1978):35–46.

D.W. Carnine, and J. Silbert, *Direct Instruction Reading* (Columbus,

Ohio: Charles Merrill, 1979).

D.W. Carnine, J. Silbert, and M. Stein, *Direct Instruction Mathematics. (Columbus, Ohio: Charles Merrill, in press).*

J.B. Carroll, "A Model of School Learning," *Teachers College Record* 64(1963):723–732.

W.M. Cheyne, "Vanishing Cues in Paired-Associate Learning," *British Journal of Psychology* 57(1966):351–359.

C.M. Clark, N.L. Gage, R.W. Marx, P.L. Peterson, N.G. Stayrook, and P.H. Winne, "A Factorially Designed Experiment on Teacher Structuring, Soliciting, and Reacting. Final Report," ERIC Document Reproduction Service No. ED 134 591 (Stanford, Calif.: Center for Research and Development in Teaching, 1976).

S. Coopersmith, *The Antecedents of Self-Esteem* (San Francisco: W.H. Freeman, 1967).

J. Cowart, D.W. Carnine, and W.C. Becker, "The Effects of Signals on Attending, Responding, and Following in Direct Instruction" (Unpublished manuscript, Follow Through Project, University of Oregon, 1973).

V.C. Crandall, W. Katkowsky, and V.J. Crandall, "Children's Beliefs in Their Own Control of Reinforcements in Intellectual-Academic Achievement Situations," *Child Development* 36(1965):91–109.

L.J. Cronbach, *Essentials of Psychological Testing,* 3rd ed. (New York: Harper & Row, 1970), pp. 292–293.

M. Crozier and A. Youngberg, "Acceleration of Low-Achieving Students in Reading and Arithmetic." Edmonton, 1974.

R. Crozier, "Some Effects of Direct Instruction on the Academic Performance of Educable Mentally Retarded Students." Edmonton, 1974.

R. Dixon *Morphographic Spelling* (Eugene, Or.: E–B Press, 1977).

R. Dixon and W.C. Becker, "A Proposal for the analysis of a basic vocabulary to facilitate instruction in the language arts" (Unpublished manuscript, University of Oregon, 1977).

H.F. Dupuy, "The Rationale, Development, and Standardization of a Basic Word Vocabulary Test," DHEW Publication No. [HRA] 74–1334 (Washington, D.C.: U.S. Government Printing Office, 1974).

R. Durling and C. Schick, "Concept Attainment by Pairs and Individuals as a Function of Vocalization," *Journal of Educational Psychology* 68((1976):83–91.

S. Engelmann, "The Effectiveness of Direct Instruction on IQ Performance and Achievement in Reading and Arithmetic," in *Disadvantaged Child,* vol. 3, ed. J. Hellmuth (New York: Brunner/Mazel, 1968), pp. 339–361.

S. Engelmann and W.C. Becker, "Forward from Basics: The Case for Direct Instruction" University of Oregon.

S. Engelmann, *SRA Corrective Reading* (Chicago: Science Research Asso-

ciates, 1977, 1978, 1979).
S. Engelmann, and D. Steeley, *E–B Press Math Series* (Eugene, Or.: E–B Press, 1978, 1979).
C.B. Ferster and C.E. Hammer, Jr., "Synthesizing the Components of Arithmetic Behavior," in *Operant Behavior: Areas of Research and Application,* ed. W.K. Honing (New York: Appleton-Century-Crofts, 1966).
W. Fink and K. Bryce, "A Comparison of the Effects of Two Programming Strategies on the Acquisition and Recall of Academic Tasks of Handicapped Preschoolers," *Journal of Mental Deficiency,* in press.
J. Flanders, D.W. Carnine, and A. Maggs, "The Effects of Misrules in Teaching Plurals to a Non-Institutionalized EMR Child" (Unpublished manuscript, University of Oregon, 1979).
L.T. Frase and B.J. Schwartz, "Effect of Question Production and Answering on Prose Recall," *Journal of Educational Psychology* 67(1975): 628–635.
M.D. Gall, B.A. Ward, D.C. Berliner, L.S. Cahen, K.A. Crown, J.D. Elashoff, G.C. Stanton, and P.H. Winne, *The Effects of Teacher Use of Questioning Techniques on Student Achievement and Attitude* (San Francisco: Far West Laboratory for Educational Research and Develment, 1975).
T.L. Good and T.M. Beckerman, "Time on Task: A Naturalistic Study in Sixth Grade Classrooms," *Elementary School Journal,* in press.
T.L. Good and D.A. Grouws, *Process-Product Relationships in 4th Grade Mathematics Classes* (Columbia: College of Education, University of Missouri, 1975).
T.L. Good, D.A. Grouws, and T.M. Beckerman, "Curriculum Pacing: Some Empirical Data in Mathematics," *Journal of Curriculum Studies,* in press.
K.S. Goodman, "A Linguistic Study of Cues and Miscues in Reading," *Elementary English* 42(1965):639–643.
I. Gordon, *Early Child Stimulation through Parent Education: A Final Report to the Children's Bureau* (Gainesville: University of Florida Press, 1969).
A.C. Granzin and D.W. Carnine, "Child Performance on Discrimination Tasks: Effects of Amount of Stimulus Variation," *Journal of Experimental Child Psychology* 24(1977):332–341.
T.M. Gruenenfelder and J.G. Borokowski, "Transfer of Cumulative-Rehearsal Strategies in Children's Short-Term Memory," *Child Development* 46(1975):1019–1024.
D. Guess, W. Sailor, G. Rutherford, and D. Baer, "An Experimental Analysis of Linguistic Development: The Productive Use of the Plural Morpheme," *Journal of Applied Behavior Analysis* 1(1968):225–235.
H. Hawke, A. Maggs, and J. Moore, "Disadvantaged Turned into Advan-

taged: A Three Year Study" (Unpublished manuscript, Macquaire University, 1978).

H. Hawke, A. Maggs, and R. Murdock, "The Effects of Teaching Morphographic on Learning to Spell," *Special* 5(1979):pages.

E.R. House, G.V. Glass, L.D. McLean, and D.F. Walker, "No Simple Answer: Critique of the Follow Through Evaluation," *Harvard Educational Review* 48(1978):128–160.

J. James and S. Stier, "A Comparative Description of the DISTAR, Head Start and Follow Through Early Education Programs" Seattle School District Report #75-40 (Seattle, Wash.: Seattle Public Schools).

E.J. Kameenui, D.W. Carnine, and R. Ludlow, "Rule Saying, Concept Application, and Rule Application Training in Relation to Rule Application Transfer Performance" (Unpublished manuscript, Follow Through Project, University of Oregon, 1978).

E. Kameenui, D.W. Carnine, and A. Maggs, "Task Analysis Instructional Procedures for Reversible Passive and Clause Constructions" (Unpublished manuscript, University of Oregon, 1979).

C. Keith, D.W. Carnine, and A. Maggs, "Miscues and Oral Language Proficiency" (Unpublished manuscript, University of Oregon, 1979).

J. Kryzanowski, and D.W. Carnine, "The Effects of Massed versus Spaced Formats in Teaching Sound-Symbol Correspondences to Young Children," in *Formative Research Studies on Direct Instruction* (Eugene: Follow Through Project: University of Oregon, 1978).

L.L. Lessinger, "Quality Control. The Missing Link in Educational Management," mimeographed (Washington, D.C.: Council of Chief State School Officers, 1976).

A. Maggs and R.K. Maggs, "Direct Instruction Research in Australia," *Journal of Special Education Technology* (in press).

A. Maggs and P. Morath, "The Effects of Direct Verbal Instruction on Intellectual Development of Institutionalized Moderately Retarded Children: A 2-Year Study," *Journal of Special Education* 10(1976a): 357–364.

A. Maggs and P. Morath, "Improving Problem Solving Skills in 130 Modately and Severely Mentally Retarded Schoolaged Children," *Rehabilitation in Australia* 12(1976b):22–24.

A. Maggs and P. Morath, "Use of Experimental Kits among Children with Moderate Mental Retardation," *Schools Cmmission Innovations Program,* 1976, 74/33, 1–43, Australia.

A. Maggs, and R. Murdock, "Teaching Low Performers in Upper Primary and Lower Secondary to Read by Direct Instruction Methods," *Reading Education* (September 1979).

R.K. Maggs, "An Effective Intervention Program for Children with Learning Difficulties in Regular and Special Classes," *Schools Commission Innovations Program,* Final Report (Australia 1978), pp. 1–39.

R. Marliave, C. Fisher, N. Filby, and M. Dishaw, "The Development of Instrumentation for a Field Study of Teaching" Technical Report I-5 (San Francisco: Far West Laboratory for Educational Research and Development, 1977).

Metropolitan Achievement Tests (New York: Harcourt, Brace, Jovanovich, 1970).

K.D. O'Leary and W.C. Becker, "Behavior Modification of an Adjustment Class: A Token Reinforcement Program," *Exceptional Children* 1(1967):287-307.

K.D. O'Leary, S.G. O'Leary, and W.C. Becker, "Modification of a Deviant Sibling Interaction Pattern in the Home," *Behavior Research and Therapy* 5(1967):113-120.

S. Paine and D.W. Carnine, "Covertization of Strategies for Working Column Multiplication Problems" (Unpublished manuscript, University of Oregon, 1979).

S. Paine, F. Falco, and D.W. Carnine, "A Comparison of Low and High Meaningfulness Algorithms for Column Multiplication" (Unpublished manuscript, University of Oregon, 1979).

J.C. Raven, *Coloured Progressive Matrices* (Dumfries, England: The Crichton Royal, 1956), sets A, AB, and B.

F. Restle, "Additivity of Cues and Transfer in Discrimination of Consonant Clusters," *Journal of Experimental Psychology* 57(1959):9-14.

Bruce Richards, "The DISTAR Experimental Program: Report for 1970-71" (Prince George's County School District, Prince George County, Maryland).

B.V. Rosenshine, "Classroom Instruction," in *The Psychology of Teaching Methods,* Seventy-fifth yearbook of the National Society for the Study of Education, ed. N.L. Gage (Chicago: University of Chicago Press, 1976).

B.V. Rosenshine and D.C. Berliner, "Academic Engaged Time," *British Journal of Teacher Education* 4(1978):3-16.

R.S. Soar, *Follow Through Classroom Process Measurement and Pupil Growth (1970-71): Final Report* (Gainesville: College of Education, University of Florida, 1973).

J.A. Stallings and D. Kaskowitz, *Follow-Through Classroom Observation Evaluation, 1972-73* (Menlo Park, Calif.: Stanford Research Institute, 1974).

M. Stein and D.W. Carnine, "Manipulatives and Strategy Teaching of Simple Subtraction" (Unpublished manuscript, University of Oregon, 1979).

M. Stein, D.W. Carnine, and A. Maggs, "Using Word Lists to Teach Identification of Complex Regular Words" (Unpublished manuscript, University of Oregon, 1979).

R.D. Tennyson, F.R. Woolley, and M.D. Merrill, "Exemplar and Non-

Exemplar Variables which Produce Correct Classification Behavior and Specified Classification Errors," *Journal of Educational Psychology* 63(1972):144–152.

D.R. Thomas, W.C. Becker, and M. Armstrong, "Production and Elimination of Disruptive Classroom Behavior by Systematically Varying Teacher's Behavior," *Journal of Applied Behavior Analysis* 1(1968): 35–45.

W. Tikunoff, D.C. Berliner, and R.C. Rist, "An Ethnographic Study of the Forty Classrooms of the Beginning Teacher Evaluation Study Known Sample," Technical Report No. 75-10-5 (San Francisco: Far West Laboratory for Educational Research and Development, October 1975).

T. Trabasso and G.H. Bower, *Attention in Learning: Theory and Research* (New York: John Wiley & Sons, 1968).

United States Office of Education, *Annual Evaluation Report on Programs* Administered by the U.S. Office of Education, FY 1975 (Washington, D.C.: Capital Publications, Educational Resources Division, 1976).

United States Office of Education, Annual Evaluation Report on Programs Administered by the U.S. Office of Education, FY 1977 (Washington: D.C. USOE Office of Planning, Budgeting and Evaluation, 145–46).

J.M. Warren, "Additivity of Cues in a Visual Pattern Discrimination by Monkeys," *Journal of Comparative and Physiological Psychology* 46(1953):484–486.

B.B. Weber, and M. Fuhrmann, "A Study of District A's Former Follow Through Students' Retention of Basic Skills after Six Years out of Program" (Paper presented at the National Conference on Urban Education, Philadelphia, November 1978).

H. Weisberg, "Short-Term Cognitive Effects of Head Start Programs: A Report on the Third Year of Planned Variation 1971–72" (Cambridge: Mass.: Huron Institute, 1973).

P. Williams and D.W. Carnine, "The Effect of Negative Examples on Overgeneralization" (Unpublished manuscript, University of Oregon, 1979a).

P. Williams and D.W. Carnine, "Effects of Uniform and Variable Instructions on Preschoolers' Concept Acquisition" (Unpublished manuscript, University of Oregon, 1979b).

L. Zoref and D.W. Carnine, "A Comparison of Visual Discrimination and Letter-Sound Correspondence Training with Letter-Sound Correspondence Training Only," in *Formative Research on Direct Instruction* (Eugene: Follow Through Project, University of Oregon, 1979).

Editors' Epilogue

A child's world constantly expands. From the moment of birth, increasing social and intellectual demands promote this expansion and require an increasing repertoire of skills to match the escalating demands. In the social arena the child moves rapidly from being a quivering, crying mass to being a responsive infant who both affects and is affected by his or her surrounding social world (Lewis and Rosenblum 1974). We have seen in the previous chapters the potentially disastrous consequences that greet the child who fails to meet the demands of the social world. Indeed, the reach of the child's failure may extend well beyond the kindergarten classroom into adolescence and adulthood, foreboding severe forms of later psychopathology.

In the intellectual arena, the child experiences an equally rapid and parallel development as she acquires knowledge about her world. Failure to meet the intellectual demands can have as devastating an effect as failure to meet the social demands. Children who are seen as slow learners, or dull, not surprisingly tend to persist in that role throughout their schooling.

Educators and researchers have attempted to break these persistent expectations and their consequences for the child's educational attainment. Raffaniello, Shultz, and Steffen (1981) have developed a communication-based analysis of this problem and suggest that a child's failure in school and subsequent labeling (for example, learning disabled) may result from a mismatch uncommunication pattern between the child and teacher. Raffaniello and her colleagues suggest that children can be better prepared for their entry into school through the exposure to the communication expectations to be encountered there and that teachers and other school personnel can be trained to understand the different communication patterns used by their students.

In a similar vein, Becker et al. challenge several assumptions about children's intellectual deficiencies. They argue, in essence, that children fail to learn not because they are dull but rather because the methods used to teach them are dull. Further, they argue and provide convincing evidence that children previously thought to be dull can be brought to a level of academic achievement equal to that of their normal peers through the application of systematic instructional methods. The educational approach they present in this chapter, Direct Instruction, may well be one of the most significant advances in educational technology in recent times.

We do not make the previous assertion lightly or in the absence of substantiating data. Throughout this chapter we encounter repeated demonstrations of the profound impact that the Direct Instruction approach has had upon the achievement of its students across a wide variety of academic topics such as reading, arithmetic, and spelling. Perhaps most compelling are the findings of Abt Associates reports from the national Follow Through Project. In this project, which compared a variety of traditional and skill-oriented instructional methods, Direct Instruction emerged as clearly superior to the other methods in most analyses. Maggs and his associates' efforts in Australia further serve to strengthen the impression that Direct Instruction is an exceptionally powerful method of remedying academic deficiencies by virtue of their work with groups of children as disparate as the retarded, aboriginal, and socially disadvantaged.

Convinced of the potent and wide-ranging impact these instructional methods can have upon children's academic achievement, we must wonder why Direct Instruction is not more widely used in educational settings. One clue may be the assumption held by many educators and, more important, by educational policymakers that classrooms should reflect a humanistic atmosphere. Being humanistic in the classroom may certainly promote good feelings between teacher and student, but it may not do well in helping children to accomplish their maximum level of academic achievement. Hopefully, promulgation of the effects and effectiveness of Direct Instruction will sensitize educators to the power of these teaching methods.

References

M. Lewis and L.A. Rosenblum, *The Effect of the Infant on its Caregiver* (New York: Academic Press, 1974).

E. Raffaniello, J. Schultz, and J. Steffen, "Learning How to Go to School: An Ethnographic-Behavioral Analysis" (Unpublished manuscript, University of Cincinnati, 1981).

5 Improving Memory Skills in Mentally Retarded Children: Empirical Research and Strategies for Intervention

Joseph C. Campione,
Kathy Nitsch, Norman Bray,
and *Ann L. Brown*

The poor memory skills of mentally retarded children have attracted widespread research and practical interest. Research in this domain can be traced back as far as Galton's (1887) and Binet's (1904) pioneering studies of intellectual performance. Almost from the beginning of the intelligence-testing movement, memory items like digit span have been included on standardized intelligence tests. It became clear, however, that the acknowledgment of memory retardation neither explained the source of memory deficits nor implied that the deficits were unmodifiable. Accordingly, during the past fifteen years, attention has been directed toward investigating why the memory skills of mentally retarded persons appear to be inefficient and how the deficits might be remedied through training. The current research interest in the remediation of memory defects marks the beginning of a convergence of the concerns of the researcher with the interests of practitioners in educational and clinical settings.

In light of this shared interest, the goals of this chapter are twofold: first, to present an overview of advances in empirical research and theoretical accounts of the memory performance of retarded school-aged children and, second, to discuss the practical implications of the improvement of memory skills through training. Since there are a number of recent, detailed reviews of research relevant to this topic (for example, Borkowski and Cavanaugh 1979; Brown 1978; Brown and Campione 1978a; 1978b; Campione and Brown 1977; Detterman 1979; Glidden 1979), our discussion presents a selective, less-technical review of this literature. Instead of striving for completeness, we have selected research paradigms and investigations of

---

Preparation of this manuscript and much of the research reported therein was supported by Grants HD-05951, HD-06864, and HD-00111 from the National Institute of Child Health and Human Development.

particular relevance to those interested in practical applications of this research in educational and clinical contexts.

A Statement about Memory Theories

Although a detailed discussion of memory theories would not be appropriate here, it is useful to introduce a few distinctions and indicate the kind of research that we consider. Many different memory theories have been proposed, but researchers agree that at least two components of memory exist. One has been called long-term memory and is presumed to be a store of accumulated knowledge. A person's long-term memory is conceived of as having enormous capacity and stored information that is presumed to be fairly permanent.

The fact that information is available in memory, however, does not guarantee that a person will be able to draw upon that information when it is required. We return to this distinction later because one major component of intelligence is the access to stored information on the occasions when the information would be relevant. As will be seen, retarded children frequently fail to use relevant knowledge even when we know it is available, a fact that causes them problems in many areas including those requiring deliberate memorization (Brown and Campione 1980; Campione and Brown 1978).

In addition to long-term memory, the other major component of the memory system is working memory (also referred to as either short-term or primary memory). This is a limited-capacity system from which information is lost rapidly. The loss of information may be due to displacement by incoming information or to simple fading. Retention cannot be ensured unless some overt attempt is made to maintain the information. The capacity limitation reflects the fact that a person can only keep so many things in mind at any given time. An additional complication is that the effectiveness of working memory is limited by both the amount of information being maintained and the demands imposed by the operations required for that maintenance. The more effortful the operations being carried out, the less room there is for the information being processed. One popular metaphor is that working memory consists of a fixed number of bins and that each unit of information takes up one of them. Maintenance operations may require one or more bins, depending on the efficiency with which the person can perform operations.

Much of intentional memorizing, including memorizing that goes on in school, in the laboratory, or in the clinical-testing situation, involves the use of procedures designed to circumvent the bottleneck imposed by the limits of working memory. On a general level, there are two kinds of situations to consider. In one, the task is to remember a small amount of information, all of which fits into working memory, for a relatively brief time. In the other, the total amount of information to be retained exceeds the capacity of working memory. In such cases, the individual can keep only a portion of the information alive at any time. This is more difficult and requires that the information be acted upon in some way (while it is present in working memory) to make it more memorable. To be more specific, types of information that require explicit effort to remember include facts for a test, remembering a person's name after an introduction, remembering a new telephone number, and other arbitrary information. Verbatim recall of facts can usually be accomplished only when a memory strategy (an explicit plan to remember) is used. Examples of simple memory strategies include underlining the main points in a text in order to remember them for a test, associating some distinctive physical features with a person's name when introduced, and repeating a telephone number several times until it can be remembered in sequence.

Whenever a memory task requires the recall of a number of pieces of information, an efficient memorizer might have to introduce even more-complex or sophisticated mnemonic strategies. For example, he or she might elaborate the material so that it fits into a meaningful context (for example, make up a story to embed the to-be-remembered items) or perhaps look for redundancies, repeated elements, or categories of information to help organize the material. Remembering that there were four animals in a list of words will help the memorizer to recall those items later; noting the repetition in the sequence 349349 will reduce memory load by about half; and noting that 149217761941 is not simply a list of twelve arbitrarily chosen numbers but rather three well-known historical dates will make this list easily retainable. These strategies help the memorizer to make more-efficient use of a limited ability for verbatim recall.

As it turns out, good memorizers use a variety of strategies for making meaningless material more memorable. We would like to point out that much of what is learned in school is, at least when originally presented to the student, relatively meaningless. Facts, principles, and rules become meaningful only when some organizational scheme into which they fit is built up. The items may be nearly meaningless to the student during that building process and thus more difficult to remember. After the organizational scheme is learned, new information relevant to that structure is more readily remembered, frequently without any special effort.

A View of the Retarded Child

Having sketched an overview of memory components, we need to ask where in this system retarded children experience specific problems. Although we cannot review the entire literature here, we can indicate what seem to be the major strengths and weaknesses. To do this, we introduce another distinction—that between involuntary and deliberate memorization (see Brown 1975) or automatic and effortful memory (see Hasher and Zacks 1979). The main point is that much of what a person remembers about the world finds its way into long-term memory with no apparent effort. People and places may be recognized, the details of personally experienced events may be recalled (including when and where they took place), and the essential gist of a conversation or story may be remembered without any deliberate attempt to remember them at the time these events were experienced. The memory system on these occasions seems to function automatically and requires minimal effort in order to function. These situations tend to involve meaningful information and require recall of general details. While there is not enough research upon which to base any strong claim, there is at least some reason to believe that, in memory situations like these, mildly retarded children tend to perform quite well (Brown 1974). The suggestion is that this aspect of the memory system is relatively intact; the entire memory system of the mildly retarded adolescent is not necessarily in some way defective.

In contrast, in many situations we are forced to deal with information that is not meaningful or we need to recall events in greater detail than would be the case if we were to fall back on automatic memory processing. In such cases, effortful processing is required, and we often run into problems imposed by the properties of working memory. Thus, we have two potential sources of problems for the retarded child. The first is the capacity of working memory. Although it is clear that there are functional differences in the use of working memory (for example, the well-known problems retarded children have with many memory-span tests, most notably digit span), it is not clear whether the differences are due to the actual number of bins available or to the efficiency with which maintenance operations are carried out. The second potential source of problem is the availability of memory strategies to overcome the capacity limitations of working memory regardless of their size. The data on this issue are very clear: in general, mildly retarded children fail to produce such strategies spontaneously even when they are obviously necessary (see any of the reviews mentioned earlier). We now review some of this research.

The most general and optimistic view can be proposed is that, while the retarded child's memory system appears to function relatively well in automatic-memory situations, problems result when the child is required to employ any of a number of strategies designed to overcome working-memory limitations. This view is an optimistic one since it indicates that the major problem underlying retarded child's poor performance is in the area of strategy use. If this is the case, then it should be possible to improve his performance by teaching him to use these devices. This possibility has motivated recent research, and a large proportion of memory studies with retarded children in the past decade have included a training component. Before looking at some of that literature in detail, we would like to place it into historical context to account for what seems to be a paradoxical limitation in that research. Specifically, while many training studies have been conducted, it is in some sense true that only a small proportion of that research is really relevant to the question of whether memory improvements of any practical significance can be achieved through instruction. To understand why this is so, it is necessary to consider briefly the history of the training study and its use in comparative/developmental research.

The Training Study (and Its Limitations)

In many areas of cognitive development, the training study has served as an important theoretical tool; in fact, its use has been more theoretical than practical. The typical situation in which the training study has been used is as follows: We have a specific task and indications that different groups of subjects (young versus older children, retarded versus nonretarded children, and so on) perform differentially on that task. We would like to know why. To deal with this question, we need a theory of what individuals must do to perform well on that task and some hypothesis about the specific source(s) of individual differences. As an example, consider a memory task wherein we assume that effective performance requires, among other things, the use of a rehearsal strategy. We also assume that young children perform more poorly than older ones because of a failure on their part to rehearse. We can test both of these assumptions simultaneously by training the younger children to rehearse. If their performance does improve significantly, we are in a position to conclude that our original analysis of the task was correct (if rehearsal were not an important component of performance on that task, instructing children in its use would not lead to improved performance) and that young children perform poorly, at least in part, because they fail to rehearse without prompting (if they did rehearse spontaneously, training would not have been necessary).

These theoretical questions can be evaluated on the basis of the subjects' immediate response to the training, but the majority of the studies stops at this point. If, however, we are concerned with the practical implications of that training, we need to ask other questions. Specifically, we need to know if the effects of the training are durable and generalizable. Will the instructed subjects continue to use the trained strategy on the same task given subsequent unprompted occasions? Will they generalize the use of that strategy to other tasks on which it would be beneficial? If the answer to these questions is negative, then the positive effects of the training have limited potential for practical application.

The great majority of the studies about retarded children has looked only at the immediate effects of training, and we are thus better able to answer the theoretical, as opposed to the practical, questions. This is probably not surprising as the initial motivation for research was primarily the theoretical one of identifying the sources of memory problems in the retarded. It was first necessary to show that retarded children did not tend to use memory strategies appropriately on their own and that instructing them to use strategies would indeed improve performance. The results of these studies have been encouraging because investigators have been able to design training procedures leading to much improved memory performance in many situations. This was no small step because it indicated both the type of instruction that might be necessary and that success was possible.

Following these studies, a number of experimenters have begun to consider the evidence for durability and generalizability. While the results here are less encouraging, we have reasons to believe that the situation is more optimistic than the data would lead us to believe. We elaborate upon this conclusion later and speculate on the form that more-successful instructional routines would take. Before that, however, we review a number of studies that show the effects of training on specific tasks and that demonstrate how large the potential for improvement is.

Studies Investigating the Training of Mnemonic Strategies

Rehearsal

Rehearsal-strategy training consists of having the learner continue to repeat the names of items that are no longer available to keep them alive in working memory. As indicated earlier, there are several uses for these strategies. One is when the amount of information to be remembered is small enough to fit into working memory. In such cases, the learner can attempt to keep all the information available until it is needed. If the amount of information to be retained exceeds the capacity of working memory, more-elaborate strategies will be necessary because the learner will be able to maintain and work on only a portion of the material at any time. We consider two cases that demonstrate how the two situations can be handled.

The first task to be reviewed is the keeping-track task. This task is similar to everyday situations that require us to keep track of several things at once. The task requires rehearsal of the present instances of the variables and no rehearsal of the previous instances of the variables. For example, in an early study of keeping-track performance with mildly retarded adolescents, Brown (1972) presented sequences of four pictures, each representing a different category (for example, animals, foods, vehicles, or clothing). On one sequence the participants might be shown pictures of a horse, pie, car, and shirt. Following this sequence, they would be asked to recall the instance presented for one of the four categories (for example, animals). On the next trial, they might see a cat, then a boat, then a tie, and finally a cake and be asked to indicate which food they had seen. Across trials the order and instances of each category changed so that the person was required to keep track of the changing states (instances) of four different variables (categories). Of interest here is the composition of the set of pictures used in the experiment. A total of sixteen pictures consisted of two examples, or states, of one variable (for example, foods: pie, cake); four examples of each of two variables (for example, vehicles: train, boat, plane, car); and six states of the final variable. Thus, specific pictures would recur frequently over the series of trials.

The most efficient strategy for this type of task is to rehearse the four items presented in the current set, keeping them available until the test occurs. Yntema and Mueser (1960) found that the keeping-track performance of nonretarded adults was not influenced by the number of states of each variable. The adults apparently used a rehearsal strategy to update the information on each trial and were able to disregard previously presented instances. They would consider only the items presented on the current trial and determine which of those was an example of the category being probed. With retarded adolescent subjects, however, Brown (1972) found that accuracy decreased as the number of states per variable increased. These results suggested that all of the states of the variable were being considered at the time of the test. It appeared, then, that the retarded subjects were not using a rehearsal strategy to keep track of the states of the variables.

This early research on keeping-track performance led to one of the more-intensive strategy-training studies with mentally retarded adolescents. Brown et al. (1973) trained one group of mildly retarded adolescents to use a rehearsal strategy in a keeping-track task. This rehearsal group was trained to repeat the first three items in each sequence three times in order and then to look only at the last item. The logic in this strategy was that looking only at the last item would be sufficient to lead to good memory since the lag time between its presentation and the test item would be very short. A second group was given no rehearsal training. Consistent with the findings reported in Brown (1972), the performance of the no-rehearsal-training group decreased as the number of states per variable increased. Performance in the rehearsal-training group was higher and not influenced by the number of states per variable. Thus, the pattern of results for the rehearsal-training group was the same as the results obtained with nonretarded adults (Yntema and Mueser 1960).

The accuracy data were supplemented by some speed-of-responding data. Brown et al. (1973) measured the amount of time that elapsed between the presentation of the probe question (What was the animal?) and the beginning of the subject's response. For the nonrehearsing subjects, the amount of time increased as the number of states included increased from two to six. In the rehearsal group, however, the response time was uninfluenced by this variable. Again, the implication is that rehearsing subjects consider only the items presented on the current trial; thus, it does not matter how many states the requested variable has. In the absence of rehearsal, however, the most recently presented items will not be available in working memory, and the subject will have to check through all the possible states to determine which had been seen most recently. This task should be more difficult and more time consuming as the number of alternatives increases from two to six.

The data from the experiment indicated that the retarded subjects did not use the rehearsal strategy when left on their own but that they were able to use it successfully when they were instructed to do so. Recall that they were instructed to rehearse just the first three items. Students given no rehearsal training were correct approximately 58 percent of the time when tested on these items, whereas the students trained to rehearse averaged about 85 percent correct in the same conditions.

In a second experiment, Brown et al (1973) tested nonretarded adolescents under two conditions. A rehearsal-prevention group was tested as well as a no-rehearsal-prevention, or free-strategy, group. In the rehearsal-prevention group the participants repeated the name of the pictures aloud for the duration of picture presentation. This prevented the cumulative repetition (rehearsal) of the item names. There were no constraints on the study activities of the free-strategy group. Recall in the rehearsal-prevention condition was dependent on the number of states per variable, whereas recall was not influenced by the number of states per variable in the free-strategy condition. The same pattern of results was obtained with the response-time measure. When prevented from rehearsing, nonretarded adolescents performed like untrained mentally retarded adolescents.

The results from these two experiments seemed to provide good evidence that effective keeping-track performance is dependent on the use of a rehearsal strategy. Of most importance, however, the results indicated that mentally retarded adolescents could use a rehearsal strategy following relatively simple and brief training.

One other important point illustrated by these two experiments is that, in some situations, not every aspect of a memory strategy needs to receive explicit training. The keeping-track task has two strategic components: rehearsing the sequence presented and retrieving the correct response from the inspection set. Mentally retarded subjects who were not trained to rehearse apparently searched the states of the relevant variables (as indicated by longer response latencies and lower recall accuracy). Nonretarded subjects who were prevented from rehearsing were apparently forced to use the same strategy. This strategy seems to be the only alternative when the picture names included in the most recently presented inspection set are not readily available due to lack of rehearsal. When mentally retarded individuals were trained to use a rehearsal strategy, however, there was no need to train them to retrieve items from the inspection set rather than by category.

Rehearsal and Retrieval

In some situations it may be necessary to teach both an acquisition strategy (for example, rehearsal) and a systematic way of retrieving the to-be-remembered information. A training study by Butterfield, Wambold, and Belmont (1973) provides an excellent illustration of this point. Mildly retarded adolescents were given sequences of six letters, each appearing on separate projection screens arranged in a horizontal array. Note that six items was more than these children could hold simultaneously in working memory. A subject-paced procedure was used in which the participant pressed a button to view each item for a fixed exposure before it terminated, but the subject was allowed to pause as long as he or she wished before pressing the button to expose the next item. At the end of each sequence, one of the letters was exposed in a so-called probe window. The subject was to indicate the location of the probe letter in the sequence.

Belmont and Butterfield (1971) had previously found that mentally retarded adolescents paused very briefly, if at all, between presses, whereas nonretarded adults exhibited a systematic pause pattern. Adults rehearsed the early items in the sequence and then quickly exposed the last few items. The adult strategy is well adapted to the task requirements since, for a short time after presentation, the last few items are easily recalled without rehearsal. Rehearsal of the first few items in that list helps to maintain these items until the recall test.

Butterfield and his co-workers (1973) first trained their subjects to use a 3-3 rehearsal strategy similar to that used by adults: The subjects were trained to repeat the first three letters cumulatively, pausing to do so following the third letter, and then to expose the last three letters quickly before an immediate test. This strategy raised the level of performance, especially for the first three letters in the sequence, but recall of the last items was still poor. The Butterfield study hypothesized that although the subjects were using the trained rehearsal strategy, they were not using an appropriate retrieval strategy. The most effective retrieval strategy would have two parts. First, when the probe item was presented, the last three items would be searched, taking advantage of the fact that these items would not yet have faded from the memory. Second, if the letter were not in the last three, the first three rehearsed items would be searched.

The training procedure used by the Butterfield study required several steps. The subjects were initially trained to rehearse a sequence of three letters cumulatively and to count to ten before recalling the position of the probe item in that set. This gave the subject practice in searching a set of three rehearsed items following a delay between the rehearsal and the test. Next, the participant was given six letters and was instructed to use the 3-3 rehearsal strategy, rehearsing the first three and exposing the last three letters with very short pauses between each of the last three letters and between the last letter and the probe. During this phase the subject was told that the test item would always come from the last three items. To aid performance, the subject was instructed to point to screen numbers four through six, in sequence, trying to identify the position of the probe letter by saying the names of the letters to himself. After practicing this, the subject was told that a probe letter might be taken from any of the six positions. To deal with this, the person was instructed to recall the letters, saying them to himself beginning with letters four through six and then one through three. The combined rehearsal-and-retrieval-strategy training resulted in a substantial increase in recall for all six items, whereas the rehearsal training alone facilitated recall only on the first three items.

The Butterfield group experiments illustrate that the effective use of an acquisition strategy, while relatively easy to train, cannot always be expected to be coordinated with an effective retrieval strategy. Although subjects in the Brown et al. (1973) study required instruction on the acquisition strategy, they did not require retrieval-strategy training. In contrast, the retrieval strategy necessary for the Butterfield task did require special training. Also, it is interesting to note that, with the type of training used by the Butterfield group, the mentally retarded subjects were able to perform at the same level as persons with average intelligence. In fact, recall following training was 114 percent of that obtained with nonretarded subjects of comparable chronological age who were not given training.

Categorization

In the rehearsal-training studies such as those by Brown et al. (1973) and Butterfield, Wambold, and Belmont (1973), cumulative repetition (rehearsal) was taught as a method for remembering a small set of ordered items. In other types of tasks, rehearsal strategies may not be as effective because the number of items to be remembered is relatively large. In one such task—the free-recall paradigm—the number of items presented can easily exceed a nonretarded adult's ability to repeat a sequence cumulatively. In this situation, a relatively large set of words (usually ten or more) is presented, and after studying the set, the person is free to recall the items in any order. Nonretarded adults usually try to use some inherent relatedness of the stimuli as a basis for remembering the words. For instance, presented with a sixteen-item list containing four items from each of four different taxonomic categories (such as food, clothing, flowers, and occupations), adults will tend to use the categorical structure of the list as a means of organizing recall. Words from each category will tend to be recalled together, even though they were presented in a random order. The analysis of this clustering of recall by categories has been the predominant method for studying organizational strategies in free recall.

Research has consistently indicated that mentally retarded subjects (and nonretarded young children) do not spontaneously adopt strategies that utilize the categorical structure of a list. Several studies have attempted to induce the use of an organizational strategy by presenting the items by category during stimulus presentation (blocking) rather than using a random order of presentation (for example, Bilsky, Evans, and Gilbert 1972; Gerjuoy and Spitz 1966). Other investigators have tried to induce organizational strategies by cuing the subject at the time of testing to recall the items by category (for example, Green 1974). Although these procedures increased the amount of category clustering, they resulted in only small improvements in recall. In most cases, there was no transfer of the organizational strategy to new lists of words. The weakness of these approaches to strategy training seems to be that, in contrast to the rehearsal-training studies, the training techniques were indirect—that is, by blocking the stimuli according to category at input or by presenting category cues to the subject at recall, the experimenter hoped to induce an organizational strategy that would facilitate recall. However, the experimenter is being strategic in this case and manipulating the subject who can remain relatively passive. These indirect methods appear to be too subtle to manipulation to affect strategic aspects of study behavior for mentally retarded subjects.

Recently, attempts to train mentally retarded children to use actively organizational strategies have been more successful. Burger et al. (1978) devised a direct training procedure in which mildly retarded adolescents were shown sixteen cards, each presenting a picture of a common object. The pictures were from four categories (for example, clothing, foods, flowers, and tools) with four instances of each category. During the first session (baseline), the sixteen cards were presented for approximately two minutes and then covered. The subject then attempted to recall the picture names. The categorization training given to one group of subjects consisted of several components. The subject was first asked to put the pictures that go together in a horizontal row. Suggestions were given, if necessary, for arranging the cards by category. The subject was then asked to label each category represented in the sorting and to name and count the instances within each category. Next, the subject was told that the pictures could be remembered best if he or she would try to recall the pictures by the groupings. The pictures were then covered, and the subject was asked to recall the picture names. If all of the picture names were not recalled, the experimenter supplied the appropriate category name as a cue.

This training procedure was repeated three times with a different set of pictures each session. There were two follow-up tests: the first occurred two or three days following training and the second was three weeks later. Recall and clustering following training were significantly higher than for the baseline session. Performance was also higher than the recall and clustering of a group of mentally retarded adolescents who had received the same amount of practice on the same stimulus sets but who were not trained to use the categorization strategy. Whereas training studies failed when using indirect, passive manipulations such as category blocking and cuing, a substantial improvement in memory performance was obtained in more-direct training methods that demands the subject's active employment of a strategy and provided feedback about the strategy's effectiveness.

Elaboration

In many situations, material is difficult to remember because it is relatively meaningless. One way to deal with such situations is to attempt to search for or to invent some meaningful context for the information. Particular types of mnemonic techniques designed to bring this about can be used in a variety of tasks ranging from the learning of simple laboratory-type paired-associates lists to more-complex academic topics (see Bransford et al. 1980). To illustrate the efficiency of these techniques, we use some data obtained in the area of paired-associates learning. In experiments of this type, the subjects see a series of pairs of items (for example, fish and telephone) followed by trials on which one item is presented (fish), and they are required to indicate the item with which it had been paired (telephone). One way to facilitate performance on these tasks is to use either verbal or visual mediators to construct a more-meaningful context in which to embed the items being paired. For example, in the fish-telephone pair, if learners either produce the sentence, "The fish is talking on the telephone," or form a mental image of a fish talking on a telephone, retention is dramatically improved. It is by now clear from a long series of studies that older and brighter children are more likely than younger or less-intelligent ones to use these kinds of elaborative strategies (Rohwer 1973).

In an experiment by Turnure, Buium, and Thurlow (1976), educable retarded children were given twenty-one pairs of items to learn. There was one study trial on which the twenty-one paired items were presented one pair at a time. This was followed by a test trial consisting of the first item from each pair presented one item at a time. Separate groups of subjects differed in terms of the activities required of them on the study trial. (We consider only a subset of the groups here.) In the labeling condition, subjects simply repeated the names of the items (for example, soap-jacket) after the tester. This condition served as a type of control treatment and simulated the type of study activity that can be presumed to be typical of the educable retarded child who is given a paired-associates task. In three other conditions, the subjects were required to answer what or why questions about the pair—for example, "What is the soap doing under the jacket?", "Why is the soap hiding in the jacket?", and so forth. The aim of these procedures was to lead the subjects to think about the meaning of the individual items and to force them to search for possible relationships between the members of each pair. Requiring this kind of "deep processing" (Craik and Lockhart 1972) about items or pairs of items usually leads to good retention, even in cases in which subjects do not know they will be given later memory tests (Murphy and Brown 1975)—that is, if materials are presented in such a way as to lead subjects to think in some depth about them, recall of those items will be good, independent of any intention to commit the materials to memory.

In the Turnure and co-workers (1976) experiment, the differences among the conditions were highly significant. The children in the labeling condition averaged 2 items correct (out of twenty-one), whereas those in the what and why groups were correct on an average of 14.4 items, an increase in recall of over 600 percent. The Turnure experiment also included groups of nonretarded children matched for chronological age (CA) (around 7.5) with the retarded groups. Children of this age have not yet begun to use these kinds of elaborative strategies spontaneously, and in fact, their performance was not different from that of the retarded sample. They performed poorly unless given the questioning procedures during study and improved dramatically in these conditions. Again, the conclusion is that retarded children's memory systems are not usually deficient. When the requisite strategy for the task is not employed by nonretarded children, no performance differences between retarded and nonretarded are apparent.

Summary

The data from these experiments (and many others) are clear and quite consistent in indicating both the causes of poor memory performance by retarded children and ways of improving that performance. When memory tasks requiring the use of any of a number of mnemonic strategies are presented to retarded children, the children seem to remain passive and fail to produce active memory routines. These difficulties can be overcome by one of two general ways. One is to teach the children the necessary strategies; this was the procedure employed in the rehearsal and categorization examples. The other, exemplified in the elaboration example, is to force the subjects to think more deeply about the to-be-remembered material when it is presented. Here the burden is on the instructor or experimenter rather than on the subject. Subjects do not have to carry out any plan on their own, but simply by answering the questions reasonably (for example, the Turnure study) they have a more-durable memory representation.

In either case, the data indicate that the memory performance of retarded children can be improved, often dramatically, as a result of well-designed training procedures. It is not the case that the memory system of these children is defective but rather that they experience major problems when task-appropriate strategies are necessary—problems that can be greatly diminished by instruction. Before claiming that there are significant practical implications of these results, however, we need to consider the criteria for effective training in more detail.

Beyond the Immediate Effects of Training

The previous discussion focused upon a single index of successful mnemonic-strategy training—initial strategy mastery. Without denying the importance of this criterion as noted previously, we argue for the consideration of additional criteria. Merely demonstrating an initial improvement in performance is not sufficient to establish the practical utility of a training program. The effectiveness of a program should be evaluated against three basic criteria: (1) performance must improve as the result of training, both in terms of accuracy and in terms of the activities (strategies) used to effect this accuracy; (2) the effects of this training must be durable since it is obviously desirable to show that what has been learned through training is still applied after a reasonable time period has elapsed; and (3) training must result in generalization to a class of similar situations wherein the trained activity would be appropriate, because, without evidence of transfer, the practical utility of any training program must be called into question.

Maintenance of Instructed Strategies

Most of the studies reviewed in the previous sections successfully demonstrated that training improved performance. Among those studies that have explicitly assessed whether trained mnemonic strategies are maintained over time, the results are also encouraging, at least for the more-intensive training efforts. For instance, studies of rehearsal training in which multiple practice sessions were used have resulted in clear evidence for strategy maintenance. In a study reported by Turnbull (1974), for example, a series of fourteen instructional sessions was followed by a retention test four weeks later. Turnbull reports that all the children in the instructed group were observed to continue with the rehearsal strategy. The subjects in the Brown et al. (1973) experiment referred to previously were also tested for retention of the instructed rehearsal strategy. In this case (Brown, Campione, and Murphy 1974), the subjects were tested for retention six months after the last of a series of twelve instructional sessions. With the retention test, they were brought back to the laboratory and simply told that they were going to play the game again. No mention was made of the rehearsal strategy they had been taught to use. After six months, the performance of the instructed children was still significantly better than the performance of the uninstructed children. Analysis of individual subjects' data showed that eight of the ten instructed children continued to rehearse and were correct in 82 percent of the trials compared with 65 percent correct for the uninstructed control group. Note that 82 percent correct was almost identical to performance during training—that is, the subjects who continued to rehearse did so with no appreciable decrease in accuracy, even six months after training.

Studies employing relatively brief periods of instruction, however, frequently demonstrate only temporary improvements in performance. With brief training, the mentally retarded memorizer may show a marked tendency to abandon a trained strategy when not explicitly instructed to continue its use. This can be illustrated by situations in which retarded children are taught a strategy for a task and are then given a series of follow-up tests: in test 1, they are reminded to use the instructed strategy; in test 2, they are given no such reminders; and in test 3, they are again reminded. In a series of studies (Brown and Barclay 1976; Brown, Campione, and Barclay 1979), children with a mental age (MA) of six years performed well on tests 1 and 3 but poorly on test 2. Note that there was no additional training during these tests; performance levels were determined simply by the provision of reminders by the experimenter. The strategy was evidently available to the children on test 2, but they did not use it without prompting. In these cases the task remained the same throughout. The problem of accessing stored information would be expected to be even more problematic when the learner encounters a new task on which the strategy is relevant. The proposal that this ability to access stored information for use in multiple situations is one major component of intelligence has been outlined in more detail in Campione and Brown (1978) and Brown and Campione (1980).

Overall, maintenance of a trained strategy seems to occur following extended strategy training. In fact, somewhat more-fine-grained analyses by Borkowski, Cavanaugh, and Reichhart (1978) suggest that the amount of training necessary may vary with the subject. They found that maintenance was a function of the efficiency and precision with which the strategy was carried out during training. Those subjects who executed the strategy well at the time of training were more likely subsequently to maintain the strategy. These results indicate that training for individual children should continue until some criterion of strategy use is achieved—rather than the usual procedure of instructing all subjects for a fixed number of trials or sessions. While some additional fine tuning is necessary to implement the overall situation, the current data are encouraging: Maintenance can be achieved with a sufficient amount of training.

Attempts to Assess the Generalization of Training

The third criterion of effectiveness of training in mnemonic strategies—generalization or transfer to appropriate new situations—presents the most recalcitrant problem for training programs. Researchers usually agree that evidence for flexible generalization to new situations is lacking. Inflexibility in the use of trained skills in new situations is such a pronounced problem for most retarded children that it has come to be viewed as an almost universal cognitive deficit. Both U.S. and Soviet psychologists, not to mention parents and teachers, have repeatedly observed the difficulty that even mildly retarded children experience with generalization. Successfully training a mentally retarded child to use a simple mnemonic skill in one specified situation seems to be well within our competence as instructors; getting the child to use the information appropriately in other settings appears to be the major obstacle.

Campione and Brown (1977) concluded that almost no evidence in the literature indicates successful generalization of trained strategies by educable retarded children. This pessimistic note can be offset, however, by a number of considerations. The most important of these is that many of the studies with negative results were not designed specifically to assess generalization and certainly were not done for the purpose of achieving generalized effects of training. As noted previously, initial training studies were conducted to determine if strategy training would facilitate performance. When tests for generalization were included, they were simply tacked on at the end of a study. It became apparent from these studies that generalization was not something that would be achieved readily and that if it was an aim, the training procedures would have to be modified to take this into account.

In retrospect, this is not surprising; indeed, it now seems unclear why generalization would be expected if the typical training procedures in the literature were used. In the design of the standard experiment, the subjects are simply given a memory task and are told to employ some strategy. No attempt is made to explain why the strategy was necessary or how it may have affected performance, much less that it may be useful in other situations. Essentially, the students are required to induce all this information on their own. Retarded children do not readily fill in such gaps (Brown 1978; Butterfield, Wambold, and Belmont 1973), so perhaps the results of such experiments should have been predictable.

The minimal instructions and explanations employed might have led us to expect no generalization for yet another reason. Recall that one of the conditions in which strategies are necessary obtains when the amount of material to be retained exceeds the capacity of working memory. Data are available that indicate that retarded children frequently considerably overestimate their memory capacity and capabilities. For instance, when shown an array of ten pictures and asked how many of them they will subsequently recall, they frequently indicate all ten when in fact they can only recall three or four (Brown, Campione, and Murphy 1977). Given the childrens' overestimation of their capability, it is not surprising that they fail to use any strategy to assist their recall. It would follow that they would not understand why trained strategy was necessary, and hence, there would be no reason for them to generalize it.

Another factor that might be expected to impede generalization concerns the nature of the skills that have been trained. Although the various strategies that have been investigated are important vehicles for the study of strategy training, they are not especially general. In fact, in many situations the use of the strategy training would be inappropriate. A rehearsal strategy, for example, is not appropriate for tasks with a large number of to-be-remembered items. Effective generalization of a rehearsal strategy would, therefore, require that the trainee be able to discriminate situations in which rehearsal would be appropriate from those in which it would not.

For purposes of training, it seems possible that generalization would be more likely to occur if more-general skills were trained—that is, if the activities being instructed were truly transsituational. In such cases, the children could apply what they had learned without having to analyze the task to determine whether or not it was appropriate. There are reasons to believe that this might be effective. Proponents of cognitive behavior modification (Meichenbaum 1977) have investigated the effects of training self-regulation behavior such as having students ask themselves if they understand what they are supposed to be doing or if they are remaining on task, and it appears that instructing such general routines results in more generalization than training more-specific behaviors.

Theorists have recently taken the approach that attempts to bring about generalized effects of training require a reanalysis of the design of the instructional component of the research; it should be designed with the goal of generalization in mind (Stokes and Baer 1977). As just indicated, there seem to be two general directions: (1) improvements in the design of training studies (including the type of instructions and explanations given) and (2) a reconsideration of the types of skills that are trained. A detailed discussion of these two avenues can be found in a paper by Brown and Campione (1978), and we give only the highlights here. There is no available study, to our knowledge, that satisfies all the conditions we believe are necessary for a completely adequate training study. Thus, the negative outcomes in the literature may be due to the faulty design of the training rather than to an inability of the subjects to generalize. To document this, we will show that some of the factors we regard as important influence generalization when manipulated individually. We then propose that simultaneous manipulations of several factors will produce greater effects.

First, consider the design of training studies and the hypothesis that the failure to obtain generalization is a result of inappropriate training regimes. Brown and Campione (1978) have listed a series of requirements for an adequate study if the aim is to produce generalization, and we review a number of them here. The first set takes place before intervention begins and involves a detailed diagnosis of the original problem. It should be established that the skill being trained is one that is important in a variety of situations and that is lacking in the immature learner. Even when these conditions are met, the specific causes for the lack should be considered. For example, a child may not use a rehearsal strategy for several different reasons. The child could be unaware of the need for any strategy, or the child could appreciate that a strategy was necessary but not realize that rehearsal would be appropriate. This in turn may be true because a rehearsal strategy was not used by the child in the past. Even if the child had rehearsed some task previously (spontaneously or in response to instruction), the child may lack sufficient mastery over this strategy for a variety of reasons, including a failure to recognize the new task as one demanding rehearsal or an inability to modify the old strategy to fit the precise demands of the new task. Simply designating a trainee as a nonrehearser is an inadequate diagnosis of the original state of competence. Very different forms of training would be indicated for children in various starting states.

A number of recommendations concerning procedures during the instructional period warrant consideration. First, include a statement about why the strategy is needed, ideally with examples of how performance would be affected without it. Second, include a detailed specification of the various components and their assembly since students may not develop the strategy in its full detail—that is, they may not fill in the missing steps themselves (compare Butterfield, Wambold, and Barclay 1973). Third, use some criterion to ensure that the learner has mastered the skill within the original context before expecting generalization to a new context. Fourth, provide feedback about the effectiveness of the strategy by clearly indicating the level of performance achieved with it versus without it, because students are not likely to transfer the use of some procedure unless they are aware that it is helpful. Fifth, train in multiple settings since instructed strategies may remain welded to the training task unless the child is shown that the strategies are in fact useful in a number of tasks. Sixth, provide direct instructions about generalization so that the learner understands that transfer is an important part of learning. All of these recommendations are based on the fact that retarded children do not tend to go beyond the information given. Without these training procedures there is no reason to believe that the children will infer that generalization is possible or desirable.

Instruction ideally should be tailored to the beginning competence of the learner. However, it may not be possible to describe that competence completely before training, causing it to fail. One final feature of a good training study is that it be designed to distinguish between different possible causes of transfer failures. The instructional procedures may be effectively redesigned if the reason for failure can be specified.

In addition to suggesting design modifications to maximize generalization, Brown and Campione (1978) advocated a reconsideration of the skills trained. They suggested a concentration on more-general skills likely to be transsituational. The specific suggestions were based on the pervasiveness of young children's problems with self-regulation and control of their goal-directed activities (Brown 1975; 1978; Brown and DeLoache 1978; Meichenbaum 1977; Mischel and Patterson 1976). Slow-learning children in particular experience major problems when required to orchestrate and regulate the use of strategies (Campione and Brown 1977; 1978). An alternative or supplement to training specific skills would be to train general "metacognitive" skills that are notably absent in the children's academic problem solving (Brown 1975; 1978). "Metacognitive" skills such as checking, planning, asking questions, self-testing, and monitoring current activities rarely appear in the protocols of slow-learning children, but they are very general skills applicable in a wide variety of situations. In addition, the failure of learners to employ these overseeing functions seems to be a major reason for their failure to transfer learned information (Brown 1974; 1978; Campione and Brown 1977; 1978). Given this analysis, the logic for directing training at these skills seems important.

There is another reason why training attempts directed at general skills might be more likely to result in transfer. One problem with specific skills is that they are just that—specific to a very small class of situations. For learners to generalize the effects of instruction in the use of specific routines, they should be able to discriminate situations in which the routine would be appropriate as opposed to those in which it would not. Adequate generalization of specific strategies would require both extended use in novel situations and decisions not to use the trained routines in other situations in which it would not be beneficial (Brown 1978; Campione and Brown 1974; 1978). This discrimination should not be necessary in the case of general skills since the skill or routine could simply be used in a whole battery of problem-solving situations without regard to any subtle analysis of the task being attempted. In this sense, general "metacognitive" skills might be the most likely to lead to transfer across task boundaries.

As a final comment, these two suggestions regarding design of training studies and choice of skills are not mutually exclusive. In fact, we believe the best programs will be those that include both the well-designed training of skills together with the training in procedures for overseeing those skills. We argue that instructing specific skills without explicit instruction in their use and management is unlikely to lead to generalization. Also, we do not see how management of skills can be taught in the absence of specific skills to be overseen. Again, the implication is that both should be considered when instructional routines are being developed.

While no studies have incorporated all these features, studies taking some of them into account have begun to appear. The result has been an increase in the likelihood of obtaining transfer, allowing much more-optimistic forecasts about our ability to engender practically important improvements in memory performance.

Recent Research on Generalization

In this section we indicate some of the factors that have been shown to influence the likelihood of obtaining strategy transfer. In a number of studies with nonretarded children (for example, Borkowski, Levers, and Gruenenfelder 1976; Kennedy and Miller 1976), an instructed strategy was more likely to be maintained in the absence of experimenter prompts if it had been made clear that the use of the strategy did result in improved performance. Apparently, for these subjects, the utility of the strategy was not appreciated without explicit feedback, and simply providing that information resulted in increased transfer. In a pair of studies with nonretarded (Kestner and Borkowski 1979) and retarded children (Kendall, Borkowski, and Cavanaugh 1978, cited in Borkowski and Cavanaugh 1979), training centered on the use of elaborative strategies to facilitate paired-associates learning. The training extended over four days and involved a number of features including explicit feedback about the strategy's effectiveness. A generalization task was also employed; the difference here was that the children were required to learn triads, rather than pairs, of words. In both experiments, children given the elaboration training outperformed control children in both the training and generalization tasks.

We turn now to a study by Belmont, Butterfield, and Borkowski (1978) that investigated the role of training in multiple, rather than single, contexts. They were concerned with the use of a variety of rehearsal strategies to be used on some similar short-term memory tasks. In each case, the subjects, 12-to-15-year-old retarded children, saw a series of seven letters—one in each of a row of windows. They were allowed to go through the list at their own pace. This trial was then followed by one of the memory tasks. In three of them, they were required to recall all seven items but in different orders. The three conditions were 3/4, 4/3, and 2/5. In the 3/4 condition, for example, the subjects were to recall the last three items of the set, followed by the first four items. In a probed recall task, the set of seven items was followed by a test letter, and they were told to indicate the window in which that letter had appeared. The point is that rehearsal processes were necessary on each of these tasks, although the specific form of the strategy had to be modified to take into consideration the specific demands of each. For example, in the 3/4 case, the optimal strategy would be to view the first four items and then pause and rehearse them as a group until they are learned. Following this the last three items should be viewed more rapidly, and the subjects should attempt recall of the set immediately. Going from a 3/4 recall to a 4/3 recall required the learner both to recognize the continued need to rehearse and to modify the strategy to conform to the changing response requirement.

In the Belmont and Borkowski (1978) study, two groups of retarded children were involved: one that received training on only the 3/4 task and one that was taught to deal with both the 3/4 and 4/3 tasks. While the group trained on only the 3/4 case did not show evidence of generalization, the twice-trained group continued to rehearse on the 2/5 and probed-recall tasks. In these tasks, they showed study patterns consistent with rehearsal usage, and their recall scores were about 170 percent of those of the singly trained group. While the variations in the tasks employed here are small and thus the amount of generalization somewhat limited, the results are impressive and indicate the potential gains to be achieved through training in multiple contexts.

The final study to be described assessed the effects of instructing mildly retarded children in the use of a general "stop-test-and-study" routine (Brown, Campione, and Barclay 1979). The initial task that included instruction was one in which subjects were required to study a large list of pictures until they believed they were ready to recall all the pictures in order. The pictures were presented in a series of windows, and the subjects could view any picture by pressing its window. Only one picture was visible at a time, but the subjects could investigate the windows in any order and as frequently as they wished. They were also told to ring a bell when they thought they were ready to be tested for recall. In a series of preliminary sessions, the maximum number of pictures each child could recall in this situation was determined individually for each child. From this point on, each child was given a series of trials in which he or she was required to recall one and one-half times the maximum number; thus, if a child could recall five items without aid, eight items would be presented on each experimental trial.

Performance was initially poor on this more-difficult task, even though the children were free to study for as long as they liked. During the training portion of the study, the children were taught strategies that could be used to facilitate their learning of the lists along with the overseeing or monitoring of those strategies. The latter aspect of training was accomplished by employing strategies that included a self-testing component and instruction to monitor their state of learning. For example, in a rehearsal condition, the subjects were told to break the list down into manageable subsets (three items) and to rehearse those subsets separately. They were also instructed to continue rehearsing the group of subsets until they were sure they could recall all the items. Keep in mind that one can only continue to rehearse all the items if he or she can remember them well enough to produce them for rehearsal. Thus, in this situation, rehearsal serves both to facilitate learning and to provide a check on the state of that learning. Another strategy, anticipation (which included similar self-testing features), was included. Children in a final condition, labeling, served as a control group. In this condition, children were told to go through the list repeatedly, labeling each item as they exposed it, and to continue that activity until they were sure they were ready to recall.

We present here the data for only an older group of educable retarded children (mean IQ = 70, mean MA = 8). Children who were taught the strategies that involved a self-testing component improved their performance significantly, whereas those in the control condition did not. These effects were extremely durable, lasting over a series of posttests, the last one occurring a year after the training had ended. Shortly after the one-year follow-up test, the children were tested for generalization to a more-typical school task—studying and recalling prose materials. Those students given either rehearsal or anticipation training outperformed a pair of control groups. They showed both better comprehension and recall of the texts. Thus, the effects of instruction given in the context of learning to recall a series of pictures generalized to the very different situation of studying texts.

Practical Implications of Strategy-Training Research

Given this body of research, what can we say about the modifiability of the memory capabilities of the retarded child? We believe quite a lot. It is by now abundantly clear that, while retarded children perform poorly in a wide variety of memory tasks, these tasks tend to be ones in which particular strategies must be used to effect efficient performance. Fortunately, if they are induced to carry out the appropriate operations during study and retrieval, their performance improves. This can be achieved in either of two ways, the choice of which depends upon exactly what the aim of intervention is.

The first case is one in which retarded children must learn and remember some specified set of facts or items. We now have a considerable understanding of the processes necessary to bring about durable memories. Individuals who engage in deep processing (Craik and Lockhart 1972) or broad elaborative processing (Anderson and Reder 1979) of to-be-retained material show good retention. It is important that this outcome does not depend upon the individual's intention to remember—that is, good retention is an automatic result of such processing. For example, Murphy and Brown (1975) showed four-year-old children a set of sixteen items, four from each of four categories. In one condition, the children were instructed to remember the items and were given two minutes to study them. In two other conditions, the children were given two minutes to sort the items into categories—that is, forced to think about the meaning of the items and to note some similarities and differences between them. They were told in one of these two conditions that they would later be tested for their memory of the pictures; in the other, no warning about the impending memory test was given. The main outcomes were that (1) the latter two conditions led to better recall (50 percent) than the simple instructions-to-remember condition (34 percent); and (2) the two categorization groups did not differ—that is, the children who did not know they would be tested for memory recalled as many items as those who were forewarned.

The conclusion from these data is that the way in which the learner interacts with the material determines the accuracy of recall. It does not seem to matter whether the learner engages those activities in an attempt to remember or is tricked into doing so. Thus, in the Turnure, Buium, and Thurlow (1979) experiment, leading the subjects to think in some depth about the pairs of items resulted in superior performance. If the goal is to produce good memory of some specified set of material, we do not need to rely on the student's producing the necessary mnemonic pyrotechnics. If, during instruction, we force them to carry out the appropriate operation, good memory should result.

Our second goal might be to teach retarded children how to employ spontaneously some of the strategies and operations necessary for good retention rather than having them rely on external agents. To do this, we must provide them with the skills and strategies upon which memory relies and teach them how to go about recognizing situations in which the skills, or simple variants of them, are appropriate—that is, teach them to generalize. While we have much to accomplish in this area, we are making a beginning. Recent work has begun to show that generalization is achievable and to indicate some of the factors that should be included in any training program. Our feeling is that we know enough about both memory and the retarded child's cognitive profile that we can devise a memory curriculum, aimed at achieving this goal, and we have begun doing this. We do not have any data yet, and we do not have space here to describe the overall program, but we can indicate the form the instruction will take.

In describing this curriculum, we also summarize the chapter because the design of such a program depends upon our knowing what the source of the retarded child's memory problems are and upon our hypotheses about which aspects can be improved and how we might go about this. Our beginning point is that retarded children experience memory problems because they do not produce the mnemonic strategies necessary on a number of tasks, possibly because they do not have a good understanding of the strengths and weaknesses of their memory system or how it works, and they do not systematically regulate their own activity, either as general problem solvers or, more specifically, as intentional memorizers.

The first step is to teach the children that, for anyone, to remember is very difficult and limited in some situations, whereas in other cases, good retention is relatively easy to achieve (for example, recalling the names of a set of twenty-five pictures is very hard, but simply recognizing that you have seen the pictures before is extremely easy; recalling a series of two digits is easy, but of ten digits is difficult). They can also be taught how to recognize the areas in which they will have problems—that is, some of the factors that make remembering difficult, the kind of memory test to be employed, amount of material, meaningfulness of the material, and so forth. After this, we outline a number of strategies for dealing with these situations. Each strategy is illustrated on a variety of problems (to minimize welding effects), and we also provide examples of problems in which that strategy would be inappropriate. This can be achieved by giving explicit feedback about recall when the child does, or does not, use the strategy. This component of the program consists of comparing and contrasting the kinds of tasks in which one or another strategy would be appropriate. The aim is to indicate to the trainees that generalization is their aim and to teach them something about how they should go about it.

The preceding steps have been concerned with identifying the need for some strategy and selecting one that matches the task at hand. We then turn to the management and monitoring of the chosen strategy. For example, children will be instructed to self-test regularly to check on how well they are learning. On the bases of this testing, they can decide whether to cease studying, if learning is adequate, continue studying with the same strategy, or find that they are not improving and abandon that strategy to search for a better approach. While these various steps seem to be acquired naturally by children of average or greater intelligence, some evidence indicates that each one causes problems for the retarded child, hence the need for the kind of explicit instruction included here. (For a more-detailed description of the issues involved in selection of generalizing strategies, see Campione and Brown 1977).

Finally, in addition to providing instruction on each of these component skills, we include the kind of self-management procedures that is used with considerable success by the proponents of cognitive behavior-modification techniques (Meichenbaum 1977). These procedures are designed to maximize the likelihood that the products of our instruction will be accessed when needed to deal with memory requirements of new problems—to lead the children to think systematically about what they need to do in their current situation. In our application, instead of instructing general self-management skills ("Do I understand the task?", "Am I attending?", and so forth), we will introduce more memory-specific questions. When confronted with a memory situation, children will be taught to ask themselves: (1) "Can I remember easily?" and to self-test if not sure; (2) "If not, what do I need to do?"; (3) "Is this task like any others I have worked on?"; (4) "What did I do there, and can I do something like that here?"; and (5) "Am I making acceptable progress?" The aim here is to introduce a plan for managing the child's memory resources and to make explicit the way in which the various activities should be considered and arranged to deal with some novel or even old tasks.

Summary

In this chapter, we have considered some of the research aimed at understanding and remedying the memory performance of mildly retarded children. We found areas in which their retention seemed quite good and concluded that the overall memory system was not just generally deficient. When, however, mnemonic strategies were required, retarded children did perform poorly. Teaching them the relevant strategies or leading them to engage in appropriate activities resulted in much improved recall, indicating the potential for improving memory. While the results are sufficient if the goal is to achieve retention of some specified material, we maintained that they are not sufficient if we want more-widespread effects. In this case, practically important benefits would accrue only if we could also provide evidence for the maintenance and generalization of training effects. While early data were not encouraging in this regard, more-recent work aimed at producing generalization has been more successful and has served as the basis for optimism.

As a final comment, we try to practice what we teach and have engaged in some checking and monitoring activities ourselves with regard to the current state of our memory and instructional theories. We feel that theories are developed sufficiently enough that we are willing to try to develop a memory package that we might take into the classroom with some hope of success. While we may turn out to be wrong, this willingness is at least a measure of our evaluation of the current state of knowledge. A few years ago, we would not have been quite so willing, an the inference is that the field as a whole is making progress toward some significant practical applications. Further, we would expect more-rapid advances in the future, as many workers in the field have come to view such practical success as an important yardstick against which to evaluate theories, resulting in a convergence of *basic* and *applied* research goals; we anticipate that this distinction will become even more blurred with time.

References

J.R. Anderson and L.M. Reder, "An Elaborative Processing Explanation of Depth of Processing," in *Levels of Processing in Human Memory,* eds. L.S. Cermak and F.I.M. Craik (Hillsdale, N.J.: Lawrence Erlbaum Associates, 1979).

J.M. Belmont and J.C. Borkowski, "Instructing Retarded Children on Examples of a Memory Method (vs. only One) Improves Maintenance and Generalization of that Method" (Paper presented at the Eleventh Annual Gatlinburg Conference on Research in Mental Retardation, Gatlinburg, Tenn., March 1978).

J.M. Belmont and E.C. Butterfield, "Learning Strategies as Determinates of Memory Deficiencies," *Cognitive Psychology* 2(1971):411-420.

L. Bilsky, R.A. Evans, and L. Gilbert, "Generalization of Associative Clustering Tendencies in Mentally Retarded Adolescents: Effects of Novel Stimuli," *American Journal of Mental Deficiency* 74(1970): 771-776.

A. Binet, "Les frontieres anthromponetriques des anormaux," *Bulletin de la Societe libre pour l'ètude psychologique de l'enfant* (1904):430-438.

J.G. Borkowski, and J.C. Cavanaugh, "Maintenance and Generalization of Skills and Strategies by the Retarded," in *Handbook of Mental Deficiency, Psychological Theory and Research,* ed. N.R. Ellis (Hillsdale, N.J.: Lawrence Erlbaum Associates, 1979).

J.G. Borkowski, J.C. Cavanaugh, and G.J. Reichhart, "Maintenance of Children's Rehearsal Strategies: Effects of Amount of Training and Strategy Form," *Journal of Experimental Child Psychology* 26(1978): 288-298.

J.C. Borkowski, S.R. Levers, and T.M. Gruenenfelder, "Transfer of Mediational Strategies in Children: The Role of Activity and Awareness during Strategy Acquisition," *Child Development* 47(1976):779–786.

J.D. Bransford, B.S. Stein, T.W. Shelton, and R.A. Owings, "Cognition and Adaptation: The Importance of Learning to Learn," in *Cognition, Social Behavior and the Environment,* ed. J. Harvey (Hillsdale, N.J.: Lawrence Erlbaum Associates, 1980).

A.L. Brown, "A Rehearsal Deficit in Retardates' Continuous Short-Term Memory: Keeping Track of Variables that Have Few or Many States," *Psychonomic Science* 29(1972):373–376.

A.L. Brown, "The Role of Strategic Behavior in Retardate Memory," in *International Review of Research in Mental Retardation,* vol. 7, ed. N.R. Ellis, (New York: Academic Press, 1974).

A.L. Brown, "The Development of Memory: Knowing, Knowing about Knowing, and Knowing How to Know," in *Advances in Child Development and Behavior,* vol. 10, ed. H.W. Reese (New York: Academic Press, 1975).

A.L. Brown, "Knowing When, Where, and How to Remember: A Problem of Metacognition," in *Advances in Instructional Psychology,* ed. R. Glaser, (Hillsdale: N.J.: Lawrence Erlbaum Associates, 1978).

A.L. Brown, and J.C. Campione, "Memory Strategies in Learning: Training Children to Study Strategically," in *Psychology: From Research to Practice,* eds. H.E. Pick, Jr., H.W. Leibowitz, J.E. Singer, A. Steinschneider, and H.W. Stevenson (New York: Plenum Press, 1978a).

A.L. Brown and J.C. Campione, "Permissible Inferences from Cognitive Training Studies in Developmenal Research," in *Quarterly Newsletter of the Institute for Comparative Human Behavior,* eds. W.S. Hall and M. Cole, Rockefeller University, 1978b.

A.L. Brown and J.C. Campione, "Inducing Flexible Thinking: A Problem of Access," in *Intelligence and Learning,* eds. M. Friedman, J.P. Das, and N. O'Connor (New York: Plenum Press, 1980).

A.L. Brown, J.C. Campione, and C.R. Barclay, "Training Self-Checking Routines for Estimating Test Readiness: Generalization from List Learning to Prose Recall," *Child Development* 50(1979):501–512.

A.L. Brown, J.C. Campione, N.W. Bray, and B.L. Wilcox, "Keeping Track of Changing Variables: Effects of Rehearsal Training and Rehearsal Prevention in Normal and Retarded Adolescents," *Journal of Experimental Psychology* 101(1973):123–131.

A.L. Brown, J.C. Campione, and M.D. Murphy, "Keeping Track of Changing Variables: Long-Term Retention of a Trained Rehearsal Strategy by Retarded Adolescents," *American Journal of Mental Deficiency* 78(1974):446–453.

A.L. Brown and J.S. DeLoache, 'Skills, Plans and Self-Regulation," in *Children's Thinking: What Develops?,* ed. R. Siegler, (Hillsdale, N.J.: Lawrence Erlbaum Associates, 1978).

A.L. Burger, L.S. Blackman, M. Holmes, and A. Zetlin, "Use of Active

Sorting and Retrieval Strategies as a Facilitator of Recall, Clustering, and Sorting by EMR and Nonretarded Children," *American Journal of Mental Deficiency* 83(1978):253–261.

E.C. Butterfield, C. Wambold, and J.M. Belmont, "On the Theory and Practice of Improving Short-Term Memory," *American Journal of Mental Deficiency* 77(1973):654–669.

J.C. Campione and A.L. Brown, "Memory and Metamemory Development in Educable Retarded Children," in *Perspectives on the Development of Memory and Cognition,* eds. R.V. Kail, Jr., and J.W. Hagen (Hillsdale, N.J.: Lawrence Erlbaum Associates, 1977).

J.C. Campione and A.L. Brown, "Toward a Theory of Intelligence: Contributions from Research with Retarded Children," *Intelligence* 2(1978):279–304.

F.I.M. Craik and R.S. Lockhart, "Levels of Processing: A Framework for Memory Research," *Journal of Verbal Learning and Verbal Behavior* 11(1972):671–684.

D.K. Detterman, "Memory in the Mentally Retarded," in *Handbook of Mental Deficiency, Psychological Theory and Research,* ed. N.R. Ellis (Hillsdale, N.J.: Lawrence Erlbaum Associates, 1979).

J.H. Flavell "Cognitive Monitoring (Paper presented at Conference of Children's Communication, University of Wisconsin, October 1978).

F. Galton, "Supplementary Notes on 'prehension' in Idiots," *Mind* 12(1887):79–82.

I.R. Gerjuoy and H. Spitz, "Associative Clustering in Free Recall: Intellectual and Developmental Variables," *American Journal of Mental Deficiency* 70(1966):918–927.

L.M. Glidden, "Training of Learning and Memory in Retarded Persons: Strategies, Techniques, and Teaching Tools," in *Handbook of Mental Deficiency, Psychological Theory and Research,* ed. N.R. Ellis (Hillsdale, N.J.: Lawrence Erlbaum Associates, 1979).

J.M. Green, "Category Cues in Free Recall: Retarded Adults of Two Vocabulary Age Levels," *American Journal of Mental Deficiency* 78 (1974):419–425.

L. Hasher and R.T. Zacks, "Automatic and Effortless Processes in Memory," *Journal of Experimental Psychology: General* 108(1979): 356–388.

C. Kendall, J.C. Borkowski, and J.C. Cavanaugh, "Maintenance and Generalization of an Interogative Strategy by EMR Children" (Paper presented at the Tenth Annual Gatlinburg Conference on Research in Mental Retardation, Gatlinburg, Tenn., March 1978).

B.A. Kennedy and D.J. Miller, "Persistent Use of Verbal Rehearsal as a Function of Information about Its Value," *Child Development* 47 (1976):566–569.

J. Kestner and J.C. Borkowski, "Children's Maintenance and Generalization of an Interogative Learning Strategy," *Child Development* 50 (1979):485–494.

D. Meichenbaum, *Cognitive-Behavior Modification: An Integrative Approach* (New York: Plenum Press, 1977).

W. Mischel and C.J. Patterson, "Substantive and Structural Elements of Effective Plans for Self-Control," *Journal of Personality and Social Psychology* 34(1976):942–950.

M.D. Murphy and A.L. Brown, "Incidental Learning in Preschool Children as a Function of Level of Cognitive Analysis," *Journal of Experimental Child Psychology* 19(1975):509–523.

W.D. Rohwer, "Elaboration and Learning in Childhood and Adolescence," in *Advances in Child Development and Behavior,* vol. 8, ed. H.W. Reese (New York: Academic Press, 1973).

T.F. Stokes and D.M. Baer, "An Implicit Technology of Generalization," *Journal of Applied Behavior Analysis* 10(1977):349–367.

J.E. Turnure, N. Buium, and M.L. Thurlow, "The Effectiveness of Interrogatives for Promoting Verbal Elaboration Productivity in Young Children," *Child Development* 47(1976):851–855.

A.P. Turnbull, "Teaching Retarded Persons to Rehearse through Cumulative Overt Labeling," *American Journal of Mental Deficiency* 79 (1974):331–337.

D.B. Yntema and G.E. Mueser, "Remembering the Present State of a Number of Variables," *Journal of Experimental Psychology* 60(1960): 18–22.

Editors' Epilogue

One way to characterize current mental-health practice is to acknowledge the ideological division that separates those who do research on psychopathology from those who offer care to the people judged to be pathological. The usual complaint is that researchers seldom care about the day-to-day concerns of the practicing clinician, preferring instead to pursue esoteric modes of inquiry that appear to have limited usefulness for on-line caregivers. However, clinicians are criticized for their know-nothing attitude toward recent research advances and their dogged adherence to outdated and less-than-effective modes of intervention. An obvious interpretation of this division is that both parties have evolved to such a specialized state that neither is able to understand what the other is up to (Steffen 1980). As clinical researchers become more methodologically and conceptually sophisticated, they leave the clinical practitioner lost in the multivariate dust of their escape from the inexactness and uncontrollability of the consulting room. At the same time, clinicians have embraced the reality of daily life in the clinic, back ward, or community and have developed and perfected methods of treatment that are both pragmatic and timely—but empirically unevaluated.

The chapter by Campione, Nitsch, Bray, and Brown represents an important effort to bridge this researcher-clinician division in suggesting methods to improve the memory skills of mentally retarded children. Building upon their work and that of other cognitive psychologists, the authors have derived a set of useful suggestions for those who would help mentally retarded children to develop skills that may allow them to compete in the real world. While it had once been thought that the retarded were marginal members of our society due in part to their limited cognitive capacity, Campione et al. have shown in that if one painstakingly analyzes the components of memory, such knowledge can be used to train the retarded child in more-efficient memorization skills.

In addition to providing us a wealth of information regarding possible memory-training strategies with the retarded, Campione and his colleagues have, perhaps more importantly, shown that the researcher-clinician division can be bridged through research that is simultaneously rigorous and practical. An important aspect of their presentation is the manner with which they use research findings like the retarded child's inefficient use of retrieval strategies to suggest possible forms of intervention to remedy these deficiencies. In other words, rather than assuming that retarded children are incapable of ever performing as well as normal children on most tasks, these authors have shown that a retarded child's memory capacity can be improved through training in the use of memorization strategies similar to those used by normal children.

Potentially beneficial, as well, might be the recent analyses of speech production in severely disturbed children. Bartolucci (forthcoming) for example, has analyzed the syntactic structure of retarded and autistic children's speech. Both groups of children were found to differ dramatically from normal children of comparable ages. The structure of a retarded child's speech (for example, use of nouns, verbs, sentence construction) was found to be similar to that of normal but younger children. The speech structure of autistic children, however, revealed deficits that could be attributed not to a developmental delay but rather to a more-basic impairment of their comprehension of speech. The comparability of Bartolucci's findings with those of Campione et al. are striking in the evidence that retarded children may be cognitively immature. This would suggest, then, that one could improve the speech production of the retarded in a fashion similar to that reported in this chapter.

The research reported here complements the work presented by Becker and his colleagues in their discussion of Direct Instruction (chapter 4). Both groups of researchers have show us that considerable practical benefit can be gained from the application of experimental rigor to problems of childhood adaptation.

References

G. Bartolucci, "Formal Aspects of Language in Childhood Autism," in *Autism and Severe Psychopathology,* eds. P. Karoly and J.J. Steffen (Lexington, Mass.: Lexington Books, D.C. Heath and Company, forthcoming).

J.J. Steffen, "Bridging the Practitioner-Researcher Gap" (Review of *Empirical Clinical Practice* by S. Jayaratne and R.L. Levy), *Contemporary Psychology* 25(1980):494–495.

6 Developing Self-Regulation in Retarded Children

Alan J. Litrownik and
Bradley I. Steinfeld

Discontent is the want of self-reliance.—Emerson

The basis for behavioral approaches to the understanding and treatment of psychopathology and/or handicapping conditions no longer rests solely on established S-R learning theory. Rather, the popularity of mediational or cognitive processes has resulted in the embracing of what some researchers term *social learning* (for example, Bandura 1977; Kanfer 1977); others use *cognitive learning* (for example, Mahoney 1977); and still others use *cognitive social-learning theory* (for example, Mischel 1973).

Although proponents of these cognitive perspectives (Bandura 1977; 1978; Kanfer 1977; Mahoney 1977) argue that the integration of the behavioristic and phenomenological traditions leads to our best conceptualization of human behavior, they point out that a number of precautions must be taken when we admit internal variables into an analysis of behavior and technology of change—that is, we need to describe fully the internal processes that are proposed, as they typically possess much surplus meaning. In addition to defining these processes in a clear and precise manner, we must acquire information about how they are related to, as well as affect, overt behaviors (see Kanfer 1977).

Self-regulation has received much attention due not only to our willingness to admit internal variables into our analysis and treatment but also to our concern about external control and long-lasting treatment effects (for example, Kanfer 1979b; Meichenbaum and Asarnow 1979; Thoresen and Mahoney 1974). Traditional S-R approaches have relied primarily on managing—that is, changing—behavior via externally controlled manipulations of one's social-personal environment. While these manipulations have led to desired changes, the effects have been short lived and confined to specific

The program of research reported herein was supported by Grant No. GOO-75-00670 from the U.S. Office of Education, Bureau of Education for the Handicapped. The authors acknowledge the assistance and cooperation of the administrators, teachers, staff, and students of Fairhaven Schools, San Diego, California. In addition, we gratefully acknowledge the invaluable contributions of Catherine Cleary, Louis Franzini, Janet Freitas, and Gregory Lecklitner.

situations. In addition, ethical and moral questions have been raised by the public sector in response to what some see as an inappropriate use of powerful manipulative techniques. These techniques result in externally determined behavior that further limits our real and/or perceived personal freedom.

Social-learning theory not only admits internal constructs into its conceptualization of human behavior but also gives these personal constructs some explanatory value. Thus, from this perspective our behavior is not viewed as being determined solely by environmental factors. Instead, our overt behavior, the environment, and our cognitions are reciprocally determined (see Bandura 1977; 1978)—that is, our environment determines, in part, how we label a situation (cognition) and our overt behavior. Conversely, how we label a situation and behave will affect our environment as well as each other. As a result, individuals are afforded more responsibility for their actions and greater personal freedom. The appropriate use of this freedom (independent functioning) is one valued goal of socialization (see Kanfer 1979a; Mahoney and Mahoney 1976)—that is, skills that allow us to regulate our own behavior; adapt to problems as they arise; and, in general, allow us to function independently are highly valued outcomes of our development. Bandura (1977) pointed out that the ability to function independently is determined by the number of options or alternative courses of action available, as well as the right to exercise these options. The greater the number of alternatives, the more choice, or freedom, one has. Constraints are placed upon our personal freedom when choices are restricted because of personal deficiencies; societal prohibitions; socially condoned discrimination of certain groups (for example, persons labeled as retarded); and self-determined restraints (for example, unwarranted fear; see Bandura 1977).

No longer are we satisfied with treatment interventions (externally controlled change) that further restrict options or choices of individuals who already have limited personal freedom. Approaches to treatment that allow for greater freedom are not only congruent with the current mood of the people but also are likely to have a more-pronounced effect. In other words, increased personal freedom and the ability to utilize appropriately this freedom should result in longer-lasting effects that are also generalized to other situations.

Meichenbaum and Asarnow (1979) cautioned that these claimed benefits of cognitive behavior modification or treatment approaches based on social-learning theory remain to be demonstrated. While our hopes have been raised, we must recognize that we must deal with developmental issues and concern ourselves with individual needs as well as identify general strategies for developing self-regulatory skills (see Karoly 1977). In an effort to begin to deal with these issues, we undertook the task of developing self-regulatory skills in a population that supposedly cannot function independently (namely, the moderately retarded). After reviewing the evidence for this claim, we present a conceptual model of self-regulation, a strategy for its development, and the results of our attempts to apply this strategy.

Self-Regulation in Retarded Individuals

Retarded persons are typically characterized as being unable to control their own behavior (Kurtz and Neisworth 1976); dependent (that is, in need of constant supervision from caretakers even when performing the simplest task) (Mahoney and Mahoney 1976); and outer-directed in their problem-solving orientation. In fact, Robinson and Robinson predicted that moderately retarded children "will not achieve any measure of social or economic independence as adults" (1976, p. 374). Although there may be unanimity in agreement that retarded persons in general and moderately retarded persons specifically can be characterized as dependent, there is some debate about the source of this dependence.

In general, deficits can be attributed either to structural features of the individual or to processes under the direct control of the individual (see Hagen and Stanovich 1977). Structural features, or the general hardware, are not modifiable like control processes. As Meichenbaum and Asarnow (1978) recognized, at times we have a tendency to jump to the conclusion that individual possess a structural defect when our initial attempts at modification are unsuccessful. As a result, we limit the opportunities that a person might have to develop appropriate skills. For example, Ross and Ross (1972) claimed that we underestimate the self-reward capabilities of retarded persons and, as a result, that caretakers typically set minimal external standards for a retarded child's performance while inconsistently administering external consequences. Thus, retarded persons may, as a group, have their personal freedom or options restricted not only because of skill deficits but also because of socially accepted limits placed on their right to exercise self-determination.

If self-regulatory skills could be developed in retarded persons, then we would suggest that the reported lack of independent functioning reflects limits that we have imposed on these individuals. However, failure to develop such skills could be due to relatively stable structural limitations in functioning or to inadequately designed and/or applied training procedures. A brief examination of studies examining self-regulation in retarded populations should help to clarify the proposed deficits as well as give us information as to whether these deficits are modifiable (that is, a result of structural features or control processes).

Delay of Gratification

The ability to postpone immediate gratification for larger delayed rewards is thought to be central to self-regulation. Kanfer (1977) and Mischel (1974) have proposed similar two-stage models of delay of gratification or self-control. In the first stage—decisional self-control—a choice is made either to seek larger delayed rewards or to obtain immediately available smaller rewards. If a decision is made to seek larger delayed rewards, then the second stage—protracted self-control—emerges (Kanfer 1977); that is, the individual must be able to withstand the self-imposed delay interval if the delayed reward is to be obtained.

Some empirical evidence suggests that decisional self-control is related to IQ (Mischel and Metzner 1962) and that mildly retarded students are less likely than emotionally handicapped students to choose to delay reward attainment (see Morena and Litrownik 1974). When we looked at decisional self-control in a moderately retarded sheltered-workshop population (mean IQ = 37), we found that our subjects did not always choose the immediate option and that their choices appeared to be determined, in part, by the reward options (see Franzini, Litrownik, and Magy 1978).

An additional study indicated that decisional self-control could be modified in this workshop population if the participants had an opportunity to experience delay intervals prior to making their choices (see Litrownik et al. 1977). Finally, a preliminary attempt to develop protracted self-control in ten chronic nondelayers from this population indicated that they could learn to endure a delay interval—evidence of protracted self-control (see Franzini, Litrownik, and Magy 1979).

Self-Observation

A number of studies indicate that retarded persons cannot reliably record their own behavior or the consequences of their behavior. For example, Zegiob, Klukas, and Junginger (1978) attempted to teach a 17-year-old mildly retarded girl and an 18-year-old moderately retarded girl to record nose and mouth picking and head shaking, respectively. Neither accurately recorded these undesirable responses, and in fact, after the first few self-recording sessions, both ceased to do any recording. In a group study, Singer (1963) assessed the ability of mildly retarded students to record the consequences of their performance (namely, scores they obtained on a game). He reported that the students were unable to report correctly their scores. Nelson, Lipinski, and Black (1976) had twelve mildly retarded (IQ = 43–80) adults record their conversations, participation in activities, and tidiness of their bedroom. Correlations of these recordings with those made by external observers suggested that the retarded adults were extremely unreliable in their recording (*r*s ranged from .23 to −.10).

While these studies suggest that retarded persons are unreliable observers of their own behavior, some reports suggest that self-monitoring skills can be developed. For example, two borderline retarded boys were taught to count the number of homework problems in arithmetic they completed each night (Mahoney and Mahoney 1976); more severely retarded children were taught to add a pop bead to a chain each time they finished a simple problem (Kurtz and Neisworth 1976); and four mildly retarded adolescents, who were provided with specific training, learned how to record their appropriate classroom verbalizations (Nelson, Lipinski, and Boykin 1978).

Not only does it appear that retarded persons can acquire self-monitoring skills but also that these skills, even if they are not reliably or accurately applied, lead to changes in the responses to be recorded; that is, Zegiob and her associates (1978) found that both of their subjects decreased their undesirable target behaviors when they were supposed to be monitoring them even though they did not do any self-recording. Similarly, the twelve retarded adults who were supposed to record three positive target behaviors increased their performance of these responses although they did not reliably record their activity (Nelson, Lipinski, and Black 1976).

Reactive effects have also been reported when retarded subjects were more reliable in their self-recording. Specifically, five retarded adults were found to talk more during a ten-minute period when they recorded their verbalizations than during two baseline periods, and five other retarded adults spent more time touching objects during a ten-minute period when they recorded this behavior than during two baseline periods. Finally, Nelson, Lipinski, and Boykin (1978) reported that their nine subjects tended to engage in more-appropriate classroom verbalizations when they were monitoring this behavior.

While these reports are promising, we should be cautious in making any claims about the negative effects of self-monitoring in retarded persons. These reports are preliminary since they involve small numbers of subjects, they utilize within-subject comparisons, and the reports of reactivity indicate that it is minimal at best.

Self-Reward

Mahoney and Mahoney (1976) reported that two young (6- and 8-year-old) emotionally disturbed boys learned to reward themselves for brushing their teeth and that the self-administered rewards (for example, money) maintained brushing at a higher level. Additionally, they reported a successful attempt to teach a borderline retarded 11-year old to evaluate and consequate his behavior with the aim of decreasing aggressive responses.

In the only group study reported to date, Helland, Paluck, and Klein (1976) had ten retarded adults (mean CA = 28 years) collate papers for three minutes. Following a five-day baseline period, one group of five subjects was externally rewarded each time they collated ten sets while the other five subjects were taught to self-administer rewards (for example, 10^{c} or a candy) after ten sets were completed. The differential treatments continued for four days and were followed by a second four-day baseline with no rewards available. The results indicated that the retarded adults could learn appropriately to administer rewards to themselves when a cue (a pink sheet of paper) was provided after each set of ten. In addition, both external and self-reward groups increased their output during reward conditions, as compared to baseline with no differences between the two. Thus, retarded adults appear to be able to maintain their output by self-administering rewards at a level equal to that when rewards are externally dispensed.

Standards and Self-Evaluative Responses

Although some investigators (like Rosen et al. 1971) have proposed that retarded persons do not set realistic standards for their performance, only one study has actually examined the suitability of predicted outcomes. Campione and Brown (1977) described a study in which mildly retarded students predicted how many pictures they would be able to recall after being shown ten pictures. The students then had an opportunity to recall as many of the items as they could. Actual and predicted scores were compared with a realistic estimation being defined as one that was within two items of actual recall. Using this criterion, less than 30 percent of the population was classified as realistic. Subsequently, some of the older students (MA = 8) became more realistic with additional experience and specific feedback.

The importance of realistic or appropriate standards is suggeted when we see the setting of standards, or levels of aspiration, appears to facilitate performance in mildly retarded students (see Rosen, Diggory, and Werlinsky 1966; Warner and de Jung 1971).

Examining self-evaluative responses on a match-to-sample task, Brodsky et al. (1970) reported that their mildly retarded subjects could not initially evaluate their performance appropriately. A group that received contingent reinforcement for their responses, however, subsequently showed appropriate evaluations.

Cue Regulation

In an anecdotal case report, Mahoney and Mahoney (1976) described the application of cue-regulation procedures to a brain-damaged 15-year old who was being treated for hysterical outbursts. Maladaptive thoughts (for example, self-criticism) that apparently triggered the outbursts were successfully supplanted by positive thoughts or cues.

Guralnick (1976) used modeling and rehearsal-training procedures to teach mildly retarded (mean IQ = 63) students (mean CA = 11.1) self-instructional statements. These cues were to be applied when the students worked on a match-to-sample task (go slowly, pick out relevant dimensions, eliminate choices), and selections were to be followed by positive self-statements. Students who were trained to emit these instructional signals and positive evaluations made significant gains in their performance from pre- to post-assessment as compared to groups that received feedback on their performance, had a model demonstrate the task for them, and served as no-contact controls.

Implications

The results of these few, mostly preliminary, studies suggest that retarded persons may not initially engage in self-regulatory skills but that these skills can be developed. In addition, there is some indication that, once acquired, these skills can be used by retarded persons effectively to regulate their own behavior. Of course, we must recognize that these results are tentative, limited to mildly retarded individuals, and based on small samples.

Based on these suggestive studies, we argue that the lack of independent functioning in retarded persons (at least midly retarded) is due, in part, to the limited opportunities they have to develop appropriate self-regulatory skills—that is, it appears that limited self-regulation is not a function of structural deficits in retarded persons but rather that limitations in self-regulation result from a lack of opportunity and inadequate training and/or the absence of training. If we are to develop appropriate self-regulatory skills in retarded persons we need to have a clear conceptualization of what it is we hope to develop; determine what would be the best approach to developing these skills (that is, strategy); evaluate attempts to develop these skills; and evaluate the effects of these skills, if acquired, on the behaviors to be controlled (that is, behaviors that are targeted for self-regulatory control).

Self-Regulation: A Conceptualization and Strategy for Its Development

As we suggested, our first task should be one of trying to identify what it is we intend to develop. Our attempts to understand and conceptualize self-regulation are based on a number of previously proposed working models (Bandura 1977; 1978; Kanfer 1977; Karoly 1977; Meichenbaum and Asarnow 1978; Thoresen and Mahoney 1974). Each has added to our understanding while also leaving us with some unanswered questions. The general conceptualization that follows hopefully serves the same function for others. We present it not as a formalized theory but rather as a working model that helps to put our work in the proper perspective—how it relates to self-regulation and what we need to do in the future.

We propose that, in general, self-regulation involves the application of a problem-solving strategy (see D'Zurilla and Goldfried 1971). The application of this strategy can result in a change of behavior, as well as serve to maintain performance that is relatively independent of environmental influences (see Kanfer 1977; Karoly 1977). Thus, we must distinguish among the various effects of self-regulation. In addition, we need to recognize that self-regulation involves a number of problem-solving stages, each stage requiring a variety of specific skills.

Self-regulation and the specific skills involved in problem-solving are cued, according to Kanfer (1977) by any disruption in the smooth flow of behavior. Thus, unexpected events—those that elicit high emotional arousal, as well as situations that require new learning—all serve as cues for the implementation of the self-regulatory process. This is the first stage: An individual must be aware that a problem exists and that there is a need for regulating his or her performance. To determine that a problem exists, individuals must be able to monitor their behavior, its antecedants, and consequences, as well as to evaluate the situation in relation to a prescribed standard ("There is a problem I need to solve"). The source, as well as the stringency of one's standards, will necessarily influence or determine whether a problem is identified (see Bandura 1978). Once a problem has been identified, a commitment to solve the problem must be made (see Karoly 1977). This second stage (commitment) requires a decision to experience some immediate aversive consequences (for example, time, effort, withholding of positive consequences) with the anticipation that more-valued positive outcomes will result at some later time. A commitment is made to try to obtain this later, desired outcome. Thus, a commitment to solve a problem requires a decision to delay gratification—that is, a person must show decisional self-control and have a general standard or goal.

During the third (executive) stage, an individual appraises the problem (characterizes the problem, what is required, and predicts his own capacity) and generates a number of possible solutions (see Campione and Brown 1977). The number and appropriateness of these possible solutions or routines for dealing with a specific problem are not only a function of an individual's repertoire of routines but also of his or her awareness of their utility; that is, the selection of an appropriate solution depends upon an individual's developing some knowledge about how behavior is controlled (metacontrol).

In the next stage, the selected plan or routine is applied, and in the final stage, the effectiveness of the routine is evaluated. The evaluation is based on prescribed goals from the commitment stage and may lead to a return to the executive stage to select another plan, continuance of the routine, or abandonment of the routine.

As we indicated, each stage requires a number of specific skills. In addition, the same skill, in some cases, may be required at a number of different stages. For example, self-observation is involved in problem identification and the evaluation of a routine's effectiveness as is standard setting that is also required at the commitment stage. We may also find that these same skills are involved when a specific routine is applied.

Our ultimate goals is one of developing general problem-solving or self-regulatory skills in moderately retarded persons. Initially, the question we had to answer was where to start. Since we hoped that our efforts would allow retarded persons to exercise more personal freedom, we decided to begin by developing a number of options or routines that they could utilize to regulate their own behavior.

As this was the initial venture in this area, we decided to focus upon a routine that we considered to be relatively easy to develop (namely, self-reinforcement) with the more modest aim of having our retarded students utilize it to maintain their behavior with a minimum of environmental control. Now that we had decided on the routine we hoped to develop, we needed to specify what it required. Bandura has described self-reinforcement as "a process in which individuals enhance and maintain their own behavior by rewarding themselves with rewards that they control whenever they attain self-prescribed standards" (1977, p. 130). We identified four component skills necessary for self-reinforcement: (1) self-observation, (2) standard setting, (3) self-evaluation, and (4) self-reward. We then attempted to operationalize each of them, determine if we could develop them singly and in combination, and evaluate the effects of these skills and self-reinforcement on task performance.

A Program for Developing Self-Reinforcement

With this conceptual framework in mind, we began our programmatic effort to develop self-regulatory skills in moderately retarded individuals. Our strategy was one of focusing on individual skill development prior to training in self-reinforcement.

Skill Acquisition

During this stage of the program, we operationalized each of the four component skills and then evaluated attempts to develop them in a young, moderately retarded population.

Population. Approximately 150 trainable mentally retarded (TMR) students between the ages of 7 and 14, attending Fairhaven-McCandles School, were individually administered the Slosson Intelligence Test (Slosson 1963). Those children (approximately 75) with IQs between 30 and 50 and MAs between 3 and 5½ years served as our pool of potential subjects for subsequent skill-acquisition studies. We should also mention that certain prerequisite skills required for participation in these studies were assessed and, if necessary, taught to subjects prior to their participation in a study. These skills included the ability to discriminate between numbers, shapes, parts of the body, and schoolwork that was finished or not finished. Those who did not acquire necessary prerequisite discriminations within one session (approximately 30–40 minutes) were excluded from participation in a given study. Groups from the remaining pool of students were established, based on a stratified match of means and variance for IQ, MA, and CA.

General Training Approach. Training in these initial skill-acquisition studies utilized demonstration, prompting, and rehearsal procedures with primary reinforcers (edibles). The training was divided into a sequence of steps and demonstrations, and/or prompting continued at each step until a criterion (four consecutive correct responses) was reached. When reaching criterion at one step, students moved on to the next step. This process continued until they reached criterion on the last step or until a certain amount of time had elapsed. Thus, the training was criterion based within a limited period of time.

Prior to participating in these studies, we presented our potential subjects with a variety of consumables (nuts, raisins, chips, candies, cheeses, fruit) and had them select three items to sample. When students participated in a study, they selected two edibles that they wanted to work for prior to each session. The demonstration-training procedures that we used had been developed previously (see Litrownik et al. 1978b); Litrownik, Franzini, and Turner 1976). They included distributed trials (that is, imitation training) where an experimenter-model demonstrated a single response or instance of the required skill and the subject had an immediate opportunity to perform. If the subject matched the model's performance he was rewarded and thus given one of the selected edibles. In addition to these distributed demonstrations that result in response matching, we also included massed-demonstration trials. In these massed demonstrations, a model (either live or on tape) demonstrated skills as they were required over a number of trials or instances before the subject had an opportunity to perform. Again, correct performance was followed with the subject's obtaining an edible. While these massed demonstrations do not lead to as much matching as the distributed demonstrations, some evidence indicates that they lead to superior concept acquisition (see Litrownik, Franzini, and Turner 1976). Training usually began with distributed demonstrations, proceeded through massed demonstrations, and finally ended with a rehearsal step (no demonstrations preceded performance).

Self-Monitoring. We began with self-monitoring, as it has been identified, as the crucial first step in self-reinforcement (for example, Thoresen and Mahoney 1974). Not only is it required if an individual is to engage in subsequent component skills such as setting standards based on past performance and evaluating subsequent performances based on these standards, but also some evidence indicates that self-monitoring in itself can affect task performance.

Self-monitoring requires observation of covert and/or overt events, a discrimination cued by these events, and a self-recording response (see Nelson 1977). Like external monitoring, self-monitoring can involve any number of responses to be observed, as well as various ways to record them. Both the target response and the self-recording response can vary from the complex (for example, describing behavior, along with its antecedents and consequences) to the simple (for example, recording a check for each problem completed).

In contrast to prior studies, we attempted to teach our moderately retarded subjects a more-complex self-monitoring task. Specifically, they had to finish a task and then discriminate between the kind of problem they completed and the consequences of their performance (for instance, score obtained). These discriminations were to determine whether a self-recording response was to follow.

A demonstration-training program was developed in an attempt to teach these skills. In order to evaluate the effectiveness of this program, ten TMR children were exposed to the training, ten served as yoked attention controls, and ten served as no-contact controls. Self-monitoring performances of all thirty children were assessed at three times: (1) prior to the intervention; (2) following training, yoked attention, or an appropriate interval of time; and (3) after a retention interval of approximately one week (see Litrownik, Freitas, and Franzini 1978).

A seat-work-discrimination task and a bowling game similar to the one employed by Bandura in his investigations (1976) were used to assess self-monitoring skills. On the seat-work task, the children were to match a figure on the top of the page with one of two figures below that was the same. All figures could be categorized as either parts of the body (arm, leg, ear) or simple shapes (triangle, circle, square). Each time students drew a line between matching parts of the body (sixteen of twenty-four problems), they were to self-monitor by placing a red ring over a peg. Following the matching of two shapes (eight of the problems), students were to proceed to the next problem without recording.

On the bowling game, students rolled a small ball down a 1-meter alley that had ten pins set up so that the bowling ball traveled below them over marks on the alley. After each roll, a score was shown on a lighted scoreboard directly above the game. Scores were predetermined with all children receiving the same number of scores on fifteen bowling trials (two scores of 1, three scores of 5, and ten scores of 10) in the same sequence. Each time a score of 10 was obtained, students were to self-monitor by placing the ring on the peg.

Two generalization tasks were used. One assessed transfer to a new task (pursuit rotor), employing the same criterion or cue for the self-monitoring response (a score of 10). Scores were presented in the same manner via the lighted scoreboard as for the bowling game. The second generalization task consisted of seat work with figures of either vehicles or letters and involved a different criterion for self-monitoring. Children were to self-monitor each time they drew a line between two vehicles.

All children were initially pretested on both the bowling (fifteen trials) and seat-work (twenty-four trials) tasks. At this pretesting and during each subsequent testing (post, retention, and transfer) the children were given two practice trials. One required a self-monitoring response; the other did not. The children were not only instructed to self-monitor appropriately but also verbally and/or physically prompted to do so. One to two weeks after pretesting, the training and attention-control groups were exposed to the live and taped demonstrations.

The training group was exposed to two training sessions: first the bowling and later the seat-work task. The first session for each task involved live demonstrations of appropriate self-monitoring by a female experimenter-model. Training continued either until the child correctly monitored on six consecutive trials without prior demonstrations or until forty minutes of training time had elapsed. The second session included the showing of a ten-minute color videotape in which Sparky the Clown demonstrated correct self-monitoring behaviors on the task.

The ten children in the *attention-control* group were each yoked to a child in the training group based on a match of gender, CA, MA, and IQ. They were then given an opportunity to perform an equal number of live bowling trials, seat-work trials, and self-monitoring responses (putting the ring on the peg) as their yoked partner from the training group. However, no instructions or demonstrations of appropriate self-monitoring responses were provided. In addition, the attention-control children viewed two control tapes that showed Sparky either bowling or doing seat work. Following her performance on fifteen bowling trials, Sparky placed ten rings on the peg, and following the twenty-four seat-work problems, she placed sixteen rings on the peg. Thus the yoked attention-control group was exposed to a taped model who bowled, completed seat-work problems, and put rings on a peg. However, the self-monitoring response was not associated with a particular score on the bowling game or with a particular type of seat-work problem.

Posttesting on the task followed the ten-minute tape (training or control) for that task. Retention and transfer of self-monitoring responses were assessed one week (±two days) following the seat-work posttest. Performances of the no-contact group on the bowling, seat-work, and transfer tasks were assessed at the same intervals as the training and attention-control groups (for example, day 1, day 3, day 11, respectively).

At each assessment (pre, post, retention, and transfer), the number of correct self-monitoring responses (putting a ring on the peg following a 10 score or following completion of a matching problem that involved a part of the body or a vehicle) and the number of self-monitoring errors of overinclusion (putting a ring on the peg following a score of 1 or 5 or following the completion of a shape- or letter-matching problem) were recorded. An appropriate self-monitoring score for each task at each assessment was obtained by subtracting two times the number of overinclusion errors from the number of correct self-monitoring responses. This correction yielded a score of zero if the child self-monitored on every trial (for example, twenty-four seat work or fifteen bowling) of if he never self-monitored. Thus, at each assessment, scores could range from −10 to 10 on the bowling game and from −16 to 16 on the seat-work task. At pretesting, the three groups were self-monitoring at the same level—that is, all three groups were correctly monitoring their bowling (means ranged from −.3 to .7) and seat-work (means ranged from −.1 to 1.2) performances at a chance level. At post-, retention, and generalization assessments, the training group significantly outperformed the two control groups. No differences between the control groups were evident, both continuing to correctly self-monitor at a chance level (means ranged from −.3 to 1.6 on the bowling game and −1.1 to .9 on the seat-work task).

Based on these results it appears that moderately retarded students cannot differentially self-monitor the consequences of their performance (bowling game) or the problem or activity that they have completed (seat-work task) when provided only with instructions to do so. These failures are even more pronounced when we consider that the two control groups were assessed four times on each task and that each assessment included two practice trials with detailed instructions. Although they were provided with a total of eight shaping trials and four sets of instructions for each task, these two control groups appropriately self-monitored at a chance level during all assessments.

Though these students could not initially correctly self-monitor, we found that those who were exposed to a brief one-hour demonstration-training program were able to acquire, retain, and transfer these skills. In this study, students learned a complex differential self-monitoring skill. Not only did they have to observe whether they had completed a task (matching seat work) or engaged in a single response (bowled), but also they had to observe and discriminate between the type of task completed and the consequences of their behavior. Such differential self-monitoring skills should prove to be quite functional as they can be adapted to a number of relevant situations. For example, retarded students in a classroom could learn to monitor correct versus incorrect performance, high versus low scores, and completion of a task within a specified time.

Our population was restricted to TMR students of a certain MA (3 to 5.5 years) who did not have severe visual or motor handicaps. In addition, we excluded students who could not perform necessary prerequisite behaviors (for example, draw a line between two objects or discriminate between shapes and parts of the body and between the numbers 1, 5, and 10). While the results of the present study cannot be generalized to TMR students with severe visual and/or motor handicaps, we can assume that a student who has acquired the necessary entering behaviors will benefit from the demonstration-training program. Thus, it appears that most moderately retarded students can learn to monitor accurately such relevant consequences of their behavior. Acquisition of differential self-monitoring skills by TMR students specifically, and retarded students in general, can relieve classroom instructors of the task of always having to monitor externally each student's performance. If instructors can rely more on their students to monitor their own performances, then additional time should be available for instruction, while at the same time the retarded individual would have an opportunity to function more independently.

In addition to fostering independence and aiding classroom instruction, self-monitoring may also lead to desired changes in the behaviors that are being observed—that is, it is reactive. Of course, further work needs to be done to demonstrate that self-monitoring is indeed reactive in a moderately retarded population.

Standards for Performance. In the next study (see Litrownik et al. 1978a), we focused upon developing standards for performance. These standards are acquired sets of criteria that serve as incentives as well as guides for personal action (Kanfer 1977). As mentioned previously, retarded individuals typically have other people set minimal and/or inconsistent standards for them. If the setting of appropriate standards for performance is important in the self-reinforcement process (Bandura 1977; Brownell et al. 1977; Masters, Furman, and Barden 1977; Spates and Kanfer 1977) and if standards are acquired via modeling, then it is understandable why retarded persons fail to control or regulate effectively their own behavior. If retarded persons are to function more independently, they must then be given the opportunity to learn to set appropriate standards for their own performance.

How can these important internal, or self-set, standards be acquired or developed? Bandura (1977) claims that our standards for performance can be based on social referents (observing how others perform and the standards they set), our own past performances, or a combination of the two. While numerous studies (Bandura 1977) have shown that normal developing preschool and elementary-school-aged children can acquire self-reward patterns (that is, standards) via observation of others, there have not been any reports of retarded individuals acquiring standards in this manner. Thus, our first aim was to determine if our moderately retarded students could adapt standards for their performance based on the observation of others.

Three groups of eight students each were established with one group randomly assigned to experience live and then taped demonstrations, taped then live demonstrations, and no training demonstrations. Students in the two training groups were brought individually to our mobile laboratory where they watched a ten-minute color videotape that showed five colorful clown models (two boys, three girls) playing the same bowling game. Before bowling, each clown said, "I'm going to try for a 6," while placing a green arrow next to the 6 on a yellow felt scoreboard. After viewing this tape, the training groups were given an opportunity to set a standard before they took a turn on the bowling game. The eight control students were also given an opportunity to set a standard and to bowl, but they did not watch the tape of the clowns.

Eleven of the sixteen students in the training group set their standard at 6. None of the children in the control group set their standard at this score. A chi-square analysis revealed that the training group was more likely than the control group to set the standard at 6—the standard the clown models set. These results are the first presented, to our knowledge, indicating that TMR students can acquire standards via observation of others. We realized that basing standards on others' performance would be appropriate for retarded students only if they were allowed to observe models of comparable skill (that is, limit them to special classes or groups). A reasonable alternative is to teach TMR students to set standards based on their own past performance. In the second phase of this study, we attempted to teach our students a relational concept (between) that would allow them to do just that.

On the first day of this second phase, students in the first training group individually observed a twelve-minute color videotape in which three clowns demonstrated the concept. Each of nine demonstrated trials (three trials per clown) included two practice rolls of the bowling ball, with the clown models receiving predetermined scores that were two digits apart (for example, 3 and 5, 6 and 8). Following each practice trial, the models recorded the score obtained by placing a blue ring around the number on the yellow felt scoreboard. The clowns then verbalized the concept between while placing the green arrow next to the score they were trying for on the next roll. On this final roll, the clowns met their standard and placed a red star next to the number on the scoreboard. Students in the second training group were exposed to live demonstrations of this concept. The experimenter-model bowled twice, received scores that were two digits apart, recorded these scores, set her standard between the two predetermined scores while verbalizing the concept, bowled again, and met her standard. Students then had an opportunity to match the model's performance, receiving the same predetermined scores as the model. These demonstrations and student performances continued until the model was matched on four consecutive trials or until twenty minutes of training time had elapsed. On the second day, the training procedures were reversed for the two training groups. A five-trial assessment followed each day's training and six ($\pm$ one) days later. On the day following this retention assessment, the students' ability to transfer the standard-setting concept to one picture-story trial and five pinball trials was assessed.

The picture-story game was adapted from MacMillan (1975) and involved the identification of one of three choice pictures that went with a sample picture. All three choice stimuli could, in fact, go with the sample since all four pictures were of animals. Two sets of eight trials were utilized, with students being told after the first set that they were correct on four of eight trials, whereas for the second set they were told that on six of the eight trials they had identified the correct picture. The students were then asked to indicate how many they would try to get correct on the next trial. The pinball game was similar to the bowling game in that there were wires running from it to the electric scoreboard. After each pinball trial, an observer flashed the predetermined score (1 to 10) on the scoreboard. At each post-, retention, and generalization assessment, the two training groups were more likely to set their standards between than the control group. The mean correct standard-setting score for the control group varied from 0 to .2 over the four assessments, while the two training groups had means in the range of 2–3 for each of the five trial assessments. On the one picture-story task, we found that only the first training group was more likely to set their standard between than the control group.

Thus, these TMR students did acquire, retain, and generalize a concept that allowed them to set a standard based on their own past performance. Although the students used the concept to set their standards, we do not know if they understood the meaning of the standards they set because we did not look at the effects of these standards on other kinds of behavior. We observed that many of the students appeared pleased when they met their standards, but no other indication of the meaningfulness of the standards was obtained. In any case, we found that our retarded students would set standards for their performance based on the observation of others and that they could learn to set standards based on their own past performances.

Self-Evaluation and Self-Reward. In the third study, we attempted to train our students to evaluate their own performance (Litrownik et al. 1978c) and then to administer conditionally fully accessible rewards. We also collected data that we hoped would give us some preliminary indication as to whether the acquisition and performance of these skills had any effect on task performance.

The students were required to perform two tasks, symbol matching (training) and block design (transfer). For the symbol-matching task, students were presented with one work page at a time. Each page contained a variety of numbers, letters, and shapes in addition to a sample number, letter, or shape at the top of the page. Students were to cross out as many of the numbers, letters, or shapes that they could that matched the sample before a bell rang. The bell was controlled by the experimenter so that the number of items that were crossed out by each child could be controlled. After each trial, the experimenter informed students as to whether they had successfully completed the page (finished or not finished). In front of both the experimenter and the child was a felt scoreboard with their names. In addition, eight circular yellow felt happy faces and eight green felt squares were available. If students finished before the bell rang, they were to put a felt happy face on the scoreboard (that is, positive self-evaluation, "I finished"). If the student did not finish, a green felt square was to be placed on the scoreboard (that is, negative self-evaluation, "I have to try harder"). Two clear plastic cups, each containing twenty edibles selected by the student, were placed within reach. Following a positive self-evaluation, students were to reinforce themselves by taking one edible. Students were to abstain from administering themselves a reward following a negative self-evaluation. Thus, self-reward was properly self-administered only after students had successfully crossed out all of the items before the bell rang and had correctly self-evaluated their performance by placing a happy face on the scoreboard.

On the transfer task, students were required to match a block design (sequence of colors) that was constructed by the experimenter before the bell rang. Six ten-block designs of varying difficulty were presented twice to each child in random order. Students were allowed fifteen to thirty seconds to complete each design. Each trial was timed by the experimenter who signaled the end of the trial by ringing the bell. As with the symbol-matching task, the experimenter informed students as to whether they had correctly completed the design. Students were then to self-evaluate and self-reward as they had on the symbol-matching task.

Two groups of eight students each were administered a pretest for both the training and transfer tasks. Two practice trials (one success and one failure) on which the experimenter instructed the child and prompted correct self-evaluative and self-reward responses preceded the twelve symbol-matching-test trials. On each trial the experimenter rang the bell after the child had crossed out a predetermined number of figures. In this manner the child was presented with six failure and six success trials in random order.

The block-design, or transfer, task was similarly administered. Following the two practice trials, students were presented with twelve test trials (six different ten-block designs with a fifteen- and thirty-second time limit). On the transfer task, the success or failure of the subject was not directly controlled by the experimenter, allowing the performance of the child to vary with his ability and effort. After each test trial, the child was told whether or not he had correctly completed the design before the bell had rung.

On the day following this pretest, the eight students in the training group received a maximum of thirty minutes of training (demonstrations and practice) for self-evaluation. On the next day, all sixteen students' self-evaluations on both the symbol-matching and block-design tasks were again assessed. These posttests were identical to those administered in the pretest with the exception that no reference to or expectation of self-reward was made. On the fourth day, self-reward training began. Students were instructed to put either a happy face or green square on their scoreboard and were administered edibles by the experimenter when they put the happy face on the board. They were then instructed to take an edible themselves following a trial when they put a happy face on their scoreboard. Finally, students put happy faces or green squares on their scoreboard and were allowed to self-administer rewards. Errors were corrected by the experimenter-trainer. Following a maximum of ten minutes of training or criterion performance (four out of five correct), the two components were trained in combination; that is, the experimenter-model demonstrated what was to be done on failure (for example, green square had no reward) and success (for example, happy face meant reward) trials, and then the students had a chance to perform. This training continued until students were able to perform correctly on nine out of ten trials, or until thirty minutes had elapsed.

On the fifth day, both training and control groups were posttested on the two tasks. The posttest was identical to the pretest as was the retention test administered four days later. Finally, one week after the retention test, six of the eight control students were exposed to the training program and then assessed again.

At each assessment (pre, self-evaluation post, self-evaluation and self-reward post, and retention), the number of correct self-evaluative responses on the training (symbol-matching) and transfer (block-design) tasks was recorded. In addition, at each assessment (except the self-evaluation posttest) the number of correct self-evaluation and self-reward trials was recorded.

We found (see figures 6-1 and 6-2) that both groups of students were initially evaluating and rewarding themselves at the same level of appropri-

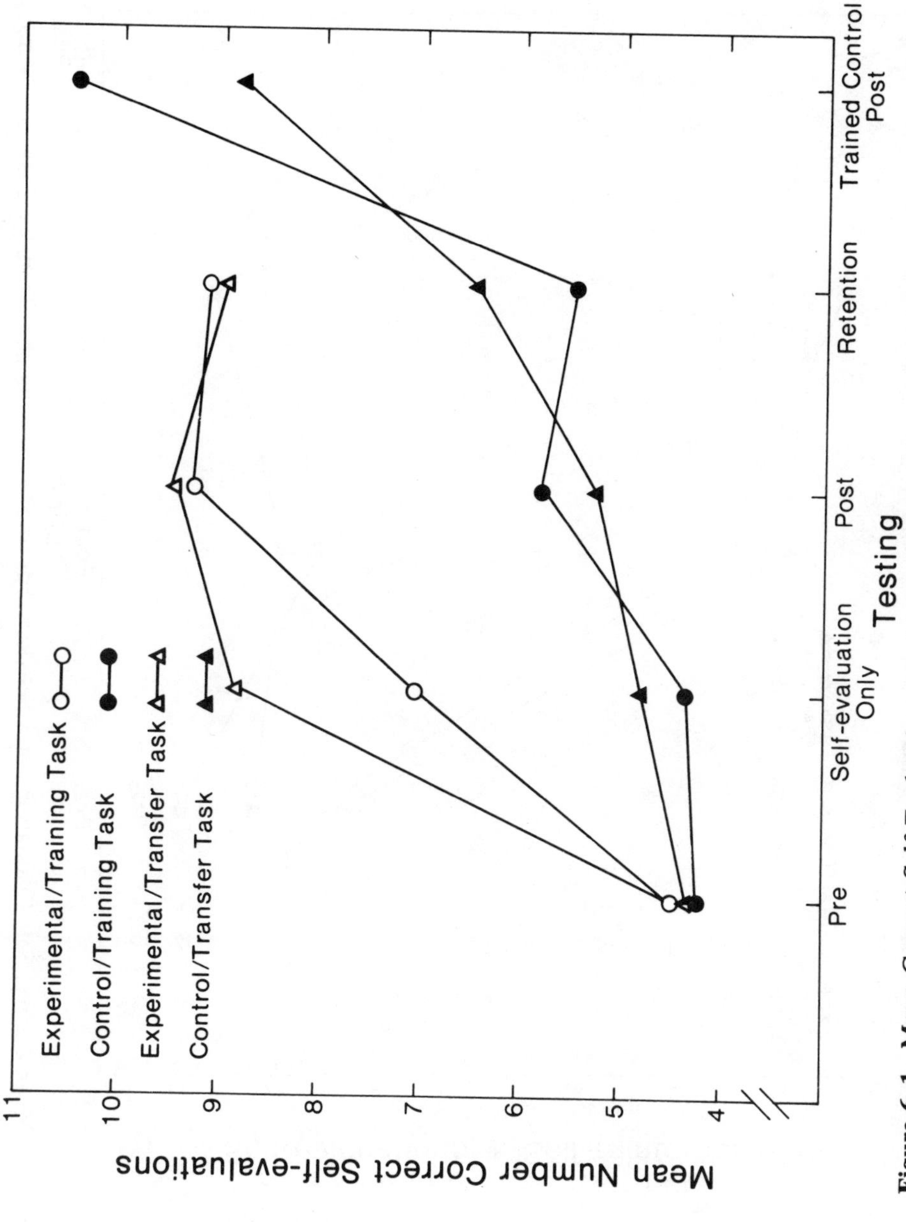

Figure 6–1. Mean Correct Self-Evaluations on the Training and Transfer Tasks at Each Assessment

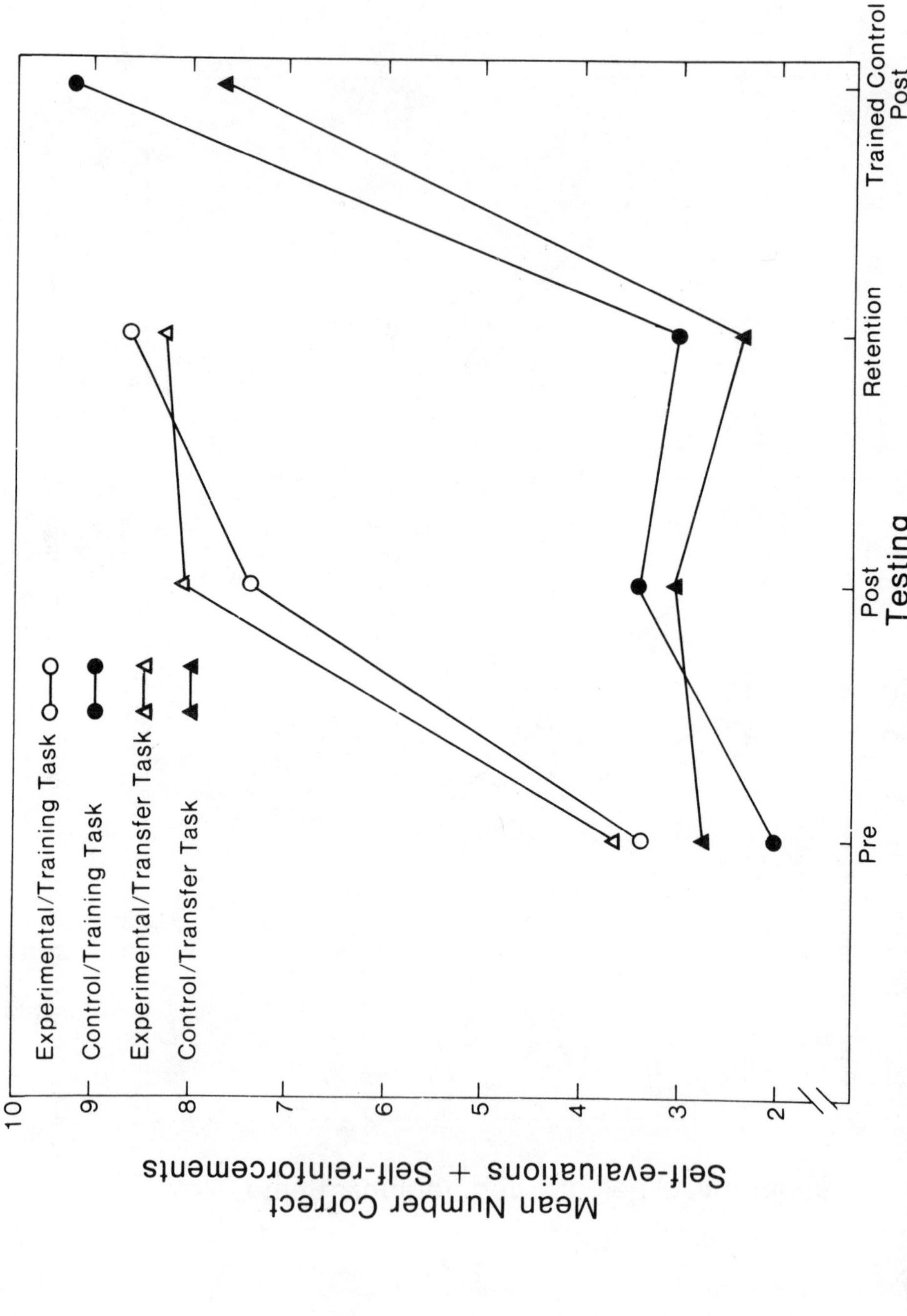

Figure 6–2. Mean Correct Self-Evaluations plus Self-Rewards on the Training and Transfer Tasks at Each Assessment

ateness—that is, chance. Subsequently, students who were exposed to the training program correctly evaluated and rewarded themselves on both the training and transfer tasks while the control students appropriately evaluated and rewarded their performances following exposure to the training program. Thus the training effect was replicated.

Four measures of task performance on the block design were obtained: (1) total number of blocks placed, (2) number of blocks placed in the correct position, (3) number of blocks placed in the correct sequence, and (4) total number of designs correctly completed. In order to evaluate the effects of acquired self-evaluation and self-reward skills on block-design performance, we conducted separate two-group discriminant analyses (see Kaplan and Litrownik 1977) at each assessment. These analyses indicated that the training and control groups did not differ at pre-and posttesting but differed at retention testing. The groups were differentiated at retention, based primarily on the training group's better serial placements and greater number of designs completed correctly.

Thus, this study not only demonstrated that self-evaluative and self-reward skills could be developed in our moderately retarded students but also that retarded persons can effect changes in their behavior as a function of engaging in these skills. The fact that differences in task performance occurred only at retention testing and not at posttesting suggests that these skills need to be applied over a period of time before changes in behavior can be observed.

Summary. The results of these first three studies suggest that (1) TMR students cannot appropriately self-monitor, set standards, or self-evaluate and self-reward their own performances when directed to do so; (2) these skills can be developed; and (3) the acquisition of self-evaluative and self-reward skills can affect task performance.

Effects of Skills on Task Performance

The next two studies we conducted in our program focused on the effects of two specific component skills—self-evaluation and self-monitoring—on task performance. We had found that our young, moderately retarded students could acquire these skills, and evidence suggested that they might, having acquired affect targeted behaviors (Nelson, Lipinski, and Black 1976; Nelson, Lipinski, and Boykin 1978; Litrownik et al. 1978c).

In order to evaluate the effects of these skills on task performance, we taught older (adolescent) moderately retarded students to emit self-evaluative statements following performance on a task (Lecklitner 1977) or to monitor their performances (Litrownik and Freitas 1980).

Self-Evaluative Statements. Masters and Santrock (1976) recently reported a series of studies designed to investigate the reinforcing or punishing characteristics of evaluative and affective self-statements made by 4-year-old children. They trained children to emit various task-relevant and task-irrelevant statements, containing differing affective quality following a task, and observed the effect of these statements on persistence at the task. In one of the studies children either said, "I'm really good at this" or "I'm no good at this," while performing a handle-turning task. Those children who verbalized the positive self-statement chose to perform the task for a longer period of time (that is, persisted) than either those who administered neutral or negative self-statements. Task persistence was not differentially affected by neutral versus negative statements. Thus, the positive self-statements or evaluations appeared to serve a reinforcing function while the negative self-statements did not.

Interestingly, these same authors also found that task-irrelevant verbalizations associated with positive or negative affect seemed to exercise the same systematic control over task persistence as the self-evaluative statements. As a result, Masters and Santrock proposed that evaluative statements may function to control behavior via the affect associated with the evaluations rather than the content of the evaluations. Further support for this contention comes from another study in which they found that children who evaluated the task as fun persisted longer at the task than those who did not (Masters and Santrock 1976).

Based on our last study (Litrownik et al. 1978c) and the work of Masters and Santrock, it appeared that moderately retarded students might be able to control their performances on a task by emitting various self-evaluative statements. The next study that we conducted specifically examined the effects of self-evaluative statements on task performance (Lecklitner 1977).

Thirty students between the ages of 14 and 21 from Fairhaven School, Mission Beach, and McCandles (both in San Diego, California) served as subjects. Each student was administered the Slosson Intelligence Test (Slosson 1963) prior to participation in the study. Students were assigned to one of the three groups based on a stratified match of means and variances for IQ, MA, and CA. We should point out that these students not only were older than those who participated in prior studies but also had higher IQs (group means ranged from 45.1 to 47.5). One group was then randomly assigned to make positive, negative, or neutral self-statements following their performance on a task that had little, if any, intrinsic reward value. A handle-turning task similar to the one employed by Masters and Santrock was utilized. Each turn of the handle activated a step relay, and after ten turns a bell was rung. This served as the signal for the students to verbalize their assigned self-statement. Individuals in the positive self-evaluative group were asked to verbalize the phrase, "I'm really good at this!" This phrase was modeled with positive affect by the experimenter in an attempt to reflect enthusiasm and pride. Students in the negative self-evaluation condition were asked to repeat the statement, "I'm not very good at this." The experimenter attempted to model this phrase with negative affect to connote self-criticism and disappointment. The neutral group was shown how to follow each ten handle turns by counting "One-two; one-two."

The experimenter modeled the evaluative statement (along with the affect) appropriate for each group until students were able to repeat the phrase correctly on three consecutive attempts. Due to the qualitative nature of the affective content of the statement, the students were not required to imitate the affective characteristics of the statement as delivered by the experimenter.

When students could verbalize the descriptive content of the self-statement, the experimental task was introduced. The experimenter demonstrated how to perform the task and emit the self-statement on eight consecutive trials without prompting or correcting.

The experimenter then explained that he was going to sit down at a table in another area of the room to do some work. The students were told that they could work at the task just as before for as long as they wanted. In order to minimize demand characteristics possibly associated with these instructions, the experimenter added, "Some people work for a long time and others for just a little bit." Students were instructed to join the experimenter at this table whenever they wanted to stop working.

As the experimenter sat down at a table located approximately twenty feet away, he started a stopwatch to record the amount of time each student worked at the task. The experimenter also recorded whether or not the appropriate self-statement was verbalized at the proper time and whether the statement appeared to be spoken with the proper effect.

After a student had voluntarily terminated the task or worked for a maximum of thirty minutes, an evaluation of the task was obtained; that is, three cards were placed in front of the students (happy, neutral, and sad face), and they were asked to pick the face that showed the way they would look if they were telling a friend about what they had just done. Following this evaluation, students were instructed to take as many pennies from a large bowl that they thought they deserved for the work they had just completed. Students were then allowed to exchange the pennies that were taken, regardless of how many, for a prize (toys, books, records). To reduce any possible negative effects associated with the repetition of the negative self-evaluative statement, students in this condition were told that they really did do a good job, such a good job that they could exchange their pennies for a prize.

Analyses of the performance measures (total number of handle turns, handle turns per minute) and evaluations of the task (pennies taken, face selected) revealed that the three groups did not differ on any of these dependent measures; that is, the self-evaluative statements that all students correctly verbalized at least 80 percent of the time did not differentially affect task performance or evaluation of the task.

The experimenter recorded his subjective impressions of the affect accompanying each student's self-evaluative statement. These anecdotal recordings suggested that only 30–40 percent of the positive and negative self-evaluations appeared to be intoned with the desired affect. Thus, the relative absence of appropriate affect associated with the self-evaluative statements apparently may offer the best explanation for the lack of significant findings in this study. If the motivational component of self-evaluation is largely moderated by the affect associated with these evaluations, as Masters and Santrock (1976) and Rosenhan (1972) suggest, then the absence of affect would suggest that the self-evaluations made by the students in this study would not act as reinforcers or punishers.

It is possible that this absence of affect or motivational control associated with the self-evaluations may be related to the socialization of these retarded students. Specifically, retarded persons are typically rewarded inconsistently. If rewarded inconsistently by others, their self-evaluative statements may not acquire meaning (that is, secondary reinforcing value) since the statements are not paired with consistent outcomes. If this is the case, we would need initially to pair self-evaluative statements with rewards in order for the self-evaluative stastements to become functional (that is, meaningful). One way of accomplishing this would be to develop self-reward and self-evaluative skills simultaneously in retarded persons and then to allow them to engage in (rehearse) both over a prolonged period of time. With this exposure we might expect that self-evaluative statements will come to acquire some meaning while the performance of the skills in combination will lead to effective control (see Litrownik et al. 1978c).

Self-Monitoring. In one of our prior skill-acquisition studies (see Litrownik, Freitas, and Franzini 1978), we found that younger TMR students could learn a complex differential self-monitoring skill. At the same time, we suggested, based on prior within-subject reports (for example, Nelson, Lipinski, and Black 1976; Nelson, Lipinski, and Boykin 1978; Zegiob, Klukas, and Junginger 1978), that the application of this skill might effect changes in the behaviors being monitored. Much evidence is accumulating that suggests that self-monitoring may lead to changes in the behavior being observed (see Kanfer 1977; McFall 1977; Nelson 1977). Both the degree and direction of these changes, as well as the accuracy of an individual's self-monitoring, appear to be a function of the valence of what is monitored (Greiner and Karoly 1976; Hayes and Cavior 1977; Kanfer 1977; Kazdin

1974; McFall 1977; Nelson 1977; Nelson et al. 1977). This means that responses with a negative valence are monitored less accurately since attention to these responses necessarily leads to negative self-evaluations that can be avoided by inaccurate monitoring. In addition, behaviors with a positive valence that are monitored increase, while responses with a negative valence decrease as a function of self-monitoring (see Hayes and Cavior 1977; Nelson et al. 1977; Sieck and McFall 1976).

In our next study (Litrownik and Freitas 1980), we attempted to examine the differential effects of valence on the accuracy and reactivity of self-monitoring in moderately retarded adolescents. Students strung as many beads as they could within a limited amount of time and either did not self-monitor or recorded positive, negative, or neutral outcomes of their performance.

Forty students from Fairhaven School, Mission Beach, who were between the ages of 15 and 21, had MAs between 4 and 8 years, and IQs between 20 and 55 (as measured by the Slosson Intelligence test) served as subjects. All were initially trained on three discriminations (red versus blue, large versus small, and work that was finished versus not finished) necessary for participation in the study. Four groups of ten subjects each were established, with one group randomly assigned to monitor each time they finished stringing a tray of beads, monitor each time they did not finish a tray, monitor when they had strung red beads, and string beads without any self-monitoring.

Students were brought to individual work stations, two or three at a time, for a maximum of sixty minutes per day over a total of five to seven days. Following each session they were given ten tokens for their participation that could be traded in for various items. In the first session, each student's bead-stringing speed was assessed. Five trials of twenty-five beads each were presented, and the number of beads strung in 125 seconds was recorded. For the second session, students in the three self-monitoring groups (finish, not finish, and red) were taught to record following a trial when they had strung large as opposed to small beads. Training continued until all students were correctly self-recording (that is, putting a marble in a tube) on ten of twelve consecutive trials. In order to equate bead-stringing experience during training, each control student was yoked to three partners, one from each self-monitoring group, based on gender, IQ, MA, and CA. The yoked students had an opportunity to string beads on as many trials as the average of their three partners. Next, the three self-monitoring groups were presented with twelve bead-stringing trials, with one group being told to self-monitor when they finished, one when they did not finish, and one when they had strung red beads. Performance was predetermined (the experimenter allowed the child to finish on six of the twelve trials). Students who monitored correctly on at least ten of twelve trials moved on to the next phase, while those who did not were provided with additional demonstration training. This training continued until the student was self-monitoring correctly on at least ten of twelve consecutive trials.

Persistence at the bead-stringing task was then assessed. Students were instructed to continue keeping track each time they finished, did not finish, or strung red beads, but after each trial they were to indicate whether or not they wished to continue to work on the task. This choice was made by pointing an arrow at a picture of a door (discontinue task and go back to class) or pointing an arrow at three beads (continue stringing beads). To ensure that students understood how to indicate what they wanted to do, the experimenter asked them to indicate what they would do if they wanted to string more beads or what they would do if they wanted to go back to their class. When students had correctly responded on four consecutive questions, they were presented with a maximum of thirty-four bead-stringing trials, each followed by a choice. Finally, a ten-trial (ten beads/trial) posttest was presented. Each student was given forty-five seconds to work on each tray of ten beads. The number of beads strung and the subsequent accuracy of self-monitoring was recorded.

The amount of training required for students to learn to monitor large-bead trials indicated that the three self-monitoring groups were equally capable of acquiring differential self-monitoring skills—that is, the groups required the same amount of training to learn this skill. Subsequently, the group that monitored not-finished trials did not take longer to learn this differential self-monitoring skill, and they were no less accurate in their self-monitoring on the posttest or assessment of task persistence than the other self-monitoring groups. Based on prior claims, we should have found that they were less accurate in their monitoring, but possibly due to the presence of external observers, valence did not appear to affect self-monitoring accuracy.

Self-monitoring did not differentially affect persistence on the bead-stringing task. It is interesting to note that we found that students tended either to persist for the maximum number of trials (thirty-four) or to choose not to string any beads at all (0 trials). Additionally, those students who did choose to string beads either continued for all thirty-four trials or stopped within thirteen trials (see table 6–1). None of the forty students persisted on more than fourteen trials but less than the maximum of thirty-four. Thus, it appears that factors other than the valence of what was monitored determined whether a student would first choose to perform a task (decisional self-control) and then actually persist (protracted self-control).

Analysis of the proportion of beads strung (with a recommended arc sin transformation) at pre- and posttesting indicated that the group that monitored finished trials significantly outperformed the group that monitored unfinished trials. In addition, examination of performances by the four groups (see figure 6–3) reveals that all the groups improved from pre- to

Table 6–1
Number of Students from Each Group who Chose to Perform 0, 1–13, or 34 Bead-Stringing Trials

	Number of Trials Performed		
Group	*0*	*1–13*	*34*
Self-monitor finish	4	2	4
Self-monitor not finish	4	2	4
Self-monitor red	3	4	3
No self-monitor	1	4	4

posttesting. Of interest is the observation that the finish- and red-monitoring groups improved more than the control group while the group that monitored unfinished trials did not improve as much as the control group.

Initially, we viewed this result as consistent with the findings and claims of others (for example, Hayes and Cavior 1977; Kanfer 1977; Kazdin 1974; Nelson et al. 1977; Thoresen and Mahoney 1974). In other words, monitoring of socially acceptable responses leads to an increase in performance, and monitoring of socially unacceptable responses leads to a decrease in behavior. However, further consideration reveals that the relationship between reactivity and valence in the present and in prior (Gottman and McFall 1972; Kirschenbaum and Karoly 1977) studies is not that simple. In each of these studies, monitoring of a positive behavior (such as finishing, talking, and correct problem solving) led to increases in the monitored behaviors, while monitoring of negative outcomes such as not finishing, not talking, and incorrect problem solving also led to increases in the behaviors monitored, such as more not talking and more incorrect solutions, or no change. If the monitoring of negatively valenced outcomes leads to decreases in the behavior, we would expect just the opposite. The students should have decreased their not finishing, decreased their not talking, and decreased their incorrect problem solving; that is, we would expect these self-monitoring students to finish stringing more beads, to talk more in class, and to solve more math problems correctly. Instead, the outcomes or behaviors that were monitored increased. Perhaps accurate self-recording had been followed by positive consequences like praise from the experimenters and thus the response of self-recording acquired reinforcing value. Thus, self-recording might have functioned as a reinforcer, increasing responses that it followed such as finishing and not finishing. Or, perhaps focusing attention on failure along with certain attributions for this failure, such as task difficulty, ability, or luck, led to giving up and subsequent inferior performance. Further work, of course, is needed to verify these interpretations.

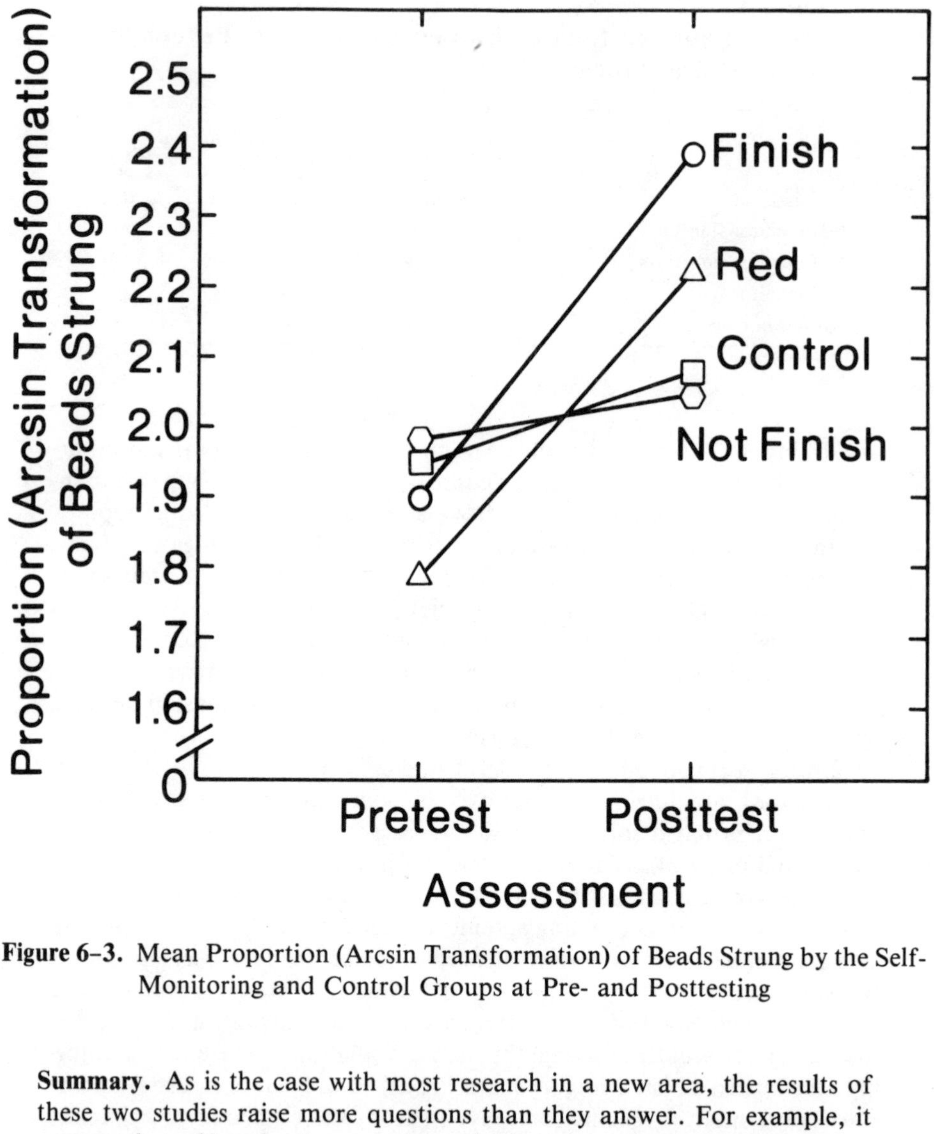

Figure 6–3. Mean Proportion (Arcsin Transformation) of Beads Strung by the Self-Monitoring and Control Groups at Pre- and Posttesting

Summary. As is the case with most research in a new area, the results of these two studies raise more questions than they answer. For example, it appears that self-evaluative statements do not serve a reinforcing function in moderately retarded adolescent students. Based on our work, we can suggest that the consistent pairing of appropriate self-evaluations and self-administered rewards might remedy this, but additional work is needed.

It does appear that these same students are differentially affected by the valence of behavioral outcomes that they self-monitor. The relationship between valence and reactivity does not appear to be simple one. Outcomes with a positive valence appear to increase when monitored while those with a negative valence also increase, resulting in even poorer performance. Not only do we need to replicate these findings but also to examine various explanations for the observed reactive effect (perceived control). In any case, some evidence indicates that moderately retarded persons can acquire component self-reinforcement skills and that these skills can affect task performance. With these studies as a foundation, we next attempted to teach our TMR population a self-reinforcement routine.

Development and Application of a Self-Reinforcement Routine

In developing our training package, we utilized information that was obtained from the results of prior studies as well as from our general experience—for example, when we identified those children who had not benefited from training and compared them to those who did in the previous studies where we noticed that the groups differed. The children who acquired the skills were all able to sit and attend to a model for a minimum of ten to fifteen minutes. They also possessed certain concepts or were able to make certain discriminations. They could discriminate between numbers, colors, when they finished a task, and so forth. Based on these observations, we identified a number of entering behaviors required for self-reinforcement training.

In addition to identifying these requisite skills, our previous research had demonstrated the effectiveness of taped modeling demonstrations. Therefore, in our training package we attempted to develop component skills first by providing our retarded students with a tape that demonstrated the appropriate skill. Their performance of the specific skill that had been demonstrated was then assessed, and only if they did not demonstrate mastery did we provide more-detailed live-demonstration training.

The advantages of this procedure are twofold: (1) those students who can learn via taped demonstrations are not required to go through a long unnecessary training program, and (2) the retarded students could be trained in groups. Finally, we decided that the training should be individualized or criterion based; that is, the training was broken down into small steps, and mastery at one step was required before moving on to the next. We anticipated that every student who possessed the requisite entering behaviors could be taught all of the necessary component skills for self-reinforcement.

The Training Package. In order to make operational the skills we hoped to develop, we designed an apparatus (see figure 6-4) that would allow us

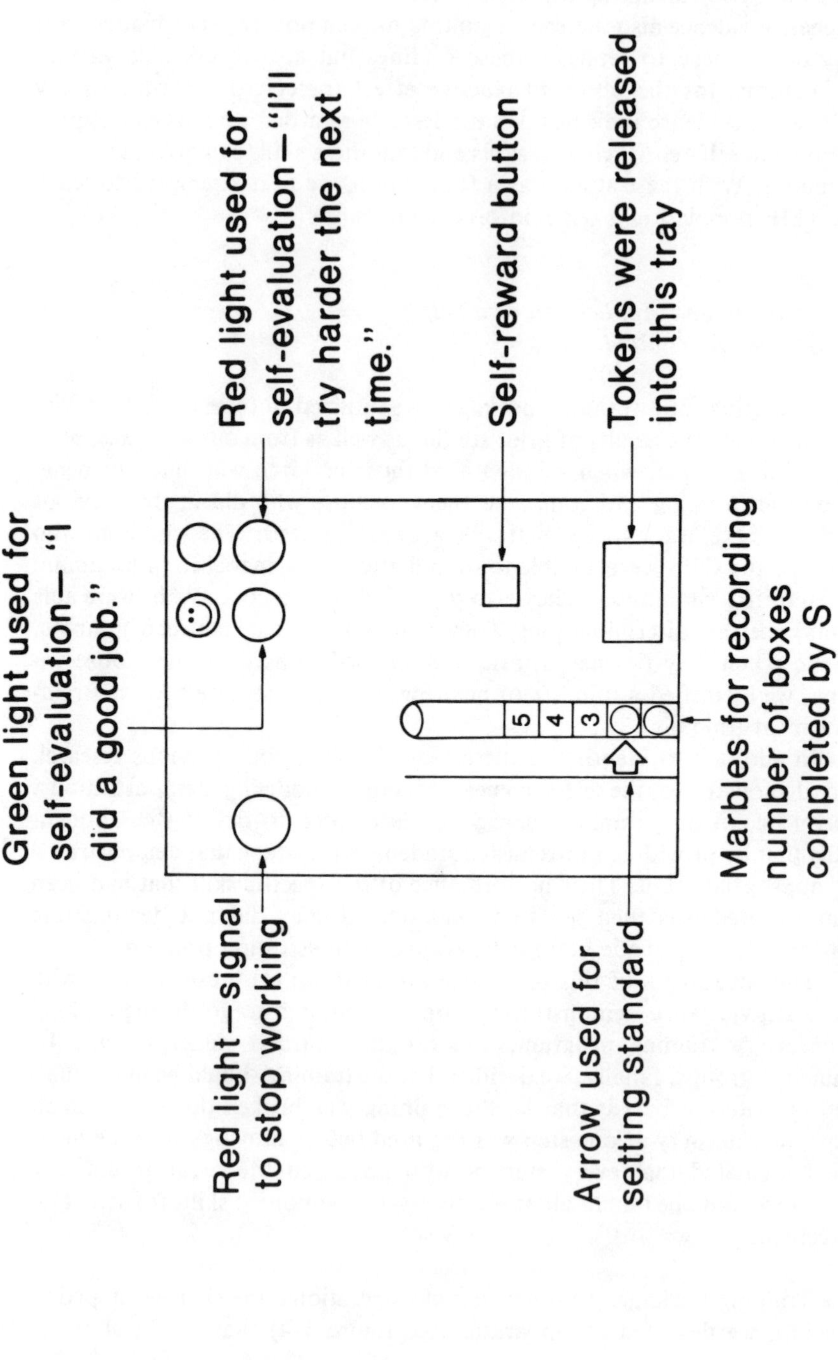

Figure 6–4. Apparatus Designed and Utilized for Training Self-Reinforcement

directly to observe student performance, to facilitate training, and to be adaptable to a number of situations or tasks to which students might be exposed in their classrooms. The apparatus we designed contained various manipulanda—each corresponding to a component skill. The plastic tube was used for the self-monitoring component. Marbles could be placed in the tube (maximum of fifteen) to indicate recordings of how many problems had been completed, completed correctly, and so forth. A standard for performance could be set by moving the arrow that was attached to a metal rod adjacent to the plastic tube up or down along the length of the tube. Self-evaluations or comparisons between actual performance and performance standards were indicated by flipping a switch that would light either a green light and green happy face (positive self-evaluation) or a red light (negative self-evaluation). Tokens were self-administered by pressing the reward button and collecting dispensed rewards in the tray. The final feature of our apparatus was the red light in the upper left-hand corner. It was controlled externally and signaled that a trial was over (that is, students were to stop working and to begin monitoring or evaluating their performance).

The task we selected for our training was bead stringing. Our objective was to have students learn to apply appropriately a self-reinforcement routine to their performances on this task. For example, if a standard of three was set (that is, finish three trays) and two trays were completed, then a marble for each completed tray of beads was to be dropped into the tube. Since the standard of three was not met, the red light, indicating that the student had to try harder next time, was to be turned on by the student, and no token was self-administered. However, if the standard was three and all five trays were completed, then five marbles were to be put into the tube, one for each tray completed, the green light was to be turned on ("I did a good job"), and a token self-administered.

In order to develop this routine, we broke our training into five steps (see figure 6–5). At step 1, each trial consisted of a single tray of five beads. Students were to put a marble in the tube only when they finished the single tray of beads before the red light went on. The self-evaluation component was added at step 2. If a training student finished a tray of beads, then the green light with the happy face was to be turned on. The red light was to be turned on when the tray was not finished. In step 3, the self-reward component was added to the single-tray trial. If a tray was finished and the green light turned on, then the student was to press the self-reward button and obtain a token. A not-finished trial was to be followed by a red light, indicating that the student had to try harder next time and was not to be followed with the pressing of the self-reward button. At steps 4 and 5, we presented students with five trays of five beads each. Students were to drop in

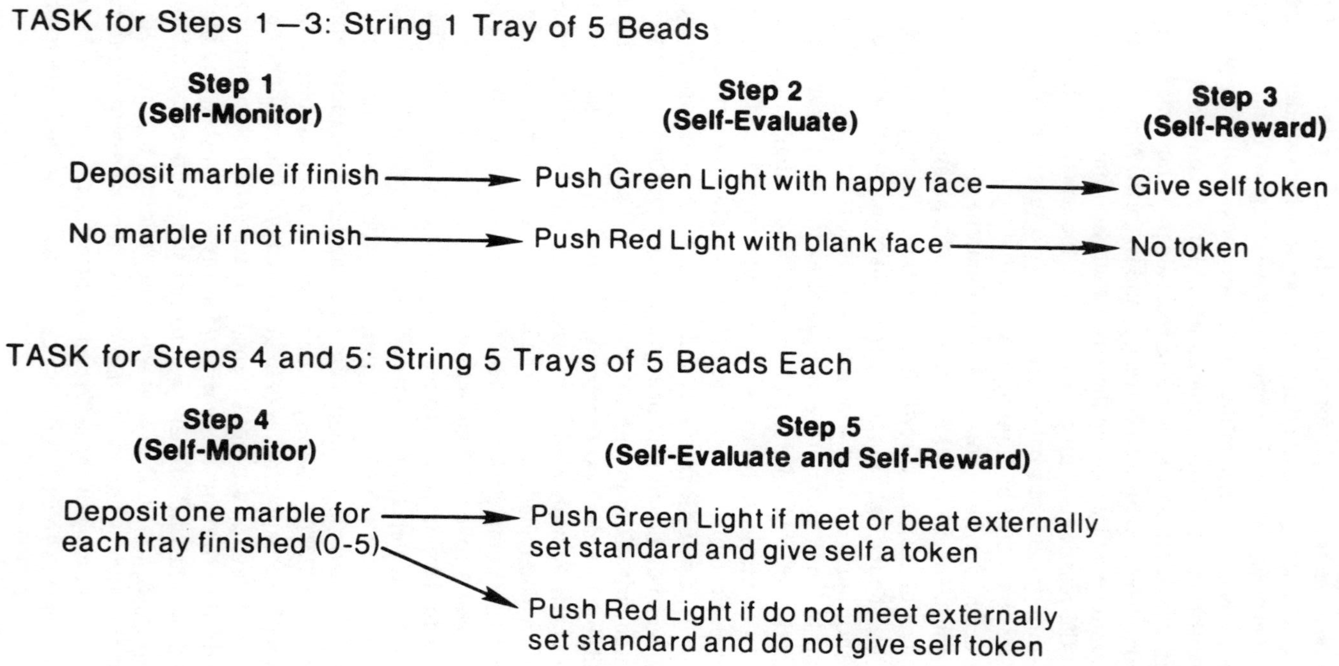
TASK for Steps 1—3: String 1 Tray of 5 Beads
Step 1
(Self-Monitor)
Step 2
(Self-Evaluate)
Step 3
(Self-Reward)
Deposit marble if finish
Push Green Light with happy face
Give self token
No marble if not finish
Push Red Light with blank face
No token
TASK for Steps 4 and 5: String 5 Trays of 5 Beads Each
Step 4
(Self-Monitor)
Step 5
(Self-Evaluate and Self-Reward)
Deposit one marble for each tray finished (0-5)
Push Green Light if meet or beat externally set standard and give self a token
Push Red Light if do not meet externally set standard and do not give self token

Figure 6–5. Training Steps

one marble for each tray completed during step 4. At step 5, the students were to evaluate their performance, after a standard had been set for them, and to administer rewards contingent on this evaluation.

The criterion-based training procedures that we used at each of these five steps are outlined in figure 6–6. At step 1, students were provided with a series of live demonstrations on how to monitor or record when they had finished a single tray of beads. Following these demonstrations, they were allowed to monitor their bead-stringing performances. They continued until they were correct (only put a marble in the tube when they finished a tray of beads) on ten of twelve trials. A brief ten-minute film was presented to students at step 2 after they had reached criterion on the first step. In this film a colorful clown model was shown stringing beads, monitoring her performance, and then evaluating her performance on ten trials. On five of the trials she finished stringing the single tray of beads, put a marble in the tube, and turned on the green light while saying, "I did a good job." For the remaining five trials our clown model did not finish stringing all the beads in her tray before the red light came on, she did not put a marble in the tube ("not this time, I still have some beads left"), and turned on the red light while indicating that she would "have to try harder next time."

Following this tape, students were presented with twelve single-tray trials. They were instructed to string the beads in the tray until the red light went on signaling them to stop. When they stopped, they were to monitor when they finished and to evaluate their performance as the clown had done. The trainers controlled the onset of the stop light, and in half of the twelve trials allowed students to finish and on half stopped them before they finished. Students who correctly self-monitored and self-evaluated on at least ten of these twelve trials proceeded to step 3. Students who failed to reach criterion performance (10/12 at this assessment) were exposed to more-detailed live-demonstration training procedures. The live training began with three massed demonstrations; the trainer demonstrated appropriate self-monitoring and evaluative responses for three trials. These massed demonstrations and subsequent student performances continued until six consecutive correct matches were accomplished by the students or they made three consecutive errors. If a student was incorrect on three consecutive trials following these massed demonstrations, he was exposed to single-trial or distributed demonstrations until correct on six consecutive trials. Once they reached this criterion they were exposed to the massed demonstrations again. The same criterion for moving on from the massed demonstrations was in force—six consecutive correct. When students reached this criterion, they moved on to the rehearsal stage of step 2. At this point, students were presented with individual trials without prior demonstrations until correct on ten of twelve consecutive trials. When this criterion was reached, students proceeded to step 3. Thus, all trainees were per-

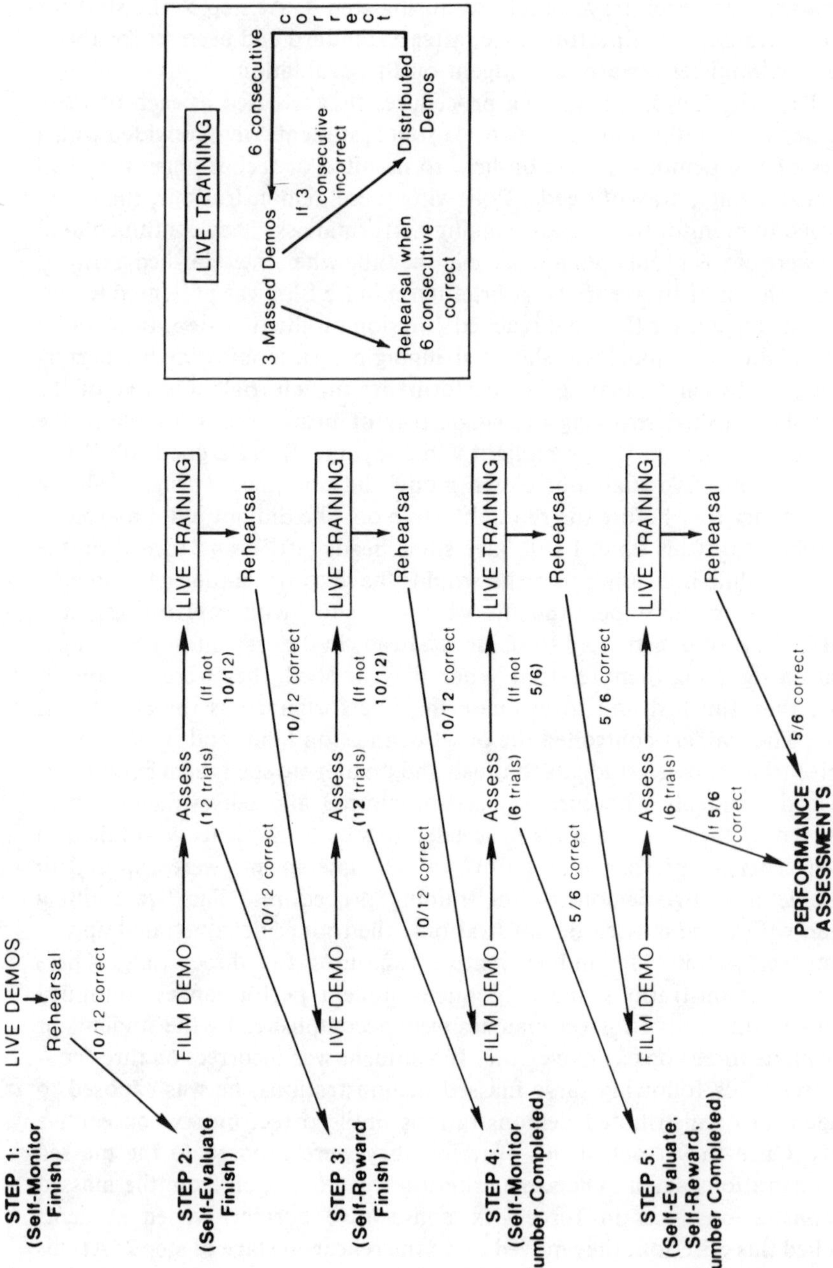

Figure 6-6. Criterion-Based Training Procedures

forming at the same level (ten out of twelve correct trials or better) when they were introduced to training at step 3.

At steps 3, 4, and 5, the same procedures, with minor modifications, were in effect. For example, at step 3 a live rather than film demonstration preceded initial assessment, and at steps 4 and 5, criterion for moving on (to step 5, or performance assessments) was five out of six correct.

Throughout the live training, students were provided with prompts to ensure that they engaged in the appropriate component responses. A prompted trial was considered an incorrect trial. During assessments following film demonstrations (steps 2, 4, and 5) and following the live demonstrations at step 3, students were not provided with corrective prompts so that the effects of these demonstrations could be evaluated.

Population and Design. The same students who served as subjects in the previous self-monitoring study participated in our next study (Litrownik, Cleary, and Steinfeld 1978). They were assigned to one of four groups randomly, with the requirement that MAs, CAs, and IQs were equivalent across groups and that approximately equal (that is, 2 or 3) numbers of students from the four self-monitoring groups were assigned to each of the four new groups. Mean IQs for the groups ranged from 38.5 to 39.8, while MAs ranged from 74.4 to 76.4 months. In order to evaluate the training program and the effects of the self-reinforcement routine on targeted responses, the following design, presented in table 6–2, was utilized: One group was trained to self-monitor, self-evaluate, and self-reward and was also allowed to set its own standards for performance—the internal group. The second group was also trained in each of these component skills; but performance standards were set for them by the trainer. These appropriate external standards were set based on the individual's immediate past performance. The standard was set at the individual's last performance with the requirement that the standard could never be lowered, only raised. The third group was trained in self-monitoring only and yoked for experience with the other components to students in the first two groups. Finally, the yoked control group did not receive training in any of the component skills but was exposed to the task.

This design allowed us to evaluate the effectiveness of the live and film demonstrations in developing specific skills at steps 2 through 5, whether the training resulted in the acquisition and transfer of the self-reinforcement routine, and whether training in this routine affected performance on the training and transfer tasks. We should point out that the two transfer tasks were quite similar to the training task, and with the first transfer task, all students were instructed to self-monitor, -evaluate, and -reward their performances. On the second transfer task, no such instruction was provided. Thus, the first transfer task assessed whether students could apply the rou-

Table 6–2
Design: Acquisition and Effects of Skills

Groups	Acquisition: Step 1	Step 2	Step 3	Step 4	Step 5
Internal: Self-monitor, self-evaluate, self-reward	Train	Train	Train	Train	Train
External: Self-monitor, self-evaluate, self-reward	Train	Train	Train	Train	Train
Self-monitor only	Train	Control	Control	Train	Control
Control	Control	Control	Control	Control	Control

	Performance Assessments
Pretest:	5 trials of 5 trays, 125 seconds/trial; groups 1, 2, 3, and 4 performed without SM, SE, SR, or standard.
Posttest:	10 trials of 5 trays, 125 seconds/trial; all groups instructed to SM, SE, and SR; group 1 set own standard prior to each trial; groups 2, 3, and 4 had an external appropriate standard set prior to each trial.
Transfer I:	10 trials of 4 formboards (3 pieces/formboard), 45 seconds/trial; all groups instructed to SM, SE, and SR; group 1 set own standards; groups 2, 3, and 4 had external standards.
Transfer II:	10 trials of 5 puzzles (3 pieces/puzzle), 60 seconds/trial; nobody instructed to SM, SE, or SR; group 1 set own standards; groups 2, 3, and 4 had external standards.

tine (namely, component skills) to a similar task, while the second transfer task assessed not only their ability to apply the routine but also whether they utilized the routine spontaneously.

Acquisition of Self-Reinforcement. Analysis of performances following exposure to the live or film demonstrations indicated that the two training groups (means = 7.5, 10.4, and 2.3) significantly outperformed the two control groups (means = 1.7, 1.7, .5) at steps 2, 3, and 5, respectively. These results suggest that the demonstrations were an effective part of the training program. In addition, the training program was effective in terms of bringing all students in the two training groups to criterion performance at step 5. This was accomplished in a minimum of five sessions and a maximum of fifteen. Thus, we were able to develop component skills required for self-reinforcement in all students who had the necessary entering behaviors.

To determine if these skills, once acquired, would be maintained, we examined the performance of our students on the three postassessments. The first included ten trials on the training task, while the other two ten-trial assessments used different tasks (formboards, wood puzzles). On the formboard task, all students were instructed to engage in the component skills; no such instructions were provided for the puzzle task.

On each posttest trial, the appropriateness of each component (self-monitoring, self-evaluation, self-reward) was recorded. In addition, the standards set by the internal group were recorded as well as the total number of trials on which each student appropriately utilized self-reinforcement (correctly self-monitored, self-evaluated, and self-rewarded).

Planned orthogonal comparisons were conducted to evaluate the effects of the training program (two training versus two control groups). We found that students in the training groups were more likely to self-evaluate, self-reward, and in general, apply self-reinforcement on all three tasks than the control groups (see figures 6–7, 6–8, and 6–9). An additional comparison (two training and self-monitoring control versus control) for self-monitoring similarly indicated that the groups that were trained on a component skill continued to engage in it on each of the three posttests. Thus the students who were exposed to our training package acquired each component skill, transferred these skills to another task when instructed to do so, and (most important) utilized these acquired skills to regulate their performances on a task when no instructions were provided. While the training students significantly outperformed the control students on the second transfer task (see figure 6–9), it appears that the group provided with standards for their performance was primarily responsible for this effect. It is possible that the external group was more likely to engage in the component skills when not instructed to do so because the external standard functioned as a cue. In any case, the results indicate that moderately retarded students can acquire a self-reinforcement routine and appropriately apply it to other tasks and situations.

Effects of Self-Reinforcement on Task Performance. In order to determine the effects of self-reinforcement training, locus of standards set, and self-monitoring on task performance, three a priori planned orthogonal comparisons were chosen to evaluate the dependent measures: two training versus two control groups, internal training versus external training, and self-monitoring versus control. These comparisons were applied to performances on the training (bead-stringing) and two transfer (formboard and puzzle) tasks. On the bead-stringing and puzzle tasks, the training groups significantly outperformed the control groups—that is, they strung more beads and put together more puzzles than the control and self-monitoring groups (see figures 6–10, 6–11, and 6–12).

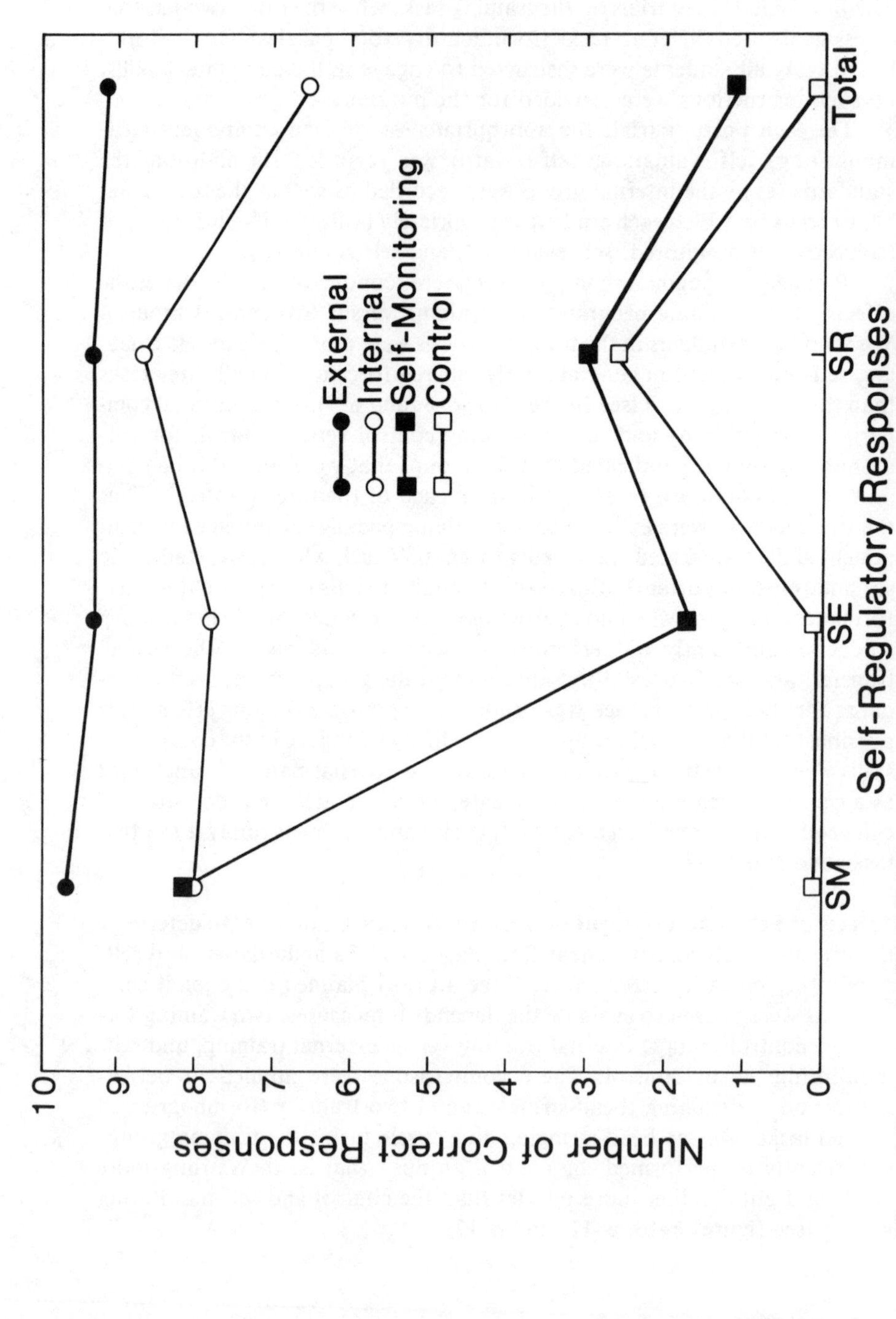

Figure 6–7. Accuracy of Self-Reinforcement (Total) and Component Skills (Self-Monitoring, Self-Evaluation, and Self-Reward) on the Bead-Stringing (Training) Task

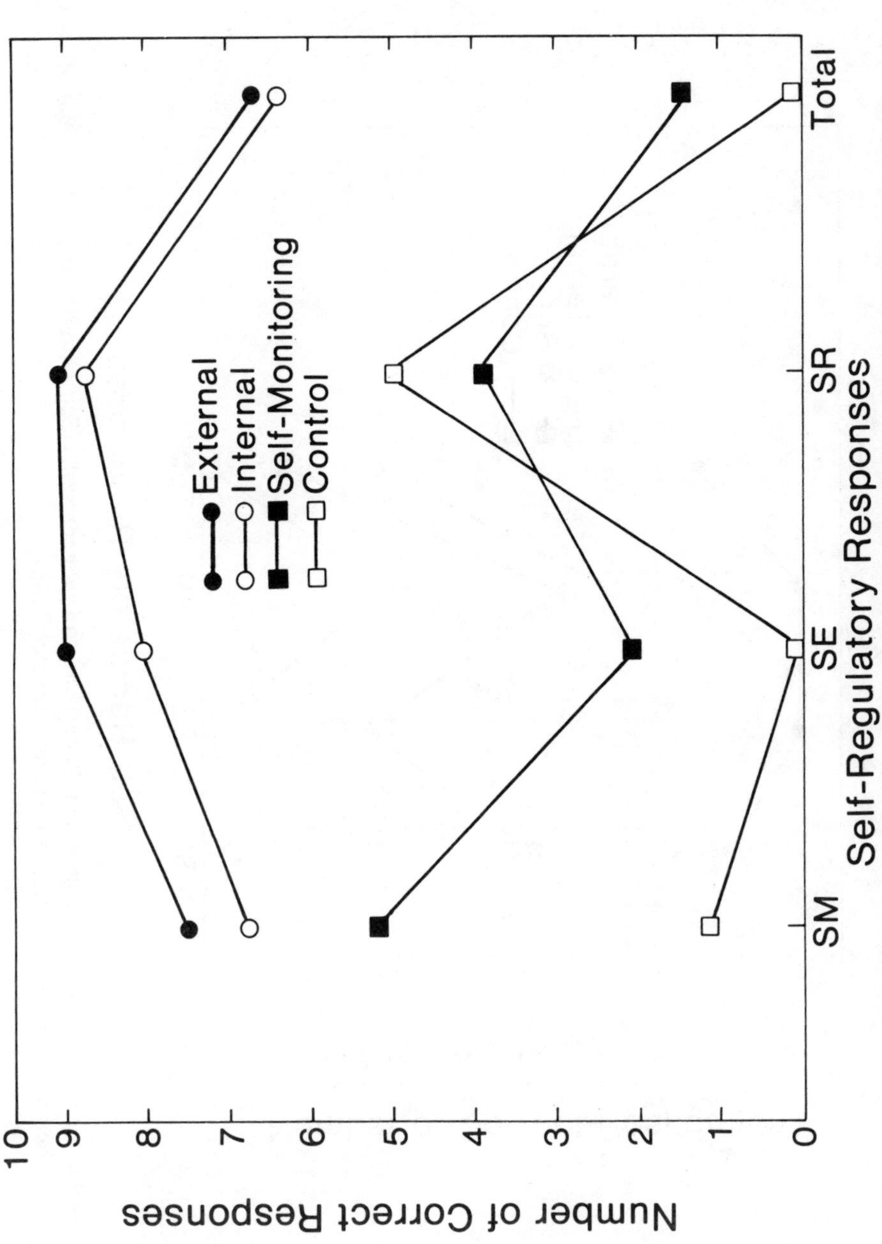

Figure 6–8. Accuracy of Self-Reinforcement (Total) and Component Skills (Self-Monitoring, Self-Evaluation, and Self-Reward) on the Formboard (First Transfer) Task

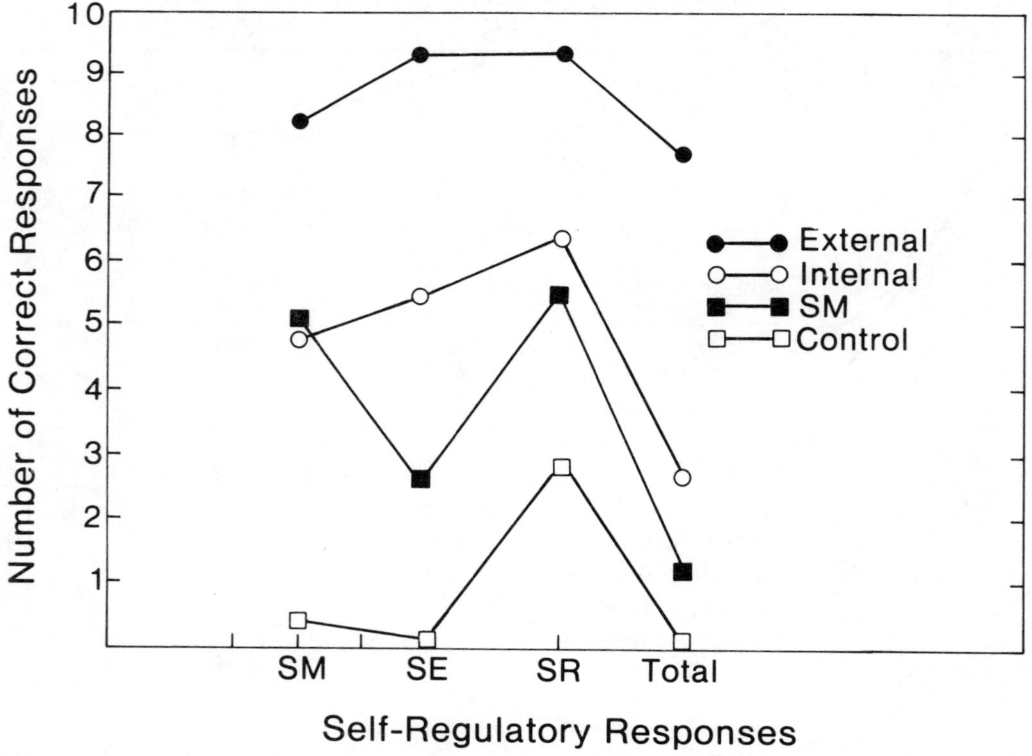

Figure 6–9. Accuracy of Self-Reinforcement (Total) and Component Skills (Self-Monitoring, Self-Evaluation, and Self-Reward) on the Puzzle (Second Transfer Task)

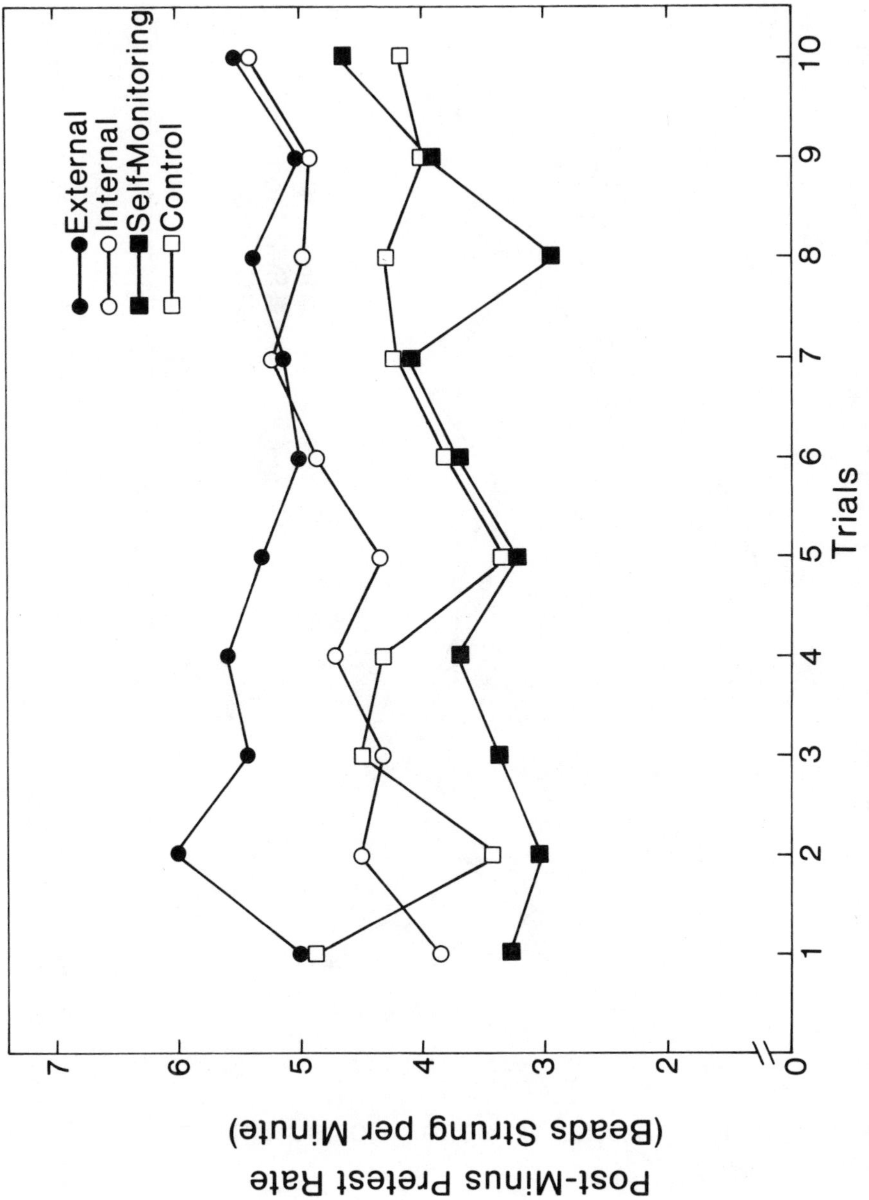

Figure 6–10. Post-Minus Pretest Rate of Beads Strung per Minute by the Four Groups at Each Trial

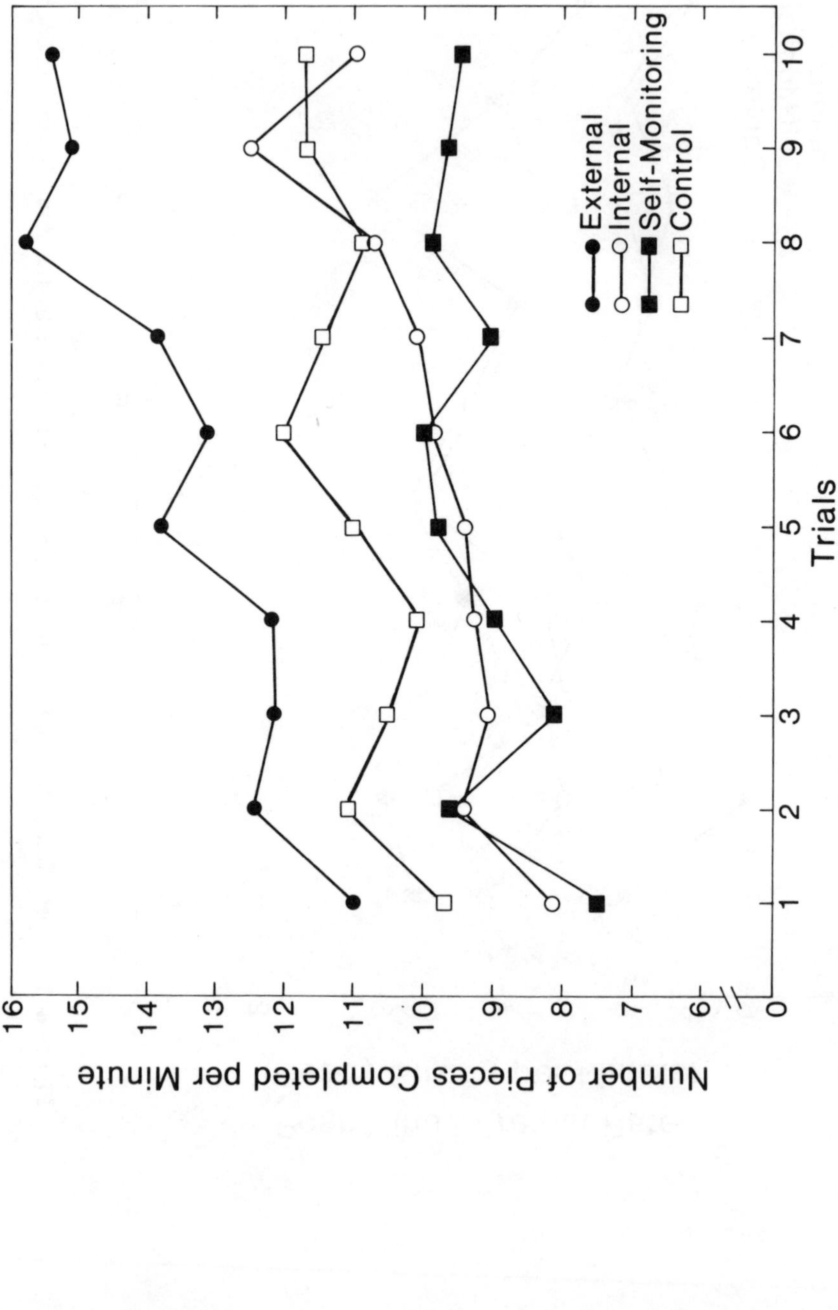

Figure 6–11. Mean Number of Forms Placed Correctly per Minute on the First Transfer Task by the Four Groups on Each of the Ten Trials

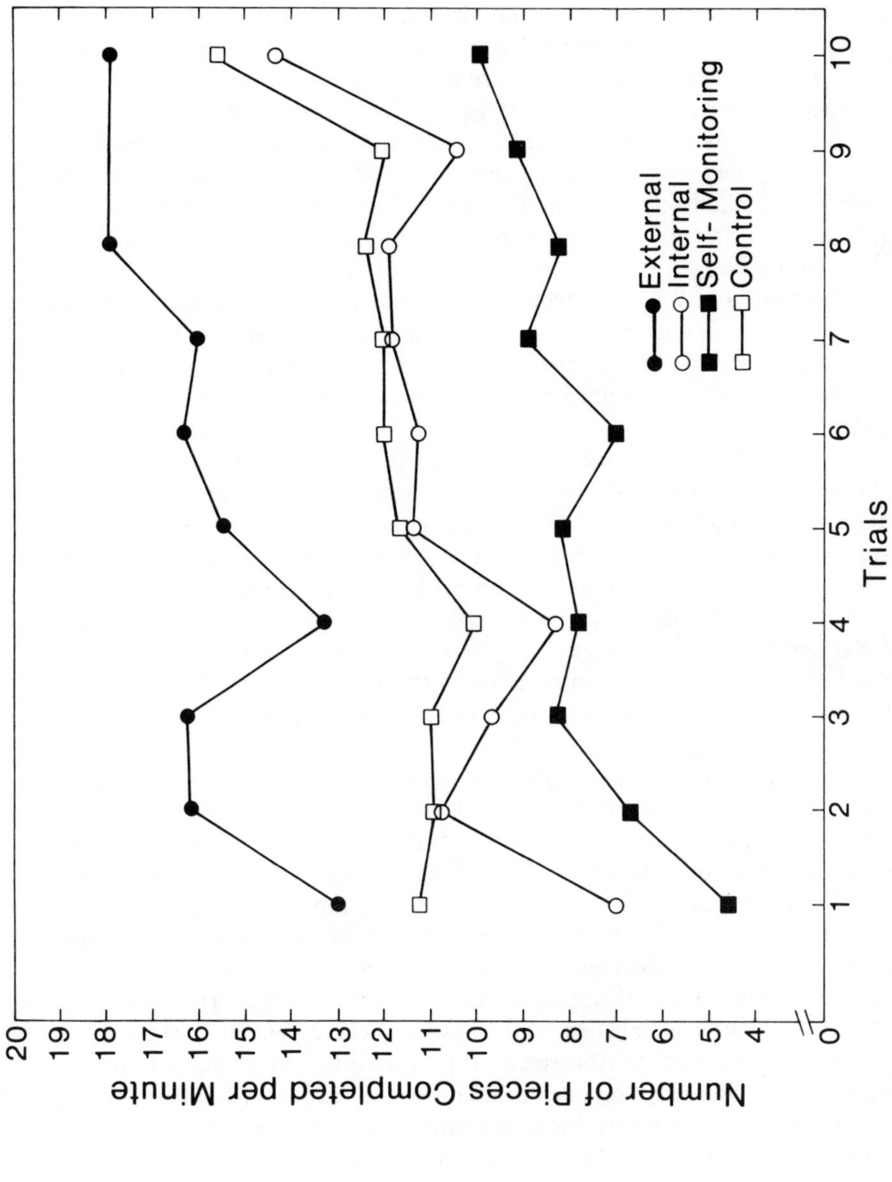

Figure 6–12. Mean Number of Puzzle Pieces Put Together per Minute at Each Trial by the Four Groups

The performances of the two control groups did not differ on any of the tasks. The two training groups did not differ on the bead stringing, and although the external group tended to outperform the internal group on the puzzle task, the difference was not significant. This difference was significant on the formboard task. These two training groups did differ in terms of the locus of their standards, and it is also possible that they had different standards. That is, the external group had standards set by the experimenter-trainer based on a general rule, whereas the internal group set its own standards on an unknown basis. Thus, we attempted to examine the standards set by this group. First, we defined what we thought, based in part on the rule used for setting external standards, should be considered an appropriate standard—a standard that was the same or one greater than the individual's immediate past performance. For example, if a student finished three formboards, a standard of three or four on the next trial was considered appropriate. We then identified students in the internal group who set appropriate standards on at least 70 percent (that is, seven out of ten) of the trials for each task. Five of the ten students in this group were thus identified as appropriate standard setters on the bead-stringing task (see table 6–3).

On the formboard task, most of the students set inappropriately high standards (see table 6–4). In fact, only three students were identified as appropriate standard setters. When we compared the performances of these students to those of the remaining seven students, using a Mann-Whitney test of ranks, we found that the appropriate standard setters significantly outperformed the inappropriate standard setters. Thus, it appears that the lower performances of the internal group relative to the external group were due to the inappropriate standards set by this internal group. In addition to having only three students (see table 6–5) set appropriate standards on the second transfer task (puzzles), a number of training students (both internal and external) did not appear to utilize acquired self-reinforcement skills on a majority (60 percent) of the trials. When we compared performances of the twelve students who utilized self-reinforcement to the eight who did not, we found that students who appropriately applied self-reinforcement put together more puzzle pieces than those who did not.

The results of this study can be summarized as follows: (1) Groups trained in self-reinforcement significantly outperformed control groups that had appropriate external standards set for them; (2) these differences were observed on the training task and on a task where students were not instructed to utilize self-reinforcement; (3) the training groups did not outperform the control groups on one of the transfer tasks; (4) the failure to find a difference on this task was due to the inferior performance of the internal-training group relative to the external-training group; (5) this difference was likely due to the inappropriateness of the standards set by the internal-

Table 6–3
Bead Stringing: Standards Set by the Internal-Treatment Group Relative to Past Performance

Standard	*M.R.*[b]	*L.H.*[a]	*B.L.*[a]	*D.G.*[a]	*L.A.*[a]	*S.G.*	*P.M.*	*E.F.*	*C.J.*[a]	*N.I.*
4 over										
3 over										
2 over	1			3						
1 over	3	8	4	5				4		
Same	1	2	3	2	7	3	2	2	9	6
1 under	4		1		2	3	2	1	1	4
2 under	1		1		1	3	2	2		
3 under						1	2	1		
4 under			1				2			

[a]Student who set appropriate standards (standard was equal to or one over immediate past trial or at least 7/10 trials).
[b]Letters stand for students' initials.

Table 6–4
First Transfer Task (Formboard): Standards Set by the Internal-Treatment Group Relative to Past Performance

Standard	*M.R.*[b]	*L.H.*	*B.L.*	*D.G.*	*L.A.*[a]	*S.G.*	*P.M.*	*E.F.*[a]	*C.J.*[a]	*N.I.*
4 over										
3 over	7		1	1						
2 over	1	8	4	4	1	3	2		1	5
1 over	1		4	3		4	4	4	8	4
Same	1	2	1	2	9	2	2	6	1	1
1 under						1	2			
2 under										
3 under										
4 under										

[a]Student who set appropriate standards (standard was equal to or one over immediate past trial or at least 7/10 trials).
[b]Letters stand for students' initials.

Table 6–5
Second Transfer Task (Puzzle): Standards Set by the Internal-Treatment Group Relative to Past Performance

Standard	*M.R.*[b]	*L.H.*	*B.L.*	*D.G.*	*L.A.*[a]	*S.G.*	*P.M.*	*E.F.*[a]	*C.J.*[a]	*N.I.*
4 over	1									
3 over	2					1				4
2 over	2					1	2			5
1 over	3					3	4	4	1	1
Same	2	2	9	3	10		2	3	8	
1 under		4	1	4		1	2		1	
2 under		4		2		2				
3 under				1		2				
4 under										

[a]Student who set appropriate standards (standard was equal to or one over immediate past trial or at least 7/10 trials).
[b]Letters stand for students' initials.

training group; and (6) students who utilized self-reinforcement, regardless of which training group they were in, outperformed those who did not.

An Additional Study. Based on the preceding study, we (Steinfeld and Litrownik 1978) decided to continue working with members of this same population in an attempt to teach them to set appropriate standards for their performance. It appeared that our population of moderately retarded adolescents would not set reasonable, yet challenging, standards for their performance even though they had been exposed to a training program in which the setting of appropriate standards was modeled (by the experimenter-trainer). Sagotsky, Patterson, and Lepper (1978) similarly found that their fifth- and sixth-grade students could not set reasonable standards and, as a result, did not outperform control-group students. They, too, recognized the need to provide more-extensive training in the setting of reasonable standards. (Not only did we focus upon developing appropriate standard-setting responses, but we also hoped to ensure that students trained on self-reinforcement utilized it when performing a task.)

The same students who participated in the preceding two studies served as subjects in this follow-up study. A summer break intervened between the end of the last study and the beginning of this study. During this time, twelve of the original forty students either moved, graduated, or for one reason or another, did not return in the fall. Of the twenty-eight who returned, fourteen had been in the training groups and fourteen in the control groups. The fourteen students who had received previous training in self-reinforcement were assigned to two groups of seven students each, and the fourteen control students were assigned to two groups of seven students each based on a stratified match of means and variances for bead-stringing-pretest performance, IQ, MA, and CA.

The two groups who had received prior training were then randomly assigned to self-reinforcement-training groups that either had external standards set for them or set their own standards. One control group was randomly assigned to receive only an external standard while the other served as a no-standard control group.

The same apparatus (see figure 6–4) was adapted for use with a design-matching task. The task required students to match seven designs (five pieces/design) presented on each trial via a stimulus card. Each design on the stimulus card was drawn to scale and consisted of five component pieces that varied in color (light blue, dark blue, white, green, orange, red, black, or yellow) and shape (square, rectangle, triangle, or parallelogram). These pieces were presented in various positions with the only requirement being that each piece always touch at least one other piece. A wooden tray that contained seven small compartments for each design and one large compartment, containing thirty-five foam rubber shapes needed to match all seven designs, was presented to the student on each trial. During performance trials, students were given two minutes in which to put as many designs together as possible.

Students in the two training groups were initially presented with twelve trials but did not actually perform on the design task. They were presented with a predetermined number of design pieces completed on each trial and told to self-reinforce, based on the number of designs completed. If students correctly self-monitored, self-evaluated, self-rewarded, and set standards (internal-standard group only) on ten of the twelve trials, they proceeded to the performance-assessment stage. Failure to meet this criterion resulted in the student being trained to engage in the appropriate component skills required for self-reinforcement on this task. The training was criterion based, utilized live demonstrations, verbal feedback, and praise—as in the previous study (see Litrownik, Cleary, and Steinfeld 1978). For example, training began with massed demonstration where the experimenter-model correctly self-monitored, self-evaluated, self-rewarded, and set standards (at the last score obtained) on three consecutive trials with corresponding verbal instructions. The student was then instructed to match the experimenter's performance on the same three trials. If students matched experimenter's performance on all three trials (without corrections) for the two consecutive turns, they moved on to the rehearsal stage of training. If a student could not match the experimenter's performance on the three trials during any of four consecutive turns, the student was provided with single distributed demonstrations; that is, the experimenter demonstrated one trial, followed by an identical trial for the student. When there consecutive single trials were correctly performed, the student was then provided with massed demonstrations again. During rehearsal, students were presented with twelve trials, and if they engaged in the appropriate component skills on at least ten out of twelve trials, they proceeded to the performance assessment. However, failure to reach criterion resulted in their being provided with massed demonstrations again.

Students had an opportunity actually to work on the design-matching task during the performance assessment. They were presented with ten trials per day over a four-day period. A different stimulus card was presented on each trial so the student never had the opportunity to put together the same design twice. Prior to each day's assessment, the two training groups had to reach criterion (five out of six correct) on a self-reinforcement accuracy-assessment test. Students who did not reach criterion on this accuracy assessment were provided with additional self-reinforcement training until criterion was reached. Overall, both self-reinforcement groups appropriately applied self-reinforcement to their performances (approximately 80 percent of the trials) during the four-day assessments with no differences between the two groups. Thus, the internal-training group did learn to set

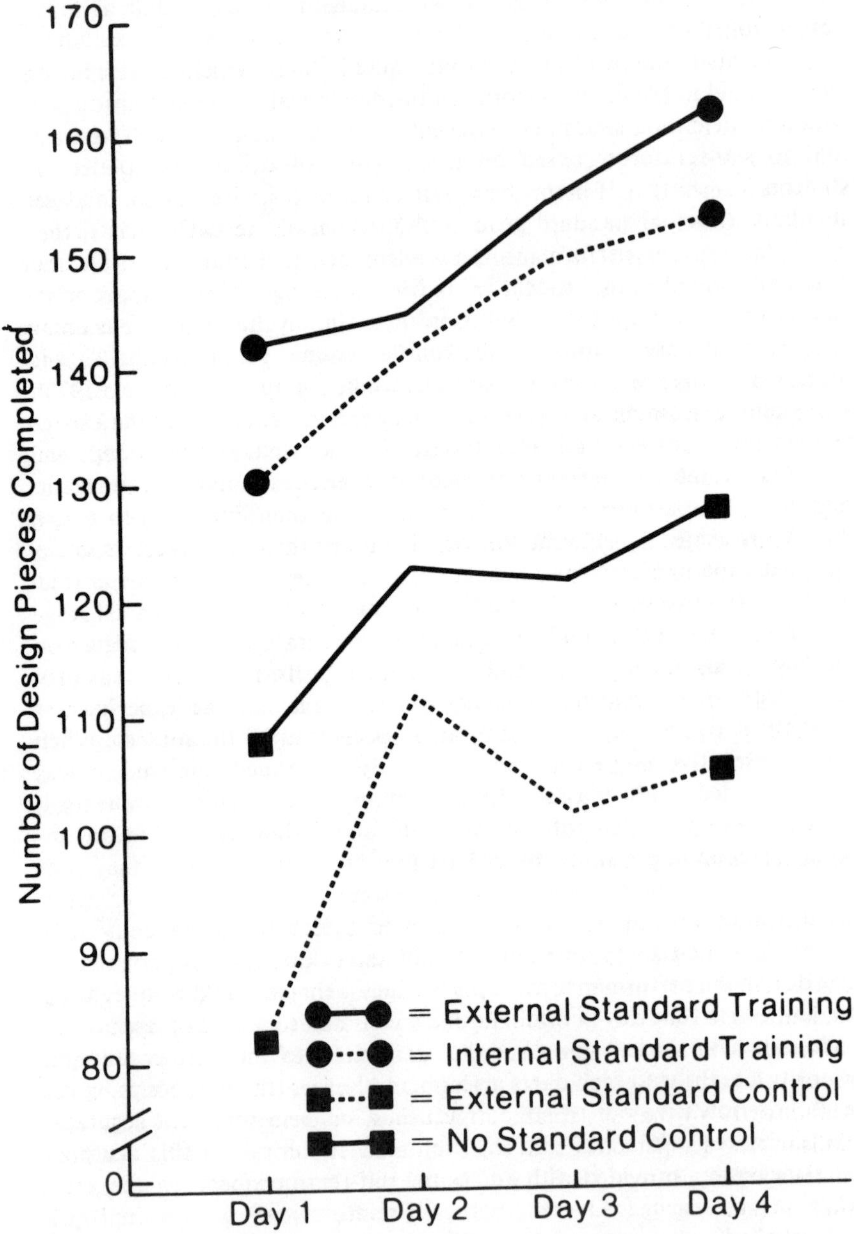

Figure 6-13. Mean Number of Design Pieces Completed at Each Day by the Four Groups

their own appropriate standards, and they, along with the external-training group, utilized self-reinforcement on the design-matching task.

In order to evaluate the effects of self-reinforcement and standards (that is, their presence and who sets them), three a priori planned orthogonal comparisons were conducted: (1) internal- and external-training versus control groups, (2) internal versus external training, and (3) external standard only versus control. Each comparison was applied to the two dependent measures, number of pieces completed, and accuracy of placement (position, color, and so forth). The analyses revealed that performance accuracy was not affected by self-reinforcement training, locus of standards, or the presence of an external standard. This was not unexpected since we did not focus on, or provide any training for, accurate placement of design pieces. Similarly, the presence of a standard (that is, standard versus control group) did not affect the number of pieces completed and neither did the locus of standards (that is, internal versus external training). We did find that, at each day, the two training groups who were appropriately applying self-reinforcement to their performance significantly outperformed the two control groups in terms of their output (see figure 6-13). Specifically, the training groups put more pieces together in the time alloted than the control groups, but they were no more accurate in their placements.

Thus, we found that we could teach our moderately retarded adolescent students to set appropriate standards for their performance and that they, along with other students trained in self-reinforcement, utilized this self-regulatory routine that led to greater performance output relative to students who had not been trained.

Summary and Implications for the Future

Retarded persons, in general, have been characterized as dependent and in need of constant supervision. While some evidence supports these characterizations, more-recent reports suggest that the failure of retarded individuals to develope more independence is due to a lack of opportunity rather than to some stable structural deficit. Based on these encouraging reports, it had been suggested (see Kurtz and Neisworth 1976; Mahoney and Mahoney 1976) that systematic approaches for developing self-regulatory skills in retarded persons ought to be initiated. In fall 1975, with the support of the USOE, Bureau of Education for the Handicapped, we undertook such a task.

We first concerned outselves with identifying what it was that we hoped to develop and our strategy for developing it—that is, we conceptualized self-regulation or independent functioning as a general problem-solving strategy with various stages and component skills. The development of these specific skills and their application to the stages of problem solving were distinguished from the effects of these skills—namely, influence of self-regulatory skills on behavior that is to be controlled. With this conceptualization, we began by focusing on self-control routines or methods that can be utilized by individuals when attempting to control their own behavior. Further, we decided to concentrate on self-reinforcement with the aim of developing this routine that would lead to effective maintenance of behavior.

For component skills—self-monitoring, standard setting, self-evaluation, and self-reward—required for self-reinforcement were identified. In the first studies, we found that our moderately retarded students could not initially perform these skills when provided with detailed verbal instructions and several practice trials or appropriate demonstrations. However, we did find that most of these same students could acquire, retain, and generalize these skills when provided with a brief (approximately one hour) training experience. This training included stepwise development of skills via live and taped demonstrations, prompting, and contingent feedback.

Not only did we find that our students could acquire these skills but also that some evidence indicated that their application influenced task performance. Specifically, self-administered rewards appeared to result in superior performance on a block-design task while the monitoring of positive outcomes led to faster bead stringing than the monitoring of a negative outcome. Additionally, we found that self-evaluative statements do not appear to serve a reinforcing function in this population as task performance was not affected by such statements. Based on the results of these preliminary studies, we designed a training program that had as its aim the development of self-reinforcement (that is, one specific self-control routine).

While the program centered on developing a self-reinforcement routine that could be applied in a given situation to a specific task, a number of general features make the training program appropriate for almost any task in a structured situation (for example, the classroom). These features included specification of necessary entering behaviors (such as ability to attend to a task or a taped demonstration for a minimum of fifteen minutes, ability to discriminate between various colors, numbers, and work that was finished or not finished; analysis of required skills as they apply to a task and breaking down of the training into many steps; criterion-based training procedures to ensure that each student could perform the required behaviors at a given training step before progressing to the next step; and use of taped demonstrations that would allow for groups of students to be trained at the same time. In addition, we designed a self-reinforcement apparatus that could be adapted for use with a number of tasks.

The apparatus allowed us to observe directly each component skill. For example, marbles were placed in a plastic tube for monitoring response, a red or green light indicated the students' evaluation of their performance relative to a standard that was provided by placing an arrow at a particular point on the plastic tube, and finally a reward button was pushed in order to administer a token reward. This apparatus and the general training features were adapted for use on a bead-stringing task. In other words, we attempted to develop a self-reinforcement routine that could be applied to a specific task. In addition, we were interested in determining whether this routine would be utilized when the students performed other tasks and whether the use of this routine affected task performance.

We found that our training program was effective in bringing all students to criterion on the last training step. Skills like self-reinforcement were maintained and applied to different tasks even when students were not instructed to do so. Additionally, we found that training in self-reinforcement led to superior task performance. Further analysis indicated that students who had been exposed to the training program and applied the routine outperformed those who did not utilize it. The appropriateness of the self-set standards also appeard to be related to task performance.

In a subsequent study, we were able to teach our moderately retarded students to set appropriate standards on a different task. We adapted our training procedures and apparatus to this new task and once again found that students who were exposed to the training program outperformed those who were not.

In sum, it appears that moderately retarded students can acquire skills necessary to utilize a self-reinforcement routine to maintain task performances. We must keep in mind that this is only one self-control routine and that its application resulted in behavioral maintenance. This is a most important initial step in the development of self-regulation in retarded students. While our findings leave us quite optimistic, we should point out that much more work needs to be accomplished before we can claim that moderately retarded children can, in fact, regulate their own behavior. For example, we must evaluate the effectiveness of our training as we move from the laboratory to more-natural settings such as, class, home, and community. We must determine if we can adapt our training procedures and apparatus to tasks that are typically assigned to TMR students in the classroom. To accomplish this, teachers must become involved in identifying activities, adapting procedures, and implementing the training. In order to adapt our procedures for home use, parents need to be brought into the program.

We must try to develop other self-control routines in TMR students. Self-reinforcement is only one of a number of self-control procedures or routines (such as self-instruction, self-monitoring, self-control, self-punishment, and self-directed stimulus control) that have been identified (Goetz and Etzel 1978). There is some indication that educable mentally retarded students can learn effectively to utilize self-instructional techniques to modify their conceptual style and resultant task performance (Guralnick 1976), but thus far only self-reinforcement and self-monitoring have been developed and effectively applied by moderately retarded students.

We must develop skills that can be utilized to engage in problem solving in other stages (for example, problem identification). Such training, we suggest, should come after a number of options or alternative routines have been acquired. With a variety of self-control routines available, retarded students would be able to exercise greater self-determination when attempting to solve a problem.

References

A. Bandura, "Self-Reinforcement: Theoretical and Methodological Considerations," *Behaviorism* 4(1976):135–155.

A. Bandura, *Social Learning Theory* (Englewood Cliffs, N.J.: Prentice-Hall, 1977).

A. Bandura, "The Self-System in Reciprocal Determinism," *American Psychologist* 33(1978):344–358.

G. Brodsky, T. LePage, J. Quiring, and R. Zeller, "Self-Evaluative Responses in Adolescent Retardates," *American Journal of Mental Deficiency* 74(1970):792–795.

K. Brownell, G. Colletti, R. Ersner-Hershfield, S.M. Hershfield, and G.T. Wilson, "Self-Control in School Children: Stringency and Leniency in Self-Determined and Externally Imposed Performance Standards," *Behavior Therapy* 8(1977):442–455.

J.D. Campione and A.L. Brown, "Memory and Metamemory Development in Educable Retarded Children," in *Perspectives on the Development of Memory and Cognition,* eds. R.V. Kail and J.W. Hagen (Hillsdale, N.J.: Lawrence Erlbaum Associates, 1977).

T.J. D'Zurilla and M.R. Goldfried, "Problem Solving and Behavior Modification," *Journal of Abnormal Psychology* 78(1971):107–126.

L.R. Franzini, A.J. Litrownik, and M.A. Magy, "Immediate and Delayed Reward Preferences of TMR Adolescents," *American Journal of Mental Deficiency* 82(1978):406–409.

L.R. Franzini, A.J. Litrownik, and M.A. Magy, "Training Adolescent TMRs in Delay Behavior," *Mental Retardation* (1979).

E.M. Goetz and B.C. Etzel, "A Brief Review of Self-Control Procedures: Problems and Solutions," *The Behavior Therapist* 1(1978):5–8.

J.M. Gottman and R.M. McFall, "Self-Monitoring Effects in a Program for Potential High School Dropouts: A Time-Series Analysis," *Journal of Consulting and Clinical Psychology* 39(1972):273–281.

J.M. Greiner and P. Karoly, "Effects of Self-Control Training on Study

Activity and Academic Performance: An Analysis of Self-Monitoring, Self-Reward, and Systematic-Planning Components," *Journal of Counseling Psychology* 23(1976):495–502.

M.J. Guralnick, "Solving Complex Discrimination Problems: Techniques for the Development of Problem-Solving Strategies," *American Journal of Mental Deficiency* 81(1976):18–25.

J.W. Hagen and K.G. Stanovich, "Memory: Strategies of Acquisition, in *Perspectives on the Development of Memory and Cognition,* eds. R.V. Kail and J.W. Hagen (Hillsdale: N.J.: Lawrence Erlbaum Associates, 1977).

S.C. Hayes and N. Cavior, "Multiple Tracking and the Reactivity of Self-Monitoring: I. Negative Behaviors," *Behavior Therapy* 8(1977): 819–831.

C.D. Helland, R.J. Paluck, and M. Klein, "A Comparison of Self and External Reinforcement with the Trainable Mentally Retarded," Mental Retardation 14(1976):22–23.

F.H. Kanfer, "The Many Faces of Self-Control, or Behavior Modification Changes Its Focus," in *Behavioral Self-Management: Strategies, Techniques, and Outcomes,* ed. R.B. Stuart (New York: Brunner/Mazel, 1977).

F.H. Kanfer, "Personal Control, Social Control and Altruism, or Can Society Survive the Age of Individualism?" *American Psychologist* 34(1979a):231–239.

F.H. Kanfer, "Self-Management: Strategies and Tactics," in *Maximizing Treatment Gains: Transfer-Enhancement in Psychotherapy,* eds. A.P. Goldstein and Kanfer (New York: Academic Press, 1979b).

R.M. Kaplan and A.J. Litrownik, "Some Statistical Methods for the Assessment of Multiple Outcome Criteria in Behavioral Research," *Behavior Therapy* 8(1977):383–392.

P. Karoly, "Behavioral Self-Management in Children: Concepts, Methods, Issues, and Directions," in *Progress in Behavior Modification,* vol. 5, eds. M. Hersen, R.M. Eisler, and P.M. Miller (New York: Academic Press, 1977).

A.E. Kazdin, "Self-Monitoring and Behavior Change," in *Self-Control: Power to the Person,* eds. M.J. Mahoney and C.E. Thoreson (Monterey, Calif.: Brooks/Cole, 1974).

D.S. Kirschenbaum and P. Karoly, "When Self-Regulation Fails: Tests of Some Preliminary Hypotheses," *Journal of Consulting and Clinical Psychology* 45(1977):1116–1125.

D.D. Kurtz and J.T. Neisworth, "Self-Control Possibilities for Exceptional Children," *Exceptional Children* 42(1976):212–217.

G.L. Lecklitner, "Self-Regulation in the Mentally Retarded. Effects of Self-Evaluative Statements" (Master's thesis, San Diego State University, 1977).

A.J. Litrownik, C.P. Cleary, G.L. Lecklitner, and L.R. Franzini, "Self-Regulation in Retarded Persons: Acquisition of Standards for Performance," *American Journal of Mental Deficiency* 83(1978a):86–89.

A.J. Litrownik, L.R. Franzini, M.K. Livingston, and S. Harvey, "Developmental Priority of Identity Conservation: Acceleration of Identity and Equivalence in Normal and Moderately Retarded Children," *Child Development* 49(1978b):201–208.

A.J. Litrownik, G.L. Lecklitner, C.P. Cleary, and L.R. Franzini, *Acquisition of Self-Evaluation and Self-Reward Skills and Their Effects on Performance* (Unpublished manuscript, San Diego State University, 1978).

A.J. Litrownik, L.R. Franzini, S. Geller, and M. Geller, "Delay of Gratification: Decisional Self-Control and Experience with Delay Intervals," *American Journal of Mental Deficiency* 82(1977):149–154.

A.J. Litrownik, L.R. Franzini, and G.L. Turner, "Acquisition of Concepts by TMR Children as a Function of Modeling, Rule Verbalization, and Observer Gender," *American Journal of Mental Deficiency* 80(1976): 620–629.

A.J. Litrownik, C.P. Cleary, and B.I. Steinfeld, "Self-Regulation in Mentally Retarded Persons. Acquisition and Effects of Self-Reinforcement" (Unpublished manuscript, San Diego State University, 1978).

A.J. Litrownik, J.L. Freitas, and L.R. Franzini, "Self-Regulation in Retarded Persons: Assessment and Training of Self-Monitoring Skills," *American Journal of Mental Deficiency* 82(1978):499–506.

A.J. Litrownik, and J.L. Freitas, "Self-Monitoring in Moderately Retarded Adolescents: Reactivity and Accuracy as a Function of Valence," *Behavior Therapy,* 11(1980):245–255.

D.L. MacMillan, "Effect of Experimental Success and Failure on the Situational Expectancy of EMR and Nonretarded Children," *American Journal of Mental Deficiency* 80(1975):90–95.

M.J. Mahoney, "Reflections on the Cognitive-Learning Trend in Psychotherapy," *American Psychologist* 32(1977):5–13.

M.J. Mahoney and K. Mahoney, "Self-Control Techniques with the Mentally Retarded," *Exceptional Children* 42(1976):338–339.

J.C. Masters, W. Furman, and R.C. Barden, "Effects of Achievement Standards, Tangible Rewards, and Self-Dispensed Achievement Evaluations on Children's Task Mastery," *Child Development* 48(1977): 217–224.

J.C. Masters, and J.W. Santrock, "Studies in the Self-Regulation of Behavior: Effects of Contingent Cognitive and Affective Events," *Develmental Psychology* 12(1976):334–348.

R.M. McFall, "Parameters of Self Monitoring," in *Behavioral Self-management: Strategies, Techniques, and Outcomes,* ed. R.B. Stuart (New York: Brunner/Mazel, 1977).

D. Meichenbaum and J. Asarnow, "Cognitive-Behavior Modification and

Metacognitive Development: Implications for the Classroom," in *Cognitive-Behavioral Interventions: Theory, Research, and Procedures,* eds. P.C. Kendall and S.D. Hollon (New York: Academic Press, 1979).

W. Mischel, "Toward a Cognitive Social Learning Reconceptualization of Personality," *Psychological Review* 80(1973):252–283.

W. Mischel, "Process in Delay of Gratification," in *Advances in Experimental Social Psychology,* ed. L. Berkowitz (New York: Academic Press, 1974).

W. Mischel and R. Metzner, "Preference for Delayed Reward as a Function of Age, Intelligence, and Length of Delay Interval," *Journal of Abnormal and Social Psychology* 64(1962):425–431.

D.A. Morena and A.J. Litrownik, "Self-Concept in Educable Mentally Retarded and Emotionally Handicapped Children: Relationship between Behavioral and Self-Report Indices and an Attempt at Modification," *Journal of Abnormal Child Psychology* 2(1974):281–292.

R.O. Nelson, "Assessment and Therapeutic Functions of Self-Monitoring," in *Progress in Behavior Modification,* vol. 5, eds. M. Hersen, R.M. Eisler, and P.M. Miller (New York: Academic Press, 1977).

R.O. Nelson, D.P. Lipinski, and J.L. Black, "The Reactivity of Adult Retardates' Self-Monitoring: A Comparison among Behaviors of Different Valences, and a Comparison with Token Reinforcement," *The Psychological Record* 26(1976):189–201.

R.O. Nelson, D.P. Lipinski, and R.A. Boykin, "The Effects of Self-Recorders' Training and the Obtrusiveness of the Self-Recording Device on the Accuracy and Reactivity of Self-Monitoring," *Behavior Therapy* 9(1978):200–201.

R.O. Nelson, L. Rudin-Hay, W.M. Hay, and C.B. Carstens, "The Reactivity and Accuracy of Teachers' Self-Monitoring of Positive and Negative Classroom Verbalizations," *Behavior Therapy* 8(1977):972–985.

H.B. Robinson and N.M. Robinson, *The Mentally Retarded Child: A Psychological Approach* (New York: McGraw-Hill, 1976).

M. Rosen, J.C. Diggory, L. Floor, and M. Nowakiwska, "Self-Evaluation, Expectancy and Performance in the Mentally Subnormal," *Journal of Mental Deficiency Research* 15(1971):81–95.

M. Rosen, J.C. Diggory, and B.E. Werlinsky, "Goal-Setting and Expectancy of Success in Institutionalized and Noninstitutionalized Mental Subnormals," *American Journal of Mental Deficiency* 71(1966): 249–255.

D.L. Rosenhan, "Learning Theory and Prosocial Behavior," *Journal of Social Issues* 28(1972):151–163.

D.M. Ross and S.A. Ross, "An Intensive Training Curriculum for the Education of Young Educable Mentally Retarded Children," Final Report of the DHEW (Washington, D.C.: U.S. Office of Education, Bureau of Education for the Handicapped, December 1972).

G. Sagotsky, C.J. Patterson, and M.R. Lepper, "Training Children's Self-

Control: A Field Experiment in Self-Monitoring and Goal-Setting in the Classroom," *Journal of Experimental Child Psychology* 25(1978): 242–253.

W.A. Sieck and R.M. McFall, "Some Determinants of Self-Monitoring Effects," *Journal of Consulting and Clinical Psychology* 44(1976): 958–965.

R.V. Singer, "Incidental and Intentional Learning in Retarded and Normal Children" (Ph.D. diss., Michigan State University, 1963).

R.L. Slosson, *Slosson Intelligence Test (SIT) for Children and Adults* (East Aurora, N.Y.: Slosson Educational Publications, 1963).

C.R. Spates, and F.H. Kanfer, "Self-Monitoring, Self-Evaluation and Self-Regulation Model," *Behavior Therapy* 8(1977):9–16.

B.I. Steinfeld and A.J. Litrownik, "The Effects of Acquired Self-Regulatory Skills on Task Performance," (Paper presented at the Twelfh nual Convention for the Association for the Advancement of Behavior Therapy, Chicago, 1978).

C. Thoresen and M.J. Mahoney, *Behavioral Self-Control* (New York: Holt, Rinehart & Winston, 1974).

D.A. Warner and J.E. deJung, "Effects of Goal Setting upon Learning in Educable Retardates," *American Journal of Mental Deficiency* 75 (1971):681–684.

L. Zegiob, N. Klukas, and J. Junginger, "Reactivity of Self-Monitoring Procedures with Retarded Adolescents," *American Journal of Mental Deficiency* 83(1978):156–163.

Editors' Epilogue

The application of self-management techniques to various problems of childhood dysfunction is an expanding enterprise. Developing out of the so-called cognitive revolution in psychology and resting upon a learning theory foundation as well, the domain of self-management appeals to practitioners of all persuations. Its basic premise—that people can learn to direct their own thoughts, feelings, and actions through the manipulation of overt and covert cues and consequences—offers the clinician a vehicle for freeing his clients from the narrow-range, short-term control of their immediate, often oppressive, environments.

Self-management was once thought to be beyond the capabilities of children and mentally deficient adults. Recent work like that by Litrownik and Steinfeld has helped us to realize that self-management skills can be taught to individuals with limited intellectual repertoires as long as the training conditions are suited to the existing or emergent abilities of the trainees.

The underlying philosophy of this approach is quite similar to the one expressed by Becker and his colleagues in chapter 4: When the training conditions are suitably designed, children, regardless of their limitations, can be trained to reach a level of functioning far beyond society's expectations. We have seen that retarded children, for example, can be taught basic academic skills, memorization and recall strategies, and from the current chapter, self-regulatory skills as well. Indeed, it would be interesting to develop a program of rehabilitation for retarded children that combined the procedures described by Becker, Campione, Litrownik, and their colleagues.

We view self-regulatory skills as having a central position in this program since such skills can be used by children to extend and maintain the instruction in the academic and cognitive areas outlined by the previous investigators. Indeed, a hallmark of adaptive growth and development is the child's acquisition of self-directive mechanisms. As children mature, increasingly greater demands will be placed upon them to perform in circumstances that require display of self-motivated action. Litrownik and Steinfeld have shown that even moderately retarded children can be taught the rudiments of these skills.

Self-regulation and/or self-control training methods are still in the early-development stages of their growth. They have yet to demonstrate sufficiently powerful effects when applied outside the laboratory or to life tasks on an intricate or sequential nature. They have yet to prove their staying power vis-à-vis posttreatment maintenance and generalization. Also, clinician/researchers have as yet to program changes at levels higher than that of behavioral output (compare Carver and Scheier, 1982; Karoly 1981). Fortunately, there is every reason to anticipate an exponential increase in the level of sophistication of self-management research and practice in the years ahead.

References

C.S. Carver and M.F. Scheier, "An Information-Processing Perspective on Self-Management," in *Self-Management and Behavior Change: From Theory to Practice,* eds. P. Karoly and F.H. Kanfer (New York: Pergamon, 1982).

P. Karoly, "Self-Management Problems in Children," in *Behavioral Assessment of Childhood Disorders,* eds. E.S. Mash and L.G. Terdal (New York: Guilford Press, 1981).

Index of Names

Index of Subjects

List of Contributors

Wesley C. Becker, Follow Through Project, College of Education, University of Oregon

Norman W. Bray, Department of Psychology, University of Alabama, University

Ann L. Brown, Department of Psychology, University of Illinois

Joseph C. Campione, Department of Psychology, University of Illinois

Douglas W. Carnine, College of Education, University of Oregon

Michael F. Cataldo, Department of Behavioral Psychology, John F. Kennedy Institute, Baltimore

Siegfried Engelmann, Follow Through Project, Teacher Education, University of Oregon

John M. Gottman, Department of Psychology, University of Illinois

Hyman Hops, Oregon Research Institute, Eugene

Brian A. Iwata, Department of Behavioral Psychology, John F. Kennedy Institute, Baltimore

Alan J. Litrownik, Department of Psychology, San Diego State University

Alex Maggs, Macquarie University, North Ryde, New South Wales, Australia

Kathy Nitsch, Department of Psychology, Indiana University, Bloomington

Martha Putallaz, Department of Psychology, University of Illinois

Bradley I. Steinfeld, Department of Psychology, West Virginia University

Eric M. Ward, Department of Behavioral Psychology, John F. Kennedy Institute, Baltimore

About the Editors

Paul Karoly, currently professor and director of clinical training at Arizona State University, received the Ph.D. from the University of Rochester. His research and professional interests include self-regulation and self-control in children and adults, health psychology, and experimental personality and psychopathology. Dr. Karoly is on the editorial boards of several professional journals including the *Journal of Consulting and Clinical Psychology, Journal of Personality and Social Psychology, Behavior Therapy,* and *Behavioral Assessment.* He is the coeditor (with J.J. Steffen) of *Improving the Long-Term Effects of Psychotherapy, Child Health Psychology* (with John J. Steffen and D.J. O'Grady), and *Self-management and Behavior Change* (with F.H. Kanfer).

John J. Steffen, currently associate professor and director of clinical training at the University of Cincinnati, received the Ph.D. from Rutgers–The State University. He is actively involved in research on interpersonal communication and on the development of social relationships in children and adults. He is coeditor (with Paul Karoly) of *Improving the Long-Term Effects of Psychotherapy* and *Child Health Psychology,* and serves as a member of the editorial board of the *Journal of Communication Therapy.*

About the Editors

[illegible]

[illegible]